Problems in Modern Latin American History

LATIN AMERICAN SILHOUETTES

Series Editors: William H. Beezley and Judith Ewell

Recent Titles in the Series

For a complete listing of titles, visit www.rowmanlittlefield.com/series.

Problems in Modern Latin American History

Sources and Interpretations

Third Edition

EDITED BY JAMES A. WOOD AND
JOHN CHARLES CHASTEEN

ROWMAN & LITTLEFIELD PUBLISHERS, INC.
Lanham • Boulder • New York • Toronto • Plymouth, UK

ROWMAN & LITTLEFIELD PUBLISHERS, INC.

Published in the United States of America
by Rowman & Littlefield Publishers, Inc.
A wholly owned subsidiary of The Rowman & Littlefield Publishing Group, Inc.
4501 Forbes Boulevard, Suite 200, Lanham, Maryland 20706
www.rowmanlittlefield.com

Estover Road, Plymouth PL6 7PY, United Kingdom

British Library Cataloguing in Publication Information Available

Library of Congress Cataloging-in-Publication Data

Problems in modern Latin American history : sources and interpretations /
  edited by James A. Wood and John Charles Chasteen.—3rd ed.
    p.   cm. (Latin American Silhouettes)
  Includes index.
  ISBN-13: 978-0-7425-5644-7 (cloth : alk. paper)
  ISBN-10: 0-7425-5644-1 (cloth : alk. paper)
  ISBN-13: 978-0-7425-5645-4 (pbk. : alk. paper)
  ISBN-10: 0-7425-5645-X (pbk. : alk. paper)
    1. Latin America—History—1830–   2. Latin America—Social
conditions.   I. Wood, James A, 1968–   II. Chasteen, John Charles, 1955–
F1413.P76 2009
980.03—dc22   2008037725

Printed in the United States of America

∞ ™ The paper used in this publication meets the minimum requirements of
American National Standard for Information Sciences—Permanence of Paper for
Printed Library Materials, ANSI/NISO Z39.48-1992.

Contents

Preface to the Third Edition

In bringing out this new edition of *Problems in Modern Latin American History*, my main goal was to make the book more relevant to the study of contemporary Latin America. In the previous edition, you may recall, we ended with the problem of globalization, focusing specifically on the issue of North American integration. In this edition I wanted to come back to globalization, but look at it from a wider perspective. The new version explores regional integration in both North and South America and takes account of China's new role in the regional economies. I also wanted to add a new chapter on what is often referred to as Latin America's "new Left turn"—meaning the string of election victories by left-of-center presidential candidates that has completely altered the political environment in the region in the last decade. Everything else in this edition, essentially chapters I–XI, is exactly the same as in the last edition, except that I cut the old first chapter ("Legacies of Colonialism") to make room for the new material.

I owe my opportunity to create this new edition of *Problems* to my friend and mentor John Chasteen. Like his illustrious predecessor Joseph Tulchin, John graciously allowed his former advisee to take over the book (hence I get top billing this time). All of the criticism or praise for the new material should be directed my way.

There is really nothing else like this book on the market. It is not a traditional textbook, but it is designed specifically with the needs of the survey course on modern Latin American history in mind. It is a primary and secondary source reader that is intended to promote critical thinking about its subject. That is the great advantage to the "problems" approach.

I have tried to make this new edition reflect what has been going on in my own teaching in recent years. I have to admit that I am fascinated by what I have seen in Latin America in the last decade, and so are my students. That fascination, I hope, has worked its way into this edition. My thinking about contemporary Latin America has also been strongly influenced by the experience of teaching in my university's global studies and university studies programs. Teaching courses focused on current trends encouraged me to think about how Latin America's experience with globalization compared with the experiences of other world regions.

I would also like to take this opportunity to acknowledge the organizations that made possible my visits to Latin America in recent years. In 2005 I participated in the Council on International Educational Exchange's program in Chile and Argentina. The daily seminars (and meals) were outstanding, and flying from Buenos Aires back to Santiago with a delegation of Chinese trade negotiators really left an impression on me. In 2006 I went with the board of directors of Artesanía Pachamama, a nonprofit organization based in Greensboro, North Carolina, to the Peruvian mountain village of Mañazo. We were there during the presidential election, which provided me with many opportunities to discuss politics with Peruvians. Together those visits contributed greatly to my understanding of the problem of contemporary Latin American reality.

In the spirit of this book's "problematic" approach, then, I offer a few concluding questions: What are the distinguishing features of Latin America's contemporary reality? Has the region entered a new period of history? How do the legacies of the nineteenth and twentieth centuries continue to shape the present moment? I hope that the new material in this edition helps students think through those and other exciting questions.

James A. Wood

Introduction

This totally new version of *Problems in Modern Latin American History*, like its two predecessors, is intended primarily for the survey course on the history of Latin America since Independence. The post-Independence survey course presents unique challenges to both teacher and student. Few commonly taught history courses surpass it in organizational difficulty. How does one cover two centuries of life in complex, multiracial societies divided into twenty separate states? Moreover, U.S. university students typically have little background in Latin American history. Most of them crave basic structure and need basic information. Thus, not surprisingly, the usual textbooks are organized narratively by country or groups of countries. Considering particular themes or "problems" for Latin America as a whole is another way to help students find coherence in the flood of information.

We make no pretense of having identified a canon of primary problems in the region's history. If one theme stands out above all others, it is race—complex, contradictory, socially constructed—in some ways so like, and in other ways so different from, the U.S. experience of race. Overall, like the field as a whole in the first decade of the twenty-first century, our new *Problems* emphasizes cultural history. Our choice of problems has been essentially pragmatic, shaped by our observations in teaching the survey course, limited by the restrictions of the one-semester format, and motivated by our desire to raise student interest in Latin America's past. The "problems" approach requires students to develop critical skills in analyzing potentially conflicting evidence. It also lends itself to classroom discussion and short writing assignments. Therefore, problems are the ideal focus for the weekly small-group discussion sections that many teachers use to focus on issues in large lecture courses. To facilitate that application of the book, the problems appear in a clear, though not a strict, chronological order, from "Legacies of Colonialism" to "Globalization." In selecting thirteen such problems in modern Latin American history, we have favored issues that complement most survey texts and endeavored to create a geographic spread that would maximize the book's usefulness in the classroom.

Like the early versions of *Problems*, this reader combines primary and secondary sources in each of its chapters. But this new *Problems* is more unified than earlier versions and more student friendly. This time the general editors have drafted the chapter introductions and selected the readings to ensure coherence and cumulative progression from chapter to chapter. As a result, concepts learned in one chapter are applied in the next, and each problem enriches those that follow it. In addition, virtually all the readings have been adapted for undergraduates. Spanish and Portuguese terms have been translated, extraneous passages (and scholarly footnotes) omitted, and brief explanations interjected to maximize student comprehension. These omissions and insertions have not been marked in the traditional fashion with brackets or ellipses, which is another decision made with the undergraduate in mind. However, we have made sure that such adaptations never alter the intended meaning of the original text.

To meet our high standards of readability, a few classic texts have been retranslated expressly for *Problems*. While some of the materials that appear here are old standards (e.g., Simón Bolívar's proclamation of "War to the Death," poems by Pablo Neruda, and Evita Perón's *My Mission in Life*), many others have never been excerpted for a book of this type— Francisco Bilbao on the Chilean Church, for instance, or various selections by the latest generation of Latin Americanist historians.

This *Problems* reader carries on a proud thirty-year tradition begun in 1973 by Joseph S. Tulchin with the publication of *Problems in Latin American History: The Modern Period*. Tulchin's former student, John Chasteen, joined him in editing the second *Problems* reader in 1994. Chasteen's former student, James Wood, takes up the baton in this volume. The present editors offer an affectionate acknowledgment to "editor emeritus" Tulchin, who gracefully stepped aside to allow the generational relay to continue. Editorial work for all three volumes was done at campuses of the University of North Carolina, alma mater to both Chasteen and Wood, as well as several Chapel Hill watering holes, where the present editors tipped well, doodled tables of contents, and swore to assemble the most engaging *Problems* reader ever.

THE PICTORIAL EVIDENCE
Reading Images

Visual images aid the historian most powerfully when they are more than mere illustrations of facts already known from other sources. Images can sometimes provide valuable evidence of subtleties such as attitude, mood, and style that are difficult to convey in words or easily lost in translation. This book includes a number of images for students to interpret as pictorial evidence.

The images have been grouped to shed light on four problems of modern Latin American history: Nineteenth-Century Travelers, Brazilian Slaves, U.S.-Latin American Relations, and Religion and Politics. In examining them, students should recall the historian's cardinal rule: a critical approach to evidence. Drawings and photographs, like any other visual or verbal representations, embody the ideas and attitudes of their creators. Therefore, the meaning of visual evidence, like any other sort, must be interpreted partly by thinking about who produced the images, why, and in what context. Students should ask themselves first, what an image shows, and then, what it "says"—that is, what statement was the creator of this image trying to make?

Clear examples may be found in the political cartoons on pages 156–159. Most of the figures in these cartoons do not represent real people at all but instead personify nations or groups. Obviously, we do not examine these cartoons to learn what Uncle Sam or the Organization of American States "really" looked like. The way that these cartoon figures look depends on what the cartoonist wanted to say about them. Moreover, they reveal ideas and attitudes that the cartoonist brought to the drawing table, consciously or unconsciously. To one degree or another, these ideas and attitudes were certainly shared by the newspaper-reading audience whom the cartoonist aimed to amuse. Therefore, students should view these cartoons to assess U.S. attitudes toward Latin America rather than to learn about Latin America itself. Likewise, the illustrations of nineteenth-century travel books found on pages 26–27 tell us more about the writers' attitudes than about the people whom they visited.

Photographs present a somewhat but not totally different interpretive problem. They do not constitute totally transparent "windows" on reality. By choosing what, when, and how to photograph, the image maker exercises control over the result. In addition, some photographs, such as those of Brazilian slaves on pages 54–55, are carefully posed. Still, photographs are likely to offer dependable information on how the subjects really appeared. Through them, we can learn something about the slaves as well as about the photographer. In sum, whatever the image, students must approach it critically, remembering that it is a representation rather than the thing itself, and consider both the circumstances and the intention.

I

Independence and Its Consequences

When pro-independence, or patriot, leaders challenged the Spanish and Portuguese empires for control of the American colonies beginning in 1810, overall they wanted not to "revolutionize" the social order of Latin America but simply to rule it themselves. Liberalism, a new set of political ideas associated with the French Revolution and the newly independent United States of America, offered a persuasive, ready-made justification for Latin American independence. (We will explore liberalism's ideological impact on modern Latin America more fully in chapter IV.) At the time, liberalism promised a truly revolutionary break with the colonial past. Liberals believed in popular sovereignty, the idea that "the People" of any given nation had the right to rule themselves. In essence, by rebelling against Spain, patriot leaders staked a claim to nationhood as well as a claim to represent the will of the Mexican, Chilean, or Venezuelan people. Both were simply that—claims, and one could even call them fictions. But they were important fictions, and they became fixtures of Latin American political systems, with very few exceptions. In sum, the Wars of Independence definitively implanted liberalism as a new hegemonic idea in Latin America, a direct rival to the older hegemonic idea, Catholicism.

The rivalry between liberalism and Catholicism took a while to develop. At first, ironically, churchmen were among the primary agents of liberalism in Latin America. Both Mexico's José María Morelos and Brazil's Batista Campos were men of the cloth who used liberal ideas in a revolutionary way, to challenge the racial hierarchies of their countries. It is important to realize that these initial challenges were crushed. Latin America's newly independent nations did not create societies characterized by equality; here is one area where colonial legacies mattered. Most patriot leaders were from Creole families high in the social hierarchy. Often, these leaders privately mistrusted the indigenous Americans and Africans who composed a large part of the population. Although Creole patriots used images of equal citizenship rhetorically, to garner wide support, they did little to turn those images into reality. Their most important audience lay among the mestizos and *pardos*, who became a crucial swing group in the Wars of Independence. Overall, they swung toward the cause of independence. Men of mixed race made up the bulk of the patriot armies and figured importantly in the patriot leadership.

As a result of patriot liberalism, principles such as equality before the law became enshrined in U.S.-style constitutions in almost every Latin American country. But after Independence, once the wars had been won and the climate of emergency had passed, rich and powerful Creoles— joined now by a few mestizos—formed a new ruling class who soon experienced a resurgence of their conservative, antiliberal instincts. Often, such leaders paid only lip service to liberal ideas. In fact, the weakness of the new liberal institutions created by Latin American patriots, combined with the continuing strength and vitality of colonial institutions such as the Church and practices such as racial discrimination, lead us to wonder just how much of a rupture with the past was achieved by political independence. This is the question we put before students in this chapter.

Continuities, of course, can be found in even the most revolutionary of historical situations. For example, we cannot explain the Stalinist turn in the history of the Soviet Union without some reference to the legacy of czarist rule in Russia. In independent Latin America, continuities with the past abounded after Independence. On the land, where the huge majority of Latin Americans lived, the rhythms of agricultural life continued as before. While slavery and *repartimiento* (a form of forced labor imposed on indigenous people) were gradually phased out across the region after Independence, the more basic relationship between the owners and the workers of the land remained the same. Similarly, the basic patriarchal configuration of gender relations went unchanged after Independence. In the few cities that existed until the later decades of the nineteenth century, the patterns of daily life changed little since colonial days. The calendar, for instance, was still marked by the pageantry of Church holidays and processions. So much remained the same that many historians of Latin America have downplayed the importance of Independence altogether. What do you think? How important a break was Latin American independence? Read the following five selections to form your own opinion.

QUESTIONS FOR ANALYSIS

1. What political ideals were used to justify Latin American movements for independence?

2. Political ideals are one thing and practical situations are another. Can you contrast the two in the case of Latin American independence movements?

3. The social hierarchy of the colonial order had been based more or less on race. What were the implications of Independence for that form of hierarchy?

1. War to the Death ~ Simón Bolívar*

Simón Bolívar led the sort of patriot movement that existed in most parts of South America—a movement dominated by criollos in which indigenous people played little part. Elite-led patriot movements faced a difficult challenge in rallying the common people of Latin America to the cause of independence. The Bolívar family, for example, had been part of the colonial elite of Caracas that was involved in the effort to keep down the pardos *in the 1790s. Why should Venezuela's* pardo *majority take Bolívar's side against the Spanish king? In 1813, when the following proclamation was written, the first independent Venezuelan Confederation had already been destroyed by royalists with popular support. Bolívar's response was to draw a rhetorical line in blood separating all American-born people from all Spanish-born. Eventually, this strategy worked in Venezuela and throughout South America. Here, the "Liberator of Venezuela" addresses his fellow countrymen.*

Venezuelans: An army of your brothers, sent by the Sovereign Congress of New Granada [present-day Colombia], has come to liberate you. Having expelled the oppressors from the provinces of Mérida and Trujillo, it is now among you. We are sent to destroy the Spaniards, to protect the Americans, and to reestablish the republican governments that once formed the Confederation of Venezuela. The states defended by our arms are again governed by their former constitutions and tribunals, in full enjoyment of their liberty and independence, for our mission is designed only to break the chains of servitude which still shackle some of our towns, and not to impose laws or exercise acts of dominion to which the rules of war might entitle us.

Moved by your misfortunes, we have been unable to observe with indifference the afflictions you were forced to experience by the barbarous Spaniards, who have ravished you, plundered you, and brought you death and destruction. They have violated the sacred rights of nations. They have broken the most solemn agreements and treaties. In fact, they have committed every manner of crime, reducing the Republic of Venezuela to

From Simón Bolívar Selected Writings, 1810–1830, comp. Vicente Lecuna, ed. Harold A. Bierck Jr., trans. Lewis Bertrand (New York: Colonial Press, 1951), 31–32.

the most frightful desolation. Justice therefore demands vengeance, and necessity compels us to exact it. Let the monsters who infest Colombian* soil, who have drenched it in blood, be cast out forever. May their punishment be equal to the enormity of their perfidy, so that we may eradicate the stain of our ignominy and demonstrate to the nations of the world that the sons of America cannot be offended with impunity.

Despite our just resentment toward the iniquitous Spaniards, our magnanimous heart still commands us to open to them for the last time a path to reconciliation and friendship. Spaniards are invited to live peacefully among us, if they will renounce their crimes, honestly change their ways, and cooperate with us in destroying the intruding Spanish government and in the reestablishment of the Republic of Venezuela.

Any Spaniard who does not, by every active and effective means, work against tyranny on behalf of this just cause, will be considered an enemy and punished. As a traitor to our nation, he will inevitably be shot by a firing squad. On the other hand, a general and absolute amnesty is granted to Spaniards who come over to our army with or without their arms, as well as to those who render aid to the good citizens who are endeavoring to throw off the yoke of tyranny. Army officers and civil magistrates who proclaim the government of Venezuela and join with us shall retain their posts and positions. In a word, those Spaniards who render outstanding service to the State shall be regarded and treated as Americans.

And you Americans who, by error or treachery, have been lured from the paths of justice, are informed that your brothers, deeply regretting the error of your ways, have pardoned you, as we are profoundly convinced that you cannot be truly to blame, for only the blindness and ignorance in which you have been kept up to now by those responsible for your crimes could have induced you to commit them. Fear not the sword that comes to avenge you and to sever the ignoble ties with which your executioners have bound you to their own fate. You are hereby assured, with absolute impunity, of your honor, lives, and property. The single title, "Americans," shall be your safeguard and guarantee. Our arms have come to protect you, and they shall never be raised against a single one of you, our brothers.

This amnesty is extended even to the very traitors who most recently have committed felonious acts, and it shall be so religiously applied that no reasonable cause or pretext will be sufficient to oblige us to violate our

---

Colombia here is not yet the name of a particular nation. Rather, it refers generally to the Americas, the lands discovered by Columbus.

offer, however extraordinary and extreme the occasion you may give to provoke our wrath. Spaniards and Canary Islanders,* you will die, though you be neutral, unless you actively espouse the cause of America's liberation. Americans, you will live, even if you have trespassed.

General Headquarters, Trujillo
15 June 1813

2. The Vision of Father Morelos ~ Enrique Krause†

José María Morelos, a priest by training and a mestizo, was the leader of Mexico's tenacious popular independence movement during the years 1811–1814. Morelos succeeded another revolutionary priest, Father Miguel Hidalgo, as the leader of a true uprising from below, with indigenous and mestizo armies of the countryside rallying to an ideology of equality and popular sovereignty, while the besieged native-born white upper class huddled together with the Spanish-born peninsulares *in the cities, stubbornly royalist and fearful of the patriot armies. The ideology of Father Morelos also represents the Mexican independence movement's strong Christian resonances, a circumstance that tells us something about Mexico's past as well as about its future. Enrique Krause, a leading Mexican public intellectual of the late twentieth century, provides the following portrait.*

More than his notable but ultimately fruitless military campaigns and victories, the greatest contribution of Father Morelos was ideological. Morelos brought with him to the struggle for Mexican independence a highly original body of arguments to legitimate it. Their overall thrust was moral, but they also included quite modern economic, social, and political prescriptions—albeit sprinkled here and there with touches of old-fashioned messianic vision. The occasion in which Morelos expounded upon these ideas, giving them legal and sometimes even constitutional form, was the Congress of Anáhuac. Morelos's role as prophet and legislator revealed that he viewed the struggle for Mexican independence as more than a worldly political contest of arms. He also considered it as a *mission,* in the Christian sense of the term.

Possibly because his social position was humbler than Father Miguel

---

*Spain had earlier colonized the Canary Islands and thus the islanders were, in effect, Spaniards.
†From Enrique Krause, *Siglo de Caudillos: Biografía política de México (1810–1910)* (Barcelona: Tusquets Editores, 1994), 77–80.

Hidalgo's, and because of his ethnically mixed origins, as well, the doctrine espoused by Morelos granted as much importance to social equality among Mexicans as it did to Mexican independence from Spain. To alleviate the condition of the indigenous people who, in the words of Bishop Abad y Queipo, lived in "ignorance and misery," and the plight of the castas (of variously mixed African and indigenous descent) who bore "the indelible mark of slavery," Morelos advanced proposals similar to those that the bishop had proposed to the Spanish crown in 1799. Among them were the right to move from place to place, freedom of contract, cancelation of tributes paid by Indians and castas, and abolition of their legal inferiority. "In Mexico," the bishop had written, "all are either rich or poor, noble or infamous, with no gradations in between." Four years later, the traveler Alexander von Humboldt, who met with Abad y Queipo during his stay in Mexico, repeated the same verdict: "Mexico is the country of inequality. Possibly no other country exhibits such shocking inequality in its distribution of wealth, civilization, population, and arable land. The color of a man's skin determines the rank he will occupy in society. A white man, even barefoot, counts himself among the nobility of the country." Daily experience in the modest ecclesiastical offices exercised by Morelos shaped his attitude toward this inequality. Unlike Hidalgo, Morelos did not call for conflict among classes. His was a constructive project of concord for all the inhabitants of Mexico except for Peninsular Spaniards. Three years before the Congress of Anáhuac, in November 1810, Morelos had issued a regulation for his army that prefigured his vision of an ideal society:

> If any movement is detected among the Indians and castas to attack whites, for example, or among whites to attack pardos, whoever tries to begin such a movement will be immediately punished. Our constituted officials [of all ethnic origins] must act in complete harmony . . . in complete accord and brotherhood . . . to punish public misdeeds committed against anyone.

A year later [referring to the possibility of interethnic conflict] Morelos clarified that it would be "the gravest of errors" to instigate "horrible anarchy" among the inhabitants of the area where his army operated. He therefore declared that the only purpose of his struggle was to transfer the reins of government from Peninsular to Creole hands, believing that a newly harmonious social, economic, and ethnic order would result:

> Let there be no more ethnic distinction made among our people, but rather, we shall all be called simply *americanos*. Regarding each other as brothers, we shall all live in the holy peace that our redeemer, Jesus Christ, bequeathed us when he rose triumphantly into heaven. Let there

be no motive for fighting among those who were called castas, nor between whites and blacks, nor between blacks and Indians. Such fighting would be the greatest error that those in our situation could commit, leading to our total destruction, both spiritual and temporal. The whites are our leading representatives. They were the first to take up arms in our struggle. They therefore deserve our gratitude and should not be the targets of the sort of hatred that some have tried to foment against them. It is not our way to attack the rich merely for being rich, so no one should loot the possessions of even the richest among us.

In 1812, in Oaxaca, Morelos declared with greater succinctness, in his typically ironic style: "The lovely nonsense that divided Indians, mulattoes, and mestizos into distinct 'qualities' of human beings is henceforth abolished. From now on, all are to be called *americanos*."

A day before the Congress of Chilpancingo, Morelos outlined his personal utopian vision for a trusted associate, the lawyer Andrés Quintana Roo, who was quite moved by what he heard:

I want us to declare formally that there shall be no sort of nobility in our society except for the nobility conferred by virtue, wisdom, patriotism, and brotherly love; that we all spring ultimately from the same origin and are all equal; that prestige and privilege shall no longer come from ancestry; that slavery is not right, nor rational, nor humane because the color of people's skin does not change the content of their hearts and minds; that the sons of a farm worker or miner should receive the same education as the sons of the richest landowner; that the courts should hear and defend all complainants against the injustices of the powerful. . . . Let us declare that this land is ours and our children's, so that all will have a faith, a cause, a banner for which to die before seeing it trampled as it is now.

The following day, writes Mexico's important nineteenth-century historian Lucas Alamán, Morelos said Mass, and "from the pulpit exhorted [the representatives of the Congress] to put aside their personal interests and desires and think only of the good of the Nation." A secretary then read "a document written by Morelos manifesting his principles for ending the war and laying the bases for a future national constitution." The document became known as *The Sentiments of the Nation*. The following are the most notable of its twenty-three articles:

ARTICLE ONE. America shall be free and independent of Spain or any other European nation, government, or monarchy. Let its independence be sanctioned and justified before the entire world.

ARTICLE TWO. Roman Catholicism shall be our official religion and no others shall be tolerated.

ARTICLE FIVE. Sovereignty emanates directly from the People, who shall delegate it to their representatives, observing a separation of legislative, executive, and judicial powers. National representatives shall be chosen by provincial representatives, all to be wise and moral individuals.

ARTICLE NINE. Only the American-born shall be eligible to receive public employment or become government officials.

ARTICLE TWELVE. The Laws, which shall apply to everyone, should impel patriotism and mitigate against both wealth and poverty. Let our Laws work to augment the earnings of the humble and improve their habits, banishing ignorance, theft, and robbery.

ARTICLE FOURTEEN. New laws shall be debated in the Congress and approved by a plurality of votes.

ARTICLE FIFTEEN. Slavery shall be forever abolished along with caste distinctions. All are henceforth equal. Americanos shall be distinguished from one another only by their personal vice or virtue.

ARTICLE NINETEEN. The Constitution shall establish 12 December, the day of Our Lady of Guadalupe, patron saint of our liberty, as a holiday to be celebrated throughout the country.

ARTICLE TWENTY-THREE. In a like manner, 16 September shall be commemorated yearly as the anniversary of the beginning of our movement for independence. . . .

Decades later, historian Lucas Alamán believed that he detected "communist and socialist" ideas in the creed of Morelos. But what really predominated in the ideology of Morelos—for all of its supremely modern social, political, and economic elements—was a much older concept, a desire to return to roots, envisioned as the kingdom of Christian equality.

---

3. Argentina's Black Legions ~ G. Reid Andrews*

The patriot struggles for Latin American independence always depended on the fighting power of the nonwhite majority, whether castas, slaves, or indigenous people. The offer of full citizenship to men of color thus became the price that Latin American elites had to pay for independence. Full citizenship was, in fact, something that black or indigenous patriots rarely achieved. Still, service in the patriot ranks allowed some men of color to improve their social status and income. A few even rose to positions of leadership. Overall, the military exploits of black patriots helped end slavery in Spanish America, but not in Brazil, where,

*From G. Reid Andrews, *The Afro-Argentines of Buenos Aires, 1800–1900* (Madison: University of Wisconsin Press, 1980), 113–26. © 1980 by the University of Wisconsin Press. Reprinted by permission of the University of Wisconsin Press.

as we will see in document 4, there was little fighting. Here, historian G. Reid Andrews describes the situation in Argentina, which had a significant black population in the early 1800s.

The phenomenon of armed black men has always been a troublesome one for the multiracial societies of the Americas. The spectacle of present or former bondsmen or their descendents organized into disciplined fighting units inevitably suggests the possibility that those units may acquire institutional autonomy and strike against the very government and society that created them. Armed forces always present this threat, but especially so when the members of those forces belong to a class or social group consistently exploited and confined to a subordinate position. Even if the black soldiers never use their power to redress their legitimate grievances, the fear that they will do so is a constant in the mind of the greater society.

Another drawback of black participation in the armed forces is that the services rendered the state by its black soldiers entitle those men, and the rest of the black population as well, to recognition and repayment of the collective debts owed them by their nation. Black assistance in defending the country against invasion can form the basis for demands that official and unofficial discrimination against black people be ended. This assistance, plus the potential of mutiny or rebellion if the demands are not met, can provide black people with the bargaining power to force societal change.

Thus, while black military units have proved useful and even irreplaceable as defenders of various American nations, the problem of black men serving in the armed forces has been an extremely complex and delicate issue, not only for military policymakers but for historians as well. To acknowledge black participation in a nation's military history is to acknowledge the contributions which entitle black citizens to equality with whites. Such acknowledgment is obviously undesirable in societies dedicated to maintaining racial inequality.

Afro-Argentines served in a succession of units in colonial and nineteenth-century Buenos Aires. As early as the 1660s, black men formed segregated militia units in the province; by 1801 black troops formed 10 percent of the city's 1,600-man militia. These troops were easily overcome by a British expeditionary force which occupied the city in 1806, but when the British were driven out six weeks later, free and slave Afro-Argentines fought side by side with white militiamen. A second British invasion a year later was defeated by a defending force of some 5,000 men, of whom 876 belonged to the Corps of Indians, Pardos, and Morenos.

Officers and enlisted men from these black militia units went on to fight in the independence wars. Free black troops from Buenos Aires con-

stituted two all-black units in the revolutionary army—the Sixth Infantry
Regiment of Pardos and Morenos, and the Battalion of Pardos and Morenos of Upper Peru. Both units distinguished themselves against the Spanish in Uruguay, Bolivia, and northwestern Argentina before being mauled
at the Battle of Sipe-Sipe in November 1815. In the worst defeat suffered
by Argentine arms during the revolution, over 1,000 men were killed,
wounded, and captured, while the Spanish suffered 20 dead and 300
wounded.

Another black unit, the Seventh Infantry Battalion, also fought at
Sipe-Sipe, but the Seventh was of a very different type from the free black
units, being composed entirely of slaves bought by the state or donated
by their owners. In 1813 the government initiated the first of a series of
"redemption" decrees by which owners were required to sell their able-
bodied slaves to the state in varying proportions, depending on the economic use to which the slaves were being put. Owners of domestic slaves
were to contribute one-third of their holdings; owners of bakeries and
manufacturing establishments, one-fifth; and owners of slaves engaged in
agriculture, one-eighth. In Buenos Aires province, this draft produced
1,016 slave soldiers, who were organized into two battalions, the Seventh
and the Eighth Infantry. Subsequent "redemptions" in 1815, 1816, and
1818 yielded 1,059 more fighters, who were aggregated to the Eighth
Infantry and the Second Special Infantry Battalion.

When Englishman Emeric Vidal wrote an account of his trip to Buenos Aires, as part of his discussion on the humaneness of slavery in Buenos Aires, he mentioned a particularly benevolent government program by
which slaves could be sold to the state as soldiers, whereupon they would
be free men. In one respect Vidal was quite right: slaves were free as soon
as they entered the armed forces, acquiring provisionally free status which
they would retain for the duration of their military service, afterwards
becoming completely free men. This program therefore had obvious
attractions for Buenos Aires male slaves, though there is no record of their
responding to it as enthusiastically as the slaves of Santiago, Chile, three
hundred of whom hired a lawyer in 1813 to sue the government for their
right to enter the army and win their freedom. Instances of slave resistance
to the redemption program in Buenos Aires were rare, much rarer than
those of owner resistance. After an initial flurry of enthusiasm in which a
number of Buenos Aires families donated slaves to the state as a patriotic
gesture, slave owners began to flood government offices with petitions for
exemptions for their slaves, usually based on their economic dependence
on the slaves' labor. Many owners resorted to the crime of spiriting their
slaves out of the city and hiding them in the countryside, where law
enforcement was looser. By 1816 the government had decreed the uncom-
pensated expropriation of slaves belonging to any master caught illegally

withholding eligible slave males, and an especially long term of service for any slave who failed to turn himself in when called for service. Slaves who informed on such recalcitrant owners would be released from service after a mere three-year term of duty, considerably less than the hitches served by the other freedmen.

Vidal's description of the redemption system as a benevolent one is a bit wide of the mark. Freedom came neither easily nor frequently. Freedmen drafted earliest signed up for the comparatively short term of five years; later decrees required them to serve until two years after the cessation of hostilities before acquiring complete freedom. To what extent these original terms were honored is unclear. Many black troops died during the campaigns and thus never lived to claim their freedom. The numerous freedmen discharged for medical reasons before completing their term of service did not always win their freedom, but rather were frequently returned to their owners.

Many other black soldiers deserted to escape the miserable conditions of campaign life. Those who succeeded in this enterprise may have won a precarious freedom which conceivably could have proved permanent, but those who were recaptured were usually sentenced to lengthy terms of extra service as punishment. In any case, deserting blacks forfeited hopes of legally winning their freedom through the originally established mechanism of service. There is even serious doubt that the remnants of the revolutionary regiments that made it back to Buenos Aires after years of campaigning were allowed to enjoy the freedom they so richly deserved. An official history of the black Eighth Infantry Regiment reports that when its few survivors returned to Buenos Aires in 1824 after eight years of campaigning in Chile, Peru, and Ecuador, they were promptly incorporated into regiments preparing for the approaching war with Brazil, an incorporation which must have been forced on them since it is impossible to imagine that those broken survivors would have gone off voluntarily to fight in yet another war.

Despite the shortcomings of the redemption program from the Afro-Argentines' point of view, it was undeniably successful in furnishing the revolutionary armies with much-needed manpower. Following the destruction of the free black battalions at Sipe-Sipe, the Afro-Argentine representation in the armed forces consisted almost entirely of freedmen. When General José de San Martín led his army across the Andes into Chile in 1816 to liberate that country from Spanish rule, half of his invading force consisted of ex-slaves recruited from Buenos Aires and the provinces of western Argentina and organized into the all-black Seventh and Eighth Infantry Battalions and the integrated Eleventh Infantry. San Martín's conquest of Chile and Peru is the stuff of which military legend is made.

Leading his small army with a rare combination of skill and luck, he succeeded in throwing off Spanish rule in two centers of royalist resistance and sympathy. Even more remarkable was the career of the black battalions that accompanied him. Between 1816 and 1823 they fought and won battles in Chile, Peru, and Ecuador in an odyssey of campaigning that took them as far north as Quito, thousands of miles from their homes in Argentina. By the time they were finally repatriated, fewer than one hundred fifty men remained out of the approximately two thousand black soldiers who had crossed the Andes with San Martín.

A potentially explosive question concerned with segregation and the existence of all-black units is the possibility that commanders used them as assault troops in preference to white units, consciously killing off Argentina's black population while achieving military objectives. No Argentine historian has suggested in print that such a policy existed, but several mentioned it in conversation as one explanation for the gradual disappearance of the Afro-Argentine population.

A focus on the all-black regiments, however, obscures the importance of Afro-Argentines in integrated units. Though segregation of the military was more strictly observed during the colonial period than after independence, there is considerable evidence that even prior to 1810 black and white soldiers served side by side in the local militias. It was not unusual, for instance, for well-to-do merchants or professionals to send their slaves to substitute for them at militia drills and in actual combat, so that a de facto integration resulted through slaves serving in supposedly all-white units. Sometimes integration was officially condoned. During the English invasions a company of free mulattoes was attached to the First Squadron of Hussars, a prestigious white cavalry unit. At least two petitions survive from black officers in this company appealing to the viceroy to allow them to continue to serve in "this distinguished unit" rather than be transferred back to the Battalion of Castas. So badly did these two men want to stay in the white unit that they both offered to serve without pay, supplying their armament and horses at their own expense. Despite their pleas, both men were reassigned to the Castas.

Given the liberal rhetoric of the revolution, integration of regular army units was almost inevitable. At first the revolutionary government sought to keep Afro-Argentine companies in separate battalions, allowing only the Indians to serve with the whites, but eventually they relented, and in 1811 several companies of free Afro-Argentines were aggregated to the Second Infantry Regiment. These companies were later separated from the regiment to form the basis of the Tenth Infantry, another integrated unit. The Eleventh Infantry, which accompanied the black Seventh and Eighth Battalions on their eight-year campaign through the Andean countries, was also integrated.

4. The Brazilian Path to Independence ∼
John Charles Chasteen*

Brazil's path to independence shows more continuity with the colonial legacy than that of any other Latin American country. There was little military mobilization, no need for a Bolívar-style "war to the death," no powerful movement for radical change such as the one led by Morelos in Mexico. Although free of Portuguese rule after 1822, Brazil did not become a republic but, instead, an independent empire. And the emperor, Pedro 1, was a prince of the Portuguese royal house. Moreover, Portuguese-born men continued to hold positions of power in the bureaucracy, the army, and the Church and to dominate trade. Resentment of this situation was natural among the Brazilian-born. Conflict developed rapidly. In the following selection, a historian describes what happened in Brazil's Amazonian north during the 1820s and 1830s.

Brazilian independence was carried out from the top down with a minimum of fighting. The main reason for the contrast between events in Spanish America and Brazil was the presence of the Portuguese monarch, João VI, in Rio de Janeiro, where he had fled to escape Napoleon in 1807. João's influence kept Brazilians loyal to the Portuguese Crown during the years when Spanish Americans began founding independent Republics. In 1821, [five years] after Napoleon was defeated, however, King João returned to Portugal, leaving his son, Prince Pedro, in charge of Brazil. Pedro declared Brazilian independence in 1822 and established the only durable New World monarchy, the Brazilian Empire, which lasted until 1889. This simple lead story of Brazilian independence was played out mostly in Rio de Janeiro. It contrasts enormously with the intense political mobilization surrounding independence in Spanish America.

However, Brazil did, in fact, undergo such a mobilization eventually. A 1817 rebellion in the Brazilian province of Pernambuco clearly showed the influence of liberal ideologies like those that influenced Bolívar and Morelos. Then came Portugal's 1820 revolution, a liberal challenge to King João. *Conselhos abertos* (open city-council meetings, the precise equivalents of the *cabildos abiertos* held in Spanish America during the crisis of independence) occurred throughout the Brazilian provinces during 1820–1821—a decade after the cabildos abiertos had unleashed the process of political mobilization in Spanish America. Then, in 1822, Pedro

---

*From John Charles Chasteen, "Cautionary Tale: A Radical Priest, Nativist Agitation, and the Origin of Brazilian Civil Wars," in *Rumours of Wars: Civil Conflict in Nineteenth-Century Latin America,* ed. Rebecca Earle (London: Institute of Latin American Studies, 2000), 16–21. Reprinted by permission of the Institute for the Study of the Americas.

himself declared "Independence or Death," with a wave of his sword. Supposedly, this was a triumph for the patriot movements that had sprung up across Brazil in past months. But, in practice, eleventh-hour patriots, who had accepted independence only by royal command, still controlled most provincial and local governments in the country. Many judges, bureaucrats, merchants, and military officers of the newly independent Brazilian Empire were still Portuguese-born. Although Brazilian independence vis-á-vis Portugal had already been established, the stage was set for conflicts similar, in many respects, to those that had occurred during the Spanish American independence struggles. The Amazonian province of Pará, with its capital at Belém, close to the mouth of the great river, provides a dramatic example. The patriot leader there was a radical priest named Batista Campos.

Batista Campos was a white Amazonian of modest means, ordained at the Belém seminary in 1805. With a population of only about 24,000, Belém was hardly a metropolis, so Batista Campos must have met his fellow cleric Luiz Zagala, a French priest from Cayenne who spent more than a year in Belém, between 1815 and 1817, before being deported for spreading the radical ideology of the French Revolution. Campos was also influenced by Felipe Alberto Patroni, a fellow Amazonian who was studying at a Portuguese university when Portuguese liberals made their 1820 revolution. Patroni, an ardent twenty-two year old, left school and returned immediately to Pará, where he raised support for the liberal revolution.

Soon, Batista Campos was helping Patroni found the radical liberal *O Paraense,* the first newspaper in Pará. But in May 1822, Patroni was arrested and deported, leaving Batista Campos to take over *O Paraense* and the leadership of Belém's radical liberals. For the next fifteen years, despite repeated jailings and harassment from the conservative local authorities, Batista Campos led a grassroots liberal movement in Belém. From prison, in internal exile (in the middle of the rainforest), at the barricades during frequent fighting in the Amazonian capital, and always through his articles in the press, Campos announced his radical cause. His goal was to carry out the true meaning of Brazilian independence by effectively implementing the principle of popular sovereignty enshrined in Brazil's 1824 constitution, which had been written by the emperor Pedro I himself. This goal implied a ceaseless struggle against the conspiracies of "the Portuguese party," conservatives (many of whom were Portuguese-born) who wished to retain as much as possible of the former colonial order. At least some of the Portuguese party were known to favor recolonization of Brazil by Portugal.

It is easy to see how the radical priest got started on this road. In September 1822, when news reached Belém of Pedro I's call for independence, Campos published it in *O Paraense* and got two weeks in jail for his insolence from the authorities of Belém. Loyalist tendencies were strong in Belém, a city of paved principal streets, an impressive governor's palace, large churches and convents, a seminary, and botanical garden. Prevailing winds and currents gave Belém better communications with Lisbon than with Rio.

Furthermore, the strategic importance of the Amazon region made for a strong (and generally loyalist) Portuguese military presence in the city, and there were also many Portuguese wholesale merchants who dealt in nuts and other fruits of the forest. Independence came to Belém from without, in the form of a warship sent from Rio de Janeiro. Overnight, the Portuguese province became part of independent Brazil, with its Portuguese—now "adopted Brazilian"—rulers still in place.

Campos and his movement questioned the patriotism of the provincial government and demanded a new, native Brazilian one. Only then, after it was already formally accomplished, did the social turmoil of independence really begin in Pará. In October 1823, revolting soldiers forcibly ousted the offending Portuguese-born officials and named Batista Campos the new provincial president. This patriot rebellion was put down by marines from a Brazilian warship whose commander (an English mercenary with an imperial commission) mistrusted the unruly patriotic mob. The naval commander had Batista Campos held against the mouth of a cannon (its fuse lit to dramatize matters) before sending him in chains to Rio. The rebellious soldiers who had placed Campos so briefly in power were not so lucky. Five were chosen at random for exemplary execution, then 256 others were packed so closely into the hold of a prison ship that they all smothered in one night of suffocating Amazonian heat.

Twelve years later, as Batista Campos led Pará's radical liberal movement to the brink of the most devastating civil war in Brazilian history, the "Brazilian Party" and the "Portuguese Party" were still divided along essentially the same lines. Brazil's radical liberal movement had gained strength during the 1820s and reached its zenith at the national level in the early 1830s. Violent clashes began in Belém, and Batista Campos was right in the middle of them. In April 1831, the liberals actually managed to force Pedro I to abdicate, leaving his son, Pedro II, to succeed him on the Brazilian imperial throne. The April Revolution, as Brazilian liberals called the abdication, had unseated a monarch and heartened the revolutionaries, particularly by suggesting the efficacy of popular mobilization. Batista Campos, now nearly fifty, had continued to hold notable ecclesiastical offices and to publish opposition papers during the stormy decade after the formal establishment of Brazilian independence. At the time of the April Revolution, he was a member of the Pará president's advisory council, with a significant personal following described in a hostile report to the central government as "almost all of low condition" and including "disreputable mulatos and blacks."

Batista Campos did not live to see the establishment of a Brazilian republic. Instead, imperial armed forces crushed his movement mercilessly during the years 1835–1840. Liberalism went into eclipse in post-independence Brazil, just as occurred in Spanish America. It is the nature of eclipses, though, that they do not last forever. Brazilian liberalism would rise again, in the late 1800s, as part of a hemisphere-wide trend.

---

5. What Independence Meant for Women ∼ Sarah C. Chambers*

Liberalism theoretically endowed "the People" with citizenship rights at the individual level. One important test of the meaning of Independence is the practical difference it made, or did not make, in the citizenship rights of non-elite Latin Americans. Historian Sarah C. Chambers has approached this problem through careful study of postcolonial judicial archives in the Peruvian city of Arequipa. She has found that many "plebeian" males—ordinary city dwellers of modest means, often of mixed race—did feel somewhat empowered by the new system rooted in the ideological model of liberalism. Plebeian men based claims to citizenship rights on the merit of their records as patriot soldiers. But the situation of women was quite different. Believing that a virtuous citizenry was the moral foundation of a republic, the authorities of 1830s Arequipa unleashed a repressive campaign during which poor women suffered disproportionately.

Citizenship in independence-era Peru became linked to the older Latin American concept of honor, a concept that inherently limits women's claims to political equality. Female honor underwent only subtle transformations after independence. Women continued to be judged primarily by their sexual purity and domestic virtue. When Doña Maria Rivera died in 1829, after supervising the foundling home for forty years, a full-page obituary praised her as an example of proper womanhood. At the age of twenty-one she had shut herself off from the world, to dedicate herself entirely to the care of infants whose mothers had secretly given them up (to save their *own* honor from public disgrace). "Austere with herself, sensitive and tender with the family given to her by Christian charity, never was there noted in her that hardness often produced by the effort of closing off the heart to the emotions of love. So it is that she has been the model, not the imitator, of maternal tenderness." Notables from the

---

*From Sarah C. Chambers, *From Subjects to Citizens: Honor, Gender, and Politics in Arequipa, Peru, 1780–1854* (University Park: Pennsylvania State University Press, 1999), 200–15. © 1999 by the Pennsylvania State University. Reprinted by permission of Pennsylvania State University Press.

municipality and the church attended her funeral to pay their last respects to this "virtuous" woman.

Old-fashioned female virtues became women's "republican" virtues when expressed in an "enlightened" manner. Thus, one can speak of "republican motherhood." One can see this reformulation most clearly in female education. When young women from two schools demonstrated their mathematical ability before local notables in 1833, for example, the official newspaper covered the events with long and enthusiastic articles. Although the students humbly apologized in advance for the errors they might commit, the reporter was impressed by their skill and "their dedication to a difficult and abstract science which might seem reserved for the profound meditations and arduous investigations of the sex endowed with robustness and strength." Both the reporter and the students in their speeches contrasted the education of colonial women—limited to learning the rudiments of reading and writing by rote rather than "reflection"—to the new, enlightened curriculum. Nevertheless, the goal was still to prepare them to better fulfill their traditional roles. The lack of education in the colonial period, Rosa Amat pointed out, had made the weak sex a "victim of perversity" and "motive of corruption," who substituted "frivolous pleasures for the true merit of being good wives and mothers." Even arithmetic, pointed out another student, was "necessary for domestic order."

Extending a domestic metaphor into the public realm, the same reporter noted that a local official "offered to the spectators the appealing picture of a family patriarch surrounded by his children." During the colonial period, the monarch had been depicted as a father to all his subjects, but in the republic it was primarily women and children who were under the paternal care of the state. Pupil Juliana Sanches echoed the familial theme in her address to the gathered officials: "Under your auspices, the fair sex will be, not a group contemptible for its ignorance, but rather, adorned with knowledge and virtues; it will be the compass that guides the domestic ship along the path of honor, inspiring in the family sentiments of justice and religion."

Though praising their mathematical abilities, moreover, the articles dwelled more on the beauty, modesty, and purity of the students. Indeed, as noteworthy as their earlier efforts at the blackboard was their performance at the banquets given in their honor, where the young women, "with their decency and neatness, and their dexterity in the handling of the table setting, gave an idea of the care of their breeding and to their belonging to people of Quality." Such skills were more important than book learning, to many parents; in defending the disciplinary methods of the female teacher accused of whipping her students, several parents praised her particularly for teaching their daughters manners.

The role of virtuous women was now to nurture republican virtues in members of their families, and there were occasions when they were called upon to extend this inspirational role into the public sphere. The editor of Arequipa's paper, *El Republicano*, advocated the introduction of French-style salons, where "the ladies distinguish with their esteem only he who demonstrates the most ingenuity and judgment in the resolution of difficult problems." Descriptions of civic celebrations never failed to highlight the presence of the "fair sex," who cried out praises of the parading heroes, threw flowers from balconies, and—in virginal choirs—sang patriotic anthems.

Women also played a role—albeit a limited one—in political life. Once again women were, officially, to serve primarily as an inspiration to men. Soldiers were exhorted to arms with promises that their sacrifices would be "rewarded with the civic crown of laurels woven by the lovely hands of Arequipa's fair sex." Conversely, the specter of what would happen to their wives and children at the hands of the enemy was invoked to bolster the men's fighting spirit. Women were praised, if not called upon, for their financial contributions—most commonly, the symbolic as well as valuable donation of their jewels—to political causes. In rare cases, women even participated actively in military movements. In 1839, for instance, with the restoration of strongman Agustín Gamarra to power, Doña Antonia Torreblanca requested compensation for her services to his cause over the previous five years. She related how she had infiltrated enemy troops under the pretext of selling them food. Then, in spite of the supposed "weakness of her sex," she crawled on her hands and knees to avoid gunfire and crossed the river in the middle of the night in order to relay urgent information. Finally, she had solicited donations from other women in order to serve food to the wounded soldiers in the hospital. After several military commanders testified to the truth of her claims, Torreblanca was rewarded with one hundred pesos.

Antonia Torreblanca's case reveals both the potential and the limitations of women's participation in the republican public sphere. Even if it was economic need that motivated her to request compensation, her account bespeaks a pride in her services and a desire for recognition. Yet, while praised for her "ardent and praiseworthy patriotism," Torreblanca did not describe her virtues as those of republican citizenship, merely proclaiming her allegiance to "the present regime so just and beneficent to the fatherland."

The failure to identify women, even figuratively, as citizens or republicans was typical. While the female superior of the foundling home was eulogized solely for her maternal virtues, for example, the priest with whom she served was paid homage as a "good patriot" and "virtuous citizen," dedicated to national independence and republican institutions.

Although some women had been involved in the wars of independence at
the national level, they never called for political inclusion in the new state,
and male politicians never raised the issue of female suffrage. Either it did
not occur to most women to identify themselves as citizens or they realized
that such claims would have fallen on deaf ears. After all, the new republican constitutions excluded women and so did the entire discourse of honorable citizenship.

Women probably realized that they could use the language of domesticity, instead, to better advantage. María Seballos, a self-declared merchant, claimed ignorance of a new regulation against distilling alcohol,
"as a woman who does not deal with anyone and lives withdrawn in the
refuge and care of her family." In point of fact, her account reveals that
she had not heard of the new order because she was away on business, her
motherly reclusion being, in this case, a rhetorical gambit. Flora Tristán, a
sophisticated traveler with family in Arequipa, commented on the appear-
ances prized by her aunt there: "Joaquina's great gift is to persuade everybody, even her husband, shrewd as he is, that she knows nothing, that she
is concerned only with her children and her household. Her great piety,
her humble and submissive air, the kindness with which she speaks to the
poor, the interest she shows in the unimportant people who greet her in the
street, all make her seem a modest woman without ambition." Republican
discourse rewarded virtuous ladies, if not with citizenship, with the right
to an education and a recognition of their social value as mothers and
arbiters of morality.

Plebeian women were in a different situation. While plebeian men
asserted their inclusion in the discourse of honorable citizenship, poor
women rarely spoke the language of republican motherhood. Whereas
men met and communicated in the workplace, the military corps, and the
tavern, there were few opportunities, outside of household service, for
dialogue among women of different classes. Only families with substantial
means could afford to send their daughters to school, where they would
be exposed to the new ideas. Even if plebeian women were aware of the
subtle shifts in gender ideology, moreover, most forms of employment
made it difficult to maintain even the appearance of being retiring keepers
of the home and family. Although poor women probably did not accept
elite stereotypes, challenging them within the official discourse of republicanism was not an effective strategy.

Not only was it difficult for poor women to base claims upon their
rights or duties as mothers, but the mitigating factors used by plebeian
men were also denied them. A work ethic failed to redeem women, since
their virtue depended upon fulfilling their domestic roles. María Toledo,
an "anguished mother," was denied a request for early release from
imprisonment although she supported her children on the income she

earned as an agricultural laborer. Just months before her request was
denied, the sentence of an "honorable" man was reduced for that very
reason. The role of hardworking provider was reserved for men.

Also reserved for men were the honors of military service, which
(with rare exceptions, such as Torreblanca) usually *dis*honored women
because of the assumption that their morals would be corrupted by a soldier's life. Despite the critical support that they provided to the troops and
their occasional participation in combat, the female "camp followers"
were more likely to be scorned than appreciated. This exclusion was critical because of the importance of military service in plebeian claims to
honor and, by extension, to citizenship rights.

Plebeian women bore the brunt of efforts to enforce the new, stricter
republican morality. While it is unlikely that their behavior changed in
any significant way from that in the colonial period, their sexuality was
increasingly seen as a threat to public order. When María Samudio was
arrested for assaulting her lover, soldier José Valdez, even the prosecutor
considered the wounds so inconsequential that the charges should be
dropped. He argued, nevertheless, that Samudio should be punished for
her loose morals, saying such crimes stemmed from "toleration of the
public immorality of these women, who, abandoning modesty, social considerations, and family obligations, have the impudence to present themselves in public as prostituted persons." By exiling Samudio, the judges
both punished her and rid the city of what they considered her immoral
influence.

Similarly, a female target of violence evoked little sympathy if she did
not meet elite standards of respectability. When Benedicto Munós was
arrested for stabbing his lover, Antonia Perula, for example, the prosecutor
did not believe the charges were much cause for concern, particularly as
the fault lay with Perula for her "long illicit relationship with the aggres-
sor." Thus female victims could be recast as delinquents. When petty vendor Felipa Galdos accused the child of a merchant of stealing a piece of
fruit, the indignant father allegedly struck her with a stick, breaking her
arm. Although the merchant was initially fined twenty-five pesos to cover
her medical expenses, the fiscal requested that the money be paid to the
court and that Galdos be made to apologize publicly for "her constant
provocations." When Antonio Vilca was arrested for stabbing his wife, he
was not the only one to receive a warning. After "making him understand
that he should correct his wife using the moderation prescribed by marital
love, and by the considerations due to her weak sex," the court also
advised his wife that she respect and obey her husband "avoiding occasions for displeasing him."

The differential treatment of men and women by the republican
authorities is epitomized in the official attitude toward domestic violence.

Given the emphasis, after independence, on respectability, one might expect the state to come to the aid of women who complained of dissolute, profligate, and abusive husbands. According to the constitutions, to abandon one's wife or to be at fault in an ecclesiastical separation was considered cause for the suspension of citizenship. Republican officials in Arequipa did increasingly claim the authority to oversee marital affairs, a matter previously left primarily to the church. As judge José Miguel Salazar argued, "The jurisdiction of our Prelates is purely in spiritual matters, and it is the responsibility of the Government to make sure that its subjects committed to the conjugal state comply with their pacts and do not offend each other." Nevertheless, the civil authorities were hesitant to interfere with a male citizen's patriarchal rights, including his prerogative to "correct" his wife. As one judge optimistically affirmed of a man accused of beating his wife, "the fear of scandalizing the community with actions foreign to an honorable citizen, will be sufficient to moderate in the future the vigor of his temper, and to make him more exact in the fulfillment of his duties in Holy Matrimony." A shocking degree of violence was commonly permitted to husbands, and republican courts defined the crime of domestic "assault" narrowly, indeed. When Francisca Obiedo complained that her husband beat her with sticks, stones, and whips and committed incest with her daughter, the fiscal asserted that even if the charges proved true, they would not constitute a public crime that could be tried by the state.

There was, at least, some improvement regarding another crime against women, rape. Only after independence did judges in Arequipa begin actively prosecuting rape.

Although the number of rape trials was small, and only minors were deemed worthy of protection, such cases marked a significant change from colonial practice and reflected the increased concerns over sexuality. About half of the accused rapists were convicted, despite the efforts of defense lawyers to depict their victims as promiscuous women. Even eighteen-year-old Maria Nuñez, who accused tailor José Maria Peralta of sneaking into her room and getting her drunk in order to take advantage of her, convinced the judge of her honorable reputation. Furthermore, the penalties for rape convictions were, generally, more strict than those for simple assault: several months in jail while performing public labor and/or providing a dowry for the young woman.

Remarkably the courts were willing to defend the honor even of poor girls. Indeed, in one case the superior court increased a sentence from the time already served to a one-hundred-peso dowry, precisely because the girl was "an unfortunate one who belongs to the lowest class and lacking in fortune deserves more consideration and more legal protection" The language used by judicial officials to describe such crimes provides a stark contrast to their attitude toward plebeian women beaten by their husbands or lovers. In 1834, for example, the justices were outraged when a tailor attempted to rape a seven-year-old girl. Even if he had not been able to consummate the act, argued the fiscal, "he reveals the utmost immorality and corruption which if not repressed and punished, its contagion could upset the order of families and cause serious damages to innocence." When defendants and their lawyers protested that such charges should be pursued only at the initiative of private plaintiffs, the justices countered that rape, like theft or homicide—but apparently not like wife abuse or incest—could be prosecuted by the state as "a true public crime because in addition to damaging the honor and morals of families, it attacks the liberty and the very person of an individual."

The transformation of the code of honor under republicanism provided a new hegemonic language but did not, by any means, create an egalitarian or democratic society. On the contrary, repressive forms of social control actually intensified after independence, and republican leaders often fell short of putting liberal principles into practice. Nevertheless, the dialectical tension between elites and plebeians forged a new republican pact, in which some working men were granted the status of citizens. The recognition of citizenship was not only contingent upon conduct, but was also based upon the exclusion of those identified as socially dependent. The legal system denied the benefits of "honorable labor" to slaves and indigenous domestic servants. Slaves and servants, like women, were legally subject to patriarchal control and so could not be free and equal citizens.

Women found their private virtues subject to increasing public scrutiny. Elite women who were able to maintain the appearance of fulfilling high republican standards of sexual purity, modesty, and maternal nurturing were still denied citizenship but were, at least, recognized as arbiters of morality within the public sphere as well as the home. Poor women, however, who often lived beyond the control of a patriarch and continued to carry out their lives in public, bore the brunt of repressive public moralism.

READING IMAGES
Nineteenth-Century Travelers

Because Spain and Portugal had routinely prohibited outsiders from visiting their colonial domains in the New World, once those domains become independent in the 1820s, travelers from the United States, England, and France, especially, reported on their Latin American experiences to an eager reading public at home. For the rest of the nineteenth century and into the twentieth, travel books were probably the primary source of public information on Latin America in Europe and the United States. Like the texts of their accounts, the travelers' illustrations were often heavily freighted with ideas that the artists brought with them in their mental "baggage." Some travelers were captivated by the idea that Latin America was romantic and mysterious—a storybook place not governed by the same human logic and daily realities of Europe and the United States. It was reasonable, after all, for artists to depict what they found as "picturesque" and "exotic." But if exoticism could be attractive, it also could be repellent. And for male travelers (the majority), "romantic" and "mysterious" were qualities more engaging in women than in men. The tone of many illustrations, like the tone of most of these texts, was critical, especially of the men. How are these various elements visible in the two illustrations that appear here? In addition, what details of each drawing suggest that travel illustrations often depicted things that the artist knew imperfectly at best?

"Customs of Bahia." Bavarian artist Johann Moritz Rugendas was not yet twenty when he traveled to Brazil as part of a scientific expedition in 1821. Once in Brazil he left the expedition and wondered extensively for several years, later publishing a book of illustrations, *Voyage pittoresque dans le Brésil* (1835), on his return to Europe. Rugendas then went back to Latin America and visited seven countries, from Chile to Mexico, staying fourteen years and becoming the region's most important travel illustrator of the century. "Customs of Bahia" was almost certainly a composite of various social types rather than any real-life scene witnessed by the artist. To "read" this image, students should know that the central figure is a Catholic priest. Rugendas seems to have shared the scornful attitude of many visitors about the Brazilian clergy. *Source:* "Customs of Bahia," *Voyage pittoresque dans le Brésil* (1835), copied from João Maurício Rugendas, *Viagem pitoresca através do Brasil* (São Paulo: Livraria Martins, 1941), plate 2/26.

"Simple and Innocent Indians." Englishman William Bullock sailed for Mexico on a scientific and commercial information-gathering trip in 1822, within months of the country's independence from Spain. In his baggage he carried both primitive photographic equipment and a book of fashion plates. On his return to England he published *Six Months Residence and Travels in Mexico Containing Remarks on . . . Natural Productions, State and Society, Manufactures, Trade, Agriculture, and Antiquities, &c.* His "camera lucida" apparently did not produce any pictures worth printing. The book's few illustrations, like this one of "simple and innocent Indians," were etchings made by a London artist at Bullock's direction. *Source:* "Simple and Innocent Indians:" I. Murray, London, 1824, copied from W. Bullock, *Six Months Residence and Travels in Mexico* (London: Kennikat Press, 1971), between pp. 196–97.

II

Slavery and Culture

There can be no doubt that African slavery, the same "peculiar institution" so deeply rooted in the history of the United States, had a profound impact on Latin American history. From the 1520s to the 1880s, the institution of African slavery left a lasting impression on the social relations, cultural values, and economic development of the numerous Latin American societies in which it thrived. Enslaved men, women, and children of African descent were a ubiquitous presence from the tropical islands of the Caribbean to the cane fields of Brazil to the bustling city of Buenos Aires. In all, somewhere from nine to fifteen million Africans survived the tragic Middle Passage across the Atlantic to take up residence in the completely alien lands of the New World. Millions more did not survive the voyage (some say as many as 20 percent), and even more died in captivity before embarking on that infamous journey. In fact, prior to the massive wave of European immigration to the Americas in the nineteenth century, more Africans crossed the Atlantic Ocean than people from any other continent.

How did enslaved Africans cope with their dreadful experience? This chapter's approach to the problem recognizes two recent trends in the historical literature. First, the approach is cultural. In recent decades, historians in the United States and elsewhere have become more attuned to questions of culture: How is it generated? How is it transmitted? And how is meaning determined? In the case of slave culture, in particular, historians of the present generation, influenced by earlier studies of slave and peasant resistance, were not satisfied with existing interpretations. So they set out to reinterpret the role that culture—in all of its individual and collective dimensions—played in the history of American slavery. Some examples of their work are included here. Second, the approach is transatlantic. The transatlantic approach to the history of American slavery, by emphasizing the importance of dynamics on both sides of the Atlantic Ocean, allows us to understand its true complexity. As we will see, the commonalities of slave culture throughout the Americas, brought to light by the transatlantic approach, force us to ask basic questions about the ways in which culture is carried from one place to another. Historians of slave culture often weigh the relative importance of practices brought from Africa, on one hand, and practices invented in the diaspora, on the other.

A final point of comparison will certainly interest students. Whereas slavery in the United States was ended only by a major civil war, slavery in Latin America declined more gradually. In 1807 the United Kingdom, bowing to reformist pressure, outlawed the commercial trade in slaves that it had dominated for a century. With the passage of this law (and the indomitable Royal Navy enforcing it on the high seas), slave importers in the Americas had to take great risks in securing their human cargoes. Some turned to smuggling operations, while others turned away from the trade altogether. In most of Spanish America, laws were passed to gradually phase out or abolish (hence the terms "abolition" and "abolitionist") the entire institution. The Wars of Independence, in which thousands of slaves earned their freedom on the battlefield, had already done much to shake up the "peculiar institution."

In two particular places, however, African slavery lived on. In Brazil, which achieved the status of an independent monarchy as a result of the Napoleonic invasion of Spain and Portugal, slavery survived until the Golden Law of 1888 freed all slaves unconditionally. In Cuba (still part of the Spanish empire until 1898), slavery remained legal until 1886. Brazil and Cuba imported more slaves overall than did any other countries. Brazil, in fact, was the destination for roughly one-third (or 3.6 million) of all African slaves brought to the New World after 1500. Cuba took in roughly 8 percent (or 0.7 million) of the total, most of them brought in illegally after the Spanish ban on the slave trade in 1815. Thus, African slavery shaped Latin America's modern history. And like the United States, many countries of the region still struggle with the legacies of that vicious system of labor and social control.

QUESTIONS FOR ANALYSIS

1. What, culturally speaking, did enslaved Africans bring with them to the Americas?

2. In what sorts of living and working situations did slave culture take shape? How did such situations affect the development of slave culture?

3. How did the collective experience of enslavement reshape African cultural traditions into African-American ones?

1. The Beginnings of African-American Culture ~
Sidney W. Mintz and Richard Price*

The centuries-long ordeal of slavery had a direct and immediate impact on African American culture. According to the eminent cultural anthropologists Sidney Mintz and Richard Price, this impact began even before the arrival of the enslaved Africans in the New World. In this excerpt from their influential work (originally published in 1976 as An Anthropological Approach to the Afro-American Past), *Mintz and Price show that enslaved Africans had already begun to think and behave cooperatively on the Atlantic shores of their homeland. And this cooperative spirit continued through the terrible Middle Passage, despite its brutalizing effects on individuals. Mintz and Price also emphasize the importance of the cultural heterogeneity of the (mostly West) African slaves for the development of African American cultures. Because of the diversity of beliefs and practices brought to the Americas by slaves, they argue, African American cultures developed an extremely open attitude toward innovation and change.*

Before any aggregate of plantation slaves could begin to create viable institutions, they would have had to deal with the traumata of capture, enslavement, and transport. Hence the beginnings of what would later develop into "African-American cultures" must date from the very earliest interactions of the newly enslaved men and women on the African continent itself. They were shackled together, packed into dank "factory" dungeons, squeezed together between the decks of stinking ships, separated often from their kinsmen, tribesmen, or even speakers of the same language, left bewildered about their present and their future, stripped of all prerogatives of status or rank (at least, so far as the masters were concerned), and homogenized by a dehumanizing system that viewed them as faceless and largely interchangeable. Yet we know that even in such utterly abject circumstances, these people were not simply passive victims. In the present context, we are thinking less of the many individual acts of heroism and resistance which occurred during this period than of certain simple but significant *cooperative* efforts which, in retrospect, may be viewed as the true beginnings of African-American culture and society.

Various shreds of evidence suggest that some of the earliest social bonds to develop in the coffles [slaves chained together in line], in the factories, and, especially, during the long Middle Passage were of a dyadic (two-person) nature. Partly, perhaps, because of the general policy of

*From Sidney W. Mintz and Richard Price, *The Birth of African-American Culture: An Anthropological Perspective* (Boston: Beacon Press, 1992), 42–51. © 1976 by the Institute for the Study of Human Issues. Reprinted by permission of Beacon Press.

keeping men and women separate, they were usually between members of the same sex. The bond between shipmates, those who shared passage on the same slaver, is the most striking example. In widely scattered parts of Afro-America, the "shipmate" relationship became a major principle of social organization and continued for decades or even centuries to shape ongoing social relations.

In Jamaica, for example, we know that the term "shipmate" was "synonymous in the slaves' view with 'brother' or 'sister.' "It was "the dearest word and bond of affectionate sympathy amongst the Africans," and "so strong were the bonds between shipmates that sexual intercourse between them," in the view of one observer, "was considered incestuous." We know also that the bond could extend beyond the original shipmates themselves and interpenetrate with biological kin ties; shipmates were said to "look upon each other's children mutually as their own," and "it was customary for children to call their parents' shipmates 'uncle' and 'aunt.' "

In Suriname, to cite a different case, the equivalent term "*sippi*" was at first used between people who had actually shared the experience of transport in a single vessel; later, it began to be used between slaves who belonged to a single plantation, preserving the essential notion of fellow sufferers who have a special bond. Today in the interior of Suriname, among the Saramaka people, "sippi" (now "*sibi*") continues to designate a special, nonbiological dyadic relationship with very similar symbolic content; when two people find themselves victims of a parallel misfortune (e.g., two women whose husbands desert them at about the same time), they thenceforth may address each other as "sibi" and adopt a special prescribed mutual relationship.

Other examples of the "shipmate" relationship in Afro-America can be cited—from the Brazilian "*malungo*" and Trinidadian "*malongue*" to Suriname "*máti*" to Haitian "*batiment.*" But we have said enough already to support the following assertions. It is not surprising that same-sex dyadic ties should have loomed large in the earliest context of African-American enslavement and transport (given that such ties seem often to develop when random individuals are thrust into an institutional, depersonalized setting—such as boot camp or prison). What may make this case unusual is the extent to which such initial bonds could develop into basic principles which probably helped to shape the institutions of such societies and which, even today, in many areas appear to retain their original symbolic content. We believe that the development of these social bonds, even before the Africans had set foot in the New World, already announced the birth of new societies based on new kinds of principles.

The initial cultural heterogeneity of the enslaved doubtless had the effect of forcing them at the outset to shift their primary cultural and social commitment from the Old World to the New, a process which often took their European masters centuries to accomplish. The quite radical cultural reorientation that must have typified the adaptation of enslaved Africans to the New World was surely more extreme than what the European colonists—with their more intact institutions, continuing contacts with the homeland, and more coherent family groupings—experienced. Even in those special situations in which some members of a particular ethnic or linguistic group could remain in close contact, such orientation must have remained a secondary focus of commitment, with the new African-American culture and its concomitant social ties being primary. All slaves must have found themselves accepting, albeit out of necessity, countless "foreign" cultural practices, and this implied a gradual remodeling of their own traditional ways of doing many things. For most individuals, a commitment to, and engagement in, a new social and cultural world must have taken precedence rather quickly over what would have become before long largely a nostalgia for their homelands. We remind ourselves and our readers that people ordinarily do not long for a lost "cultural heritage" in the abstract, but for the immediately experienced personal relationships, developed in a specific cultural and institutional setting, that any trauma such as war or enslavement may destroy. A "culture," in these terms, becomes intimately linked to the social contexts within which affective ties are experienced and perceived. With the destruction of those ties, each individual's "cultural set" is transformed phenomenologically, until the creation of new institutional frameworks permits the refabrication of content, both based upon—and much removed from—the past.

We have been suggesting that distinctive, "mature" African-American cultures and societies probably developed more rapidly than has often been assumed. The early forgings of "shipmate" ties or ritual complexes, as we have phrased them, are intended as arbitrary (though central) examples of much more general processes. Even in the realm of the arts, to choose a less likely example, it could be shown that new cultural subsystems were worked out through the interaction of slaves who had not yet set foot in the Americas. Not only was drumming, dancing, and singing encouraged for "exercise" on many of the slavers, but [John Gabriel] Stedman tells us how, at the end of the nightmare of the Middle Passage, off the shores of Suriname: "All the Slaves are led upon deck . . . their hair shaved in different figures of Stars. half-moons, &c, /which they generally do the one to the other (having no Razors) by the help of a broken bottle and without Soap/." It is hard to imagine a more impressive example of irrepressible cultural vitality than this image of slaves decorating one another's hair in the midst of one of the most dehumanizing experiences in all of history.

We have stressed some of the ways in which the early stages of African-American history fostered the rapid development of local slave cultures. But we believe that this distinctive setting also stamped these cultures with certain general features that strongly influenced their subsequent development and continue to lend to them much of their characteristic shape today. Our speculation runs as follows. While the greatest shock of enslavement was probably the fear of physical violence and of death itself, the psychological accompaniment of this trauma was the relentless assault on personal identity, being stripped of status and rank and treated as nameless ciphers. Yet, by a peculiar irony, this most degrading of all aspects of slavery seems to have had the effect of encouraging the slaves to cultivate an enhanced appreciation for exactly those most personal, most human characteristics which differentiate one individual from another, perhaps the principal qualities which the masters could not take away from them. Early on, then, the slaves were elaborating upon the ways in which they could be individuals—a particular sense of humor, a certain skill or type of knowledge, even a distinctive way of walking or talking, or some sartorial detail, like the cock of a hat or the use of a cane.

At the same time, as we have seen, the initial cultural heterogeneity of the enslaved produced among them a general openness to ideas and usages from other cultural traditions, a special tolerance (within the West African context) of cultural differences. We would suggest that this acceptance of cultural differences combined with the stress on personal style to produce in early African-American cultures a fundamental dynamism, an expectation of cultural change as an integral feature of these systems. Within the strict limits set by the conditions of slavery, African-Americans learned to put a premium on innovation and individual creativity; there was always a place for fads and fashions; "something new" (within certain aesthetic limits, of course) became something to be celebrated, copied, and elaborated; and a stylistic innovation brought by a newly imported African could be quickly assimilated. From the first, then, the commitment to a new culture by African-Americans in a given place included an expectation of continued dynamism, change, elaboration, and creativity.

---

2. Rethinking Palmares ~ Stuart B. Schwartz*

During the seventeenth century, an extraordinary kingdom—Palmares—developed in the midst of the Portuguese colony of Brazil. What made Palmares extraordinary was the fact that it was composed mostly of slaves who had

*From Stuart B. Schwartz, *Slaves, Peasants, and Rebels: Reconsidering Brazilian Slavery* (Champaign: University of Illinois Press, 1992), 124–28. © 1992 by the Board of Trustees of the University of Illinois. Reprinted by permission of the University of Illinois Press.

escaped from the sugar plantations along Brazil's northeastern coast. In other words, Palmares was a quilombo, *the Portuguese word for a community of runaway slaves. In this selection, historian Stuart Schwartz lays out a revisionist interpretation of the kingdom's connections to African (particularly Angolan) culture. Utilizing new research on African history and a subtle analysis of language (African and Brazilian), Schwartz explores the question of ethnicity within the "neo-African" community of Palmares. His findings, while not definitive, clearly suggest the existence of a fascinating network of cultural linkages across the Atlantic Ocean.*

In many ways Palmares seems to have been an adaption of African cultural forms to the Brazilian colonial situation in which slaves of various origins, African and *crioulo*,* came together in their common opposition to slavery. Within Palmares people called each other *malungo*, or comrade, a term of adoptive kinship also used among slaves who had arrived together on the same slave ship.

In Palmares we can see the attempt to form a community out of peoples of disparate origins. Such an attempt had to be made by all fugitive communities, but in the case of Palmares there are some specific features that help to explain its particular history as well as the history of slave resistance in colonial Brazil as a whole. The search for "African" elements at Palmares and in the cultural "survivals" of slaves or fugitives as a whole has too often focused on specific cultural or ethnic identities. In fact, much of what passed for African "ethnicity" in Brazil were colonial creations. Categories or groupings such as "Congo" or "Angola" had no ethnic content in themselves and often combined peoples drawn from broad areas of Africa who before enslavement had shared little sense of relationship or identity. That these categories were sometimes adopted by the slaves themselves indicates not only the slaves' adaptability, but also the fact that African societies had considerable experience with, and a variety of institutions for, the integration of disparate peoples and the creation of solidarities across ethnic lines.

There is, I believe, a deeper story in Palmares and one with broad implications for the subsequent history of slave resistance in Brazil. A key to the problem lies in the etymology of the word *quilombo*. This term came to mean in Brazil any community of escaped slaves, and its usual meaning and origin is given as the Mbundu word for war-camp. By the eighteenth century the term was in general use in Brazil, but it always remained secondary to the older term *mocambo*, a Mbundu word meaning hideout. In fact, the word quilombo does not appear in any contemporaneous document until the end of the seventeenth century except for its mid-

---

*Here the Portuguese word for Creole refers to people of African descent born in the New World.

century use by the poet Gregório de Mattos, who employed it with the meaning of any place where blacks congregated. The first document I have seen with the term quilombo used for a fugitive community is dated 1691 and it deals specifically with Palmares. The chronology and the connection with Palmares are not accidental. Within the term quilombo is encoded an unwritten history that only now because of recent research in African history can be at least partially understood.

While Palmares combined a number of African cultural traditions and included among its inhabitants *crioulos*, mulattoes, Indians, and even some renegade whites, or mestiços, as well as Africans, clearly the traditions of Angola predominated. Its residents referred to Palmares as *angola janga* (little Angola) in recognition of that fact, and in a complaint of 1672 the municipal council of Salvador referred to the "oppression we all suffer from the gentiles of Angola who live in Palmares." But, within the context of Angolan history, what is the significance of that connection for the history of Palmares?

The kingdom of Ndongo, which the Portuguese came to call Angola in the late sixteenth century, was a land in turmoil, invaded from the coast by the Portuguese and from the interior by bands of marauding warriors from Central Africa. The dissolution of the old Kingdom of Kongo and the Luanda state in Kitanga created a period of military struggle and disruption that destroyed villages and uprooted peoples. Powerful groups of uprooted warriors calling themselves "Imbangala" or "Yaka," and called by the Portuguese "Jaga," swept into present-day Angola, disrupting existing states and eventually creating a series of new polities.

The precise origins and cultural traditions of the Imbangala and even the relationship of the designations Jaga, Imbangala, and Yaka have been a matter of debate among Africanists for some time, but some aspects of Imbangala/Jaga society were noted by contemporary observers that are of direct interest to historians of slave resistance in Brazil, and especially to those interested in Palmares. First, the Imbangala raiders lived on a permanent war-footing. Reportedly, they killed the babies born to their women, but integrated adopted children into their ranks so that over time they came to be a composite force of large numbers of people of various ethnic backgrounds united by an organized military structure. That organization and a reputed military ferocity made them the scourge of the region, highly effective and greatly feared. Imbangala–Portuguese relations were alternately hostile and friendly. Between 1611 and 1619, Imbangala lords served as mercenaries for the Portuguese governors and supplied a flow of captives to the slave traders at Luanda. New states were formed by an Imbangala fusion with the indigenous lineages as the Imbangala conquered or created a number of kingdoms among the Mbundu peoples of the Congo–Angola region. Two of these states were the kingdom of

Kasange and the kingdom of Matamba, ruled by Queen Nzinga, with whom the Portuguese first fought until the mid-seventeenth century when an alliance was formed. These states battled each other for control of the Kwango River basin, a struggle that opened up this region to increased slaving.

As the Imbangala moved southward into Angola in the early seventeenth century they encountered among the Mbundu people an institution that they adopted to their purposes. This was the *ki-lombo*, a male initiation society or circumcision camp where young men were prepared for adulthood and warrior status. The Imbangala molded this institution to their own purposes. Torn from ancestral lands and gods, sharing no common lineage, living by conquest and according to European observers rejecting agriculture, the traditional basis of societies in this region, the Imbangala needed an institution that provided cohesion to the disparate ethnic elements comprising their bands. The ki-lombo, a military society to which any man by training and initiation could belong, served that purpose. Designed for war, this institution created a powerful warrior cult by incorporating large numbers of strangers who lacked a common ancestry. The Imbangala ki-lombo was distinctive because of its ritual laws. Lineage and kinship, so important to the other basically matrilineal peoples of the region, were denied within its confines, and although European observers spoke of infanticide, strictly speaking, women could leave the confines of the ki-lombo itself to bear their children. What was prohibited was a legal matrilineal link within the ki-lombo that might challenge the concept of a society structured by initiation rather than by kinship. Historian Joseph Miller believes that the Imbangala "killing" of their own children was a metaphor for the ceremonial elimination of kinship ties and their replacement with the rules and proscriptions of the ki-lombo.

The creation of a social organization based on association created risks. The inhabitants of the ki-lombo stood in a special spiritual danger since they lacked the normal lineage ancestors who might intercede with the gods on their behalf. Thus a chief figure in the ki-lombo was the *nganga a nzumbi*, a priest whose responsibility was to deal with the spirits of the dead. The Ganga Zumba of Palmares was probably the holder of this office, which was in effect not a personal name but a title. There are other echoes from the descriptions of Angola that seem suggestive. In the Imbangala, quilombo leadership depended on some kind of popular acclaim or election just as some of the Brazilian accounts suggest. Most curious is the observation of Andrew Battell, who lived among the Imbangala and who noted that their chief luxury was palm wine and that their routes and camps were influenced by the availability of palm trees. His comment makes the association of the maroon community with a region of Palmares (the word means palm trees) seem more than coincidental.

If the founders of Palmares had used the Imbangala ki-lombo as the basis for their society, their version of it was incomplete or at least a variation on the basic model. A number of features associated with the Imbangala ki-lombos had no parallel in Brazil. The Imbangala were always referred to as cannibals who practiced cannibalism and human sacrifice to terrorize their enemies. These practices were strictly controlled as was the preparation of *magi a samba*, a paste made from human fat and other substances which supposedly made the ki-lombo warriors invincible. A strict set of ritual laws (*kijila*) surrounded the ki-lombo. Women were prohibited from the interior compound of the ki-lombo and there were strict ritual proscriptions against menstruating women. None of these customs are mentioned in the surviving documentation on Palmares.

The use of the term *quilombo* in reference to Palmares does not necessarily mean that all the ritual aspects of that institution as they were practiced in Angola were present in Brazil or that the founders or the subsequent leaders of Palmares were necessarily Imbangala. Many aspects of the Imbangala ki-lombo could be found in other Central African institutions like the *kimpasi*, secret initiation camps of the Kongo, which also created new social bonds by association. Much of what was inherent in the ki-lombo would have been understood by non-Imbangala. As noted, Imbangala dynasties and institutions were incorporated in a number of Mbundu states, and the quilombo came to symbolize the sovereignty of these states. Our best source in this regard is Antonio de Oliveira de Cadornega, the principal chronicler of seventeenth-century Angola. Cadornega used the term *quilombo* to describe Jaga troops, *quilombos de Jagas*, or *gente e quilombos de Jagas*, but also as a descriptive term for the kingdoms of Matamba and Kasange. The use of the phrase "kingdom and quilombo" of Matamba was a general descriptive use of quilombo that referred to these Imbangala-influenced polities but did not necessarily suggest the full existence of the original institution nor its ritual practices. Quilombo was becoming a synonym for a kingdom of a particular type in Angola.

Given the poor documentary record of Palmares much of the above hypothesis is admittedly tenuous, but I believe there is enough evidence to suggest that the introduction of the term *quilombo* into Brazil in the late seventeenth century was not accidental and that it represented more than simply a linguistic borrowing. If true, then we must deal with the African aspects of Palmares not as "survivals" disembodied from their original cultural milieu, but a far more dynamic and perhaps intentional use of an African institution that had been specifically designed to create a community among peoples of disparate origins and to provide an effective military organization. Surely, the fugitive slaves of Brazil fitted such a description, and the attacks made upon them by colonial governments made the military organization of the quilombo essential for survival. The success of quilombos varied as greatly as the quilombos themselves in size, leadership, longevity, and internal organization. Taken together, Palmares and the smaller fugitive communities constituted a continuous commentary on the Brazilian slave regime.

---

3. Africans in the American World ~ John Thornton*

During the eighteenth century, the traffic in slaves across the Atlantic grew explosively. In this selection, historian John Thornton examines the impact of this growth on the development of slave culture in the Americas. Thornton makes the point that, due to the tremendous increase in the number of first-generation Africans living in the Americas, African cultures were not only surviving in the eighteenth century; some were, in fact, just arriving. Such a situation amounted to a "re-Africanization" of American slave culture. Thornton explores this phenomenon in the areas of language, nationality, and religion. He finds that enslaved Africans maintained many of their cultural traditions as a way of adapting to the extremely hostile realities of their lives in bondage.

From 1680 to 1800, the Atlantic slave trade grew immensely. From about 36,000 persons per year at the beginning of the century, the trade had more than doubled by the 1760s, and it reached a high point of nearly 80,000 per year in the last two decades of the century. Of the six trading regions identified by David Richardson in his study of the volume of the slave trade (Senegambia, Sierra Leone, Gold Coast, Bight of Benin, Bight of Biafra, and West Central Africa), West Central Africa had consistently the largest volume of exports, running between 30 and 45 percent of the overall trade. The Bight of Benin, mainly from the ports around the Kingdom of Dahomey, was the second most important, with nearly 40 percent of all exports in 1700, which declined to just over 10 percent by century's end. The Bight of Biafra, whose export trade grew rapidly during this time, supplying only 6 percent at the start of the period but peaking at nearly 30 percent in the 1780s, was close behind it. Among them, these three regions supplied nearly three-quarters of all the Africans transported across the Atlantic during the eighteenth century to labor in the Americas. Of the remaining areas, Sierra Leone provided more than one-fifth of the exports for a brief period between 1760 and 1780, at other times less than 10 percent; the Gold Coast never supplied more than 15

---

*From John Thornton, *Africa and Africans in the Making of the Atlantic World, 1400–1800,* 2nd ed. (New York: Cambridge University Press, 1998), 304–5, 318–24. Reprinted by permission of Cambridge University Press.

percent of the exports; and the exports from Senegal exceeded 10 percent only in the 1720s. The causes of the prodigious growth of the slave trade are not hard to find. There was certainly a great rise in the demand for slaves in the Americas, especially from the Caribbean islands, settled in the second half of the seventeenth century and transformed economically in the eighteenth, and from Brazil, constantly growing first as a sugar and tobacco producer and then as a mining colony. Sugar in the Caribbean and gold in Brazil paid the increasingly high prices for slaves demanded by those Africans in a position to sell them and, as higher prices brought larger numbers of slaves, promoted continued growth and still higher slave prices in an upward cycle that continued throughout the century.

In the Caribbean and Brazil, the newly arrived Africans were often slated to maintain labor forces on sugar estates and in mines whose owners had been unable to keep up the slave populations by natural increase. In addition to the mortality caused by problems of labor and nutrition, women on sugar-producing estates often had very low fertility rates, and their offspring often suffered very high rates of infant and child mortality. This was true even of the large estates of Peru carefully managed by the Jesuits in the last half of the century.

In addition, the recently arrived were employed to open new enterprises as the economy spread to new land and put larger and larger areas under cultivation. In almost all the colonies, the eighteenth century witnessed increasing density of settlement, as well as colonization of new lands in a relentless movement to take over all the land available for crops that could be profitably grown with slave labor. In these frontier areas, a combination of the newly arrived and creoles* would form the colonizing group. The cultivation of coffee, which allowed the exploitation of new areas in existing colonies, brought largely African labor forces to these frontier areas. In Virginia, where the population of African descent soon became self-sustaining and even growing within a generation of the accelerated arrival of slaves, movement inland and up rivers still brought a mix of the newly imported and a minority of creoles.

The flood of African arrivals often Africanized the areas to which they came. Even areas where there was a preexisting population of African descent were "re-Africanized," as Ira Berlin characterized the early eighteenth-century influx around the Chesapeake. The re-Africanization was dramatic in Cuba. The colony had a well-established, even ancient Afro-creole population, but its subsequent transformation into coffee- and sugar-producing colonies in the 1770s brought thousands of Africans in,

---

*Like the Portuguese *crioulo* used by Schwartz in document 2, this word here refers to the people of African descent born in the Americas.

raising the population of slaves of African origin from just under 40,000 in 1774 to 212,000 by the early nineteenth century.

The demography of the eighteenth-century Americas points to an important fact—that African-born people, socialized and bearing African culture, were often the majority in American societies among those of African descent in places like North America, where there was a large European or Euro-American population, and in absolute terms in areas like the Caribbean islands and Brazil. In cultural terms the point is vitally significant. Although many scholars discuss the possibility of the survival of African culture into the present day, an important issue to be sure, the fact is that in the eighteenth century African culture was not surviving: It was arriving. Whatever the brutalities of the Middle Passage or slave life, it was not going to cause the African-born to forget their mother language or change their ideas about beauty in design or music; nor would it cause them to abandon the ideological underpinnings of religion or ethics—not on arrival in America, not ever in their lives.

The newly arrived Africans, like those who had come before them, used this African culture to adapt to the Americas. In the New World they were subject to a restrictive regime created by slavery. Slave owners, concerned to the point of paranoia about security, were often hostile to group activities outside of labor, a factor that might restrict many cultural activities, as seen in the formal statements like the French *Code Noir* or the Spanish *Código Carolina*. More importantly, these Africans came to America to work, and the slave regime often made incredibly heavy labor demands, pushing them to, and sometimes beyond, their physical capacity, shortening life spans, and reducing time for cultural life. Nevertheless, masters were not always willing or able to restrict cultural life, group meetings, or networks of friendship. Within the space that the slave regime allowed, the Africans re-created an African culture in America, although it was never identical with the one they had left in Africa.

Of course, the Africans retained their native languages, and African languages were widely spoken in eighteenth-century America. There were more first-language speakers of African languages in many parts of America than speakers of English, French, Dutch, Spanish, or Portuguese. Many of these Africans developed a certain necessary proficiency in the colonial language, the European language of their masters and other European or Euro-American settlers, after some years' residence, but it was always a second language, spoken with an accent. They were like the runaway woman, described in a late eighteenth-century Jamaican newspaper advertisement, who "speaks not altogether plain English; but from her talk she may easily be discovered to be a Coramantee." She, like other African-born Americans, probably thought, dreamed, and communicated more often in her native language than in the colonial language.

These African languages formed the basis for the nation,* which along with the estate was one of the two groups that had claims on every new African's time, loyalty, and service. It was in the context of the nation that the African cultures of the Americas reemerged, albeit in a new form. Since the sixteenth century, African religious and aesthetic ideas (music and dance especially) were displayed in gatherings of people from the same nation. The nation was the locus for the maintenance of those elements of African culture that continued on American soil.

Yet, in America these African distinctions were put aside, and linguistic loyalty formed a first order of contact and companionship. Although the linguistically formed nations often united those whose relatives in Africa might have been at war with each other, as the Coromantee nation certainly did, they were real enough entities in America. At Pinkster, a Dutch celebration observed in New York, dancers in 1737 "divided into Companies, I suppose according to their different nations." The distinctions were sufficiently significant for a certain rivalry between groups to be noticeable: One South Carolina observer about 1775 noted how "Ibas" and "Gully" often chided each other. A mid-eighteenth-century Virginia preacher urged his flock to "not only pray for your Country-men, who are with you in America but . . . for all the inhabitants of your own Native land."

A nation could also form the locus of a religious community to the degree that it organized funerals. In the seventeenth century, nations were likely to be associated with the cult of ancestors, which was fairly ubiquitous in Africa. In 1765, a planter named Monnereau noted that most assemblies of nations in St. Domingue were to honor the dead. Descendants of a dead person would announce the ceremony, which friends and members of the deceased's nation would attend. Funeral services, conducted according to the "custom of the coast," that is, following national religious norms, were common in the Danish West Indies and elsewhere.

There were also specific religious ideas particular to each nation that made them distinctive. The Anglican bishop Griffith Hughes noted that the Africans of Barbados in the mid–eighteenth century followed the "Rites, Ceremonies and Superstitions of their own Countries." The Kongolese of St. Jan in the Danish West Indies in the 1750s, as Christians of many generations' standing, took it upon themselves to baptize all newly arrived slaves, serving as godparents of sorts to them. Father Jean Baptiste le Pers, an early Jesuit missionary in St. Domingue, identified three different national religious groups there: the Congos, who were Christians (even if all did not properly know the faith); the Senegalese, who were Muslims; and the Ardas (Fon-speaking peoples), who were "idolatrous" snake wor-

---

*Nation, here, indicates group identities shared by Africans of similar regional origin.

shippers. On the eve of the revolution, [Médéric Louis Elie] Moreau de Saint-Méry grouped these various nations under the general term "Voudou." People from the cultural area around Dahomey (the Jeje nation in Brazil) were indulging in religious practices from their homeland when authorities in Cachoeira, Bahia (Brazil), invaded and seized their goods in 1785.

Many Brazilian slaves, as well as those of Spanish colonies, expressed their national identities in ethnically specific lay brotherhoods. The rules of these brotherhoods, which were intended by the clergy to promote Christian life and charitable works, often specified that members of only one or another nation could be members, and often their charitable works were directed toward the nation at large, presumably even toward those who were not official members of the brotherhood (a minority, and the richest at that). In addition to doing charitable work, brotherhoods proudly paraded on saints' days, performing dances of their nation and singing in their national language.

For the newly arrived, the nation formed a surrogate for the family left behind in Africa. Within that group there were often shipmates who had traveled together to America probably, given shipping patterns, from the same nation—which facilitated communication on board ship. Advertisements in Jamaica often noted that runaways could name "their shipmates and country-men" or might be going to where "shipmates and country-men" live. National solidarity provided moral support, cultural reinforcement, and familiarity of practices. Often slaves chose their spouses or other domestic partners from their home nation or closely related ones, as they had earlier.

---

4. A Day on a Coffee Plantation ~ Stanley J. Stein*

Most African slaves brought to the Americas ended up in Brazil, and most Brazilian slaves worked on plantations. In the colonial period, sugar plantations dominated, but by the nineteenth century coffee was on the rise, especially in the south, inland from Rio de Janeiro, the location of Vassouras county. In this passage from his classic study of a nineteenth-century coffee plantation in Brazil, historian Stanley Stein takes us inside the daily routine of plantation slaves. The selection begins with daybreak, follows the slaves through a day in the fields, and ends with nightfall and the return to their quarters. Stein captures not only the rhythm of a typical day but also the way slave culture made the workday

*Adapted from Stanley J. Stein, *Vassouras: A Brazilian Coffee County, 1850–1900* (Cambridge, MA: Harvard University Press, 1957), 161–69. Reprinted by permission of Harvard University Department of History.

more bearable. Students should notice the subtle forms of slave resistance in the passage.

S lave life on the average Vassouras plantation (called a _fazenda_) of approximately eighty to one hundred slaves was regulated by the needs of coffee agriculture, the maintenance of work buildings and slave quarters, and the processing of coffee and subsistence foodstuffs. Since the supply of slaves was never adequate for the needs of the plantation either in its period of growth, prosperity, or decline, the slaves' work day was a long one begun before dawn and often ending many hours after the abrupt sunset of the Paraíba plateau.

Cooks arose before sunup to light fires beneath iron cauldrons; soon the smell of coffee, molasses, and boiled corn meal floated from the outdoor shed. The sun had not yet appeared when the overseer or one of his Negro drivers strode to a corner of the _terreiro_* and reached for the tongue of a wide-mouthed bell. The tolling of the cast-iron bell, or sometimes a blast from a cow horn or the beat of a drum, reverberated across the terreiro and entered the tiny cubicles of slave couples and the separated, crowded dormitories of unmarried slaves. Awakening from their five- to eight-hour slumber, they dragged themselves from beds of planks softened with woven fiber mats; field hands reached for hoes and bill hooks lying under the eaves. At the large faucet near the slave quarters, they splashed water over their heads and faces, moistening and rubbing arms, legs, and ankles. Tardy slaves might appear at the door of their quarters muttering the slave-composed verse which mocked the overseer ringing the bell:

> That devil of a _bembo_ taunted me
> No time to button my shirt, that devil of a bembo.

Now, as the terreiro slowly filled with slaves, some standing in line and others squatting, awaiting the morning prayer, the _senhor_ appeared on the veranda of the main house. "One slave recited the prayer which the others repeated," recalled an ex-slave. Hats were removed and there was heard a "Praised-be-Our-Master-Jesus-Christ" to which some slaves repeated a blurred "Our-Master-Jesus-Christ," others an abbreviated "Kist." From the master on the veranda came the reply: "May-He-always-be-praised." The overseer called the roll; if a slave did not respond after two calls, the overseer hustled into the quarters to get him or her. When orders for the day had been given, directing the various gangs to work on certain coffee-covered hills, slaves and drivers shuffled to the nearby slave kitchen for coffee and corn bread.

---

*A wide patio where the coffee beans were sun-dried.

The first signs of dawn brightened the sky as slaves separated to their work. A few went into the main house; most merely placed the long hoe handles on their shoulders and, old and young, men and women, moved off to the almost year-round job of weeding with drivers following to check stragglers. Mothers bore nursing youngsters in small woven baskets on their backs or carried them astraddle one hip. Those from four to seven trudged with their mothers, those from nine to fifteen close by. If coffee hills to be worked were far from the main buildings, food for the two meals furnished in the field went along—either in a two-team ox-cart, or in iron kettles swinging on long sticks, or in wicker baskets or two-eared wooden pans on long boards carried on male slaves' shoulders. A few slaves carried their own supplementary articles of food in small cloth bags.

Scattered throughout the field were shelters of four posts and a grass roof. Here, at the foot of the hills where coffee trees marched up steep slopes, the field slaves split into smaller gangs. Old men and women formed a gang working close to the rancho; women formed another; the men or young bucks (*rapaziada nova*), a third. Leaving the little boys and girls to play near the cook and assistants in the rancho, they began the day's work. As the sun grew stronger, men removed their shirts; hoes rose and fell slowly as slaves inched up the steep slopes. Under the gang labor system of *corte e beirada* used in weeding, the best hands were spread out on the flanks, *cortador* and *contra-cortador* on one, *beirador* and *contra-beirador* on the other. These four lead-row men were faster-working pace-setters, serving as examples for slower workers sandwiched between them. When a coffee row ended abruptly due to a fold in the slope, the slave now without a row shouted to his overseer, "Throw another row for the middle" or "We need another row"; another passed on the information to the flanking lead-row man who moved into the next row giving the slave who had first shouted a new row to hoe. Thus lead-row men always boxed-in the weeding gang.

Slave gangs often worked within singing distance of each other and to give rhythm to their hoe strokes and pass comment on the circumscribed world in which they lived and worked—their own foibles, and those of their master, overseers, and slave drivers—the master-singer of one gang would break into the first "verse" of a song in riddle form, a *jongo*. His gang would chorus the second line of the verse, then weed rhythmically while the master-singer of the nearby gang tried to decipher the riddle presented. An ex-slave, still known for his skill at making jongos, reported that "Mestre tapped the ground with his hoe, others listened while he sang. Then they replied." He added that if the singing was not good the day's work went badly. Jongos sung in African tongues were called *quimzumba*; those in Portuguese, more common as older Africans diminished in the labor force, *visaria*. Stopping here and there to "give a lick" of the lash to

slow slaves, two slave drivers usually supervised the gangs by crisscross-
ing the vertical coffee rows on the slope and shouting, "Come on, come
on"; but if surveillance slackened, gang laborers seized the chance to slow
down while men and women slaves lighted pipes or leaned on their hoes
momentarily to wipe sweat away. To rationalize their desire to resist the
slave drivers' whips and shouts, a story developed that an older, slower
slave should never be passed in his coffee row. For the aged slave could
throw his belt ahead into the younger man's row and the youngster would
be bitten by a snake when he reached the belt. The overseer or the master
himself, in white clothes and riding boots, might ride through the groves
for a quick look. Alert slaves, feigning to peer at the hot sun, "spiced
their words" to comment in a loud voice, "Look at that red-hot Sun" or
intermixed African words common to slave vocabulary with Portuguese
as in "*Ngoma* is on the way" to warn their fellow slaves, who quickly set
to work industriously. When the driver noted the approaching planter, he
commanded the gang, "Give praise," to which slaves stood erect, eager
for the brief respite, removed their hats or touched hands to forehead,
and responded, "Vas Christo." Closing the ritual greeting, the master too
removed his hat, spoke his "May He always be praised," and rode on.
Immediately the industrious pace slackened.

To shouts of "lunch, lunch" or more horn blasts coming from the
rancho around 10 A.M., slaves and driver descended. At the shaded rancho
they filed past the cook and his assistants, extending their bowls (gourds
split in two). On more prosperous fazendas, slaves might have tin plates.
Into these food was piled; drivers and a respected or favored slave would
eat to one side while the rest sat or sprawled on the ground. Mothers used
the rest to nurse their babies. A half hour later the mother was ordered
back to the sun-baked hillsides. At 1 P.M. came a short break for coffee, to
which slaves often added the second half of the corn meal cake served at
lunch. On cold or wet days, small cups of cachaça (raw rum) distilled from
the plantation's sugarcane replaced coffee. Some ex-slaves reported that
masters often ordered drivers to deliver the *cachaça* to the slaves in a cup
while they worked, to eliminate a break. Supper came at 4 P.M. and work
was resumed until nightfall when to drivers' shouts of "Let's quit" the
slave gangs tramped back to the terreiro. Zaluar, the romantic Portuguese
who visited Vassouras, wrote of the return from the fields: "The solemn
evening hour. From afar, the fazenda's bell tolls Ave-Maria. (From hilltops
fall the gray shadows of night while a few stars begin to flicker in the sky).
. . . From the hill descend the taciturn driver and in front, the slaves, as
they return home." Once more the slaves lined up for roll call on the
terreiro, where the field hands encountered their slave companions who
worked at the plantation center rather than in the fields.

5. A Cuban Slave's Testimony ~ Esteban Montejo*

Working in the fields was the main activity of most enslaved Africans, but not the only one. On Sundays and Catholic holidays, slaves were often allowed to rest and celebrate in their own manner. Such recreational and religious activities were yet another venue for the reworking of African cultural traditions into African-American ones. This selection, taken from the testimony of a runaway Cuban slave named Esteban Montejo, takes us inside a barracoon, or living quarters used to house slaves in Cuba, on a typical Sunday on the Flor de Sagua plantation. Montejo's testimony is fascinating for the insight it provides on such Sunday rituals as bathing, music and dance, and religion. Montejo is also a valuable source on the divisions (especially religious) within this nineteenth-century Cuban slave community.

S unday was the liveliest day in the plantations. I don't know where the slaves found the energy for it. Their biggest fiestas were held on that day. On some plantations the drumming started at mid-day or one o'clock. At Flor de Sagua it began very early. The excitement, the games, and children rushing about started at sunrise. The barracoon came to life in a flash; it was like the end of the world. And in spite of work and everything the people woke up cheerful. The overseer and deputy overseer came into the barracoon and started chatting up the black women. I noticed that the Chinese kept apart; those buggers had no ear for drums and they stayed in their little corners. But they thought a lot; to my mind they spent more time thinking than the blacks. No one took any notice of them, and people went on with their dances.

The one I remember best is the *yuka*. Three drums were played for the yuka: the *caja*, the *mula*, and the *cachimbo*, which was the smallest one. In the background they drummed with two sticks on hollowed-out cedar trunks. The slaves made those themselves, and I think they were called catá. The yuka was danced in couples, with wild movements. Sometimes they swooped about like birds, and it almost looked as if they were going to fly, they moved so fast. They gave little hops with their hands on their waists. Everyone sang to excite the dancers.

There was another more complicated dance. I don't know whether it was really a dance or a game, because they punched each other really hard. This dance they called the *maní* or peanut dance. The dancers formed a circle of forty or fifty men, and they started hitting each other. Whoever

---

*From Esteban Montejo, *The Autobiography of a Runaway Slave*, ed. Miguel Barnet and trans. Jocasta Innes (New York: Pantheon Books, 1968), 20–25. © 1968 by The Bodley Head, Ltd. Reprinted by permission of Pantheon Books, a division of Random House.

got hit went in to dance. They wore ordinary work clothes, with colored print scarves round their heads and at their waists. (These scarves were used to bundle up the slaves' clothing and take it to the wash: they were called *vayajá* scarves.) The men used to weight their fists with magic charms to make the *maní* blows more effective. The women didn't dance but stood round in a chorus, clapping, and they used to scream with fright, for often a Negro fell and failed to get up again. *Maní* was a cruel game. The dancers did not make bets on the outcome. On some plantations the masters themselves made bets, but I don't remember this happening at Flor de Sagua. What they did was to forbid slaves to hit each other so hard, because sometimes they were too bruised to work. The boys could not take part, but they watched and took it all in. I haven't forgotten a thing myself.

As soon as the drums started on Sunday the Negroes went down to the stream to bathe—there was always a little stream near every plantation. It sometimes happened that a woman lingered behind and met a man just as he was about to go into the water. Then they would go off together and get down to business. If not, they would go to the reservoirs, which were the pools they dug to store water. They also used to play hide-and-seek there, chasing the women and trying to catch them.

The women who were not involved in this little game stayed in the barracoons and washed themselves in a tub. These tubs were very big and there were one or two for the whole settlement.

Shaving and cutting hair was done by the slaves themselves. They took a long knife and, like someone grooming a horse, they sliced off the woolly hair. There was always someone who liked to clip, and he became the expert. They cut hair the way they do now. And it never hurt, because hair is the most peculiar stuff, although you can see it growing and every-thing, it's dead. The women arranged their hair with curls and little part-ings. Their heads used to look like melon skins. They liked the excitement of fixing their hair one way one day and another way the next. One day it would have little partings, the next day ringlets, another day it would be combed flat. They cleaned their teeth with strips of soap-tree bark, and this made them very white. All this excitement was reserved for Sundays.

Everyone had a special outfit that day. The Negroes bought themselves rawhide boots, in a style I haven't seen since, from nearby shops where they went with the master's permission. They wore red and green vayajá scarves around their necks, and round their heads and waists too, like in the maní dance. And they decked themselves with rings in their ears and rings on all their fingers, real gold. Some of them wore not gold but fine silver bracelets which came as high as their elbows, and patent leather shoes.

The slaves of French descent danced in pairs, not touching, circling slowly around. If one of them danced outstandingly well they tied silk scarves of all colors to his knees as a prize. They sang in patois and played two big drums with their hands. This was called the French dance. I remember one instrument called a *marímbula*, which was very small. It was made of wickerwork and sounded as loud as a drum and had a little hole for the voice to come out of. They used this to accompany the Congo drums, and possibly the French too, but I can't be sure. The marímbulas made a very strange noise, and lots of people, particularly the *guajiros*,* didn't like them because they said they sounded like voices from another world.

As I recall, their own music at that time was made with the guitar only. Later, in the Nineties, they played *danzones* on pianolas, with accordions and gourds. But the white man has always had a very different music from the black man. White man's music is without the drumming and is more insipid.

More or less the same goes for religion. The African gods are different, though they resemble the others, the priests' gods. They are more powerful and less adorned. Right now if you were to go to a Catholic church you would not see apples, stones, or cock's feathers. But this is the first thing you see in an African house. The African is cruder.

I knew of two African religions in the barracoons: the Lucumí and the Congolese. The Congolese was the more important. It was well known at the Flor de Sagua because their magic-men used to put spells on people and get possession of them, and their practice of soothsaying won them the confidence of all the slaves. I got to know the elders of both religions after Abolition.

I remember the *Chicherekú* at Flor de Sagua. The Chicherekú was a Congolese by birth who did not speak Spanish. He was a little man with a big head who used to run about the barracoons and jump upon you from behind. I often saw him and heard him squealing like a rat. This is true. Until recently in Porfuerza there was a man who ran about in the same way. People used to run away from him because they said he was the Devil himself. You dared not play with the Chicherekú because it could be dangerous. Personally I don't much like talking of him, because I have never laid eyes on him again, and if by some chance . . . Well, these things are the Devil's own!

The Congolese used the dead and snakes for their religions rites. They called the dead *nkise* and the snakes *emboba*. They prepared big pots called *ngangas* which would walk about and all, and that was where the secret of their spells lay. All the Congolese had these pots. The ngangas had to work with the sun, because the sun has always been the strength

---

*Country people usually not of African descent.

and wisdom of men, as the moon is of women. But the sun is more important because it is who gives life to the moon. The Congolese worked magic with the sun almost every day. When they had trouble with a particular person they would follow him along a path, collect up some of the dust he walked upon, and put it in the nganga or in some little secret place. As the sun went down that person's life would begin to ebb away, and at sunset he would be dying. I mention this because it is something I often saw under slavery.

If you think about it, the Congolese were murderers, although they only killed people who were harming them. No one ever tried to put a spell on me because I have always kept apart and not meddled in other people's affairs.

The Congolese were more involved with witchcraft than the Lucumí, who had more to do with the saints and with God. The Lucumí liked rising early with the strength of the morning and looking up into the sky and saying prayers and sprinkling water on the ground. The Lucumí were at it when you least expected it. I have seen old Negroes kneel on the ground for more than three hours at a time, speaking in their own tongue and prophesying. The difference between the Congolese and the Lucumí was that the former solved problems while the latter told the future. This they did with *diloggunes*, which are round, white shells from Africa with mystery inside. The god Elegguá's eyes are made from this shell.

The old Lucumís would shut themselves up in rooms in the barracoon and they could rid you of even the wickedness you were doing. If a Negro lusted after a woman, the Lucumís would calm him. I think they did this with coconut shells, *obi*, which were sacred. They were the same as the coconuts today, which are still sacred and may not be touched. If a man defiled a coconut, a great punishment befell him. I knew when things went well, because the coconut said so. He would command *Alafia* to be said so that people would know that all was well. The saints spoke through the coconuts and the chief of these was Obatalá, who was an old man, they said, and only wore white. They also said it was Obatalá who made you and I don't know what else, but it is from Nature one comes, and this is true of Obatalá too.

The old Lucumís liked to have their wooden figures of the gods with them in the barracoon. All these figures had big heads and were called *oché*. Elegguá was made of cement, but Changó and Yemayá were of wood, made by the carpenters themselves.

They made the saints' marks on the walls of their rooms with charcoal and white chalk, long lines and circles, each one standing for a saint, but they said that they were secrets. These blacks made a secret of everything. They have changed a lot now, but in those days the hardest thing you could do was to try to win the confidence of one of them.

The other religion was the Catholic one. This was introduced by the priests, but nothing in the world would induce them to enter the slaves' quarters. They were fastidious people, with a solemn air which did not fit the barracoons—so solemn that there were Negroes who took everything they said literally. This had a bad effect on them. They read the catechism and read it to the others with all the words and prayers. Those Negroes who were household slaves came as messengers of the priests and got together with the others, the field slaves, in the sugar-mill towns. The fact is I never learned that doctrine because I did not understand a thing about it. I don't think the household slaves did either, although, being so refined and well-treated, they all made out they were Christian. The household slaves were given rewards by the masters, and I never saw one of them badly punished. When they were ordered to go to the fields to cut cane or tend the pigs, they would pretend to be ill so they needn't work. For this reason the field slaves could not stand the sight of them. The household slaves sometimes came to the barracoons to visit relations and used to take back fruit and vegetables for the master's house; I don't know whether the slaves made them presents from their plots of land or whether they just took them. They caused a lot of trouble in the barracoons. The men came and tried to take liberties with the women. That was the source of the worst tensions. I was about twelve then, and I saw the whole rumpus.

There were other tensions. For instance, there was no love lost between the Congolese magic-men and the Congolese Christians, each of whom thought they were good and the others wicked. This still goes on in Cuba. The Lucumí and Congolese did not get on either; it went back to the difference between saints and witchcraft. The only ones who had no problems were the old men born in Africa. They were special people and had to be treated differently because they knew all religious matters.

Many brawls were avoided because the masters changed the slaves around. They kept them divided among themselves to prevent a rash of escapes. That was why the slaves of different plantations never got together with each other.

The Lucumís didn't like cutting cane, and many of them ran away. They were the most rebellious and courageous slaves. Not so the Congolese; they were cowardly as a rule, but strong workers who worked hard without complaining. There is a common rat called Congolese, and very cowardly it is, too.

In the plantations there were Negroes from different countries, all different physically. The Congolese were black-skinned, though there were many of mixed blood with yellowish skins and light hair. They were usually small. The Mandingas were reddish-skinned, tall and very strong. I swear by my mother they were a bunch of crooks, too! They kept apart from the rest. The Gangas were nice people, rather short and freckled.

Many of them became runaways. The Carabalís were like the Musungo Congolese, uncivilized brutes. They only killed pigs on Sundays and at Easter and, being good businessmen, they killed them to sell, not to eat themselves. From this comes a saying, "Clever Carabalí, kills pig on Sunday." I got to know all these people better after slavery was abolished.

READING IMAGES
Brazilian Slaves

Photographer José Christiana de Freitas Henriques Júnior, who was apparently Portuguese by birth, had a studio in Rio de Janeiro during the 1860s. In addition to portraits of the well-to-do, he took pictures of slaves to sell as souvenirs, "a perfect item for those returning to Europe," in the words of his 1866 advertisement. Because by that time the "peculiar institution" had been abolished even in the United States, the continued existence of slavery had become a Brazilian curiosity in the eyes of the rest of the world. Not proud of this dubious distinction, Brazilian photographers had no interest in taking pictures of slaves, just as Brazilian authors tended to leave slaves out of their novels. As a result, here again we see important historical images of Latin America created by Europeans for the European gaze. The following two images suggest a wide variation in what it meant to be enslaved during the lost generation before abolition in Brazil in 1888. How can we deduce the contrasting nature of these men's experiences from their photographs?

"Field Slave." A field slave such as this one labored on a plantation under the watchful eye of an overseer, slept in barracks-like quarters, and enjoyed only a few moments of rest and relaxation. His experience probably included the violence of enslavement in Africa, the horror of the Middle Passage, and the disorientation of arrival in an entirely new and uninviting environment. Africans were more likely to work in a field gang and less likely to work as domestic servants, when compared with the Brazilian born. They were also more likely to try to escape but less likely to succeed than Brazilian-born slaves, who spoke Portuguese with native fluency and moved about with ease. Moreover, African field slaves suffered so intensely that many of them committed suicide. The grimmest comment on Brazilian slavery is the fact that the enslaved population never reproduced itself, necessitating the constant importation of new African captives. *Source:* Serviço do Património Histórico e Artístico Nacional (Brazil), copied from Paulo César de Azevedo and Maurício Lissovsky, *Escravos brasileiros do séculos XIX na fotografia de Christiano* [*sic*] Jr (São Paulo: Editora Ex Libris, 1988), plate 68.

"Slave for Hire." At the other end of the spectrum were urban slaves-for-hire, such as this man. Slaves-for-hire worked independently in the streets as carriers or vendors, reporting to their owners daily or weekly to turn over their earnings. They had greater control over their lives, more opportunities to socialize, even occasionally enough earning power to buy their own freedom. This man, more European than African in appearance, was nonetheless plainly a slave, bare feet being the unmistakable mark of slavery in urban Brazil. Very possibly, his father was white and his mother an enslaved woman of light complexion. Until the Free Birth Law of 1871, the children of enslaved mothers were inevitably slaves. Although people in this situation were clearly better off than field slaves, they faced their own special psychological torment. The plight of the almost-white slave was a poignant subject for nineteenth-century novels. *Source:* Serviço do Património Histórico e Artístico Nacional (Brazil), copied from Paulo César de Azevedo and Maurício Lissovsky, *Escravos brasileiros do séculos XIX na fotografia de Christiano* [*sic*] Jr. (São Paulo: Editora Ex Libris, 1988), plate 48.

III

Caudillos

The political history of postcolonial Latin America confronts us with a maze of shifting alliances and a succession of leaders who rise and fall by force more often than by election. The ubiquity of leaders on horseback, called caudillos, and the proliferation of political warfare pose one of the oldest riddles to confound historians of Latin America. Nineteenth-century chroniclers either sang the praises of caudillos or blasted them, depending on each author's political convictions. Many saw caudillos as a collective disorder of political culture, a view that lasted far into the twentieth century. Late twentieth-century interpretations emphasized the financial feebleness, centrifugal regionalism, and wobbly liberal institutions characteristic of Spanish America in the wake of Independence. Caudillos partly filled a power vacuum left by weak states.

Note the use of the term *Spanish* America. In contrast to the republics that had emerged from the political fragmentation of Spanish-controlled lands, Portuguese America—Brazil—had remained politically united under the only lasting New World monarchy. While not immune to political warfare, nineteenth-century Brazil saw comparatively little of it, and the central government of the empire was never overthrown. In Brazil, leaders on horseback were usually colonels in the national guard. These *coronéis* exercised strong local power, and *coronelismo* is a topic of Brazilian history comparable, in some ways, to Spanish American caudillismo. Overall, however, Brazilian coronéis were less important than Spanish American caudillos, whose heyday was the 1840s–1860s, when military leaders often occupied presidential palaces all over the region. After 1870, Latin American states consolidated their central power and gradually brought the caudillos to heel. Throughout the twentieth century, however, and even today, powerful leaders arise who sometimes win the name "caudillos" from friend and foe alike.

By definition, caudillos' followers were loyal to them personally. They had an army, we might say, with or without a general's rank. In power, caudillos were conservative, rarely questioning existing social hierarchies or hegemonic ideas. They tended to mobilize support through family and friends as well as through patronage networks that linked them to people below them in the social hierarchy. Understanding these networks is essential to all interpretations of caudillismo, a variety of patronage politics (what U.S. politicians call pork-barrel politics, or the spoils system). In a nutshell, political parties were basically competing networks of friends and followers who wanted to control the government to trade favors and reap benefits. At the top stood a national caudillo who counted the powerful heads of the country's great families among his supporters. In the next tier down, these powerful supporters had followers of their own, especially lawyers and landowners, in the regions they dominated throughout the country. Below them were clerks, artisans, and rural workers, the clients of the lawyers and landowners. Political support flowed up through the patron–client links of this multitiered social pyramid, and patronage benefits flowed down. Although ideology played a role in nineteenth-century Latin American politics, historians agree on the primary importance of patronage structures.

As often as not, politics was a matter of fighting, which made it a strictly male activity. For example, a challenger to the current government would issue a proclamation of rebellion and parade through the countryside gathering supporters. He displayed loyalty to his friends, gallantry to women, generosity to his social inferiors. In battle, he had to demonstrate (or conceal the lack of) physical courage and a commanding presence. One or two battles revealed the preponderance of power, and the weaker side saw little to be gained by persisting in a hopeless cause. Defeat would send the rebellious caudillo into exile, but if fortune smiled, he might make a triumphal entry into the national capital and assume the presidency. There he would distribute the spoils of office to his loyal friends and they, in turn, would reward their followers, down to the level of the servants and laborers who composed the bulk of each caudillo's army.

Caudillo "revolutions" became integral parts of the political process in postcolonial Spanish America. Limited goals, small armies, and a shortage of firearms kept routine political warfare from producing huge death tolls like those of the U.S. Civil War. Still, if caudillos were so popular, it makes sense to inquire: Why did people follow caudillos? For answers, students can consult samples of three generations of twentieth-century scholarship on the problem and three nineteenth-century primary sources.

QUESTIONS FOR ANALYSIS

1. Not only primary sources, but also secondary sources written by historians, can sometimes be less than objective. What kind of biases

can you see in the following documents? Can you relate them to the
time in which each historian was writing?
  2. What are main differences in the three secondary sources? Are
there any points of agreement? What do they say about the origins of
caudillismo?
  3. How do the three primary-source excerpts confirm, add to, or
raise questions about the secondary sources?

---

1. Caudillos as Scourge ∼ Charles E. Chapman*

This scholarly article exemplifies the "bad old days" of ethnocentric, chauvinistic writing on Latin American history in the United States. For U.S. historian Charles E. Chapman, caudillismo is a shortcoming, a syndrome, a pathology. He presents the caudillos as megalomaniacal madmen. He describes their frequent appearance in Latin American history as a result of the region's "retarded political development," a manifestation of its "inferior races." Caudillismo could possibly be remedied, he suggests, by the "civilizing influence" of the United States, but otherwise he holds out little hope. It is important for us to confront this sort of interpretation, despite its obsolete ideas, not so that we can feel superior (none of us can claim today's better understanding of race as a personal achievement) but so that we can recognize this discourse as a historical factor in its own right. In 1932 this view passed as expert analysis in a respected professional journal.

It is hardly necessary to say that caudillismo grew naturally out of conditions as they existed in Hispanic America. Institutions do not have a habit of springing full-blown and without warning into life. One of the essential antecedents of caudillismo is to be found in the character of the Hispanic races which carried out the conquest of the Americas. Spaniards and Portuguese, then as now, were individualists, at the same time that they were accustomed to absolutism as a leading principle of political life. *"Del rey abajo ninguno"* is a familiar Spanish refrain, which may be rendered freely "No person below the king is any better than I am." It is precisely because of the strength of this feeling that absolutism has become a necessary part of Hispanic practice, because usually only some form of strong dictatorship has been able to hold Hispanic peoples in

*From Charles E. Chapman, "The Age of the Caudillos: A Chapter in Hispanic American History," *Hispanic American Research Review* 12, no. 2 (May 1932): 286–92. © 1932 Duke University Press. All rights reserved. Reprinted by permission of Duke University Press.

check. Otherwise, in a truly democratic country of ten million Hispanic persons there would be ten million republics. Furthermore, it was the most adventurous and least conservative elements among the Spaniards and Portuguese who first came to America. Even some of their illustrious leaders were men of comparatively low origin in the mother country. In America, the conquerors were a dominant minority among inferior races, and their individualism was accentuated by the chances now afforded to do as they pleased amidst subjugated peoples. It must be remembered, too, that they did not bring their families, and in consequence not only was there an admixture of blood on a tremendous scale with the native Indians and even the Negroes, but also tendencies developed toward loose and turbulent habits beyond anything which was customary in the homeland.

In other words, Hispanic society deteriorated in the Americas. To make matters worse, there were no compensating advantages in the way of political freedom, for the monarchy was successful in establishing its absolutist system in the colonies, a system which in practice was a corrupt, militaristic control, with scant interest in, or attention to, the needs of the people over whom it ruled. The Anglo-American colonies were settlements of families in search of new homes. They did not decline in quality, as there was no such association with the Indians as there was in Spanish America and Brazil. In Hispanic America, society was constituted on the basis of a union of white soldiery with Indian or Negro elements. It tended to become mestizo or mulatto, with a resulting loss of white culture and the native simplicity of life. Soon the half-castes far surpassed the whites in numbers, and, especially in the case of the mestizos, added to the prevailing turbulence in their quest for the rights of white men. Even in the eighteenth century it was the custom in Buenos Aires for men to go about armed with swords and muskets, for the protection of both life and property depended more upon one's self than upon the law. As for the Indians and Negroes, they were usually submissive, but shared one feeling with castes and native-born whites: abomination for the government. Most persons in colonial days knew no patriotism beyond that of the village or city in which they lived. For this, in keeping with the individualistic traits of their character, they came to have an exaggerated regard.

Without taking too much space for argument, a few words might be added in order to emphasize the existence of the factor of a favorable atmosphere in colonial days for the eventual development of caudillismo. Indeed, the institution really existed throughout the pre-independence era. What were the conquistadores and even the viceroys but absolute military and political bosses? Not infrequently colonial officials continued to wield power despite higher orders to the contrary. It was a natural transition from native chiefs by way of Hispanic officialdom to the caudillos of the early republics. The social keynote was one of individualistic absolutism in all classes, instead of that love of, and subjection to, the law which were such marked characteristics of the Anglo-American colonists. In consequence, with the disappearance of the mother country governments at the time of the revolutions, all authority fell with them, and there was no legal consciousness or political capacity ready at hand to cope with the turbulence which was to facilitate the emergence of the caudillos. When the citizens of Buenos Aires came together on May 25, 1810, to begin the movement for the over-throw of Spanish control, it was the first time that the people of that part of the Americas had exercised civic functions. Only the absolutism of the mother country had existed before, and in the bitter war period after 1810 it became a habit to denounce that dominance in exaggerated fashion as a tyranny of which the last vestige should be destroyed. There was no desire for a continuance of the institutions of the mother country such as there was in Anglo America. There was little in the way of political liberty worth preserving in either Spain or Portugal anyway. So institutions were adopted which were as far removed as possible from those of their former rulers, with the result that they did not fit the peoples of Hispanic America. An attempt was made to pass immediately from colonial absolutism to pure democracy. Naturally, the effort failed. It was possible to tear down the outward forms—one might say the nomenclature—of the old system, but its inner spirit remained, for it was ingrained in the habits of the people.

Ignorance, turbulence, and what proved to be their great ally, universal suffrage, combined to assure the rise and overlordship of the caudillos. The overwhelming majority of the people of Hispanic America were illiterate. Certainly, it would be a generous estimate to assert that 10 percent of the inhabitants could read and write. With this impossible background, democratic institutions were attempted. The meetings of the cabildos became demagogic tumults, with the masses sitting in the galleries and cheering the most radical and violent. It was on this account that new institutions were adopted by law which did not fit actual conditions, a prime cause of the failure of the early independence governments. The turbulence of the new alleged democracy could accept nothing less than universal suffrage, which of course was duly proclaimed. That meant the demagogue in the city.

Much more important, it meant the caudillo in the rural districts, for the "sacred right of voting" became the principal legal basis of the power of the caudillos. Out of this there developed that curious phenomenon, the Hispanic American election. Elections were habitually fraudulent. The question about them was whether the fraud should be tame or violent. If there were no resistance, various devices were employed to obtain the vote desired. But if there were opposition, the caudillo nevertheless won, but to the accompaniment of an orgy of blood. In the beginning the masses supported the demagogue of the city or the country caudillo. In these leaders, with their rhetoric about the "rights of man," they found the vindication of their claims for political recognition. The conservative classes acquiesced. It was better to suffer the mob and grotesque usurpers than to lose one's life and property through any genuine participation in elections. All that remained for the caudillos to do was to conquer the demagogues. Then at last their work was complete.

The different leaders in no respect represented any real political or social conflict, just different leaders. Government reduced itself to dominating and to resisting the efforts of others to dominate. In point of fact this practice of exaggerated expression fitted in with the customs of the people. It was a Hispanic-American habit to conceive of causes in the name of persons. There have been far more "Miguelistas" or "Porfiristas" in Hispanic America than "Progressives" or men of other party names, at least in popular parlance. The leader, which meant the caudillo, was party, flag, principle, and objective, all in his own person. If conditions were bad, it was because another leader was needed, and for that matter each group had its "liberator" or "savior" of the country. Indeed, hyperbole of civic phrase makes its appearance in all the documentation of Hispanic-American history. All prominent men are national heroes or tyrants, according to whatever person happens to be writing. It makes research in this field a matter requiring great discrimination and critical appreciation, for hyperbole, I repeat, was and still is a Hispanic-American disease.

---

2. Caudillos as Profit Maximizers ~
Eric R. Wolf and Edward C. Hansen*

Anthropologists Eric Wolf and Edward Hansen exemplify a very different period of Latin American studies. Gone is the racism and chauvinism of the early twentieth century. Latin Americanist social scientists of the 1960s and afterward took a less judgmental approach, concentrating not on the caudillos' personal attributes but on the economic logic of the social system within which they operated. This emphasis on economic or materialist explanations of politics was typical of Latin American studies at the time. This article, which appeared in the Cambridge journal Comparative Studies in Society and History, *became the single most important statement on caudillismo to be published in English in the late twentieth century.*

*From Eric R. Wolf and Edward C. Hansen, "Caudillo Politics: A Structural Analysis," *Comparative Studies in Society and History* 9 (1967): 168–79. Reprinted by permission of Cambridge University Press.

In spite of the decline of Spanish power in the late colonial period, the New World planter class proved too weak numerically and too lacking in cohesion to oust the Peninsular forces by its own unaided efforts. To gain their own independence they were therefore forced into political alliances with the numerically strong and highly mobile—yet at the same time economically, socially, and politically disadvantaged—social strata of the population which are designated collectively as mestizos. Not without trepidation, criollo leaders armed elements derived from these propertyless strata and sent them to do battle against the Spaniards. Success in maintaining the continuing loyalties of these elements depended largely upon the ability of leaders in building personal ties of loyalty with their following and in leading them in ventures of successful pillage.

Although the alliances of criollos and mestizos was instrumental in winning the Wars of Independence, granting arms to the mestizo elements freed these to create their own armed bands. The mestizos in turn were thus enabled to compete with the criollos for available wealth. The case of Venezuela, while unique in its extreme manifestations, nevertheless demonstrates this new, and continent-wide, ability of the mestizos to act on their own behalf. There the royalists were originally victorious by granting the llanero plainsmen, formerly armed servants of the criollos, pillage rights against their masters. Having eliminated their own masters, the llaneros then turned upon the royalists and massacred them in an effort to obtain additional loot. In granting independent armament to the mestizos, therefore, the criollo gentry also sacrificed any chance it might have had to establish a monopoly of power.

We must not forget that criollo wealth was dependent upon large landholdings, or haciendas. If the hacienda provided a bulwark of defense against the laissez-faire market, the hacienda system itself militated against the development of a cohesive political association of hacienda owners. Geared to a stagnant technology, yet under repeated pressures to expand production, the hacienda tended to "eat up" land, in order to control the population settled upon the land. The aim of each hacienda was ultimately to produce crops through the arithmetic addition of workers, each one of whom—laboring with his traditional tools—would contribute to increase the sum of produce at the disposal of the estate. While in some parts of Latin America, notably in the Andes and in Middle America, the expansionist tendencies of the hacienda could be directed against Indian communities, in areas without Indians a hacienda could expand only at the expense of neighboring haciendas. Not surprisingly, therefore, we find that blood feuds among hacienda owners are a notable feature of this period. Each hacienda owner's bitterest enemy was potentially his closest neighbor. In this competition we must find the economic roots of criollo anarchy.

Such economic determinants of anarchy were reinforced further by social organizational factors. Competition and conflict on the economic plane could, to some extent, be compensated for through the workings of kinship. Arnold Strickon has noted the growth of regional aristocratic families and their role in national politics. We do not yet possess adequate data on how such alliances were formed, how many people were involved, and how much territory they covered. Theoretical considerations, however, lead us to believe that the organizing power of such alliances must have been relatively weak. If we assume that hacienda owners favored the maintenance of large estates through inheritance by primogeniture; if we assume further that the chances are equal that the chief heir will be either male or female; and if we postulate that each hacienda owner strives to maximize the number of his alliances, then it seems unlikely that the number of strategic alliances based on landed property between a hacienda family of origin and other hacienda families of procreation will exceed three. The marriage of Father with Father's Wife creates one such alliance; the marriage of the first-born son with a woman of another family swells the number to two; and the marriage of the eldest daughter with the first son of a third family brings the number of strategic alliances to three. These considerations are intended to yield a measure of insight into the inability of the criollo gentry to form a wide-ranging network of strategic alliances for political purposes.

In analyzing the caudillo mode of political organization, we are forced to rely on materials dealing with caudillos who made their influence felt on the national level. The available literature deals mainly with these national-level or "maximal" bands, but sheds little light on how the "minimal" bands of local chieftains and followers were first formed. The caudillos who emerged into the light of day are thus all leaders who proved capable of welding a series of structurally similar minimal bands into a maximal coalition, capable of exercising dominance over wide regions. The data dealing with such national caudillos, however, permit some generalizations about the patterns of coalition formation, about the distribution of wealth by the leader to his band, and about the sources of political strength and fragility. We are also enabled to make certain comparisons between the different problems faced by mestizo and criollo chieftains. To describe the model, we shall conjugate verbs in the ethnographic present.

The aim of the caudillo band is to gain wealth; the tactic employed is essentially pillage. For the retainers, correct selection of a leader is paramount. No retainer can guarantee that he will receive recompense from his leader in advance, because the band seeks to obtain wealth which is not yet in its possession. All know that the wealth sought after is finite; only certain resources are "safe game." The band cannot attack with impunity the basic sources of criollo wealth, such as land; and it cannot sequester, without international complications, the property of foreign firms operating in the area. Hence there is not only intense competition for movable resources, but great skill is required in diagnosing which resources are currently "available" and which taboo. The exercise of power therefore gives rise to a code which regulates the mode of access to resources. The code refers to two basic attributes of leadership: first, the interpersonal skills needed to keep the band together; second, the acumen required to cement these relationships through the correct distribution of wealth. Possession of interpersonal skills is the initial prerequisite; it suggests to the retainers that the second attribute will also be fulfilled.

The social idiom in which the first of these attributes is discussed is that of "masculinity": the social assertion of masculinity constitutes what has come to be known as machismo (from *macho*, masculine). According to the idiom, masculinity is demonstrated in two ways: by the capacity to dominate females, and by the readiness to use violence. These two capacities are closely related; both point to antagonistic relations between men. The capacity to dominate women implies the further capacity to best other men in the competition over females.

Assertions of dominance are tested in numerous encounters, in which the potential leader must test himself against other potential claimants. Although Latin American rural communities are frequently isolated by poor communication facilities, the local caudillos are thrown into contact from time to time. Occasionally in activities such as drinking, card playing, carousing, and brawling, a man so stands out that the others automatically accept his authority and extend to him their loyalties. Such situations are charged with potential violence, for in such antagonistic confrontations, the claimants to victory must be prepared to kill their rivals and to demonstrate this willingness publicly. For the loser there is no middle ground; he must submit to the winner, or be killed. Willingness to risk all in such encounters is further proof of masculinity. The drama involved in such tests of leadership is illustrated by the following episode in the rise of the Bolivian caudillo Mariano Melgarejo, an ignorant and drunken murderer given to the wildest sexual orgies, who ran the country from 1864 to 1871. Melgarejo got into power by killing the country's dictator, [Manuel Isidoro] Belzú, in the presidential palace. The shooting took place before a great crowd which had gathered in the plaza to see the meeting of the two rivals. When Belzú fell dead into the arms of one of his escorts, Melgarejo strode to the window and exclaimed: "Belzú is dead. Now who are you shouting for?" The mob, thus prompted, threw off its fear and gave a bestial cry: "Viva Melgarejo!"

Personal leadership may thus create a successful band. By the same token, however, the personal nature of leadership also threatens band maintenance. If the caudillo is killed or dies of natural causes, the band will disintegrate because there can be no institutionalized successor. The qualities of leadership reside in his person, not in the office. To establish a system of offices it would have been necessary to reorganize post-Independence society. Attempts in this direction were continuously thwarted by criollo arms. One has to note the defeat of the "centralists" in all parts of Latin America.

Proof of masculinity does not yet make a man a caudillo. Men will not flock to his banner unless he also proves himself capable of organizing a number of minimal bands into a maximal faction, and demonstrates his ability to hold the faction together. To this end, the caudillo must weld a number of lieutenants into a core of "right-hand men." Important in this creation of a core of devoted followers is not merely assertion of dominance, but also calculated gift-giving to favored individuals who are expected to reciprocate with loyalty. Such gifts may consist of movable goods, money, or perquisites such as the right to pillage a given area or social group. The importance of such gifts is best understood as a presentation of favors defined not merely as objects, but also as attributes of the giver. Where the receiver cannot respond with a counter-gift which would partake equally of his own personal attributes, he is expected to respond with loyalty, that is, he makes a gift of his person for a more or less limited period of time. The existence of such a core of right-hand men produces its own demonstration effect. They are living testimony to the largesse of the caudillo aspirant and to his commitment to grant riches in return for personal support.

To satisfy this desire for riches, the caudillo must exhibit further abilities. We have already discussed some of the limitations under which the caudillo labors in acquiring wealth: there are certain groups he may not attack with impunity. To cast about in quest of riches may stir resistance; resistance may imply defeat. To be successful, therefore, a caudillo needs what we may call "access vision," capabilities closely related to the "business acumen" of the North American entrepreneur. He must be able to diagnose resources which are available for seizure with a minimum of resistance on the part of their present owners. He must estimate how much wealth is needed to satisfy his retainers. He must also control the freelance activities of his followers, such as cattle rustling and robbery, lest they mobilize the resistance of effective veto groups. He must be able to estimate correctly the forces at the disposal of those presently in control of resources. And he must be able to predict the behavior and power of potential competitors in the seizure of wealth. Nor can he rest content with initial success in his endeavors. He must continuously find new sources of wealth which can be distributed to his following, or he must attach resources which replenish themselves. Initial successes are therefore frequently followed by sudden failures. Many caudillo ventures end as "one-shot" undertakings. The caudillo may be successful in seizing the government treasury or the receipts of a custom house, but then no other source of wealth is found, and the faction disintegrates. The more limited the supply of ready wealth, the more rapid the turnover of caudillos. Thus Bolivia, one of the most impoverished countries during this period, averaged more than one violent change of government every year.

Such considerations affected even the most successful caudillos, such as José A. Páez and Juan Manuel Rosas. Páez held sway in Venezuela for thirty-three years (1830–63); Rosas dominated Argentina for twenty years (1829–31, 1835–52). Both owned enormous cattle ranches which furnished large quantities of beef, the staple of the countryside. Both drew their retainers from the ranks of the fierce cowpunchers of the tallgrass prairie, the gauchos in Argentina and the llaneros of Venezuela, whose mode of livelihood provided ideal preparation for caudillo warfare. Time and again, both men defeated the attempts of rivals to set up centralized forms of government Despite the initial advantages of abundant wealth, their control of "natural" military forces, and their ability to neutralize a large number of competitors, however, both men had to beat off numerous armed uprisings, and both ultimately met defeat. Their cases illustrate the difficulties which beset caudillos operating even under optimal conditions.

---

3. Caudillos as Culture Heroes ～ Ariel de la Fuente*

The following excerpt from a recent book by historian Ariel de la Fuente takes up the subject of caudillos a generation after Eric Wolf and Edward Hansen's influential article. It is a close-up regional study of the sort that the two anthropologists called for in 1967. Focusing on the Argentine province of La Rioja during a seventeen-year period, de la Fuente's book adds a much broader investigation of culture to the economic emphasis of the 1960s. In so doing, he exemplifies the cultural emphasis of Latin American history at the turn of the twenty-first century. The work of de la Fuente (like that of several other contemporary historians whose studies are excerpted in this volume) also shows a particular interest in non-elite culture—here, the oral traditions of the illiterate majority. De la Fuente uses a major 1921 collection of Argentine folklore to probe aspects of nineteenth-century patron–client relations and attitudes toward authority.

*From Ariel de la Fuente, *Children of Facundo: Caudillo and Gaucho Insurgency during the Argentine State-Formation Process* (La Rioja, 1853–1870) (Durham, NC: Duke University Press, 2000), 115–17, 125–28. © 2000 Duke University Press. All rights reserved. Reprinted by permission of Duke University Press.

Politics occupied an important place in the oral culture of the provinces of the Argentine interior in the nineteenth century. This can be seen in many of the songs that remained in the collective memory of the provinces in the early twentieth century. For example, among the thousands of pieces collected in 1921, some 250 songs had a strictly political content, and many of those were principally concerned with nineteenth-century caudillos and their political lives. In terms of the caudillos from the province of La Rioja itself, we find eight songs about Facundo Quiroga and twenty-one about Chacho Peñaloza. The geographic location where the songs were collected reveals the extent of their circulation throughout Argentina. Songs that have as their protagonists Riojan caudillos, for instance, appear not only in the province of La Rioja but also in Córdoba, San Luis, San Juan, Catamarca, Tucumán, Salta, and Jujuy. The collection of 1921 also preserved a good number of stories featuring caudillos as protagonists: twenty-two concerning Facundo and thirteen about Chacho were collected in the provinces of La Rioja, Catamarca, and San Juan.

Testimony from some of the caudillos' contemporaries suggested the importance of such songs and stories in political life. In 1862, an observer noted that after Chacho had successfully resisted the troops from Buenos Aires, the gauchos raised the power and prestige of Peñaloza in the provinces of the interior "by singing the glories of the general." And General José Maria Paz remembered that in his campaigns in the province of Córdoba toward the end of the 1820s, besides confronting Facundo on the battlefield, he also confronted Facundo's prestige within popular culture:

> I also had a strong enemy to combat in the popular beliefs about Quiroga. When I say popular I am speaking of the countryside, where those beliefs had taken root in various parts and not only in the lower classes of society. Quiroga was thought to be an inspired man, who had well-known spirits that penetrated everywhere and obeyed his mandate . . . and a thousand other absurdities of this type.

The beliefs that circulated in the form of stories and songs, and the resulting perceptions that they generated among the rural population of Córdoba, were key elements of the gauchos' loyalty to the Riojan caudillo.

Oral culture, as Paz recognized, was a political dominion, an arena where the struggle between Unitarians and Federalists (Argentina's two parties of the era) was waged. Humor was also used as a weapon in this conflict, and Unitarian and Federalist leaders became the protagonists (as well as targets) of jokes. In the 1840s, a Unitarian from Santiago del Estero named one of his horses Juan Manuel (a reference to the caudillo Juan Manuel de Rosas) to depict the Federalist caudillo as a beast, belonging in the camp of the barbarians, the enemies of civilization. When Catamarca was occupied by Unitarian troops from Buenos Aires in 1862, a poor black of that locality defiantly called a dog "Bartolo" (short for Bartolomé Mitre, leader of the Unitarian Party) and got 500 lashes for his insolence. And after the death of Chacho, in 1863, a poem of Unitarian origin made fun of his supposed hatred of the emblematic Unitarian color, sky blue:

> Peñaloza died and
> Went straight to heaven,
> But as he saw it was sky blue
> He went back down to hell.

The Federalist color was red.

Although Unitarians and Federalists competed for primacy in the arena of popular culture, overall Federalism dominated it. Thus, a quick review of the 205 songs collected in 1921 that explicitly referred to the conflict between the two parties shows that two-thirds of them were Federalist. And if we consider the presence of leaders of both parties in those songs, the predominance of Federalism is even more pronounced: of the total number of positive depictions of leaders from both parties, more than four-fifths concerned Federalist caudillos. The names Urquiza, Facundo, Rosas, El Chacho, and Felipe Varela were most often evoked. Among the rarely mentioned Unitarians were the Taboadas, General Lavalle, General Paz, General La Madrid, Mitre, and Sarmiento. While these references do not necessarily reflect the amount of support each party enjoyed, they certainly reveal the predominance of Federalism in the oral culture; and this, in turn, signals the pervasiveness of this partisan identity among the illiterate, the main users of oral culture.

The caudillos, in their day, were perceived as the highest authority. In this respect, popular culture underscored not only their position as political leaders but also distinguished the caudillos as moral authorities and role models in the communities they ruled over. Oral culture integrated well-known motifs from folklore, and invested caudillos with qualities and connotations similar to those that popular classes attributed to kings or patrons in other societies. This association with images of kings stemmed, in part, from the repertoire of preexisting archetypes on which the images of the caudillos were formed, but it could also possibly be the product of three centuries of colonial, monarchical experience, which would have left a model and language through which to define legitimate authority, and the characteristics that holders of that authority should have .

In certain stories, Facundo, hiding his identity, appeared by surprise in various places in La Rioja, although everyone thought he had left the region. These stories attributed to him a special capacity to know what Riojans were doing, and, if necessary, reward or punish them. In one story, after the battle of La Tablada, a group of young Unitarians got together to celebrate the defeat of Facundo. The young men began to sing a song that painted the caudillo negatively, when they realized that among them was "an individual in a poncho, with practically the entire face covered by a big hat." The man in a poncho "asked them in a polite tone to finish the interesting song." When the song came to an end, "Quiroga (for it was none other in the poncho)" called his soldiers and had the singers shot. "Nobody imagined that the disguised figure was the Tiger of Los Llanos," concluded the story, "for he was thought to be thirty leagues away." Here, using the motif that folklorists have classified as "the king in disguise to learn the secrets of his subjects," oral tradition sought to explain a tragic occurrence: the fact that after the battle of La Tablada, Quiroga did have some Unitarians in La Rioja shot "under the pretext that they had been rejoicing in his defeat." The form the story took spoke of the reach of Quiroga's authority and the control that he exercised over the population of La Rioja. Thus, omnipresence was one of the supposed qualities of Facundo, which also suggests an appreciation of his power. But this capacity "to learn the secrets of subjects" may have been a quality attributed to Federalist caudillos more generally. William H. Hudson remembered that a number of stories about Rosas circulated, many of them related to his adventures when he would disguise himself as a person of humble status and prowl about the city [of Buenos Aires] by night, especially in the squalid quarters, where he would make the acquaintance of the very poor in their hovels.

Mediation in the daily conflicts of rural La Rioja was the responsibility of the caudillos. This included interventions in family disputes or conflicts between gauchos and government officials. Sometimes the caudillos proposed solutions, while on other occasions they made sure that the proper authorities intervened. Conflict resolution and justice, then, were some of the caudillos' duties, and to explain them, gauchos used archetypes clearly drawn from the King Solomon legend. Facundo was portrayed as a Solomon-like figure who used his exceptional wisdom or astuteness to resolve disputes and impart justice.

But the caudillo was the highest authority because he was also responsible, ultimately, for the material and moral preservation of the society. The extent of his authority and the nature of this responsibility were expressed in the language of caudillos and gauchos. Chacho reflected on the dimensions of his own authority:

> I have that influence [over the gauchos], that prestige, because as a soldier I fought at their side for forty-three years, sharing with them the fortunes of war, the suffering of the campaigns, the bitterness of banishment. I have been more of a father to them than a leader . . . preferring their necessities to my own. As an Argentine and a Riojan I have always been

the protector of the unfortunate, sacrificing the very last that I had to fulfill their needs, making myself responsible for everything and with my influence as a leader forcing the national government to turn its eyes toward these unfortunate people.

Penaloza's authority and status as a caudillo had evolved through the long political experience that he shared with the gauchos since the 1820s, when Chacho had entered into the party struggles as a subaltern of Facundo. His partisan leadership, however, was only one part of his relationship with the gauchos: "I have been more of a father to them than a leader." That is, he had always been "the protector of the unfortunate," putting the needs of the gauchos above his own and sacrificing for them. As a father, then, Peñaloza had made himself "responsible for everything."

The language of kinship emphasized the nature of the obligation and, especially, affective ties that bound caudillos and gauchos. This explains why references to caudillos as fathers were often articulated in an emotive language. Popular songs defined Facundo, for example, as "a dear father." Likewise, it was said of General Octaviano Navarro, from Catamarca, that "he was beloved by his province, he was the father of said province and his heart was tempered by his very warm soldiers, who loved him so much."

The authority of the caudillo as a "father" had moral and ideological dimensions, too, as reflected in a story featuring Facundo as the protagonist. Here, the caudillo was going through a village when he decided to stop and join a crowd assembled for a wedding. During the ceremony, the bride refused to accept the man her father had chosen to be her husband. She pointed out another man in the crowd and said, "He is the one I love, not [indicating her bridegroom] this one." According to oral tradition, "Quiroga sent his officers to take the girl and hang her from the highest Tala tree and to bring the one she loved to judgment, and give him six shots." It was the caudillo who castigated those who would subvert the functioning of matrimony and the authority of the father to choose a daughter's mate. In this episode, however, the "real" father was absent, transforming the tale into an explicit comment on the caudillo's authority. It was Facundo, the father of all Riojans, who exercised patriarchal authority and did what was expected of any father under the same circumstances. The caudillo was "responsible for everything" including the reproduction of patriarchy. And to fulfill that responsibility, oral culture resorted once again to Facundo's omnipresence, which allowed the caudillo to attend an apparently insignificant wedding.

The stories concerning Facundo and Chacho emphasized that these Federalist caudillos appreciated and rewarded the loyalty of the gauchos. Therefore, he who responded when his leader asked for, or needed, help was compensated beyond what a client would hope for from a caudillo. In one of the stories, collected in San Antonio, the home village of Facundo, in Los Llanos, a peon who, without recognizing the caudillo, helped Quiroga to cross a river and escape when the caudillo was pursued by government officials, was later rewarded by Facundo with "ten oxen and ten cows." Any landless worker in Los Llanos understood the significance of this compensation. It allowed the peon to begin raising cattle, thereby distancing him from the periodic specter of hunger that was part and parcel of casual wage labor and subsistence agriculture. In other words, the peon's service to the caudillo was more than amply repaid with an amount of animals that surpassed what the sons of modest ranchers received to start their own ranches. This way of rewarding gauchos appears in stories about Chacho as well. After requisitioning for his troops the "four or five cows" that a couple living in a hut had, "Chacho returned not only the five cows but as many more," doubling the stock of these small landholders.

The poor occupied a privileged and almost exclusive position in the representation of the patron–client relation, which gave the caudillo's following a clear social identity. In a story from Los Llanos about the death of Peñaloza, an elderly woman tried to warn him about the fatal event to come, telling him, "Fly from here, I don't want them to kill you, all us poor folk need you." Her warnings were not enough, and Peñaloza died. His death "was felt by all, since he had been so generous in these villages."

In other tales, elements of Chacho's personal history and his special relationship with the poor made him look almost like a saint. "Chacho was a man who had been a priest, and because he liked to sacrifice for humanity he threw off the priest's habit and took up the dress of the gaucho." With this explanation, one story recounts an episode in which Chacho went to the house of "a woman who had a good amount of livestock but she was very tight-fisted, and she had all her animals hidden." When the caudillo asked her "what she had to offer him, chickens or goats, the woman said nothing." Chacho had her punished, and then the woman admitted that she did have livestock and offered it to the caudillo, who reminded her that "with a man like him, one doesn't tell lies."

---

4. The Lions of Payara ~ José Antonio Páez*

The Venezuelan caudillo José Antonio Páez, a rural man of middling social origins, became a leader during the Wars of Independence and afterward the first

*From José Antonio Páez, *Autobiografía del general José Antonio Páez*, 2 vols. (New York, 1869; reprint ed., H. R. Elliot and Company, 1946), 2:297–301. Translated by John Charles Chasteen.

*president of Venezuela. Such social mobility was uncommon, and it usually
stemmed from fighting ability. Páez's original supporters were the mounted herds-
men, famous for their military prowess, of the Orinoco plains. Charging lancers,
roll calls of heroes, and paternalistic bonds between Páez and his followers give
his account of 1836–37 an archaic tone reminiscent of a medieval epic. In this
passage from his autobiography (written in an elevated style he would have
required assistance in composing), the caudillo describes events that occurred
between his two presidencies of the 1830s. Although out of office, he remained
the real power behind the government at the time.*

A fter the triumph of Independence, the cattle of the Province of Apure
had been distributed among the valiant warriors of the army whose
lances doomed Spanish despotism there. By distributing the herds, our
country repaid their services and gave them a stake in the prosperity of
the territory which they had conquered with heroism and defended with
unfailing courage. Cornelio Muñoz, intrepid captain of my former guard,
had property there; so did Rafael Ortega, my constant companion in hard-
ship and glory, whose recent death still grieved me at the time of these
events; then there were Francisco Guerrero (second in command of the
army in Apure), Remigio Lara, Juan Angel Bravo, Facundo and Juan
Antonio Mirabal, Doroteo Hurtado, Leon Ferrer, Andrés Palacio, Marcelo
Gómez, and others whose names I have recorded already when describing
my campaigns in the Orinoco plains. Also among them were Juan Pablo
and Francisco Farfán, who had aided me on more than one occasion to
succeed in my desperate struggle. These two were true bedouins of the
plains: gigantic in stature, with athletic musculature and valor bordering
on the ferocious, obedient only to naked force. They had served at first in
the ranks of the royalist Yáñez. But when I had offered to give the rank of
captain to any plainsman who brought me forty fighters, they enlisted with
their followers and rode with me in Apure from that time on. If I had been
strict with my troops, I would have had to punish these brothers severely,
because they often deserted for a time with their men to go on plundering
raids. Later they would reappear.

Just before the Battle of Mucuritas the Farfán brothers disappeared on
one of these escapades, and I finally threatened to lance them through if
they did not get out of my sight with all their people. That is why they did
not share in the glory of Mucuritas. Later I allowed them to return, and I
have told elsewhere how valuable the Farfán brothers proved in the capture
of Puerto Cabello in 1823. They eventually returned to their herds in
Apure, and there they lived peacefully until the year 1836.

In that year they raised the flag of rebellion—according to some, in
connivance with other rebels on the coast; according to others, in response
to a personal affront—without even a pretext of principles to justify their

uprising against the government. The government directed the governor of Apure, Gen. Comelio Muñoz, to organize a column to march against them, providing him with men, horses, arms, money, and a few troops from other provinces. The president also authorized General Muñoz to extend any sort of clemency compatible with the dignity of the government. He well knew that an insurrection based in Apure could put the whole Republic in danger. For my part, I sent several letters to the rebel leaders, reminding them of their patriotic duty. In reply, they tried to convince me that what they demanded was no more than I had promised to the people of Apure during the war of independence, that in a free Venezuela they would have to pay no taxes.

"Your demands are unjust, quite unjust," I wrote back to them. "In no American republic are taxes lower than in Venezuela. The customs house supplies our treasury. The only internal taxes are those essential for the maintenance of public works in the provinces, which must have schools to educate the young and roads for the betterment of trade. The provinces should supply these needs with their own funds. Refusal to pay taxes for ends so important would mean an eternity of backwardness and misery." The rebels finally accepted the clemency offered by Muñoz in his decree of July 9, and Francisco Farfán wrote me that "ignorance of the situation, the influence of others, and the lack of any adviser who could discern right from wrong had plunged him into an error that grieved him in his heart. He had fallen into it despite his good intentions and persisted in it thoughtlessly." He wrote: "I am aware of all the good Your Excellency has done for me, more than I can repay. But if gratitude would serve as repayment, I could bestow a wealth of it upon you, my friend and comrade, to whom I look up as a son to his father."

What happened next will show whether Farfán's repentance was sincere. Early in 1837 he rebelled again, this time in the Province of Guayana, proclaiming reunification with Colombia, the reform of the Constitution, the reestablishing of special fueros for military officers and clergy, the institution of trial by jury, the abolition of all taxes on rural property, a decree of amnesty for various conspirators fleeing justice, and finally the proclamation of General Mariño (the instigator of all of this) as Supreme Chief.

Cornelio Muñoz mobilized against Farfán, but his subordinates failed in their operations. Major Navarrete was defeated on the banks of the Orinoco and Colonel Mirabal was beaten on the plains of the Merecure. The rebels took Achaguas and obliged Muñoz to entrench himself in San Fernando. The president then decreed the formation of an army under my orders, naming Col. Agustín Codazzi chief of staff for the Division of Apure. Codazzi marched to the aid of Muñoz, besieged by Farfán in San

Fernando, and managed to force his way into that beleaguered town. I moved my troops to San Fernando as well and, on arrival, sent Captain Mirabal's infantry and Major Calderin's cavalry to reconnoiter. The enemy had crossed the river and withdrawn about a mile from the city just before my arrival. My men's horses were exhausted, so at nightfall I had the advance parties return so that the entire force would be able to resume the pursuit together. When the moon rose, I had the men take their horses across the river, and we set out at eight the next morning. Reaching the place called Rabanal, I learned that the rebels had passed hours earlier. I saw that it would be impossible to catch them with our whole army, so I took the best-mounted men on ahead, leaving the rest to come along afterward. With sixty fighters, I trotted in pursuit of a rebel force that numbered three times that. At the place called Yuca, about fifteen miles from San Fernando, I heard that they were only slightly ahead of us and, increasing the pace, I caught up with their rear guard a couple of miles from the town of Payara.

We entered the fight with that rear guard (composed of eighty men armed with carbines) and defeated them. As we chased these routed rebels through the town, my small force was divided into two groups. The enemy was waiting in a field to the west of the town: three columns of cavalry with a reserve force of infantry. The group to my right charged ahead impetuously but was repulsed, and the whole enemy army bore down upon them. Seeing this, I rushed to join them with my own group in order to face the onslaught with a compact mass of sixty lancers. In the extraordinary battle which followed, each man defended the ground within the radius he could reach with his lance, leaving an adversary sprawled there or dying there himself. Juan Pablo Farfán came personally to put me out of action, but the robust lance of my servant Rafael Salinas knocked him dead out of the saddle.

The rebels finally gave up the field, and the soldiers of the government were not less ardent in the pursuit than they had been in the heat of combat. We lost a mere two men dead and seven wounded; the rebels lost one hundred and fifty dead, among them a brother and an uncle of the ringleader, Francisco Farfán. Farfán sought his own salvation in the swiftness of his horse, and his followers fled in such disarray that one could not see ten of them together in their flight.

This deed of arms took place on April 26, 1837. I received a thousand congratulations for the victory, but they would have been more pleasant if the glory had not been won at the cost of Venezuelan blood. Such bravery, had it been displayed in the face of a foreign foe, would have moved the grateful nation to erect a battlefield monument to THE LIONS OF PAYARA.

5. Ribbons and Rituals ~ Domingo Faustino Sarmiento*

The Argentine caudillo Juan Manuel de Rosas imposed church rituals and red lapel ribbons to signify public conformity under his rule. His enemy, Domingo Faustino Sarmiento (who later became president), ridiculed Rosas's symbol-mongering in this passage taken from Facundo, or Civilization and Barbarism *(1845), the single, most influential interpretation of nineteenth-century Argentina and one of the most influential Latin American texts ever written. The apparent subject of the book was Rosas's ally, Facundo Quiroga, the Argentine caudillo found in document 3. But Sarmiento was using Facundo mostly to personify the terror of caudillo rule in Argentina under Rosas. In the following selection, Facundo himself does not appear at all.*

Finally, Rosas has the government in his hands. Facundo died a month earlier; the city has placed itself at his discretion; the people have candidly confirmed their surrender of all rights and institutions. The State is a blank slate on which he will write something new and original. He is a poet, a Plato who will now bring into being the ideal republic which he has conceived. He has meditated upon this labor for twenty years, and now he can finally bring it forth unimpeded by stale traditions, current events, imitations of Europe, individual rights, or existing institutions. He is a genius, in short, who has been lamenting the ills of his century and preparing himself to destroy them with one blow. All will be new, a work of his creative faculty. Let us observe this prodigy.

Leaving the House of Representatives, where he went to receive his staff of office, he withdraws in a coach painted red expressly for the ceremony. Yoked to the coach by cords of red silk are the men who, with criminal impunity, have kept the city in a state of continual alarm since 1833. They style themselves the People's Society, and they wear knives at the waist, red vests, and red ribbons with the slogan: "Death to the Unitarians." At the door of his house, these same men form an honor guard. Next he gives audience to citizens, and then to generals. Everyone must show his limitless personal loyalty to him, "the Restorer."

The next day, a proclamation appears with a list of proscriptions. This proclamation, one of Rosas's few writings, is a wonderful document that I am sorry not to have on hand. It was his program of government, undisguised and unambiguous: WHOEVER IS NOT WITH ME IS MY ENEMY. That is the axiom of the policy enshrined in the document, which announces that

---

*From Domingo Faustino Sarmiento, *Facundo, o civilización y barbarie* (Caracas: Biblioteca Ayacucho, 1977), 123–24, 206–8. Translated by John Charles Chasteen.

blood will flow, and promises only that property will be respected. Woe to those who provoke his fury!

Four days later, the parish of San Francisco announces its intention to celebrate a Mass to give thanks to the Almighty for the rule of Rosas, inviting the people of the neighborhood to solemnize the event with their presence. The surrounding streets are dressed with banners, bunting, and carpets. The place becomes an Oriental bazaar displaying tapestries of damask, purple, gold, and jewels in whimsical array. People throng the streets: young people who are attracted by the novelty, ladies who have chosen the parish for their afternoon stroll. The ceremony of thanksgiving is postponed for a day, and the city's excitement—the agitated coming and going, the interruption of all work—lasts for four or five days in a row. The government's *Gazette* supplies the most insignificant details of the splendid event. And eight days later, another parish announces its own ceremony of thanksgiving. The people of that neighborhood are determined to surpass the enthusiasm of the first parish, to outdo the first celebration. What excess of decoration! What ostentation of wealth and adornment! The portrait of Rosas "the Restorer" is placed on a dais in the street, swathed in red velvet, with golden cords and braid. The hubbub returns, for as many more days. In the privileged parish, people seem to live in the street. And, a few days later, there is another celebration, in another parish in another neighborhood. But how long can this go on? Do these people never tire of spectacles? What sort of enthusiasm is this, which does not subside in a month? Why do not all the parishes have their celebrations at the same time? No, it is a systematic, organized enthusiasm, administered a little at a time. A year later the parishes still have not concluded their celebrations. The official giddiness has passed from the city to the countryside. It appears endless. The government's *Gazette* is occupied for a year and a half with descriptions of Federalist celebrations. The famous portrait of Rosas appears unfailingly, pulled along by generals, by ladies, by the purest of Federalists, in a carriage made especially for the purpose.

After a year and a half of celebrations, the color red emerges as the insignia of loyalty to "the cause." The portrait of Rosas first graces church altars and then becomes part of the personal effects of each and every man, who must wear it on his chest as a sign of "intense personal attachment" to the Restorer. Last, out of these celebrations comes the terrible Mazorca, the corps of amateur Federalist police, whose designated function is, first, to administer enemas of pepper and turpentine to dissenters, and then, should this phlogistic treatment prove insufficient, to slit the throat of whomever they are told.

All America has scoffed at these famous celebrations of Buenos Aires and looked at them as the maximum degradation of a people. But I see in them nothing but a political strategy, and an extremely effective one. How does one teach the idea of personalist government to a republic which has never had a king? The red ribbon is a token of the terror which goes with you everywhere, in the street, in the bosom of the family; you must think of it when dressing and undressing. We remember things always by association; the sight of a tree in a field reminds us of what we were talking about as we walked under it ten years ago. Imagine what ideas the red ribbon brings with it by association, the indelible impressions it must have joined to the image of Rosas. . . .

The story of the red ribbon is, indeed, curious. At first, it was an emblem adopted by enthusiasts. Then they ordered everyone to wear it in order "to prove the unanimity" of public opinion. People meant to obey, but frequently forgot when they changed clothes. The police helped jog people's memories. The Mazorca patrolled the streets. They stood with whips at the church door when ladies were leaving Mass and applied the lash without pity. But there was still much which needed fixing. Did someone wear his ribbon carelessly tied?—The lash! A Unitarian!—Was someone's ribbon too short?—The lash! A Unitarian!—Someone did not wear one at all?—Cut his throat! The reprobate!

The government's solicitude for public education did not stop there. It was not sufficient to be a Federalist, nor to wear the ribbon. It was obligatory also to wear a picture of the illustrious Restorer over one's heart, with the slogan "Death to the Savage, Filthy Unitarians." Enough, you think, to conclude the job of debasing a civilized people, robbing them of all personal dignity? Ah! They were not yet well enough disciplined. One morning, on a street corner in Buenos Aires, there appeared a figure drawn on paper, with a ribbon half a yard long floating in the breeze. As soon as someone saw it, that person backed away in fright and spread the alarm. People ducked into the nearest store and came out with ribbons half a yard long floating in the breeze. Ten minutes later, the entire population was out in the street wearing ribbons half a yard long. Another day the figure reappeared with a slight alteration in the ribbon. The maneuver repeated itself. If some young lady forgot to wear a red bow in her hair, the police supplied one free—and attached it with melted tar! That is how they have created uniformity of public opinion! Search the Argentine Republic for someone who does not firmly believe and maintain that he is a Federalist!

It has happened a thousand times: a citizen steps out his door and finds that the other side of the street has been swept. A moment later, he has had his own side swept. The man next door copies him, and in half an hour the whole street has been swept, everyone thinking it was an order from the police. A shopkeeper puts out a flag to attract people's attention. His neighbor sees him and, fearing he will be accused of tardiness by the governor, he puts out his own. The people across the street put out a flag;

everyone else on the street puts one out. Other streets follow suit; and suddenly all Buenos Aires is bedecked with flags. The police become alarmed and inquire what happy news has been received by everyone but them. And these people of Buenos Aires are the same ones who trounced eleven thousand Englishmen in the streets and then sent five armies across the American continent to hunt Spaniards!

Terror, you see, is a disease of the spirit which can become an epidemic like cholera, measles, or scarlet fever. No one is safe, in the end, from the contagion. Though you may work ten years at inoculating, not even those already vaccinated can resist in the end. Do not laugh, nations of Spanish America, when you witness such degradation! Look well, for you, too, are Spanish, and so the Inquisition taught Spain to be! This sickness we carry in our blood.

---

6. Protagonist on a National Stage ～ Antonio López de Santa Anna*

The autobiography of Antonio López de Santa Anna (the same general who famously besieged the Alamo during the Texas war for independence from Mexico) constitutes an extraordinary work of self-dramatization. Writing in exile at the end of his career this caudillo presents himself not as a strongman or power broker but as a vulnerable, introspective protagonist—the leading figure on a national stage. The modern reader may recoil from the unmitigated vanity of this "leading man," but Santa Anna's obvious self-absorption does not seem to have disqualified him in the eyes of his audience. When this excerpt begins in the early 1840s, Santa Anna is about to become president of Mexico for the fourth time.

Sixty-two days after my foot had been amputated, Gen. Guadalupe Victoria called on me at the instigation of the government. He informed me that a revolution was threatening, and that the government desired me to take [Anastasio] Bustamante's place as temporary president in this time of trial. How well the people knew me! They knew I would never desert my principles and would always be on hand when my country needed me!

I was carried to the capital on a litter. Although my trip was made with extreme care, the hardships of the journey and the change of climate weakened me. However, despite my poor health, I assumed the office of president immediately. The tasks involved completely overwhelmed me, but I pulled through. The government forces triumphed throughout the country. Gen. Gabriel Valencia captured and executed the hope of the

*From Antonio López de Santa Anna, *The Eagle: The Autobiography of Santa Anna*, ed. and trans. Ann Fears Crawford (Austin, TX: Pemberton Press, 1967), 65–69.

revolution, José A. Mejia, in the vicinity of the town of Acajeta. The dreaded threat of revolution died, and peace was restored.

Bustamante once again took up the reins of government, and I retired to [my estate] to complete my recovery. However, Bustamante's loss of prestige with the people caused his government to fail. In the town of Guadalajara, in the early months of 1841, arrangements were made for Bustamante to abdicate and for the reform of the Constitution of 1824. In Tacubaya, a council of generals agreed upon basic ground rules to help bring about these reforms, and once again I assumed the office of provisional president. . . .

In order to conform to public opinion, I called together a group of prominent citizens from all states in the nation to instigate needed reforms. This group drew up *The Principles of Political Organization* on June 12, 1844. This constitution was circulated by the government, and each of the states accepted and ratified it without dissension.

In September 1844, my beloved wife died. Greater sorrow I had never known! General of Division Valentín Canalizo substituted for me while I devoted myself to family matters.

During the first session under our new Constitution, I was duly elected president and called to the capital to administer the customary oath. The election saddened me even more. My deep melancholy drove me to abhor the glamorous life of the capital and to prefer a life of solitude. I resigned the noble office to which I had been called, but the public intruded upon my privacy, pleading that I return. My friends, with the greatest of good faith, also begged me to resume my office. Their pleas led me to sacrifice myself to the public good. I withdrew my resignation.

Near the end of October, General [Mariano] Paredes rebelled against the government in Guadalajara. When the news was communicated to me by the government, they ordered me to take the troops quartered in Jalapa and march to the capital. I instantly obeyed the orders. Paredes had been relieved of his command of the Capital District due to excesses of intoxication while he was commanding his troops. He bore a grudge and was determined to take revenge. In our country one spark was sufficient to set aflame a revolution.

I was marching toward Guadalajara under orders, when I received the news of an upheaval in the capital. The situation seemed serious, and I halted my advance. Details of the revolt in the capital arrived soon after my halt. The messenger read me the following infamous words:

> The majority of Congress openly favor the Paredes revolution. The government, in self-defense or wishing to avoid revolution, has issued a decree by which the sessions of Congress have been suspended. This decree has served as a pretext for General José J. Herrera to join the

revolt. Rioters have torn down the bronze bust of President Santa Anna that stood in the Plaza del Mercado. They have also taken his amputated foot from the cemetery of Santa Paula and proceeded to drag it through the streets to the sounds of savage laughter.

I interrupted the narrator, exclaiming "Stop! I don't wish to hear any more! Almighty God! A member of my body, lost in the service of my country, dragged from the funeral urn, broken into bits to be made sport of in such a barbaric manner!" In that moment of grief and frenzy, I decided to leave my native country, object of my dreams and of my illusions, for all time.

At the head of eleven thousand well-trained and well-armed men and with partisans in the capital, I could have taken it easily. However, I was drained of all vengeance and was determined merely to leave my country forever. I countermarched toward Puebla, avoiding everyone.

IV

Liberalism and the Catholic Church

While the Catholic clergy supplied the movement for Independence with some of its most important early leaders, in general the relationship between the Church and the independent states was very troubled. Liberalism provided the intellectual playbook for the creation of the new republics. Liberals of the Independence generation and after decried the power of the Church over political life, railed against its monopoly over education, and despised its vast real estate and land holdings, its stultifying influence on banking and commerce, and the exploitative fees that its priests sometimes charged even the poorest peasant for its sacramental services. In sum, Latin American liberals, like their Anglo-American counterparts of the previous half-century, wanted to reform completely the relationship between Church and state.

In this chapter, students will explore the nineteenth-century clash between Latin America's liberals and the Church, a problem that continues to resonate in the region to this day. Indeed, in the view of many contemporary observers, Latin America is the most devoutly Catholic part of the world today, the global home of the faith's most intensely held feelings. And yet it is also a region that has embraced the ideas and values of nineteenth-century liberalism, an ideology incompatible with (or at least antagonistic toward) the worldview of the Roman Catholic Church. With this conflict in mind, let us take a step back to analyze the intellectual content of the term *liberalism*.

Nineteenth-century liberalism—or classical liberalism, as it is sometimes called—is based on the belief that human progress is best achieved by unleashing the energies of the individual human being. Nineteenth-century liberals sought freedom from constraints that impede each individual's innate creativity. Such a belief first arose in the European context as a consequence of the rising power of the bourgeoisie, the capitalist middle class that wanted liberation from medieval traditions and, to get it, carried forward such major historical movements as the Renaissance, the Reformation, and the French Revolution. In their belief that individual liberty was the key to human progress, European liberals called for the abolition of class privileges that had been inherited from the Middle Ages. To destroy the vestiges of Europe's unjust and unproductive old order, liberals attempted to wipe away intermediaries such as artisan guilds or religious orders that stood between the state and the individual. Human beings were to be freely constituted, rational actors who would act on their own behalf. In this clash of free and competing interests, affirmed liberal thinkers, societies would find the proper means of governing themselves.

What did classical liberalism mean in practice? In political terms, liberalism became associated with ideas of citizenship, Rousseau's social contract, constitutional government, and the will of the majority. Monarchy was a dinosaur. In economic terms, the liberal promotion of individual initiative matched the capitalist spirit of entrepreneurship. Governments, in the view of liberal theorists, were to keep out of economic matters, permitting free enterprise (*laissez-faire*) and allowing the "invisible hand" of markets to determine the allocation of resources. In social terms, nineteenth-century liberals thought of themselves as revolutionaries out to change the world. Active intervention was needed to dismantle the old ways and establish a new order based on the legal equality of all individuals. In practice, however, when nineteenth-century liberals referred to the "equality of individuals," they were really talking about the equality of literate, property-owning white men. In cultural terms, liberals strongly distrusted the traditional sources of authority, particularly the Roman Catholic Church, which they thought infested by superstition, ignorance, and empty ritual. The famous French liberal, Voltaire, summed up their attitude in his phrase against superstition: "*écrasez l'infâme*," which loosely translated means "crush the infamous thing!"

The writings of Voltaire and other influential French liberals such as Jean-Jacques Rousseau were banned from colonial Latin America. Nonetheless, Latin American liberals read them, took them to heart, and, after the break with Spain and Portugal, attempted to implement them. Civil wars between Liberals and Conservatives became commonplace in the mid-1800s. Invariably, the Church allied itself with the Conservatives, who made defense of the Church their rallying cry. How did this clash play out? The following documents give us the answers.

QUESTIONS FOR ANALYSIS

1. What were the goals of nineteenth-century Latin American liberals? What did they want to accomplish?

2. How did liberalism threaten the Church's interests, both material and spiritual, in Latin America?

> 3. What were the long-term effects of the conflict between liberalism and the Church? How might the conflict have affected the region's subsequent development?

1. A New Generation of Liberals ∼ Frank Safford*

The first generation of Latin American liberals failed in their attempts to uproot three centuries of colonialism in a single decade. But beginning around the 1840s, a new generation of liberals, newly born in the independent republics of Spanish America, arrived on the scene. This generation, many of whom were extremely militant in their opposition to the colonial past, were more successful. In this selection, historian Frank Safford explains some of the chief characteristics of this new generation of liberals, focusing on their class and geographical origins, their precarious electoral alliance with urban artisans, and their connection to political and intellectual currents emanating from mid-nineteenth-century Europe. In Safford's view, this generation was consciously completing the mission begun by the previous one.

In the 1840s, a new generation of politicians emerged, challenging the persons and policies of those who had held power since the end of the 1820s. Most Spanish American countries had been ruled by the same generation that had made independence. In Mexico, Peru, Venezuela, and New Granada presidential power seemed to be the monopoly of the military heroes of independence, with civilian elites of the same generation collaborating in the organization of politics and the management of government. Men born at the eve of independence, particularly civilians, had cause to wonder when their time might come. Tutio Halperín Donghi has suggested that the fiscal penury endured by almost all Spanish American governments limited their capacity to absorb the younger generations into public posts. Whatever the reason, the fact is that in the 1840s the younger generation began, in many places quite consciously, to challenge the existing political establishment which in some places, it should be said, had lost its will or ability to dominate. In Venezuela, by 1844, General Carlos Soublette, who currently governed for the Venezuelan oligarchy, calmly tolerated the mobilization of university students (including two of his sons) in opposition, making little effort to generate support for the established system. In Mexico, disastrous defeat in war with the United States (1846–48)

---

*From Frank Safford, "Politics, Ideology, and Society," in Leslie Bethell, ed., *Spanish America after Independence, c. 1820–c. 1870* (New York: Cambridge University Press, 1987), 91–97. Reprinted by permission of Cambridge University Press.

undermined the authority of established politicians in all the major factions and filled the new generation with a sense of the urgency of taking radical measures in order to form a strong, modern state. In New Granada in 1848–49, the government party split, thus opening the way for challenge by a new generation. In Chile, the political system also began to show signs of wear as elements in the governing party began to break away in opposition to President Manuel Montt, thus encouraging a series of liberal rebellions in the 1850s.

Although the political dynamic of the period may be seen as a challenge from a new age group within the upper social sectors, the struggle also had a class aspect in some places. Historians of the *Reforma* period in Mexico (1855–76) consider many of the liberal protagonists of this struggle to have been a "new" generation not merely in the sense of age but also in that of social origin. The new liberal generation that emerged in the 1840s is described as typically composed of mostly ambitious provincials whose social mobility was made possible by the expansion of secondary education during the early independence period. A similar generalization might be made about New Granada and, to a lesser degree, Peru and Chile. Young men of such social origins had particular reason to challenge the monopoly of power by established groups and to wish to destroy those remnants of colonial institutions that tended to block social mobility.

The emerging generation of upper-sector politicians, seeking to develop its own sense of political identity as against the older generation, was receptive to new European influences that had little appeal to the already formed, established politicians. The impact of these new external influences, along with the dynamic of intergenerational tensions, helped to polarize politics from the middle of the 1840s until 1870, by which time the new generation was thoroughly dominant.

The European political events and ideological currents influencing the new generation varied depending upon local political conditions. In much of Spanish America the powers and privileges of the Church remained a central, and unresolved, problem. Consequently, agitation in France over ecclesiastical issues in the 1830s and 1840s influenced some of these countries after 1845, most particularly Mexico, New Granada, Chile, and Peru. The attacks of [Jules] Michelet and [Edgar] Quinet on the role of the Church in higher education in the 1840s and their book assailing the Jesuits had an impact upon young democrats like Francisco Bilbao (1823–65) in Chile and also served to inflame antagonism toward the Jesuits among the younger generation in New Granada.

In Buenos Aires and Montevideo, where many of the Church's powers and privileges had already been stripped away before 1835, religio-political controversies in Europe were of relatively little concern to young intellectuals. [Giuseppe] Mazzini's Young Italy, however, had a notable influence among the dissident youth of the Rio de la Plata region; one of their intellectual leaders, Esteban Echeverría, for example, proclaimed a Young Argentina. Echeverría and his associates also found some interest in French Socialism, particularly in Saint-Simonian currents. This was much less true in other parts of Spanish America, at least until the European Revolution of 1848.

The inflammation of Church–State issues between 1845 and 1870 in some Spanish American republics, and the new, more fervent spirit with which civilian politicians approached these issues, derived in part from the influence of [Félicité de] Lamennais. His criticism of the Church as a political establishment concerned primarily with money, power, and dignities, and his advocacy of a primitive, popular, extra-ecclesiastical Christianity, inspired many in the new generation. He provided them with a rhetoric with which to attack the established Church as part of the old, oppressive order while claiming adherence to a purer democratic Christianity. His insistence upon the separation of religion and politics, and therefore upon the separation of Church and State, found echo in Mexico, New Granada, Peru, and Chile. His strongly democratic spirit, with his support of a wide extension of the suffrage, also encouraged the democratic enthusiasms of the new generation, just as his call for administrative decentralization reinforced the federalist political currents in Spanish America. Lamennais's influence, perhaps more than any other, demarcates the generation of the 1840s from its predecessors, who for the most part ignored him. Undoubtedly, Lamennais, like Mazzini, had a special appeal for the younger generation in symbolizing rebellion against established authority.

The European Revolution of 1848 both drew attention to, and crystallized the influence of, utopian Socialist ideas in Spanish America. Shortly after the European revolutions began, aspiring young politicians, influenced by European example, began to reach out to elements in the urban underclasses—and principally to the artisan class, not the very poorest—in an effort to mobilize them politically.

The Revolution of 1848 was greeted enthusiastically in New Granada, Peru, and Chile, where the new generation had to contend with established government groups that could be viewed as essentially elitist and where, consequently, democratic revolution appealed as a means of political change. In the Rio de la Plata, however, the dictatorship of Juan Manuel de Rosas in Buenos Aires, like the regimes of lesser caudillos in the provinces, had enjoyed widespread support from the popular classes. In the Plata, therefore, younger intellectual politicians tended to take a more negative view of democratic revolution. In exile in Chile in the 1840s, Domingo Faustino Sarmiento and Juan Bautista Alberdi, even before the

European revolutions, expressed the belief that popular sovereignty, in the hands of an ignorant mass, would inevitably lead to dictatorship. While Francisco Bilbao and others in the new generation of Chileans attacked their government as elitist, their Argentine contemporaries resident in Chile defended the existing regime as the rule of an enlightened minority, far preferable to the tyranny produced in Argentina by a barbarous majority. The Revolution of 1848, with the subsequent election of Louis Napoleon, served to confirm Sarmiento and Alberdi in their distrust of democracy, at least in countries where the large majority was illiterate. Thus, whereas in parts of Spanish America the new generations tended to a democratic rhetoric (not necessarily democratic practice) even after they became ascendant between 1850 and 1870, in Argentina after the overthrow of Rosas in 1852 the newly dominant intellectual elite tended to have a more conservative view of political democracy.

The new generation of liberal politicians that emerged in the 1840s in many respects pursued the same tendencies as their political progenitors, the liberal reformers of the 1820s. But they did so with a new spirit and intensity, in the belief that the earlier generation had failed in its mission to liberalize Spanish American society. Like the liberals of the 1820s, the reformers of 1845–70 affirmed essentially individualist conceptions of state, society, and economy. Like their predecessors, they were libertarian constitutionalists, in belief if not in behavior. But they tended to be more absolute in their individualism, more fervent in their libertarian rhetoric. The called not merely for individual freedoms but for an absolute freedom of conscience, of the press, of education, and of commerce—in New Granada even to the extent of sanctioning an absolute freedom of commerce in arms. They called not merely for trial by jury and the abolition of the death penalty but also for constitutional recognition of the right to insurrection. To safeguard these individual freedoms liberals in Mexico, New Granada, and Venezuela recommitted themselves to the ideal of federalism looking to the United States as a model, and they resurrected plans of 1825–35 to limit the size of the army and to establish citizens' national guards.

In economic and social policy also the mid-century reformers rededicated themselves to liberal individualism and the ideal of legal equality, both of which they felt had been compromised by their predecessors. They sought to rationalize their countries' economies in accord with nineteenth-century liberal conceptions. This meant abolishing enterprise-constricting taxes that had been allowed to hang on from the colonial period, such as the *alcabala* (sales tax), the tithe, and government monopolies. At least during the 1850s they rather dogmatically opposed government intervention in the economy, whether in the form of public enterprise, the extension of monopoly privileges to private enterprise, or protectionist tariffs.

Their affirmation of the ideal of legal equality meant the elimination of the juridical privileges of the Church and the military. They also sought the fulfillment of legal equality, as well as of individualist social conceptions, through the abolition of slavery and the incorporation of Indian communities into the dominant, capitalistic, European society. The new generation of reformists recognized that these were themes pursued by the earlier liberals of the 1820s. But they believed that the earlier generation had taken only the first tentative steps toward a necessary elimination of colonial structures. They saw themselves as carrying out a political, economic, and social revolution that would bring to completion the movement that had begun in 1810, but had been betrayed during the 1830s.

---

2. Liberalism as Anticlericalism ⁓ Helen Delpar*

In nineteenth-century Latin America, as in most places, liberalism was strongly associated with anticlericalism. Anticlericalism was based on the idea that the clergy (especially prelates who ran the administrative offices of the Church) were preventing social progress in areas such as public education and economic development. In this selection, historian Helen Delpar views Colombian liberals and conservatives largely in terms of clericalism and anticlericalism. She provides details on the types of laws and policies that liberals adopted when they took office, and the reactions that such laws and policies drew from conservatives. She is also careful to point out the divisions within the Liberal party on just how far anticlericalism could be pushed.

To ensure the proper functioning of republican institutions, most Liberals thought that three conditions were necessary. The first of these was cessation of the political disorders that had ravaged the nation since independence. Although they continued to be concerned about this problem, Liberals were optimistic about an eventual reign of peace once the two other conditions had been realized: an enlightened citizenry and economic prosperity. An editorial entitled "Needs of the Country" in 1866, for example, stressed the importance of improving primary education and hoped that at least two schools could be established in each district. "Free education for the masses—this is the motto of the true patriot and the sincere republican. Only an ignorant people can be deceived; only a brutish people can be made the victim of despotism." President [Eustaquio] Salgar expressed a similar opinion while congratulating the Chamber of

---

*From Helen Delpar, *Red against Blue: The Liberal Party in Colombian Politics, 1863–1899* (Tuscaloosa: University of Alabama Press, 1981), 68–70, 78–80. Reprinted by permission of the University of Alabama Press.

Representatives for appropriating $100,000 for the establishment of normal schools in 1870. Emphasizing the relationship between democracy and education, he declared that the former did not exist in Latin America. Instead, more or less well-educated minorities managed affairs as they saw fit while the great majority of workers and taxpayers, who lived in rural areas, bore all the burdens of the republic but received none of its benefits. What was the point, he asked, of guaranteeing freedom and individual rights if the citizens were too ignorant to be aware of their existence?

In the opinion of Liberals, the expansion of public education was but one aspect of the struggle against ignorance. If it was to be truly successful, the hold of the clergy on the masses also had to be reduced. Liberals invariably emphasized, however, that they were not antagonistic to religion itself but to the political activity of some members of the Roman Catholic clergy and to their efforts to hinder the intellectual and spiritual enlightenment of the Colombian people. An apologist for the anticlerical policies of the mid-1870s explained: "Colombian Liberalism, far from being hostile to the true religious spirit, draws inspiration from it and seeks its protection, for it knows that freedom is in essence of divine origin and that it appears, grows, and produces its fruits only among people in whom conscience—that is, moral sense—is allowed to develop fully and with complete guarantees."

Liberal leaders varied greatly in their personal religious convictions. Eustaquio Salgar and Santiago Pérez, for example, were said to be practicing Catholics. When the latter was nominated for the presidency in 1873, Medardo Rivas declared that his only blemish was the fact that he attended Mass; Rivas conceded, however, that this was a purely private act that in no way rendered Pérez unfit for the presidency. Miguel Samper has been described as a convinced Christian who became a practicing Catholic toward the end of his life. Many other Liberal leaders, however, were probably free-thinkers who, like Teodoro Valenzuela, believed that the universe is governed by a supreme intelligence; organized religion had a social value, he felt, but was otherwise meaningless.

Regardless of their personal beliefs, Liberal leaders could generally be divided into two camps with respect to religious issues. On the one hand were those who thought that the government should take an active role in extirpating clerical influence, both temporal and spiritual, and that in order to do so it should be invested with powers similar to those enjoyed by the Spanish crown in the colonial era. On the other were those who might deplore the power of the clergy but believed that extreme anticlericalism was not only futile but violated Liberal principles as well. Liberals of this school were likely to regard separation of church and state as the best solution for the religious question. This was the position of Salvador Camacho Roldán, who wrote in 1878: "What we seek in this country is not the repression of the Catholic idea but the complete emancipation of human thought, and this requires liberty for Catholics and non-Catholics, for those who believe and those who do not."

Liberal attitudes toward the Church were shaped not only by ideological considerations but also by Conservative exploitation of clerical grievances for political ends and by Liberal suspicions about the subversive designs of the clergy, which were strengthened by the condemnation of liberalism by Pope Pius IX in 1864 and by the proclamation of the dogma of papal infallibility six years later. As a result, even Liberals who favored separation of church and state at times became alarmed by the possibility of a clerical-Conservative alliance to drive them from power. In 1874 an editorialist in the *Diario de Cundinamarca* warned that if the Conservatives attempted to use religion for partisan purposes, the Liberal party would react energetically "to annihilate completely" the political power of the clergy.

The differences between these various points of view were never fully resolved while the Liberals were in power. Although separation of church and state had been decreed in 1853, the Liberal constitution empowered the federal and state governments to exercise the right of inspection over religious cults, and the law of 23 April 1863 required of all clergymen, on pain of banishment from Colombia, that they swear to obey the constitutions, laws, and authorities of the nation and the states. By 1864, however, the belief that this law was unduly harsh and vindictive had become sufficiently widespread among Liberals to permit its substitution by a milder measure (17 May 1864), which required the oath of obedience only from prelates. In addition, Manuel Murillo, who took office as president on 10 April 1864, made a conciliatory gesture by lifting the sentence of banishment decreed in 1861 against the archbishop of Bogotá, Antonio Herrán, provided he took the required oath.

Relations between the federal government and the Church again deteriorated during the presidential term of Tomás Mosquera (1866–67), but after his deposition the 1864 law was repealed. This meant that in the future, relations between church and state would be governed only by the general dispositions in the constitution. In the following years tension between the Church and the federal government was at a relatively low ebb, but became increasingly severe after 1870, mainly because of clerical opposition to the educational program launched by the Salgar administration in that year. After the Conservative revolution of 1876–77, which was openly supported by some clergymen, the "hard line" temporarily gained ascendancy, winning adherents even among Liberals who had previously eschewed extreme anti-clericalism.

Colombian Conservatives were no more uniform or consistent in their thinking than Liberals, but there were several principles basic to Conservative ideology that set them apart from Liberals. The first of these principles was a belief in the universality and infallibility of the precepts of Christianity. Secondly, Conservatives regarded the Catholic Church as the sole depository and interpreter of the divine truths of Christianity. Thirdly, they considered the Conservative party as the political agency by which the teachings of Christ and the interests of the Church might best be protected and advanced in Colombia. For both clergymen and Conservatives, this last proposition occasionally raised dilemmas that could not always be satisfactorily resolved: for the clergy, the extent to which party leaders should be encouraged to act as spokesmen for the interests of the Church, and for the Conservatives, the extent to which the interests of the party were identical with those of the Church.

Conservatives also tended to feel that Catholicism and by extension the entire fabric of society were gravely menaced by Liberalism, which, by asserting that the mind is shaped only by sensory experiences, repudiated the concept of divine will as the source of human nature and institutions. The Conservative newspaper *La América* declared in 1874 that Catholic morality was the basis of its doctrine. The editorial continued:

> Today Liberalism aims to establish a school of negation [and] seeks utility or sensationalism as [the basis of] morality, and this is where the true division between the parties lies. It is natural that we who raise as a moral banner the one left to us in the Gospel by the Son of God should form ranks around the Church which received it. Those who seek in pleasure or pain the norm for their actions are the enemies of this Church, and therefore in every political question a religious question is involved.

Convictions such as these frequently led Conservatives to assert that a Catholic could not be a Liberal. Thus a Medellín newspaper stated in 1875: "the doctrinaire Liberal party is anti-Catholic, and . . . no Catholic can vote for any of its members without betraying his conscience."

The association between Catholicism and Conservatism remained close. In fact, on occasion Conservatives did not hesitate to censure publicly clerics whom they considered lukewarm in the struggle against Liberalism. One such incident in 1873—involving the archbishop of Bogotá—led to a decision of the Second Provincial Council of Colombian bishops that Catholic writers should not anticipate the judgment of the hierarchy on any issue related to the Church and that they were to submit to the authority of the prelates should they disagree with them. To Miguel Antonio Caro, this ruling meant the imposition of "shackles" on Catholic writers.

Conservatives had no difficulty in accepting republican government, though they assigned a much higher priority than the Liberals to the maintenance of order and were uncomfortable with the extensive liberties enshrined in the 1863 constitution. While they affirmed the right of all citizens to equality of treatment before the law, they were likely to express hostility to those who condemned economic inequality. On 9 July 1848, for example, *El Nacional* of Bogotá declared that the achievement of de facto equality (as opposed to legal equality) would be the equivalent of robbery, for it meant elevating the lazy to the rank of the worker. Later, in the aftermath of the Paris Commune, *La Sociedad* of Medellín condemned "socialist equality," which it said was engendered by envy and based on injustice. "Its purpose is to level the human race, reducing all that is outstanding until it descends to the lowest, meanest, and most brutish level in society." This kind of equality, the newspaper asserted, was totally incompatible with Christian equality, which rested on the oneness of the "human race and the universality of God's moral law."

---

3. The Post-Colonial Church ∼ John Lynch*

In this survey of the post-colonial church in Latin America, historian John Lynch examines the problem of liberalism from the Church's point of view. He finds that the Church's chief concern was not the devotion of the poor masses but, rather, the faithfulness of the new states' ruling elites. Lynch also describes how the principal nineteenth-century leader of the Roman Catholic Church, Pope Pius IX, reacted to the challenge of liberalism with his famous Syllabus of Errors *(1864), a document that provided Latin American conservatives with an intellectual playbook of their own.*

The Church in Latin America after independence bore the marks of its Iberian and colonial past. From Spain, Catholics inherited a tradition of strong faith, a basic doctrinal knowledge, and an enduring piety. Observance itself was a medium of knowledge, for in the Mass, the Litanies, and the Rosary the people learned the doctrines, the Scriptures, and the mysteries of the Catholic faith. Portugal too transmitted an orthodox Catholicism, but with less doctrinal knowledge and a lower degree of observance. Everywhere, religion in Latin America was a religion of the people, and the Church continued to receive the adherence and the respect of the Indians, *mestizos*, and other popular sectors. Ruling groups were less committed, and the great fear of the Church in the nineteenth century was the apostasy of the elites, not the desertion of the masses. The Iberian

*From John Lynch, "The Catholic Church," in Leslie Bethell, ed., *Latin America: Economy and Society, 1870–1930* (New York: Cambridge University Press, 1989), 301–5, 315–17. Reprinted by permission of Cambridge University Press.

tradition in religion favored a privileged and a state-controlled Church. After independence, however, the wealth, influence, and privileges of the Church were viewed by the new states as a rival focus of allegiance, an alternative power, and a source of revenue. The threat of state control appeared in a new form. The Church had to look to its own resources—and these in the early nineteenth century were diminishing.

Independence administered a great shock to the Church. To many it was the end of an epoch, the collapse of an entire world, the triumph of reason over faith. If Iberian power was broken, could the Catholic Church survive? Independence exposed the colonial roots of the Church and revealed its foreign origins. Independence also divided the Church. While some of the clergy were royalists, many were republicans, a few were insurgents, and most were influential in encouraging mass support for the new order once the last battle had been won. The hierarchy was less divided by independence, but its unity was hardly a source of strength. A few bishops accepted the revolution. The majority rejected it and remained loyal to the crown. They might justify themselves in religious terms but they could not disguise the fact that they were Spaniards, identified themselves with Spain, and had, in effect, abandoned the American Church. From Rome they received little guidance. The papacy, pressed by Spain and the Holy Alliance, refused to recognize Latin American independence. This was a political error, the fruit of human judgment and not of Church doctrine. But it was a costly error, and when the irrevocability of independence and the need to fill vacant sees forced the papacy, from 1835, to recognize the new governments, great damage had been done.

The Church moved from Spain and Portugal to Rome in the nineteenth century, from Iberian religion to universal religion. While this avoided the emergence of national churches, it did not remove the threat of state control of the Church. The *patronato* (*padroado* in Brazil), the royal right to appoint Church officials, was now claimed by the national governments and placed in the hands of liberal and agnostic politicians.

Yet the Church survived, its mission defended if inert, its assets real if diminished, its offices intact if often unfilled. This was not a Church in decline, and, if it was temporarily weak, the state was weaker. Here was a paradox and a problem. In the aftermath of independence the Church was more stable, more popular, and apparently more wealthy than the state. The state reacted by seeking to control and to tax the Church and to restore the balance in its own favor. After a period of relatively conservative government in Spanish America, from 1830 to 1850, the advent of the liberal state heralded a more basic rupture with the past and with the Church. The principle behind liberal policy was individualism, a belief that the new states of Latin America could only make progress if the individual were freed from the prejudice of the past, from corporate constraints and privilege, privilege which in the case of the Church was accompanied by wealth in real estate and income from annuities. These gave the Church political power, retarded the economy, and stood in the way of social change. The Church was thus seen as a rival to the state, a focus of sovereignty which should belong to the nation alone. These assertions were not necessarily true, but they were the liberal perceptions of the time. And liberalism represented interests as well as principles. In Mexico, for example, where typical mid-century liberals were young upwardly mobile professionals, these considered the Church as a major obstacle not only to nation-building but also to their own economic and social ambitions.

The post-colonial Church, therefore, encountered from specific social groups a hostility which it had never experienced before. For the first time in its history, in the period 1850–80, the Latin American Church acquired enemies who hated it with an intensity born of frustrated conviction. It is true that not all liberals shared these convictions. Some were simply seeking to reform the state, to constitute the rule of law for all, and to modernize the economy. None of these objects were necessarily a threat to religion. But more radical liberals went beyond an attempt to establish the appropriate autonomy of the state: they favored an all-out attack on the Church's wealth, privileges, and institutions, for they believed that without the destruction of ecclesiastical power and the death of its accompanying dogma no real change could be made. So secularization in the nineteenth century took various forms and drew various responses, some of them violent. The battle was fought over the right to appoint bishops, over ownership of property, over the legal and political sanctions of religion, and over education. And secularism had a social base, among the elite or those aspiring to the elite. The masses, it seemed, preferred their ancient beliefs.

In reaction the Church sought allies where it could. Throughout Latin America Catholic political thought became more conservative in the mid–nineteenth century. Churchmen aligned themselves with civilian conservatives in the belief that religion needed a political defense. In turn the dominant ideology of conservatism was Catholicism, and a belief that the alleged irrationality of man created a need for strong government supported by the Church and the sanctions of religion. The conservative political philosophy was not essentially religious but an interest and an ideology. Conservatives believed that without the restraint of religion, people would be turbulent and anarchic, a defense of religion on the grounds not of its truth but of its social utility. The alliance was harmful to the Church, for it placed it among a complex of interests identified as obstacles to change by liberals and Progressives, and it shared in the reverses of its associates.

The doctrinal heritage of Latin American Catholicism was not different from that of the rest of the Church. Bishops and priests received and transmitted traditional Catholic theology and scholastic philosophy. Whatever its past service to religion in reconciling faith and reason, scholasticism had become inert and repetitive. It failed to respond to the ideas of the Enlightenment, and in the nineteenth century Latin American Catholicism did not have the intellectual tools to confront the utilitarians, liberals, and positivists, with the result that the Christian argument went by default. The Bolivian priest Martín Castro complained of the education given in the seminaries and of the dominance of scholasticism "which is rightly banned by modern civilization." The Church relied not on new philosophical expression of religious dogma but on dogmatic restatement of ancient beliefs.

The doctrinal inspiration of the Latin American Church in the nineteenth century came from Rome and standards were set by Pope Pius IX (1846–78), who, in December 1864, published the Encyclical *Quanta Cura*, with its annex, the *Syllabus of Errors*. The Syllabus condemned liberalism, secularism, freedom of thought, and toleration. It specifically condemned lay education and the idea that state schools should be freed from ecclesiastical authority. It condemned the proposition that "in our age it is no longer expedient that the Catholic religion should be regarded as the sole religion of the State to the exclusion of all others," and it condemned, too, the proposition that "the Roman Pontiff can and should reconcile and harmonize himself with progress, liberalism, and recent civilization." The attitude of the papacy, of course, had a philosophical and historical context. The liberalism of the time was seen as an assertion of man's emancipation in relation to God and a deliberate rejection of the primacy of the supernatural. As Rome was bound to deny a rationalist and purely humanist conception of man, so it opposed the political conclusions which liberals drew from this. The papacy, moreover, was itself beleaguered by the Piedmontese government which, as it annexed the papal states, systematically applied a secular regime and imprisoned priests and bishops who opposed it. The Syllabus was a defense reflex. Even so, it was a crude and uncompromising compendium.

The Syllabus was a weight round religion's neck, a burden which damaged its prospects of peaceful growth in Latin America. Catholic moderates seeking a middle way were embarrassed by its intransigence. Conservative Catholics could appeal to it against moderates. And liberals could cite it as proof of the danger from the Catholic Church. As applied to Latin America the policy of Pius IX can be seen in his reaction to the Peruvian liberal priest, González Vigil, who attacked papal power and advocated a new national and liberal organization for the Church. Pius IX banned his book and excommunicated the author for denying that the Roman Catholic faith was the only true belief, for proclaiming religious toleration, and for preferring clerical marriage to celibacy. Some of these views would have been regarded as heterodox in any age of the Church and were probably unrepresentative of Catholic opinion. The policy of Pius IX, therefore, did not introduce a new or "romanized" faith and morals to Latin America but, after a period of regalism and laxity, defined more clearly doctrines and discipline as they were and asserted the primacy of Rome. It was papal definitions which were new, not papal authority.

What were the instruments of papal influence in Latin America? Ultimately it depended upon the respect of Catholics for the successor of Saint Peter. But it also had a number of more worldly agents. First, Rome sought to retain the nomination or confirmation of bishops, and only those who looked to Rome for authority were considered. In this context it has been remarked that Rome did not always get the bishop it preferred, but it never permitted a bishop it disapproved. A second means of influence was the Catholic media in Latin America; the papal position was propagated in the Catholic press and by individual writers and clerics. A third power base were the seminaries, bastions of orthodoxy, where the faith and morals of future leaders of the Church were formed. In 1858, Pius IX established the Latin American College in Rome, and future graduates of the Gregorian University would return to Latin America as an ecclesiastical elite. Fourthly, the new religious orders, many emanating from Europe, were key agents of Rome and took modern Catholicism to the length and breadth of the subcontinent. Finally, the Holy See had its own representatives in Latin America, though its diplomatic presence was not consistently strong.

---

4. The Juárez Law and the Lerdo Law ~ Brian Hamnett*

The nineteenth-century struggle between Liberal reformers and the Catholic Church was particularly acute in Mexico. It sent the country into civil war in the 1850s and paved the way for a humiliating foreign occupation in the 1860s. The person most closely associated with the conflict in Mexico between the Church and state, and the one most responsible for creating a new relationship between them, was Benito Juárez. A Zapotec Indian from the state of Oaxaca, Juárez rose from humble origins to the presidency of his country. In the mid-1850s he and his liberal colleagues proposed major changes in the legal status of the Church. The Juárez Law (named for Juárez himself) attacked the special legal prerogatives, or fueros, *enjoyed since the colonial era by Church officials and military men. Its intent was to create legal equality for all. The Lerdo Law (named for*

*Adapted from Brian Hamnett, *Juárez* (London: Longman, 1994), 96–100. Reprinted by permission of Pearson Education Limited.

Juárez's colleague Sebastián Lerdo de Tejada) broke up the Church's collectively owned lands in an attempt to individualize landholdings, but it had the secondary effect of destroying many of the communally held lands of Mexico's indigenous people. In the following selection, historian Brian Hamnett describes the two laws and the reaction they provoked among Catholic officials in Mexico and Rome.

The celebrated Juárez Law concerning the abolition of the fuero and the administration of justice was issued by the executive authority of President [Juan] Alvarez, under whom Juárez served as Minister of Justice and Ecclesiastical Affairs. Juárez intended the law to curb the clergy's exemptions from civil law, though not to abolish their corporate privileges outright. Consequently, ecclesiastical courts remained intact for the purpose of regulating internal discipline, but the new law excluded them from hearing civil cases. Writing more than a decade later, when himself President, Juárez described his law as "the spark that produced the conflagration of the Reform." This uncharacteristically immodest claim derived from the attempt to portray himself at that time as a radical and thereby to dissociate himself from the moderate Liberals.

Yet, even allowing for the radicalization of events between 1855 and 1859, the Juárez Law even at the time of enactment amounted to a moderate, if not conciliatory, measure. It formed part of a general Liberal effort not to provoke the clergy into irreconcilable confrontation. Even so, the bishops interpreted the law differently. The archbishop of Mexico condemned it outright on 28 November 1855 as an attack on the Church and clergy. Bishop Clemente de Jesús Munguía of Michoacán argued two days later that the government did not possess any legitimate faculty of restricting the Church's fuero. Accordingly, it should apply to the Holy See in Rome for formal permission to do so. He urged the government to suspend the law until such agreement had been obtained. Juárez, however, regarded such a view as a challenge to the civil power and to national sovereignty. He replied to Munguía that the government could not discuss with one of its citizens whether a law it had enacted and considered to be in the public interest should be complied with or not. Munguía subsequently argued that the fuero was not a "privilege" but a right possessed by the Church by virtue of its divine constitution.

Bishop Pelagio Antonio de Labastida of Puebla protested to Juárez on 29 November, though not in extreme terms. Juárez replied on 6 December that the President insisted on compliance with the new law. He hoped that the bishop would not sanction disobedience of it. Events in Puebla, however, proved to be beyond the bishop's control. The National Guard put down an attempted rebellion in the city on 12 December 1855. This rebellion was designed to coincide with another rebellion in the northern Puebla sierra led by the parish priest. The rebels, calling for the defense of religion and the reestablishment of the Constitution of 1836, moved down from the mountains and on 23 January 1856 secured control of the state capital. The rebellion dealt a serious blow to the Liberal regime.

Although the Conservatives were forced eventually to capitulate, the government again overstepped the mark by levying the cost of putting down the rebellion on the diocese of Puebla. This punitive measure, taken at the end of March 1856, provoked an indignant protest from Bishop Labastida, who had not in any case identified himself with the rebels. For this protest Labastida was banished from the country. Until that time, Labastida had not been a party man. He had largely been indifferent to politics, though he found himself henceforth caught up in them without possibility of extrication. He proceeded to Rome, where the government still had not managed to place an official spokesman who might try to explain its policies. There he became a powerful enemy of the Reform movement. Labastida's stand on basic principles at a time of extreme government sensitivity made matters worse. This was serious, since both Conservative and Liberal extremists were anxious to exploit the situation for their opposing ends. The Puebla conflict remained alive throughout the year. After a forty-day siege, the city again fell on 3 December. In this way, Conservative actions managed to knock the Liberal revolution off course and expose some of its more intolerant aspects.

On 18 February 1856, the same day that the Constituent Congress opened, the president issued the *Acta de Jacala*, which declared the Juárez Law to be effective in all its parts. Juárez, however, had already returned to Oaxaca as governor for the second time. During his absence from the capital, the administration revived the legislation of the first Liberal regime of 1833–34. The most significant measure was the Lerdo Law of 25 June. Both the Juárez and the Lerdo Laws sought to avoid direct confrontation with the Church. Their authors, along with most of the Liberal administration, still hoped to persuade the ecclesiastical hierarchy to accept the Reform process. They thereby strove to include the Church in the mainstream of the modernizing project, as conceived by the Liberal Party. Both laws veered uneasily between radical objectives and Catholic sensibilities. During the years 1855–57, the moderate element in the party still remained predominant, at least at the federal level. Different situations pertained, however, in the states. The Lerdo Law, moderate in conception, had unforeseen consequences. These served to intensify conflict at all levels.

Envisaging clerical cooperation, the Lerdo Law required the ecclesiastical authorities to assess the value of their collectively owned properties, break them up, and transfer them to private ownership, with the existing tenants given preference. The intention was to convert the annual rent into an interest payment on capital values. The new owners would pay interest on these mortgages to the ecclesiastical body concerned and the state would receive the appropriate fees. If, after the lapse of three months, this procedure had not proved successful, then the ecclesiastical authorities were required to put these properties up for sale at public auction.

The ecclesiastical authorities denounced the Lerdo Law as confiscatory. Bishop Munguía argued on 26 July that the properties of the Church were independent of the wishes of governments and that they had been acquired not by a concession of the temporal power but by the nature of the social existence of the Church. He saw the law as another Liberal attempt to secure money at the expense of the Church. Social and ethnic relations markedly deteriorated after the passage of this law.

Though not made public until later, Pope Pius IX's Allocution of 15 December 1856 denounced the Juárez and Lerdo Laws, the banishment of Bishop Labastida, and the sequestration of Puebla diocesan property. It also condemned the depriving of the clergy of the right to vote in national elections, those articles of the projected Constitution deemed to be contrary to religion, and the procedure of the civil authorities with total disregard for the Holy See and the ecclesiastical authorities. This Allocution became public knowledge during the same month in which the Liberal Constitution was put into effect. The government committed a serious error by insisting that all public office-holders should take an oath to uphold it. The archbishop roundly condemned this requirement and used the fullness of episcopal power to counter it. On 15 March 1857 he declared in the cathedral that henceforth he would bind all confessors to request of their penitents whether they had taken the oath or not. If they responded in the confessional that they had, then they would be denied absolution. This extreme recourse was deeply compromising for ordinary Catholics and infuriating for Liberals. The archbishop's action compounded the Liberals' own error by escalating the conflict beyond repair.

---

5. Generational Warrior ~ Francisco Bilbao*

This selection is composed of three related primary-source documents from mid-nineteenth-century Chile. The first is an abridgment of an essay published in the Santiago magazine El Crepúsculo (The Dawn) *on June 1, 1844. Its author, twenty-one-year-old Francisco Bilbao, was a student at the newly established University of Chile and a member of one of the country's most prominent liberal*

*Adapted from Pedro Pablo Figueroa, ed., *Obras completes de Francisco Bilbao*, 2 vols. (Santiago: El Correo, 1897), 1:11–19, 28–31, 51–55, 59–61, 81. Translated by James A. Wood.

families. His essay "Chilean Sociability," aimed at inspiring his fellow students to become agents of revolutionary change, was deeply critical of the Church's influence on Chilean social development. It also owed a great intellectual debt to the French Catholic socialist, Félicité de Lamennais. The next document is the federal prosecutor's indictment of Bilbao's essay on the charges of blasphemy, immorality, and sedition. It reveals the Church's power over the state as well as the rigid orthodoxy of the 1840s (notice especially the government's reaction to Bilbao's "immoral" views on marriage). The final document is Bilbao's defense of his essay, which he presented at the jury trial that was convened to hear the case. His defense argued passionately on behalf of "innovation" and the need to push Chile into the modernity of the nineteenth century. Bilbao was found guilty of blasphemy and immorality (but not sedition) and forced to leave the country or face imprisonment. Within a month he was on his way to Paris, where he witnessed the Revolution of 1848. He returned to Chile in 1850 and tried to start a revolution of his own.

"Chilean Sociability" by Francisco Bilbao

S pain is our past.
　　Spain is the Middle Ages. The soul and body of the Middle Ages are composed of Catholicism and feudalism.

We look to the peculiar characteristics of Spain to see our own character.

The Middle Ages were completed in Spain, that is to say, they achieved their full development in the Catholic domination of Spain.

America came from Spain and carries her stamp; the Spanish past on American soil brings us to Chile.

Let us quickly review the relations that the Catholic Church sanctions with regard to the state, the customs, and the philosophy of the time in which we live.

There is no doubt that Christianity was a major advance in the religious rehabilitation of men; but Catholicism, which is oriental and reactionary with regard to symbolism and formula, reacted with hostility to the primitive purity of the doctrine of Jesus.

Under Catholicism, women are subordinated to their husbands. The result is the slavery of women. Paul, the primary founder of Catholicism, did not follow the moral religion of Jesus Christ. Jesus emancipated women. Paul subordinated them. Jesus was Western in his spirit, that is to say, liberal. Paul was oriental and authoritarian. Jesus founded a democratic religion, Paul an ecclesiastical aristocracy. From there originates the logical consequence of the slavery of women. Jesus introduced matrimonial democracy, that is to say, the equality of spouses. Paul put *authority* and the inequality of privilege in its place, in favor of the strongest, in favor of men.

Matrimonial inequality is one of the most outdated aspects of the elaboration of our customs and laws. Incessant adultery, the sentinel that announces the imperfection of our laws, is a protest against the poor organization of marriage. France is at the head of this protest, George Sand* at the head of France. She is the priestess who sacrifices herself, but her prophetic visions signal the dawn of the regeneration of matrimony.

When children are irremediably subordinated to fathers, the result is the slavery of children. This principle is of great importance in Catholic logic. In the family, the father, the elder, the old man is the authority; the power he possesses is absolute. Political laws can limit this power. Because we recognize the authority of individual reason in *every* individual, despotism is illegitimate; the child is his own person, whose liberty is sacred.

When individuals are subordinated to authority, the result is the slavery of citizens. "Obey the authorities," says Saint Paul. A diplomatic principle in origin, it began so as to avoid the persecution of pagan authorities and was converted later into an active instrument of subjugation. This also explains the union that has almost always existed between the clergy and the Catholic monarchies. Monarchy is a government of divine or heroic *tradition*, of privilege or authority; of course it needs the aid of religion. The clergy dominate individual citizens and obstruct free analysis and free thought, which are the enemies of tradition. The clergy, for its part, needs the aid of earthly power for the creation and maintenance of its private interests, for the persecution of heresy. How clearly the logic of the French Revolution appears now. The people, free individuals, free analysis, the present cut loose from the past. Bury the monarchy, the clergy, and the nobility; bury the Catholic synthesis of the past.

When thought is chained to the text and intelligence molded by beliefs the result is slavery of the mind. Education, logically, was entrusted to the convents. This also explains the predominance of Aristotle in the Middle Ages. Aristotle was logic then. One could only deduce from given principles.

What was the culmination of the eighteenth-century revolution and of the American† revolution? The liberty of men, the equality of citizens, individuals vindicated in all their rights, and the applications of those rights. The recognition of the equality of man's origins, both in means and ends. The individual, as a man, asks for the freedom of thought, where the freedom of religion is born. The individual, as a free spirit, exposed to both good and evil, needs *education* in order to recognize good. The indi-

---

*George Sand was the pen name of a female novelist in nineteenth-century France known for her criticism of traditional social institutions such as marriage.
† "American" is used here in the hemispheric sense of the word.

vidual, as a *human being*, body and soul, needs *property* in order to fulfill his purpose in life. He needs property to develop his intellectual life, his physical life, and the lives of his children. Thus he needs the necessary conditions to acquire property, and to acquire it in a complete manner, as it is owed to him. Here the destruction of privilege and feudalism is born, as well as the raising of wages to a measure that raises human dignity.

The inescapable point of departure, the foundation of all human systems, is *the equality of liberty*.

It is the Paradise from which we were dispossessed, the infiniteness of human greatness, the kingdom of heaven on earth.

The equality of liberty is a universal religion; it is the government of humanity; it is the future unity.

Indictment of Bilbao's "Chilean Sociability"

The interim prosecutor of the Court of Appeals, having seen issue number two of the periodical titled *The Dawn*, states: everything written under the title "Chilean Sociability" suffers from the odious stain of blasphemy, immorality, and sedition in the third degree in the view of this Ministry.

As the present indictment deals principally with this printed work, this Ministry feels it is necessary to enter into a meticulous analysis and a listing of the particulars of the passages that contain the crimes mentioned above.

In talking about the depredations of the feudal lords and the ferocity with which they took the lives of other men, the author refers to those who suffered punishment under that system, as expressed in this manner: "Desperation grows, but the Catholic priest says there is nothing but misery in this world. All power comes from God [say the priests], submit yourselves to his power. This is the glorification of slavery."

Next the author analyzes the symbol of the Catholic faith in a manner that attacks and ridicules all aspects of the religious dogma of the State.

He goes further, and in manifesting his audacity in combating the most sacred institutions, he questions the principles of the Christian religion, the doctrines of the wise apostle of the people, Saint Paul:

Under Catholicism, women are subordinated to their husbands. The result is the slavery of women. Paul, the primary founder of Catholicism, did not follow the moral religion of Jesus Christ. Jesus emancipated women. Paul subordinated them. Jesus was Western in his spirit, that is to say, liberal. Paul was oriental and authoritarian. Jesus founded a democratic religion, Paul an ecclesiastical aristocracy. From there originates the logical consequence of the slavery of women. Jesus introduced matrimonial democracy, that is to say, the equality of spouses. Paul put *authority* and

the inequality of privilege in its place, in favor of the strongest, in favor
of men.

Of the principles cited in the paragraph above, Bilbao infers vices in
the marriages celebrated under the Catholic rite, and from that point in the
article he becomes immoral, as well as blasphemous.

Speaking of marriage he says: "Matrimonial inequality is one of the
most outdated aspects of the elaboration of our customs and laws. Incessant adultery, the sentinel that announces the imperfection of our laws, is
a protest against the poor organization of marriage."

After reproaching the system of marital indissolubility he says that the
Catholic rites affirming arranged marriages impede the spontaneity and
liberty of the heart. These rites are maintained to give protection to the
privileged classes and so that authority and tradition are not weakened.

From the tradition of arranged marriages, he says, are born misan-
thropic isolation, and the system of life that he explains in these terms:

> The passion of youth is silenced. Such exalted passion is an instrument
> of instinctive revolution. It is taken to church, dressed in black, its face
> hidden from the street, not allowed to say hello, to look to its side. It is
> kept on its knees, told to mortify its flesh, and, what is more, the confes-
> sor examines its conscience, and imposes an authority on it that cannot
> be appealed. The chorus of old men carries on with the litany of the
> dangers of fashion, of contact with visitors, of dress, of glances and
> words. One ponders the monastic life, the stupid mysticism of God's
> acceptance of physical suffering. This is youth. What of the young man
> who comes home late, who listens to amorous words? Pity on him who
> is caught reading a banned book; in sum, on he who goes out, dances,
> falls in love! The father's whip and eternal condemnation are anathema.
> There is no rationality between fathers and sons. After work the son will
> go to pray the rosary, pass along the sacred path, go to the school of
> Christ, to hear stories about witches, spirits, and purgatories. Imagine a
> young man of robust constitution, of good health, of ardent imagination,
> under the weight of that mountain of worries.

Not content at having committed the crimes of blasphemy and immorality, the author concludes his work with sedition.

He complains that the Executive Power will not change the State religion by allowing religious pluralism, thus destroying a fundamental law:

> The Constitution, which organized the Republic in this despotic, unitary
> mode, is what rules us. The code that legally organized despotism,
> destroying all the guarantees that republicanism had conquered, still
> exists. Ecclesiastical organization exercises an influential power that is
> separate from its political influence. The Catholic system reigns without

limits. The priest still collects the tithe, the priest still sells marriages and baptisms. Ecclesiastical power has an imposing pension fund that the government tolerates. The government is hypocritical.

It is under the authority of Your Honors to proceed with the arrangements to effect a judgment on the present indictment.

Bilbao's Defense of "Chilean Sociability"

S ociety has been shaken to its core. From its profound disturbance we have come today to the surface: you, Mr. Prosecutor, the accuser; I, the accused.

The place in which we find ourselves and the accusation made against me reveal the state in which we find our institutions and ideas.

The prosecutor is trying to cover himself with the dust of Spanish laws. The jury can remove that dust with its breath.

A hand appears trying to uphold fourteen collapsing centuries, in order to destroy a face baptized in the rising dawn.

The hand belongs to you, Mr. Prosecutor; the face is mine.

Yours is the mouth through which fading subterranean echoes denounce me; I am the conscience that faces its anathema.

We have two names, accuser and accused, two names brought together by historic fate that will live on in the history of my country.

Some day we will see, Mr. Prosecutor, which of the two will have the blessings of posterity. Now then, which one of us is right to rejoice before our fellow men? History will tell us.

History always shows innovators as idols; reactionaries it paints as the snake that bites the traveler's shoe along the side of the road.

Which one of us is right to rejoice before the divinity? History, which teaches us the laws that God has imposed on humanity, will also tell us. These are the laws of innovation and disintegration.

To oppose the development of these laws I find difficult to understand. Now then, Mr. Prosecutor, you call me a blasphemer: I, who obey and try to follow the laws. But those who call on authority for help in slowing the march of innovation, I do not call them blasphemous—I call them ignorant!

I have always felt the activity of my conscience, and the reasoned application of that activity has always tormented my human existence.

Study and observation have showed me the law of duty. With my thoughts submerged in the investigation of the human mission, I found myself awakening in the nineteenth century, and in Chile, my homeland.

In my beliefs I wanted (call me foolish if you want) to take this country I love so much in my weak hands, and give it the push that the present century dictates to me—I wanted, in the audacity of my journey, to thrust the Chilean flag into the vanguard of humanity—but a hand subdued me; with its touch, it reminded me of the reality that I wanted to remove, and tried to crush me, accumulating anathema after anathema. That hand is yours, Mr. Prosecutor. Here you have me, then, before the jury, soon to be sentenced as a dangerous innovator.

I have acquired a great reputation for protecting liberty and I have sought to broaden the minds of my fellow men by giving them that understanding with its social consequences. I have cried with the tears of the people for their present state and their gloomy future: I have tried to show them the happy regions of equality. I have obeyed the sacrosanct voice of fraternity, which extinguishes pride and brings humanity together. Your Honors of the Jury, I am not a blasphemer because I love God; I am not immoral because I love and search for the obligation to perfect it; I am not seditious because I want to prevent the exasperation of my oppressed fellow men.

Your Honors of the Jury, I have looked into the grave that opens before me. I have measured the gravestone that rises in front of me and I have come with a peaceful conscience to reflect on a verdict of not guilty or resign myself to the crime of which I am condemned. But I also say, Your Honors of the Jury, that I can already envision the dawning of the day in which my country, motivated by human activity, will look upon me again, its presently lost son, and that illuminating look will imprint my name radiantly on the civilized memory of my country.

V

Race and Nation Building

In the nineteenth century, the nation-state became the standard political model in the Western world. Kingdoms, empires, and former colonies were reorganized into nations (with a specific, unified ethnic identity), each of which had its own state (an independent, usually republican, government). Latin American elites aspired, for the most part, to duplicate this nation-state model. But in Latin America the republics had become independent states before their national identities had really gelled in most people's minds. Therefore, the post-Independence 1800s were a period of nation building, in which schools, newspapers, elections, and political conflicts gradually generated a shared sense of belonging among diverse populations. Furthermore, the construction of new national identities was complicated by the prevalence of racist ideas throughout the Western world at the time.

Dreams of equality among native-born *americanos* had made a cross-racial patriot alliance possible during the Wars of Independence. But the region's hierarchies of race and class had proved resistant to transformation afterward. The patronage politics of caudillismo allowed talented mestizos to get ahead, here and there. But slavery continued in several places, as we have seen. To make matters worse, intellectually prestigious doctrines of "scientific racism" were emanating from Europe and the United States, where they had been proposed as part of the dark underside of world liberalism. Core republican principles such as citizenship, popular sovereignty, and equality before the law empowered everybody if applied fairly. As with the case of slave-owning in the United States or Brazil or Cuba, however, republican principles contradicted stubborn political realities. Powerful men committed to excluding slaves (or women, or anyone else who was not white or male) from the magic circle of equality were eager for justifying arguments, and scientific racism supplied them. Scientific racism became a rationale for slavery, an apology for colonialism, and an excuse to disempower non-Europeans around the world. Latin American elites seem to have been particularly influenced by the French thinker Gustave Le Bon, who taught that the racial traits of a population determined the character of a country. Le Bon ranked races according to a strict hierarchy, with Europeans at the top and indigenous Americans and Africans at the bottom. An advocate of racial purity, Le Bon argued that race mixing always leads to degeneration.

Therefore, the would-be nation builders of Latin America faced a great dilemma. What sort of countries could the region's white ruling classes envision in the light of scientific racism? Only countries full of supposedly second-class and third-class people, unfit for self-government—a negative prospect, indeed. In contrast, a sturdy nation-state required a positive national identity, one that inspired people to cooperate and, occasionally, make sacrifices in the name of the common good. The elite's dilemma helps to explain the chronic political instability of the region during the mid-1800s.

One solution might be to infuse the current population with European immigrants. European immigration did demographically transform a handful of countries, notably Argentina and Uruguay. Overall, however, Latin American elites had no choice but to envision nations that were largely brown and black, at least for the time being. As a result, creative thinkers in majority nonwhite countries began to challenge Le Bon's dictum about the inevitable degeneration caused by race mixing. If that were not true, they reasoned, perhaps the national stock could be improved by cross-breeding. Around 1900, it was widely expected that entire national populations would gradually "whiten" over the generations. After all, seeking partners of lighter skin color was a familiar strategy, a commonplace of Latin American life at the individual or family level. But "whitening" was merely racist wishful thinking at a collective, societal level without massive European immigration.

How do you think the nation builders' dilemma was overcome? The following readings will give you a better appreciation of the problem, followed by three looks at how Latin American writers dealt with race, and, finally, a reminder that the need for political solidarity is what always drives the idea of nation.

QUESTIONS FOR ANALYSIS

1. Why do you think Latin American intellectuals such as Carlos Octavio Bunge and Alcides Arguedas allowed themselves to be influenced by European doctrines of scientific racism in the nineteenth century?

2. Race and nation were important themes in many nineteenth-century Latin American novels. What can we learn from novels that we cannot always find in other kinds of writing?

3. Is Cuba an exceptional case in the broader picture of Latin American thinking on race and nation in the nineteenth century? If not, how does it fit in?

1. The Specter of Degeneration ~ Martin S. Stabb*

Latin American intellectuals read the prestigious European theories of scientific racism and, overall, accepted them. The following is an excerpt from a 1967 scholarly study of how the region's writers absorbed, wrestled with, and (in the mid-1900s) finally rejected those ideas. This passage deals with the period when the prestige of scientific racism still stood unchallenged in the Western world. Essayists such as Argentina's Carlos Octavio Bunge and Bolivia's Alcides Arguedas, depressingly faithful to their European sources, applied racist concepts to Latin America in a rigid manner representative of essayists throughout the region.

An important expression of positivism's scientific approach to man and his society was a strong interest in race and racial theories. The biological thought of the nineteenth century—diffused through such popularizing movements as Darwinism, social organicism, and the relatively new discipline of physical anthropology—provided abundant material upon which the racial theorizer could draw. Moreover, the fact that Spanish America had a population of great ethnic complexity naturally led her thinkers to consider race in assessing the continent's problems. The effect of the U.S.–Spanish War of 1898 must also be taken into account in this connection. Although it was Spain rather than Spanish America who had suffered the defeat, the weakness of the mother country at the hands of the vigorous and ambitious Anglo-Saxon certainly disturbed the Hispanic world. The popular mind undoubtedly saw in the defeat of a swarthy southern "race" by a blue-eyed northern "race" a good example of the triumph of a "more fit" people over an "inferior" group.

One of the most complete raciological analyses of Hispanic America to appear in this century was *Nuestra América* (1903) by the Argentine, Carlos Octavio Bunge (1875–1918). The route which Bunge's thinking will follow is indicated early in his book: "What I would call the practical objective in this book is to describe, with all its vices and all its forms,

*From Martin S. Stabb, *In Quest of Identity: Patterns in the Spanish American Essay of Ideas, 1890–1960* (Chapel Hill: University of North Carolina Press, 1967), 12–22. © 1968 by the University of North Carolina Press. Reprinted by permission of the University of North Carolina Press.

the politics of Spanish America. In order to understand this, I must first investigate the collective psychology which produces it."

When Bunge turns his attention to the nonwhite elements in Spanish America's racial composition, his deeply engrained racism is very apparent. The Indian, he feels, is characterized by "passivity" and "oriental fatalism," and these traits account for the Spaniards' easy conquest of Peru and Mexico. The Negro receives similar treatment. After a brief moment's consideration of the validity of the concept of superior versus inferior races, he proceeds to analyze the "positive facts" regarding the Negro's attainments. These he finds to be utterly lacking: the Negro has not invented anything, he is not capable of intellectual leadership or of artistic creativity. His typical traits are "servility" and "vanity." Similarly, his characterization of the mulatto plainly reveals his utter disdain for this group: "Impulsive, perfidious, petulant, the mulatto is a complex amalgam of the Spanish and African spirit. . . . He is as touchy and as fickle as a woman, and, like a degenerate, like a devil himself, he aspires to be strong but is necessarily weak. . . . He lacks personal valor. In dangerous situations he has difficulty in overcoming his fear. But by means of trickery and fraud, he can escape his enemy with reptilian undulations." The mestizo hardly fares better. He is accused of "rapacity," of intensifying and aggravating the Spaniard's arrogance, and of having a love for brutality inherited from his Indian ancestors. In short, both the mulatto and the mestizo reflect the worst of their parent stocks: "Both impure, both atavistically anti-Christian, they are like the two heads of a mythical Hydra which encircles, constricts, and strangles in its gigantic coils a beautiful and pale virgin: Hispanic America!"

A book such as *Nuestra América* would have little appeal to present-day Spanish Americans. The author's racism is only the outward manifestation of attitudes which run counter to contemporary thought and sensibility. The most striking feature of Bunge's view of the New World (at least the Hispanic portion of it) is that it cannot measure up to what he considers the only culture worthy of emulation, the European. The complete falseness of his "objective" positivistic pose is frequently revealed by violent, impassioned outbursts against specific groups, particularly mulattoes and mestizos.

Like Bunge, Alcides Arguedas (1879–1946) of Bolivia undertakes the investigation of his region's problems with a desire for a realistic, "surgical," hardheaded approach. In keeping with this spirit, he urges his compatriots to face the facts of national backwardness and political chaos directly: "we must agree frankly, vigorously, and directly that we are sick and that our total collapse may be certain." The causes of this sickness are then sketched out in broad terms: "Heredity, lack of culture, laziness, and poverty; here you have in summation the real underlying causes of the sickness of the Andean countries." Arguedas traces the ills of the Andean countries to both "inheritance" and environmental forces. Arguedas's characterization of the Indian occupies an important place in his analysis. The native American, he asserts, "carries in his blood" a marked lack of foresight. He possesses an "atrophied" aesthetic sense. And the Indian's willingness to die in battle "comes to the poor unfortunates by heredity." Although these traits are apparently considered innate in the native American, a few other characteristics are ascribed to environmental conditioning. In an early chapter of Arguedas's best known book, *Pueblo Enfermo* (*Sick People, 1909*), for example, Arguedas maintains that the "hypocrisy and deceit" of the Indian were developed as defense mechanisms against the brutality of the conqueror. In a similar manner, according to Arguedas, twentieth-century Indians find that feigned stupidity affords an escape from distasteful work.

Arguedas discusses the Bolivian mestizo, or *cholo*, at great length. Significantly, this group fares considerably worse in his view than does the pure Indian. Speaking of alcoholism and laziness, he asserts that while there is some justification in the Indian's being a sluggard and a drinker, these vices are found in the cholo simply "by inclination." Arguedas's overall characterization of the cholo stresses his "atavistic" traits, though the Bolivian writer does concede him a degree of intelligence and an "enviable" ability to adapt to his environment. Moreover, he is "generous and considerate." Having taken brief note of the few good cholo characteristics, Arguedas goes on to present the catalog of his faults. These include a lack of sense of duty, a lack of discipline, bellicosity, egocentrism, vanity, hypocrisy, servility, and lack of loyalty.

Given this view of mestizo character, it is not difficult to predict how Arguedas will "explain" his region's social and political shortcomings. In language reminiscent of Bunge, he states that "mestizo blood" has molded Bolivian society to the point that "we are burdened with imprudence, cheating, falseness, and other evils which unavoidably turn man aside from the pursuit of moral perfection, the highest goal of life." It is to miscegenation that Bolivia owes its slow development of democratic institutions. It is because of "a certain uniqueness of the Indo-Hispanic character" that the people lean too heavily upon the state for all their needs. And, had Indian blood not predominated in his country's racial composition, Bolivia would have adopted "all kinds of moral and material advances and would today be at the same level as many of the more favored nations." Again, Bunge may be recalled when Arguedas states that "with mestizos and cholos one cannot utilize institutions made for pure-blooded and thoroughly educated peoples."

The theory that miscegenation produces degeneracy and the complementary notion that racial purity leads to superior culture occupies a central place in Arguedas's thought. As late as 1937, in the third edition of *Pueblo Enfermo*, Arguedas is unequivocal in his view that racial mixing is the explanation of Bolivia's backwardness: "In short, I repeat that miscegenation is the most obvious and the most enslaving phenomenon in Bolivia, and it is the only thing that explains reasonably and satisfactorily our present backwardness." As in the 1909 edition, he seeks support for his position in the literature of European raciology. By the 1930s, however, such support could no longer be found within the ranks of scientific anthropologists and social psychologists. As the critic Zum Felde notes, Arguedas's thesis was never corrected in the light of modern race concepts. His racism, in fact, became so entrenched that he could only find substantiation for his views in the writings of that distinguished raciological "expert" of recent history, Adolf Hitler.

---

2. Civilization versus Barbarism ~ Domingo Faustino Sarmiento*

Sarmiento's classic Facundo, or Civilization and Barbarism *(1845) constitutes an early expression of the dilemma with which elite Latin American nation builders grappled in the nineteenth century. Sarmiento's famous formula, "civilization and barbarism," directly implied, in slightly expanded terms, "imported European civilization versus native American barbarism." Indirectly, however, it also expressed a racial dichotomy. For Sarmiento, Argentine civilization was defined by the cities, where people of European descent predominated. Barbarism, which supposedly had to be eliminated for Argentina to realize its national potential, was defined by the countryside, where most people were not of purely European descent. The excerpted passage exemplifies this aspect of Sarmiento's thought and also foreshadows the "solution" that Argentine elites pursued more successfully (beginning roughly with Sarmiento's own presidency in 1868–1874) than any other ruling group in Latin America.*

The question is to be or not to be savage.

One illness which afflicts the Argentine Republic is its vast expanse. The desert surrounds it. Solitude and wilderness without human habitation isolate its provinces from one another. There is immensity everywhere: immense plains, woods, and rivers, the horizon always uncertain, always blended with the earth among varicolored clouds and tenuous

---

*From Domingo Faustino Sarmiento, *Facundo, o civilización y barbarie* (Caracas: Biblioteca Ayacucho, 1977), 123–24, 206–8. Translated by John Charles Chasteen and Leslie Bary.

vapors which prevent us from determining that distant point at which the world ends and the sky begins.

The agglomeration of navigable rivers is a notable trait of the country. But these immense canals excavated by Nature's solicitous hand have left no mark on the customs of the Argentine people. An Argentine countryman considers himself imprisoned in the narrow confines of a boat. When a great river cuts off his passage, he calmly undresses, prepares his horse, and guides it swimming to an islet made out from afar. There the horse and rider rest, and from islet to islet the crossing is finished at last. Thus, the Argentine countryman disdains to navigate these river roads, the greatest favor Providence has supplied to the country, seeing them only as an obstacle to his movements.

As for the city man of Argentina, he wears a European suit and lives a civilized life. In the cities there are laws, ideas of progress, means of instruction, municipal organization, and regular government. Outside the cities, the look of everything changes. The countryman wears different clothing, not European but American. His way of life is different, his necessities peculiar and limited. Argentina is therefore composed of two entirely different societies, two peoples unconnected with each other. What is more, the countryman, far from aspiring to resemble his urban counterpart, disdainfully rejects urban luxuries and cultivated manners. All aspects of urban civilization are banned in the countryside. Anyone who dared appear in a frock coat, mounted on an English saddle, would bring upon himself the jeers and brutal aggression of the barbarous country people.

The triumph of European civilization encounters practically insuperable barriers in the Argentine countryside. It cannot, on the other hand, be denied that this situation has its poetic side, worthy of a novelist's pen. If a sparkle of national literature can shine momentarily in the new American societies, it will arise from the description of grand natural scenes, and, above all, from the struggle between European civilization and indigenous barbarity.

Great difficulties for any political organization are born from the conditions of country life. Would England like to find consumers for its products in Argentina, irrespective of its government? Fine, but what can six hundred thousand poor Argentine country people, without industry, almost without necessities, consume, under a government which, by extinguishing European customs and tastes, necessarily diminishes the consumption of European products? When there is a cultured government that cares about the national interest, then what business, what industrial movement there will be!

The principal element of order, and the main hope for the future that Argentina possesses today is European immigration, which by itself, and in spite of the lack of security offered it, rushes in daily to the Plate region. If there were a government capable of directing this immigration, it would by itself be enough to cure in no more than ten years all the wounds which the bandits who have dominated the country—from Facundo to Rosas—have inflicted upon Argentina.

3. A Brazilian Tenement ⁓ Aluísio Azevedo*

Latin American novelists were also infected with scientific racism. Here, Aluísio Azevedo, an important Brazilian novelist of the late 1800s, depicts the kind of degeneration that, according to racist dogma, resulted from race mixing. The novel is set in a tenement in Rio de Janeiro, where European immigrants and native Brazilians of African descent rub elbows in daily life. Jeronymo, a hard-working Portuguese immigrant and a married man, has fallen for Rita, a bewitching Brazilian mulata. Azevedo tries to "document" the outcome in minute detail through the technique of the naturalistic novel, a European genre. Jeronymo becomes a slacker and develops a taste for liquor—a matter of behavior, not genes. Yet, scientific racism systematically linked biology and culture. The supposed cultural degeneration of Jeronymo stands symbolically for the supposed genetic degeneration of the children he might have with Rita. The scene is a party enlivened by popular Brazilian music.

Suddenly Porfirio's mandolin, aided by Firmo's guitar, broke forth in a *chorado* of Bahia, and at the first vibrant note of the exhilarating negro music, the pulses of the tenement quickened and gloom disappeared. As it continued it became, not merely the sound of a mandolin accompanied by a guitar, but the expression of a people—moans and sighs freed in a torrent, gliding and writhing like serpents in a burning forest—the music increased in intensity, music made up of caresses, of kisses and of happy sobs, of brutal caresses of agony.

Filled with the fire of madness was this strange music, like the sharp and smarting aroma of certain poisonous plants deep in the Brazilian forest, and astonishing was its effect on its hearers. Their bodies swayed with the sensual rhythm of the melodies, their senses intoxicated with exhilaration. Dispelled was Portugal's gloom by the quick pulsing joyousness of Bahia—the clouds and shadows of old Europe routed by young America's brilliant sunshine.

Jeronymo laid aside his guitar and with rapt attention listened to the weird music, which was carrying on a strange revolution within him—a

*From Aluísio Azevedo, *A Brazilian Tenement*, trans. Harry W. Brown (New York: R. M. McBride and Co., 1926), 97–99, 120.

revolution that had begun the day he felt in his face, like a challenging blow, the dazzling sunshine of this new world; a revolution that revived the first time he heard the chirp of a tropical cricket and the song of a Brazilian bird, that progressed with the taste of the first juicy fruit he had sampled in this new, young land, and that was to be completed by the first woman here who attracted him—a half-white, whose sinuous movements fascinated him as a helpless bird is transfixed by the deadly eyes of a serpent.

"What's the matter with you, Jeronymo?" asked his [Portuguese] wife Piedade, marveling at his tense expression.

"Wait," he replied; "I want to listen." For Firmo had started singing the chorado, accompanied by the rhythmical hand claps of the others. Jeronymo arose, almost mechanically, and approached the group surrounding the two musicians, Piedade following him. With his elbows on the fence surrounding Rita's little patch of flowers and his chin resting on his clasped hands, he stood, neither moving nor speaking, giving body and soul to the seduction of the voluptuous music, as a giant tree allows itself to be encircled and bound by the caressing tentacles of a treacherous vine.

And then came Rita Bahiana, who had shed her ruffles and appeared with arms and neck bared to dance. The moon burst through the clouds at this moment, bathing the scene with a soft, silver glow and lending to the rich, warm skin of the mulata a pallor that made her really beautiful. With infinite grace she danced, simple, primitive, seemingly formed solely to delight the senses, a creature from Eden's garden, much of the woman and much of the serpent.

She danced within the circle, her hands at her waist and her entire body in movement. Now her arms were outstretched and raised, and then lowered till her finger tips touched her neck. At times she sank till she appeared to be almost sitting on the ground, while the movement of her arms and hips never ceased. Then she leaped into the air and danced, faster and faster, her arms twisting and writhing, and her blood boiling with a passion that communicated itself to the onlookers.

As she flung herself into a chair, the enthusiasm of her admirers knew no bounds. An explosion of applause rent the air and cries of delight burst from every throat. She must dance more; they would not be refused. Seizing Firmo, she dragged him into the center and made him dance. Agile and supple, seemingly made of rubber, he performed astonishing feats. He doubled his legs beneath him and danced with his body almost on the ground, then leaped aloft and cut the most fantastic capers, his arms and legs appearing about to be shaken from his trunk. The dance spirit proved to be contagious; Florinda started dancing and so did even slim Albino.

The spell of the chorado enchained them all despotically, those who did not dance as well as those who did. But none was so affected as Rita.

She only, with the sinuous grace of the cursed snake, could truly interpret and express the spirit of her native Bahia—a combination of movement, of the strange perfume of the mulata, and of the seduction of her voice—low and sweet, with no spoken words, but startling little cries and a crooning murmur, as she danced.

Jeronymo gazed and listened, spellbound, feeling his soul pour out of his eyes, which he could not turn from the mulata. She was a mystery to him, and he was dimly conscious of a confusion of impressions as he stood and stared. She was the brilliant glare at mid-day, the red heat of the plantation field; she was the aroma of the vanilla tree, filling the Brazilian forest; she was the virgin palm which lifts its head aloft and scorns contact with another living thing; she was poisonous—and marvelously sweet; she was the sapoti fruit with its juice like honey, and she was the caju nut, whose fiery oil causes running ulcers; she was the treacherous green snake, a reptile of rare beauty, which had entwined itself about him and filled him with desires beside which his longing for his old home was a sentiment poor, indeed, and its fangs had penetrated his arteries and poisoned him with a venom that he knew would make him burn with fever—a fever of passion for the mulata, for the half-white Rita, who danced to the music of Bahia.

All this Jeronymo felt but only half understood, so giddy was he with the change that had come over his spirit. The subsequent impressions of that Sunday ever remained a hazy recollection of events, of the experiences attendant upon unaccustomed drunkenness—an intoxication, not of wine, but of the bitter honey from the calyx of the baneful tropic lily. So he remained, looking on. Other girls danced, but the tall Portuguese had eyes only for the mulatta, even as she fell exhausted into the arms of her lover. Piedade, her head nodding with drowsiness, called to him to come along several times, receiving in reply only an unintelligible mutter, after which she departed alone. Hours passed by, but still he could not leave.

The circle had increased. Izaura and Leonor, on cordial terms with the tenement dwellers, were in the front row. João Romão and Bertoleza, the day's labors finally over, had come out for a moment to enjoy the scene before wearily falling into their bed. Miranda's family were at their high, next-door windows, highly diverted with the merry-making. Many passersby could not resist coming in for the frolic. But of all this Jeronymo had no consciousness; there was but one object before his eyes—the panting mulata twisting voluptuously in the arms of Firmo.

Several weeks passed, Jeronymo now taking every morning a cup of strong coffee "like Rita makes," and accompanying it with two fingers of the local liquor, paraty. A slow but relentless transformation was in progress within him, hour by hour, and day by day, silently but surely remolding him, body and soul. For his energy, even, was weakening. He became contemplative and romantic. This New-World atmosphere and his Brazilian surroundings presented to him now unexpected and seductive aspects that moved him. He forgot his early ambitions and gave himself over to the idealizing of new pleasures, sharper and more violent. He became liberal and improvident, more given to spending than to saving. He lost his old-time austerity and became pleasure-loving and, to a certain extent, indolent, no longer defying the blazing sun, the barricade of heat which the quarry wall threw back as a desperate last defense against the conquering invader. Thus were slowly modified in him the old habits of the Portuguese villager. Jeronymo's house lost its former air of severity, and friends occasionally dropped in for a little glass of paraty after work hours, while on Sundays there was now and then a dinner there. Eventually, the revolution was complete: Portuguese wine gave way to the Brazilian rum made from the cane juice. Stewed dried beef with black beans and mandioca succeeded codfish with potatoes and boiled onions, and, one by one, the other viands of old Portugal were crowded aside by dishes peculiar to Bahia, or Minas, or the shores of Guanabara. Once coffee had firmly established its welcome at No. 35, it began dragging in its twin sister, tobacco, and soon Jeronymo was contentedly puffing with the rest.

The more he dropped into the life and habits of Brazil, the finer his sensibilities became, even though his physical force weakened. He began to enjoy music and even comprehended to some extent the wilderness poets who sang of blighted love, their songs accompanied on the violin, or native guitar—indeed, Jeronymo himself had discarded the old instrument for the Brazilian. Formerly his one dream had been an eventual return to Portugal, but now, like the sailor on the high seas, his eyes became accustomed to the broad sweeps, and the turbulent Brazilian atmosphere, with its savage gaiety, no longer disconcerted him. Jeronymo had become Brazilianized.

---

4. A Mexican National Romance ~ Ignacio Altamirano*

Writing at almost the same time as Brazil's Aluísio Azevedo, in the late 1880s, Mexican novelist Ignacio Altamirano resisted racist claims of degeneration. Altamirano's novel, El zarco, *the title of which might be translated as* The Blue-Eyed Bandit, *reverses the familiar hierarchy of the nineteenth century by making its bad characters light-skinned and the good ones dark-skinned. The novel is*

---

*From Ignacio M. Altamirano, *El zarco* (Mexico City: Editorial Porrua, 1992), 5–11. Translated by John Charles Chasteen.

*set in the early 1860s, when bandit gangs were running amok in the Mexican
countryside. The following passage is straightforward. Nicolás, an honest, hard-
working indigenous man, loves Manuela, one of the two young women in this
scene, but Manuela despises him because (we eventually learn) she prefers a
blue-eyed bandit chief. She and her bandit meet a bad end, of course. And the
other young woman, Pilar, a virtuous mestiza, gets Nicolás in the end.*

On the edge of town, near the river, stood a humble but nonetheless
lovely little house, with its walled garden of lemon, orange, and
banana trees. In the internal patio of that house, a small family—composed
of an elderly señora and two young women, both quite beautiful but contrasting in appearance—sat to enjoy the cool breeze.

One was about twenty years old and fair, with that pallid whiteness
one sees occasionally in the tropical lowlands of Mexico, her eyes dark
and vivacious, her lips red and laughing, her head held high. This young
woman had a proud and disdainful look that came, no doubt, from her
slightly aquiline nose, from the frequent fluttering of her velvety eye-
lashes, and from a smile more mocking than benevolent. She sat on a
rustic bench and entertained herself by braiding red calendulas and white
roses into her black, silky tresses. One might mistake her for an aristocratic maiden shunning the prying eyes of the court, disguised and hidden
away in that tropical garden, perhaps with the intention of meeting her
suitor for a romantic tryst.

The other young woman was about eighteen, and her complexion was
darker. Her skin had the delicate tone of a true daughter of Mexico: not
purely Spanish in physical type, but not quite Indian, either. Her large,
dark eyes, her mouth that smiled sadly at her companion's mocking comments, her bowed head, and her delicate body together expressed a melancholy so intense that one could discern immediately a character
diametrically opposed to the character of the first young woman. Slowly
and listlessly, the dark beauty braided common orange and lemon blossoms into her hair. She had collected them from the orange and lemon
trees so abundant in the town, and she had hurt her hands in doing so, for
which her companion kidded her mercilessly.

"Look, Mamá," said the fair young woman to the elderly señora who
sat a bit further off, sewing in a wicker chair. "Look at this silly thing
who's been at it all afternoon and gotten nowhere. She hurt her hands
trying to get the highest, freshest blooms on the trees, and now she can't
braid them into her hair. What she wants is to get married . . . and soon!"

"Who, me?" asked the dark young woman, timidly raising her eyes
as if embarrassed by the very idea.

"Yes, you!" replied the other. "Don't pretend not to. You dream about
getting married. That's all you talk about all day long. And you choose

orange blossoms because they have that association. Not me. I'm not ready to get married yet, so I wear the flowers I like best. Anyway, a wreath of orange blossoms is for a corpse. That's what they put on girls who die unmarried."

"Maybe I like them because that's how they'll bury me," said the dark young woman.

"Girls, don't talk that way!" scolded the older woman. "With times the way they are, and the two of you talking like that, how can a person keep her spirits up? You, Manuela," she said, turning to the proud, fair one, "let Pilar wear the flowers she wants, and you wear the ones you want. You *both* took pretty . . . and nobody sees you anyway," she concluded with a sigh.

"It *is* a shame, *such* a shame," agreed Manuela with obvious feeling. "Now, if we could go out to a dance, even spend some time at the window . . . that might make a difference."

"Fine times these are," complained the señora bitterly, "for attending dances or spending time at a window. What would we do with a party since, God save us, we have to live hidden away so that those horrid bandits won't know we exist! I can't wait for my brother to come from Mexico City and take us away from here, even if we have to walk. Who can live in this place anymore? One of these days something is going to frighten me to death. The life we lead today in Yautepec, Lord knows, is no way to live. In the morning, a fright if the church bell rings and we hurry to hide in the church or the neighbor's house. In the afternoon, we've hardly had lunch, and more fright if we hear the church bell or see people running. At night, we are startled by every step, every bump, every sound of horses in the street. And if we hear a shot or a shout, we don't sleep a wink all night. It is impossible to live this way. All people talk about are robberies and murders. They've grabbed so and so and taken him into the hills, and sure enough his body appears. There is a swarm of vultures over here or there. The priest has gone to hear the confession of so and so, whom the bandits left for dead. Tonight that bandit Salomé Plasencia will be coming into town—or maybe it's Zarco or Palo Seco, instead—and we should all go hide. Then here come the government troops and they're tying people up and executing them, too. Tell me, is this any way to live? It is infernal torment . . . and my heart can't take it!"

Thus, weeping copious tears, the old woman concluded her description of life in Yautepec, a description that was only too accurate and perhaps even not quite as bad as reality. Manuela, who had blushed vividly at the mention of Zarco's name, reacted with sympathy when she heard her mother complain of heart trouble.

"Mamá, you hadn't told me your heart was bothering you. Does it hurt, really? Do you feel ill?" Manuela asked, approaching her mother with obvious conern.

"No, daughter, not sick. I'm fine. I'm just saying that this life afflicts me, saddens me, makes me feel desperate, and it really will make me sick if things go on this way. No, I haven't been sick, thank God. That's one bit of good fortune we've enjoyed, amid all the bad we've have to endure since your father died. But I'll worry myself sick about you, in this town, with all the neighbors saying: Doña Antonia, better hide Manuela or even send her to Cuernavaca or Mexico City. She's in danger here, being so pretty, if the bandits find out about her. They've got spies here who could let them know, and they'd swoop into town one night and carry her away. That's what everyone tells me, Jesus be with me! The priest himself has said it. The mayor has said it. All our relatives have said it. There's not a blessed soul in this whole town who doesn't say it every day. And here I am hopeless, with no idea what to do . . . alone . . . with no way to make a living except for our garden, which is all that keeps us here, with no other ally except my brother, who now ignores my letters, I've sent so many. Do you see, daughter, why I say my heart can't take it? If my brother weren't promising to come get us, we'd have just one way to save ourselves. . . ."

"What's that, Mamá?" asked Manuela with a start.

"Getting you married, my dear one," responded her mother with infinite tenderness.

"Me married? With whom?"

"What do you mean, with whom?" said the old woman in a tone of gentle reproach. "You well know that Nicolás is in love with you, that he would be the happiest creature in the world if you consented to marry him. Poor thing, it's two years now since he's been coming to visit us every single day, rain or shine, despite all hazards, despite the way you snub him, so often and so unjustly, hoping only that your heart will finally soften and accept his love . . ."

"So here is that topic again, no, Mamá?" interrupted Manuela energetically, who had reacted with open disgust as soon her mother mentioned Nicolás. "I should have known from the first where you were headed. You always talk about Nicolás, always propose I marry him, as the only way to remedy our situation, as if nothing else were possible!"

"But *what* else, girl?" "We could go to Mexico City with Uncle, or we could just keep on living as we have, hiding at any sign of trouble."

"But your uncle doesn't ever come! And three women can't very well travel to Mexico City by themselves, now, can they? And entrusting ourselves to anybody is dangerous now, with the roads so infested with bandits who'd probably find out in advance and lie in wait for us."

"Wouldn't it be just as risky to travel with Uncle?"

"Maybe, but he's family and would do his best to protect us. He'd probably hire armed men for an escort or come with a contingent of government troops from Cuernavaca or Mexico City. And we'd know he'd keep his lips sealed about our plans, too. He'd probably plan for us to travel by night through Totolapam or Tepoztlán. Anyway, we'd be safer. But he doesn't come, you see? And he's stopped answering my letters. He must know what's going on around here, and I'll bet his wife and children refuse to let him take risks. Still, he's our only hope. . . ."

"Well," replied Manuela, who refused to concede the point, "even if that's the way things are, Mamá, what would we gain by my marrying Nicolás?"

"Oh, daughter! You would be a married woman, under the protection of a worthy man, that's what we would gain."

"But that worthy man, as you call him, is just the blacksmith of the Atlihuayan estate. If the owner of that estate, a powerful señor, has gone to Mexico City because he is powerless against the bandits, what is the blacksmith going to be able to do against them? He's nothing but a poor artisan, Mamá," protested Manuela, her lower lip jutting out in disdain.

"He may be a poor artisan, but Nicolás is brave and every inch a man. The bandits have never dared to attack him on the road. His assistants and friends hold him in high regard. On the Atlihuayan estate, you would be safe from bandits, and if you don't want to stay around here at all, Nicolás has saved a lot of money, you know, since he's been head blacksmith. The master tradesman who taught him and left him in charge is a foreigner who now lives in Mexico City, you know. He is very fond of Nicolás, and I'll bet we could stay at his house until things get better around here."

"No, Mamá. Never!" interrupted Manuela. "My mind is made up. I'll never marry that horrible Indian. I can't stand to lay eyes on him. He repulses me and I just can't abide his presence. I'd prefer anything to being with him. I'd prefer to be with the bandits!"

"With the bandits!" cried her mother, throwing down her sewing. "May I never live to see such travesty. I'd sooner die!" To Pilar, the dark young woman who had listened throughout in silence, the old lady said: "You, who are only my goddaughter, would surely never cause me such sorrow. Horrible Indian? This princess thinks she deserves some ideal lover." And to Manuela: "How did you become so conceited? You are a poor girl, even if God did give you that white face and those eyes that get you compliments from all the storeowners in town. That horrible Indian, as you call him, is a young man of high principles, a poor orphan from Tepoztlán who learned to read and write before becoming a blacksmith. He is already in charge of the forge at an age when most are barely journeymen, with an excellent reputation and the respect even of rich men. He earned what little he has with honest labor and the sweat of his brow. That is always a fine achievement, most especially these days and around here. There isn't anyone else to compare with him. Am I right, Pilar?"

"Yes, Godmother," answered the modest young woman, "you are completely right. Nicolás is a very good man, a hard worker, who loves Manuela very much. He would give her everything she asks for and be a wonderful husband. I'm always telling her so. And he doesn't look horrible to me . . . "

"Of course not! He's not white, not Spanish, and not one to wear fancy clothing or cut a fine figure at dances and parties, that's all. He's quiet and reserved, and that doesn't seem a defect to me."

"Nor to me," added Pilar.

"Well, Pilar," said Manuela, "if you like him so much, why don't you marry him?"

"Me?" gasped Pilar, turning pale and then blushing to the point of tears. "Why do you say that? He loves you, not me." And at that instant a soft knock sounded at the door.

"Go open the door for him, Pilar," said the señora. "It's Nicolás."

---

5. A Raceless Nation ～ Ada Ferrer*

In the long run, it was political need that forced Latin American elites to broaden the racial identity of their nations. Cuba provides a good example, represented here by a recent U.S. study. Cuba did not become independent with the rest of Latin America in the first decades of the nineteenth century and remained under Spain's control until the 1890s. Most historians explain this Cuban exception by emphasizing the rising importance of slavery on the island. A war of independence was almost certain to disrupt the institution of slavery. Spectacular profits on sugar production made Spanish colonialism tolerable for the plantation-owning Cuban upper classes until the late 1860s. When Cuba's independence wars finally began, however, the patriot leaders competed with Spanish governors for the loyalty and fighting power of Cuban blacks.

Cuba's nineteenth-century revolution emerged from a society that seemed highly unrevolutionary—a society that in the political ferment of the Age of Revolution earned the designation "the ever-faithful isle." Between 1776 and 1825, as most of the colonies of North and South America acquired their independence, Cuba remained a loyalist stronghold. The story of Cuba's deviance from the Latin American norm is, by

*From Ada Ferrer, *Insurgent Cuba: Race, Nation, and Revolution, 1868–1898* (Chapel Hill: University of North Carolina Press, 1999), 1–5, 7–10. © 1999 by the University of North Carolina Press. Reprinted by permission of the University of North Carolina Press.

now, a familiar one: in the face of potential social revolution, criollo (Cuban-born) elites opted to maintain the colonial bond with Spain. With that bond, they preserved as well a prosperous and expanding sugar industry built on the labor of enslaved Africans. After the Haitian Revolution of 1791, Cuba replaced colonial St. Domingue as the world's largest producer of sugar. Content with their new position in the world market, Cuban planters did not want to emulate Haiti again by becoming the hemisphere's second black republic. Thus, colonialism survived in Cuba even as it was defeated to the north and south; and peace and slavery prevailed over insurrection and emancipation.

The colony that outlived those Atlantic revolutions was, however, a fractured and fearful one. In 1846, 36 percent of the population lived enslaved. Even well into the nineteenth century, a thriving (and illegal) slave trade continued to replenish the supply of enslaved Africans. More than 595,000 arrived on the island's shores in the last fifty years of the trade, between 1816 and 1867—about as many as ever arrived in the United States over the whole period of the trade (523,000). About half those slaves labored on sugar plantations. Under brutal work regimes, many continued to speak African languages and to have only minimal contact with the criollo world outside the plantation. Free persons of color constituted another 17 percent of the population. Though legally free, they faced numerous constraints on the exercise of that freedom: prohibitions on the consumption of alcohol, bans against marriage to white men and women, and restrictions on the use of public space, to name but a few.

At mid-century, then, enslaved and free people of color together constituted a majority of the population, outnumbering those identified as white. That white population, educated in the fear of black and slave rebellion, looked to Haiti and clung to Spain in fear. Haiti's slave revolution served as a perpetual example of what might happen to whites in the midst of armed rebellion, but there were smaller local examples as well. The most famous, perhaps, was the alleged conspiracy of 1843—said to involve a massive number of slaves, free people of color, and abolitionist statesmen from England. Even as late as 1864, only four years before the outbreak of nationalist insurgency, authorities uncovered a conspiracy in El Cobre in which slaves from seven area farms were allegedly to join forces to "kill all the whites and make war in order to be free." When the would-be rebels were captured and tried in a Spanish military court, translators had to be hired, for the enslaved suspects spoke no Spanish. In this context of slavery and division, the colonial state and many influential white creoles asserted that to risk expelling Spain was to invite a more horrible fate. Cuba, they said, would either be Spanish or it would be African. It would be Spanish or it would be another Haiti. For those with the power to decide, the answer came without hesitation: Cuba would remain a Spanish colony. There did exist a handful of prominent intellectuals willing to consider, if hypothetically, the founding of a Cuban nation independent from Spain. But, always, they were careful to specify that the Cuban nationality they desired—"the only one that any sensible man would concern himself with—[was] a nationality formed by the white race."

It was onto this world that revolution erupted on October 10, 1868. And when it did, it seemed to defy the fear and division that formed the society from which it emerged. Led initially by a handful of prosperous white men, the revolution placed free men of color in local positions of authority. It also freed slaves, made them soldiers, and called them citizens. And that was just the beginning. The movement formally inaugurated on that day went on to produce three full-fledged anticolonial rebellions over the thirty years that followed: the Ten Years' War (1868–78), the Guerra Chiquita, or Little War (1879–80), and the final War of Independence (1895–98), which ended with the Spanish-American War. All three rebellions were waged by an army unique in the history of the Atlantic world—the Liberation Army, a multiracial fighting force that was integrated at all ranks. Historians estimate that at least 60 percent of that army was composed of men of color. But this was not just an army in which masses of black soldiers served under a much smaller number of white officers, for many black soldiers ascended through the ranks to hold positions as captains, colonels, and generals and to exercise authority over men identified as white. By the end of the thirty-year period, estimates one historian, about 40 percent of the commissioned officers were men of color.

If this integrated army was one pillar of the revolution, the other was significantly less tangible. It was a powerful rhetoric of antiracism that began to flourish during the first rebellion and became much more dominant in the years between the legal end of slavery in 1886 and the outbreak of the third and final war in 1895. This new rhetoric made racial equality a foundation of the Cuban nation. Espoused by white, mulatto, and black members of the movement's civilian and military branches, it asserted that the very struggle against Spain had transformed Cuba into a land where there were "no whites nor blacks, but only Cubans." It thus condemned racism not as an infraction against individual citizens but as a sin against the life of the would-be nation. Revolutionary rhetoric made racial slavery and racial division concomitant with Spanish colonialism, just as it made the revolution a mythic project that armed black and white men together to form the world's first raceless nation.

That this revolution emerged from that slave society makes the story of Cuban independence a remarkable and compelling one. That it emerged from the late-nineteenth-century world makes it seem even more so—for the Cuban revolution unfolded as European and North American thinkers linked biology to progress and divided the world into superior and inferior races.

Those ideas, espoused or encouraged by the work of thinkers as diverse as Charles Darwin, Herbert Spencer, and Joseph-Arthur de Gobineau, had a profound influence on Latin America. Yet in that world "under Darwin's sway," the Cuban movement's principal intellectual leader, José Martí, professed the equality of all races. Indeed, he went further, boldly asserting that there was no such thing as race. Race, he and other nationalists insisted, was merely a tool used locally to divide the anticolonial effort and globally by men who invented "textbook races" in order to justify expansion and empire. Here, then, were voices raised not only in opposition to Spanish rule but also in opposition to the prevailing common sense of their time.

Furthermore, what Cuba's nationalist leaders preached and (less perfectly) practiced stood in stark and concrete contrast to the emerging racial order of its neighbor to the north. Cuban rebels spoke of a raceless nation in the period that represented the nadir in American racial politics. Thus the escalation of racial violence, the spread of spatial segregation by race, and the dismantling of political gains made during the Reconstruction of the South occurred in the United States precisely as black and mulatto leaders gained increasing popularity and power in Cuba. Arguably the most popular leader of the nationalist movement was Antonio Maceo, a mulatto who had joined the movement in 1868 as a common foot soldier and rose to the rank of general. By 1895, he led the insurgent army across the entire territory of the island and won the allegiance of white and non-white men and women—a national, multiracial following that in the United States would have been rare in local contexts and unthinkable at the national level. Thus, as the color line in the United States grew more and more rigid, and as the consequences of crossing that line became more and more brutal, a revolutionary movement in Cuba appeared willing, sometimes eager, to eradicate those lines in Cuba. And it was the victory of this revolution that American intervention helped block after 1898.

The nationalist movement thus gave rise to one of the most powerful ideas in Cuban history—the conception, dominant to this day, of a raceless nationality. In rebel camps and battlefields, as well as in memoirs, essays, and speeches, patriot intellectuals (white and non-white) made the bold claim that the struggle against Spain had produced a new kind of individual and a new kind of collectivity. They argued that the experience of war had forever united black and white; and they imagined a new kind of nation in which equality was so ingrained that there existed no need to identify and speak of races, a nation in which (to borrow the phrase of the mulatto general Antonio Maceo) there were no whites nor blacks, but only

Cubans. Thus the rebel republic declined to record racial categories of identification on army rosters, and a great many citizens repeatedly asserted (and today continue to assert) the non-existence of discrimination and the irrelevance of race. This study of anticolonial revolution, then, is also a story of the emergence of a particularly powerful racial ideology. It is the story of the tensions and transformations that produced that ideology and of those that it, in turn, produced.

As that ideology of raceless nationality emerged, it clashed with long-standing colonial arguments about the impossibility of Cuban nationhood. Since the end of the eighteenth century, advocates of colonial rule in Cuba had argued that the preponderance of people of color and the social and economic importance of slavery meant that Cuba could not be a nation. Confronted by threats to political order, they invoked images of racial warfare and represented the nationalists' desired republic as Haiti's successor. Such arguments worked well in the Age of Revolution, when Cuban elites decided to forgo independence and to maintain a prosperity built largely on the forced labor of Africans in sugar. These arguments continued to work, in modified form, even after the start of anticolonial insurgency in 1868, when nationalist leaders of the first rebellion (the Ten Years' War) began to challenge traditional formulations about the impossibility of Cuban nationhood. They established a rebel republic and placed free people of color in public office at the local level. They mobilized enslaved workers and declared (falteringly and ambivalently) the (gradual and indemnified) end of slavery. Spanish authorities and their allies responded to these challenges by deploying familiar arguments about the racial dangers of rebellion. As usual, the references to Haiti became ubiquitous. But they were almost always brief and nebulous—as if merely to speak the name sufficed to call up concrete images of black supremacy: of black men who raped white women and killed their husbands and fathers, of political authority exercised by self-anointed black emperors, of wealth and property annihilated, of God and civilization spurned.

The movement's detractors utilized the same images and arguments again—to even better effect—during the second separatist uprising known as the Little War of 1879–80. Colonial officials, however, did more than merely label the independence movement black. They also consciously and skillfully manipulated features of the rebellion to make them more closely correspond to their interpretation. They tampered with lists of captured insurgents, omitting the names of white rebels. They made surrendering white insurgents sign public declarations repudiating the allegedly racial goals of black co-leaders. And the blacker colonial officials made the rebellion appear, the more white insurgents surrendered, and the blacker the rebellion became, and so on. Race, and its manipulation by colonial authorities, are therefore absolutely central to understanding the limits of multiracial insurgency in the first half of the nationalist period.

Thus, as independence activists prepared to launch a final and, they hoped, successful rebellion against Spain, they faced not only the challenge of uniting different separatist camps and, of amassing men, arms, and money for the struggle. They faced as well the imperative of combating colonial representations of the independence movement. To succeed at anticolonial insurgency, separatists had to invalidate traditional claims about the racial risks of rebellion. They had to construct an effective counterclaim to arguments that for almost a century had maintained that Cuba was unsuited to nationhood. "The power to represent oneself," they had come to realize, was "nothing other than political power itself." The struggle for that power of representation required that patriot-intellectuals reconceptualize nationality, blackness, and the place of people of color in the would-be nation. In the process, black, mulatto, and white intellectuals constructed powerful and eloquent expressions of raceless nationality, of a nationality that had antiracism as a solid foundation. Among these intellectuals were José Marti, white son of a Spaniard and a Cuban, who in 1892 founded the Cuban Revolutionary Party in New York; Juan Gualberto Gómez, a mulatto journalist born to enslaved parents, educated in Paris and Havana; and Rafael Serra y Montalvo, a prominent journalist who began his career as a cigar worker. All wrote of the union of blacks and whites in anticolonial war, and in that physical and spiritual embrace between black and white men in battle they located the symbolic and material birth of the nation. In their vision, black and mulatto men could never threaten that nation with aspirations to a black republic. Such portrayals thus explicitly countered colonialist claims about race war and the impossibility of Cuban nationhood. To powerful notions of racial fear and unrest they juxtaposed equally powerful images of racial harmony and racial transcendence.

But if this complex process of reconceptualizing race and nationality occurred in dialogue with the racialist claims of the colonial state, it also emerged from—and produced new—tensions within the nationalist community itself. By declaring that there were no races and by asserting that racism was an infraction against the nation as a whole, nationalist rhetoric helped defeat Spanish claims about the impossibility of Cuban nationhood. That same rhetoric, however, also provided a conceptual framework that black soldiers could use to condemn the racism not only of their Spanish enemies but also of their fellow insurgents and leaders. Thus the ideology of a raceless nationality, even as it suggested that race had been transcended, gave black insurgents and citizens a powerful language with which to speak about race and racism within the rebel polity—a language with which to show that that transcendence was yet to occur. And, in fact, throughout the period of insurrection, especially during and after the final war of independence in 1895, black soldiers and officers used the language of nationalism to expose and condemn what they perceived as racism within the nationalist movement. Thus the language of raceless nationality, a language of harmony and integration, became also a "language of contention."

Just as nationalist rhetoric shaped black political behavior, so too did black participation profoundly affect both the discourse and practice of nationalism. The mobilization of free and enslaved Cubans of color helped radicalize Cuban nationalism and made the rebellion militarily viable. Black participation was even celebrated in the nationalist prose of the period. But black mobilization—in the beginning because its only precedent lay in slave rebellion and later because it was accompanied by significant black leadership—also created anxieties among insurgents and fed the forces of counterinsurgency. Black political activity and power led some white leaders to impugn the motives of black co-leaders. And it led others to abandon the movement altogether and ally with Spain to secure its defeat. Black participation in insurgency—and representations of that participation—thus had the power on the one hand to compromise the success of nationalist efforts and, on the other, to strengthen the appeal of the movement.

VI

Neocolonialism

Colonialism casts a long shadow over world history, and Latin America is a perfect example. After centuries of colonial domination and decades as a postcolonial basket case, Latin America entered a phase that historians call "neocolonialism" around 1870. The *neo* implies a new form of colonialism, without direct political control of the subject territory by the colonizing power. No Latin American country returned to being a colony in this period, strictly speaking. And Spain and Portugal mattered less than ever politically. Instead, Great Britain, France, and the United States replaced the old "mother countries" at the center of the system, while Latin American nations orbited around them like planets. The analogues of gravitational pull, in this neocolonial "solar system," were economic and ideological forces. Only rarely were armies of occupation required.

Economically, Latin American countries geared themselves to produce minerals, raw materials, and agricultural commodities for European and U.S. markets. Tin from Bolivia, bananas from Central America, sugar from Cuba, nitrates and copper from Chile, beef and wheat from Argentina, coffee from Brazil and Colombia—the list goes on. These export products dominated economic life in Latin America by absorbing capital, shaping infrastructure, defining political issues, determining patterns of migration, and setting the agenda for legislation. The result was overwhelming dependence on a few export products. A sharp price rise on the international commodities markets triggered national euphoria; a sharp fall spelled national disaster. This situation, summarized as "economic dependency," is key to understanding neocolonialism.

The industrialized countries at the center of the system benefited more securely than did the Latin American ones on its periphery. The products of industry (finished clothing, locomotive engines, fine furniture) constituted rare commodities in the international economy, while bananas or coffee or sugar could be grown in many places. Europe produced goods that Latin Americans wanted to import, whereas Venezuela or Paraguay produced only a few things that Europeans needed. Therefore, the terms of trade in this system always favored the center. In addition, European (and eventually, U.S.) companies ran the system: they were the shippers, the bankers, and the builders. Their employees were everywhere in Latin America, which they treated as a land of opportunity for smart and resourceful outsiders. Finally, the central countries could deploy greater military force, and they did so on numerous occasions to protect their economic interests in the region, a practice that earned the name "gunboat diplomacy."

Britain, France, and the United States defined the center of the neocolonial system ideologically as well as economically. In part, this was the triumph of the cosmopolitan, progressive-minded liberals who battled the conservative Catholic Church in postcolonial days. In philosophy and fashion, science and politics, literature and entertainment, British and French models reigned supreme in Latin America by the late 1800s. The region's ruling classes still identified themselves socially and culturally with imported models, but these models were no longer Spanish and Portuguese. Instead, elite women avidly copied French fashions and hairstyles. Elite men learned the parliamentary discourse of British government. A more outlandish example, to conform to the standards set by Europeans, were the men who wore heavy, black woolen suits in the tropics. The Latin American consumption of imported scientific racism discussed in chapter V must also be viewed as part of this larger tendency. Europeans claimed to be the leaders of world civilization, and the Latin American upper classes swallowed the claim hook, line, and sinker. After all, such a claim fit well with their own desire to maintain social dominance over the non-European majority populations in their own countries.

The neocolonial system lasted from around 1870 to around 1930 in most of Latin America, and it is still a powerful influence today. What were its consequences for the social, economic, and political development of the region? To answer that question, the following two readings explore neocolonial ideologies and economics. In addition, we have included five selections from accounts written by European and U.S. travelers to Latin America at the height of the neocolonial order. How do such travel accounts reflect the neocolonial dynamics at work in Latin America during this period?

QUESTIONS FOR ANALYSIS

1. How did the economic and ideological characteristics of neocolonialism reinforce each other?

2. What aspects of neocolonialism can you find in the primary source documents written by early twentieth-century travelers to Argentina, Peru, Brazil, Colombia, and Guatemala?

3. How are the five travel accounts similar? Where do they differ, and why?

1. Neocolonial Economics ~ Celso Furtado*

Brazilian economist Celso Furtado exemplifies the dominant view of neocolonialism from the 1960s to the 1980s, when many social scientists focused on the idea of economic dependency. During those years, historians of Latin America pointed to neocolonial economics as the main cause of the region's underdevelopment and eventual revolutionary ferment. The composition of a country's exports was the starting place for any analysis of its history. Decades later, historians would put less emphasis on economic determinism. But an analysis of export economies remains basic to any understanding of Latin America, most especially in the period from 1870 to 1930.

Latin American countries began to enter the channels of expanding international trade in the 1840s. The primary product-exporting economies involved in this process can be divided into three types: (a) economies exporting temperate agricultural commodities (like those grown in Europe or the United States); (b) economies exporting tropical agricultural commodities; (c) economies exporting mineral products. In each case, foreign trade helped to shape a distinctive economic structure whose characteristic features should be borne in mind when studying its subsequent evolution.

The first type is represented essentially by Argentina and Uruguay. In this case, exportable agricultural production was based on the extensive use of land and was destined to compete with the domestic production of countries undergoing rapid industrialization. Extensive use of good agricultural land made it possible to achieve high profitability from the start. On the other hand, the very extensiveness of the agriculture practiced and the sheer volume of freight involved necessitated the creation of a widespread transportation network which indirectly led to the rapid unification of the domestic market, focusing on the major ports of shipment. These countries display the characteristics of regions referred to earlier as constituting an expanding frontier of the industrializing European economy.

This frontier, to which European agricultural techniques were transplanted in the early stages, soon became an important center for developing new agricultural techniques of its own. Both the techniques of farming vast open spaces and of large-scale transportation, storage, and shipment of cereals originated in the United States. In sum, the countries in this

*From Celso Furtado, *Economic Development of Latin America: Historical Background and Contemporary Problems*, trans. Suzette Macedo (New York: Cambridge University Press, 1976), 47–51. Reprinted by permission of Cambridge University Press.

group, precisely because they competed with the domestic production of countries at a more advanced stage of development and with regions of recent European settlement enjoying a high standard of living, were from the start integrated into a productive sector of the world economy characterized by continuing technological advance. Throughout the phase of expansion in their foreign trade, these countries achieved high rates of growth.

The second type, represented by countries exporting tropical agricultural products, involves more than half the Latin American population. It includes Brazil, Colombia, Ecuador, Central America, and the Caribbean, as well as large regions of Mexico and Venezuela. Countries in this group entered international trade in competition with colonial areas and the slave-holding region of the United States. Sugar and tobacco remained typically colonial products until the last years of the nineteenth century. It was the rapid expansion of world demand for coffee and cacao from the mid-nineteenth century that enabled tropical commodities to play a dynamic role in integrating the Latin American economy into world trade during the period under consideration. The direct impact of the structural changes in the British economy was much less, since the British market continued to be abundantly supplied by colonial regions where labor was plentiful and wages were low. The role of dynamic center fell to the United States and, to a lesser extent, to the European countries. On the whole, tropical commodities were of little significance as a factor in development, although they did involve the opening up of large areas for settlement. On the one hand, their prices continued to be influenced by the low wages prevailing in colonial regions, which had long been traditional tropical commodity producers. On the other, they did not usually require the creation of a complex infrastructure; in many regions traditional means of transport continued to be used. Finally, since they were produced in areas lacking the capacity to develop new techniques for themselves, tropical products tended to remain within the framework of the traditional economies. Nonetheless, in certain regions, tropical export agriculture did manage to play an important role in development. The most notable instance is probably that of the coffee region of São Paulo, in Brazil. Here the physical and chemical qualities of the soil permitted extensive coffee planting. The relatively high productivity of labor, the vast size of the area planted, and the use of European immigrants who demanded monetary wages favored the creation of a modern infrastructure and the emergence of a domestic market. The special nature of this case becomes evident when we recall that at the end of the nineteenth century the São Paulo highlands supplied two-thirds of the total world coffee output.

The third type of economy, represented by countries exporting mineral products, includes Mexico, Chile, Peru, and Bolivia. Venezuela entered this group in the 1930s as an exporter of petroleum. The lowering of freight rates for long-distance transport and the rapid expansion of the mechanical industries, by creating an international market for industrial metals, brought about a radical change in Latin American mining. In the first place, precious metals, notably silver, rapidly lost their importance. Secondly, small-scale mining operations of the artisan or quasi-artisan type were gradually replaced by large-scale production controlled by foreign capital and administered from abroad. The considerable rise in the world demand for non-ferrous metals coincided with major technical advances in production methods which permitted or required the concentration of production in large units. This process of concentration carried out initially in the major producing country—the United States—soon spread to other areas, where local producers were marginalized by American organizations with heavy financial backing and the technical "knowhow" required to handle low-grade ores.

The three decades preceding the First World War were a period of rapid economic development and some social change in Latin America as a whole: in Mexico, where the Porfirio Díaz administration created the conditions for a large inflow of foreign capital directed mainly into mineral production; in Chile, whose victory in the War of the Pacific against Bolivia and Peru enabled her to monopolize the sources of nitrate; in Cuba, where, even before independence was attained in 1898, the country's increasing integration into the United States market had brought about a dramatic expansion in sugar production; in Brazil, where the spread of coffee over the São Paulo highlands and the influx of European immigrants hastened the collapse of the slave economy; finally, in Argentina, where the economy and society underwent drastic changes under the impact of the great wave of immigration and the penetration of substantial foreign capital.

A closer look at the three largest countries reveals the importance of the changes that occurred during this period. In Mexico, the population increased from 9.4 million in 1877 to 15.2 million in 1910. In the last of the nearly three decades of the Porfirio Díaz administration (1900–1910), the annual average growth rate of the real per capita product was 3.1 percent. During this decade the production of minerals and petroleum, the colony's basic export sector, grew at an annual rate of 7.2 percent, that is, twice as fast as manufacturing production and nearly three times as fast as agricultural production. In Brazil, the population increased from 10.1 million in 1872 to 17.3 million in 1900. In the last decade of the nineteenth century, the rate of population increase in São Paulo was over 5 percent a year, while for the country as a whole it was under 2 percent. Nearly all the 610,000 immigrants entering Brazil during this decade went to the state of São Paulo. Between 1880 and 1910, the total length of railways increased from 3.4 to 21.3 thousand kilometers. Coffee exports, which were around 4 million 60-kilogram bags in 1880, rose to almost 10 million in 1900 and to over 16 million on the eve of the First World War, a total seldom surpassed in later years. In the same period, exports of cacao rose from 6,000 to 40,000 tons, and rubber exports from 7,000 to 40,000 tons. However, it was in Argentina that the changes brought about in this phase were most marked. Between the periods 1890–1904 and 1910–1914, Argentina's population doubled, increasing from 3.6 to 7.2 million; the country's railway network was extended from 12.7 to 31.1 thousand kilometers; cereal exports rose from 1,038,000 to 5,294,000 tons, and exports of frozen meat rose from 27,000 to 376,000 tons.

In sum, during the neocolonial period, Latin America became an important contributor toward trade and a key source of raw materials for the industrialized countries. In 1913, the Latin American share in world commodity exports had reached the following levels:

Product	Percentage
Vegetable fibers	6.3
Livestock products	11.5
Cereals	17.9
Fruit and vegetables	14.2
Sugar	37.6
Rubber, furs, hides, and leathers	25.1
Coffee, cocoa, and tea	62.1

2. Neocolonial Ideologies ～ E. Bradford Burns*

"Progress," on a European model, was the central concept of neocolonial ideology. In the following excerpt from The Poverty of Progress *(1980), U.S. historian E. Bradford Burns stressed the influence of this idea on Latin American elites. His point was important, because scholars of his day tended to view neocolonialism primarily as an economic system that held peripheral countries in a state of material dependency. By signaling the power of neocolonial ideology, Burns explained why the region's upper classes became such enthusiastic collaborators in an economic system that turned out to be so detrimental to their countries. In effect, he showed that Latin America's economic dependency flowed partly from*

---

*From E. Bradford Burns, *The Poverty of Progress: Latin America in the Nineteenth Century* (Berkeley: University of California Press, 1980), 18–20, 29–34. © 1980 by The Regents of the University of California. Reprinted by permission of the University of California Press.

Europe's cultural hegemony in the region. Burns's emphasis on culture and ideology would be adopted by many historians of Latin America in coming decades.

The Latin American elites of the nineteenth century boasted of their European heritage and even those with Indian or African ancestors dwelt more on their European ties than otherwise. England and France, in particular, were their models enhanced by distance, some misconceptions, and the elites' fears of their own provinciality or inferiority. They readily understood what was happening in Europe and ably discussed the latest ideas radiating from the Old World, which they welcomed to the New. But European thought was no intellectual spring: it proved to be an ideological flood, which swept before it most American originality. Generally speaking, three major European philosophies shaped the ideology of the elites during the nineteenth century: the Enlightenment, the ideas of evolution put forth by Charles Darwin and Herbert Spencer, and Positivism. The concept of "progress," perhaps the key word for understanding nineteenth-century Latin American history, linked the three.

Stressing the vincibility of ignorance, the Enlightenment philosophers concluded that if people had the opportunity to know the truth, they would select "civilization" over "barbarism." Those influenced by Enlightenment ideas believed in a universally valid standard to judge civilization, and the criteria for such a judgment rested on European concepts of progress. Civilization and the progress that led to it became identified with Europe, or more specifically with England, France, and Germany. Moreover, a burgeoning faith in science directed judgments on progress itself away from philosophical and moral matters toward material change. The popularized idea of Darwin that organic forms developed over the course of time and represented successive states in a single evolutionary process toward perfection further heightened the interest in progress, giving it a scientific veneer. Very propitiously, Spencer, who enjoyed tremendous circulation in nineteenth-century Latin America, applied the same principle of evolution to society. To Spencer, progress signified a march toward the establishment of the greatest perfection and the most complete happiness. However, that march subsumed a great many economic changes and adaptations. As one example, Spencer advocated railroads as a vital part of the organic system of a modern society. As another, he regarded industrialization as a certain manifestation of progress. Many Latin Americans drew from Spencer the interrelationship of science, industry, and progress, a combination pointing to future glory through societal evolution. Like most European thinkers, Spencer said much that damned Latin America: his racism, for example.

Many of the ideas on progress pulled from the Enlightenment, Darwin, and Spencer, as well as other sources, seemed to converge in the form that

Auguste Comte's Positivism assumed in Latin America during the last decades of the century. To Comte that progress was attainable through the acceptance of scientific laws codified by Positivism. Outward manifestations of progress—again, railroads and industrialization—assumed great importance in Positivism and emphatically so among the Latin Americans, whether they acknowledged Comte or not.

A part of the elites had initiated a serious and escalating questioning of some of the Iberian values during the last decades of the eighteenth century. It goes without saying that they were even more critical of Indian and African contributions to Latin American life if, in fact, they ever considered them. Increased contacts with Northern Europeans, an expanding book trade, and more opportunities for foreign travel facilitated the elite's introduction to the ideas of the Enlightenment. A selective reading of those ideas buttressed the disenchantment with Iberian rule and provided ready formulae for alternatives. The intellectuals flirted with a political ideology complementary to independence, in most cases republicanism, and economic ideas harmonious with free trade specifically and with emerging capitalism generally. Latin American elites continued the search for, as well as exploitation and export of, raw materials, the continuation of a well-established pattern of thought and practice of the colonial period which augured poorly for economic independence.

Many of the intellectuals who questioned their Iberian experience while embracing various, varying, and sometimes contradictory Northern European examples held important governmental posts after political independence had been won from Spain and Portugal while others occupied secondary, but still influential, positions in the nascent governments. They found ample opportunity to put their ideas and preferences into practice.

Intensified contacts with Europe throughout the nineteenth century reaffirmed the conclusion reached by many of the elites familiar with the philosophies of the Enlightenment that the Europeans, particularly the English and the French, had confected a desirable civilization worthy of emulation. The opinion of a Bolivian visitor to the continent in 1877, José Avelino Aramayo, that Europe not only represented progress but was needed to foment a similar progress in the New World, typified the thought of most of the elites. Aramayo did not hesitate to praise those Latin American nations that most nearly seemed to duplicate Europe. In truth, Europe's rapid industrialization and technological change awed most of the impressionable Latin American cosmopolites who clamored to replicate the process in their own localities, to graft the novelties on the quite different political, social, and economic institutions and realities of the New World. The effort to acquire the outward or material manifestations of the progress they acknowledged as civilization meant that for these Latin Americans in the nineteenth century progress could be measured quantitatively by the amount of exports, the number of steam engines, railroad mileage, or gas lights. The more the capital city architecturally resembled Paris, then ipso facto the greater degree of progress that particular country could proclaim. Many a Latin American aristocrat echoed the sigh of the Brazilian Eduardo Prado in the last decade of the century, "Without a doubt, the world is Paris."

Most Latin American elites subscribed to the European racial doctrines of the day, which ranked European whites at the pinnacle of civilization while regarding the Africans and Indians as real obstacles to progress. A mixture of the European with either the Indian or black was regarded —as European social doctrine prescribed—as a sure condemnation to an inferior status. A leading cultural review published in Rio de Janeiro in 1895, *Dom Quixote*, castigated the Brazilian "race" composed of the "backward" African, the "decadent" Portuguese, and the "primitive" Indian. The authors' recommendation was standard for the times: "What we need are new forces, originating in the strong and vigorous races that on arrival here will work by absorption to improve our race." Rather than a novelty, the article simply recapitulated and reemphasized an idea current for at least half a century among urban elites. The Brazilian intellectuals put great faith in the "whitening" process, the eradication of the "weak" Indian and African genes by the "stronger," meaning "more dominant," European ones. The theory might not have squared with European anthropological thought, but it provided a necessary solution for the distraught Brazilian elite and according to its proponents offered the surest method to reproduce European civilization in their vast nation. Paralleling similar hopes in Argentina and elsewhere, the Brazilian intellectual despaired of remolding the local populations and so planned to replace them. By mid-century, the Indians had withdrawn into the Amazonian hinterlands, and the prohibition of the slave trade had stopped the African inflow. The government threw open the doors to European immigration, which in fact did change the racial characteristics of the Brazilian population.

The intellectuals of Indo-America demonstrated no greater understanding or tolerance of the Indians than their Brazilian counterparts did of the Africans. The huge Indian populations of Mexico, Guatemala, Ecuador, Peru, Bolivia, and Paraguay embarrassed the intellectuals, who regarded them as barbaric at worst and childlike creatures at best. The Indians' disdain of European civilization only intensified the suspicions of the elites. Governments and landowners felt perfectly correct in forcing the Indians to labor for them under the rationalization that it fostered contact with the elites and thus exposed the Indians to the indubitable benefits of European civilization. Whatever their professed political persuasion, the Latin American elites seldom shied away from exploiting the Indians.

Mexican intellectuals vigorously debated the "Indian problem" in the nineteenth century, a debate that accelerated during the long government of Porfirio Díaz (1876–1911), whose policies divested the Indian communities of several million acres and literally enslaved entire Indian groups. The intellectuals divided over the intelligence and ability of the Indians as well as the feasibility of integrating them into national life—that is, making Europeanized Mexicans of the indigenous inhabitants. One side emphasized the potential of the Indians and urged the government to improve their conditions. Intellectuals like Justo Sierra believed education and greater exposure to Westernization while rescuing the Indians would transform them into mestizo Mexicans. To others, however, the Indians constituted an insuperable obstacle to national progress. They particularly decried their communal spirit and lack of individualism. Writing in the 1860s Antonio García Cubas identified Indians as the "enemies" of other Mexicans and predicted that their "decadence and degeneration" could not be reversed. Decades later, Francisco Bulnes, the quintessential Social Darwinist, published his blunt and influential *The Future of Spanish American Nations* (1899), which concluded that the racial inferiority of the Indians prohibited national development. The almost universal solution to the "Indian problem" advocated the encouragement of European immigration with the hope that the new blood would dilute the Indian. The debates focused exclusively on whether or not the Indians could be Europeanized. The intellectuals entertained no other alternatives. None recognized that the Indians might want to draw on their own past rather than Europe's or perceived any attributes in the Indian community worthy of incorporation into the national ethos.

A somewhat different debate on the Indians took place in Guatemala City in 1893 at the Central American Pedagogical Congress, whose first topic for discussion was: "What would be the most efficient method of civilizing the Indian race in order to imbue it with the ideas of progress and the habits of cultured peoples?" In a preliminary study for the congress, the Guatemalan Juan Fernández Ferraz rejected the idea that the Indians were condemned to backwardness and eventual extinction. As one Honduran delegate, Professor Alberto Membreno, noted, the Organization Committee of the Congress left no doubt that the Indians possessed the aptitude for "civilization." The question before the congress revolved around how to civilize them. The delegates roundly condemned the racism prevalent in the hemisphere which hastened the extinction of the native population and castigated both the United States and Argentina for genocide. In a very perceptive speech, Ferraz denounced the alienation of the Indians from their own environment and advised that the first step toward helping them would be the return of their lands. Although the Central American intellectuals showed a far greater understanding of the problems and a more perceptive insight into the Indian mentality than their Mexican counterparts at a similar time, they, too, saw Europeanization as the ultimate fate of the Indians. Unlike many of their Mexican colleagues, however, the Central Americans judged the native population intellectually capable of adopting European ways.

While the Mexican and Central American intellectuals debated national Indian policies, the Argentine government aggressively pursued its own policy of genocide. In Argentina's so-called Conquest of the Desert, 1879–80, the army under the command of General Julio A. Roca, who later served twice as president, fanned out across the pampas to clear the land of Indians once and for all. In an Order of the Day to his troops dated April 26, 1879, General Roca left no doubt in the minds of the soldiers of their exalted duty to the fatherland, a fatherland that seemed to have no place for the original inhabitants. These few sentences from the Order revealed the full intentions of the government in Buenos Aires:

> When the wave of humanity invades these desolate fields that were yesterday the state of sanguinary and devastating raids to turn them into markets of wealth and flourishing towns, in which millions of men may live rich and happy—then and not till then the true worth of your efforts will be perceived. Destroying these nests of land pirates and taking possession of the vast region that shelters them, you have opened and widened the horizons of your country toward the Southland, tracing as it were with your bayonets an immense field for the development of future greatness.

The armies massacred Indians. A few succeeded in escaping to the Patagonian wilderness. Others were absorbed into the rural work force. Those campaigns in fact did open up vast tracts of new territory. How much they contributed to the well-being of the majority, however, is problematic. The lands promptly fell under the control of rich hacienda owners, most of whom were intimately linked to the export economy and partners in the exploitation of an increasingly dependent Argentina. For those privileged few, the public funds that financed the military campaigns proved an ideal means to expand their landholdings. For the government, the army conveniently served as the executioner of those remaining "barbarians" who continued to reject Europeanization.

The countryside, increasingly dependent on exports to insure prosperity, whether in Argentina or elsewhere in Latin America, was perfectly mirrored in the cities, whose life and looks depended to a large degree on those exports and the imports they facilitated. Those cities with their cafes, shops, theaters, operas, balls, and academies often opulently packaged in Beaux Arts architecture absorbed the attention of the elites and to an ever larger degree symbolized their nations to them. Although technology appealed the most to the elites, they also aped certain life-styles and professed the values accompanying them. The result was to graft onto Latin America those accoutrements of progress (as defined by the elite) rather than to accommodate new ideas and modes by reforming the basic national institutions or to modify the new ways to complement older institutions.

Both a contributor to and the consequence of a dependent economy, cosmetic modernization further subordinated Latin American political behavior to North Atlantic demands and degraded native cultures to accommodate imported ones. Many of these results had not been entertained by the intellectuals who wrote so glowingly of progress.

The elites steadfastly pursued their vision of progress. In their pursuit, they readily understood the need to guarantee order and stability, peace and security in order to receive the loans, investments, technology, and immigration that they required to maintain or enhance their life-styles. Thus many of their activities and decisions were more for international approval than internal improvement. To meet the costs of modernization, commercial agriculture and mining—the export sector—received priorities in attention and investment. By mid-century, the plans and policies of most governments clearly reflected those realities. President Tomás Cipriano de Mosquera of Colombia (1845–49) supported a program of road building, steam navigation on the Magdalena River, increased tobacco exports, and invitations to foreign technicians. By the 1850s, the imperial government of Brazil had embarked on a program to encourage railroad construction, foster steam navigation, reorganize banking, favor increased coffee exports, and entice European immigrants. A reform manifesto in Mexico in 1859 called for encouraging foreign immigration, capital, and technology, the restoration of law and order, renovation of mining, growth of commerce, and nationalization of Church property. The government of President Domingo Faustino Sarmiento of Argentina (1868–74) imposed order, opened the doors to immigrants, built schools, pushed the railroad into the pampas, and in general facilitated foreign trade. While all of the activities might have contributed to development, few, if any, did in practice. Rather, they served to strengthen the dynamic, but dangerous, export sector of the economy and in so doing also deepened dependency.

---

3. A Paean to Progress ～ Georges Clemenceau*

Georges Clemenceau, a former premier of France, penned his impressions of a quick trip to southern South America in the first decade of the 1900s. Clemenceau

*From Georges Clemenceau, *South America To-day: A Study of Conditions, Social, Political, and Commercial, in Argentina, Uruguay, and Brazil* (New York and London: G. P. Putnam's Sons, 1911), 28–35, 63–71, 420–24.

waxed enthusiastic at how progress, on a European model and including large numbers of European immigrants, had advanced in Argentina, Uruguay, and southern Brazil. Arguably, he had seen the areas of Latin America where neocolonialism had had the most positive effects.

B uenos Aires first. It is a large European city, giving everywhere an impression of hasty growth, but foreshadowing, too, in its prodigious progress, the capital of a continent. The Avenida de Mayo, as wide as the finest of our boulevards, recalls Oxford Street [in London] in the arrangement of its shop fronts and the ornamental features of its buildings. Every style of architecture is to be seen, from the showy, the more frequent, to the sober, relatively rare. Indeed, there is an epidemic of Italian architecture in Buenos Aires. Everywhere the eye rests on astragals and florets, amid terrible complications and interlaced lines. (An exception are the dainty villas which call public attention to the dwellings of the aristocracy.) The commercial quarter of Buenos Aires is the most crowded imaginable. Thoroughfares that seemed spacious twenty or thirty years ago for a population of two or three hundred thousand souls have become lamentably inadequate for a capital city with more than a million. Sidewalks so narrow that two can scarcely walk abreast are closely shaved by tramways that constitute a danger to life and limb. The traffic is severely regulated by careful police. But so congested do certain streets become in the afternoon that they have to be closed to vehicles. To stroll along, or still worse, to pause to look at a shop window is out of the question.

One of the peculiarities of Buenos Aires is that you can see no end to it. Since there is no obstacle on the side away from the Río de la Plata, the edge of the city extends farther and farther on to the pampas as building plots downtown—the object of perpetual speculation—rise in value. The quality of the building goes down, naturally, toward the outskirts, ending with walls of clay dried in the sun, with a roof of corrugated iron or even more primitive *ranchos* supported on empty oil cans, placed at convenient distances and roofed with boughs or thatch.

I should need a volume if I tried to describe the plan and equipment of the docks of Buenos Aires. Those who take an interest in the subject can easily get all the information they need. The rest will be grateful to me for resisting the temptation to quote long lists of figures copied from technical reports. More than thirty thousand craft, sail and steam, come in and out annually, including at least four thousand from overseas. The big grain elevators have been described over and over again by travelers. Those of Buenos Aires are not one whit inferior to the best of the gigantic structures of North America. Each can load twenty thousand tons of grain in a day. To one there is attached a mill said to be the largest in the world.

The Negra slaughterhouses form a model establishment in which not less than 1,200 animals are killed daily, without counting sheep and pigs—a faithful copy of the famous slaughterhouses of North America. The beast is felled by a mallet and slips down a slope, at the foot of which the carotid artery is cut. After this operation, the body is hooked up by a small wagon moving along an aerial rail, and is then carried through a series of stages which end in its being handed over in two pieces to the freezing chambers to await speedy shipment to England—the great market for Argentine meat. The whole is performed with a rapidity so disconcerting that the innocent victim of our cannibal habits finds himself in a sack ready for freezing, with all his insides neatly packed into tins, before he has time to think.

The recent Buenos Aires Exhibition contained, among its side shows, several that were remarkable, including the English railway exhibit and the German electrical exhibit. France, I regret to say, did not distinguish herself, although we could hardly help being well represented in the art and sculpture pavilions, of course. This is a lamentable shortcoming when one considers the market that might, in this way, have been found for our manufactures. We reckoned, perhaps, on the Argentine millionaires coming to Paris to look for the goods we failed to exhibit.

The section on Argentine produce—cattle, timber, plants, fruits, cereals, etc.—was of special interest to foreigners. To describe it would be to write an economic history of Argentina. I heard on all sides that the cattle exhibits were especially fine. I am not astonished, as I have seen here the finest of breeding stock. The rearing of horses, cattle, and sheep has developed enormously here. Grain growing (wheat and corn) has likewise developed. The pampas, with their immense stretch of arable land between the Andes and the sea, yield every kind of harvest without fertilizer and almost without labor. Wherever the locomotive makes its appearance, there blossoms forth a fertile strip of cultivated land on either side of the line, accompanied by an instant rise in the value of these properties whose produce has, henceforth, a quick means of transport to market.

France has so far managed to maintain friendly and sympathetic relations with the Argentine Republic. Latin idealism keeps the South American nations ever facing toward the great modern peoples that have sprung from the Roman conquest. But France has not yet drawn from this favorable situation all the advantage that might be derived from it, both for the Republics themselves and for Latin civilization overall, steadily drained, as it has been, by the systematic activity of the Northern races. The great Anglo-Saxon republic of North America will count more and more in the affairs of the globe. May it not be that South America, whose evolution is the result of lessons taught to some extent by the Northern races, will give us a new development of Latin civilization?

For the last twenty years there has been a prodigious increase of production and public wealth in the two Americas. I want to say a word for the creation of a line of fast ships to make the journey between France and South America. If we are to enlarge our dealings with South America, it is of capital importance to France to have a service fitted up with modern comforts. This fact accounts for the greatly increased proportion of travelers to Europe from the United States, Mexico, Brazil, Argentina, and so on. The proof is that the luxurious hotels springing up anew almost daily in Paris and on the Riviera to cater to this class of customer are almost always crowded.

Brazil and Argentina have most especially benefited from a rise in land values. In the course of the last ten years, from 1900 to 1909, their working railways have gone up from 14,027 kilometers to 19,080 in Brazil, and from 16,563 to 25,508 kilometers in the Argentine Republic. These new railroads have opened the door to agriculture, cattle-breeding, and forestry in immense regions, and the results may be traced in the increase of their foreign trade: up 1071 million francs for Brazil and up 2161 million francs for Argentina. To reap the advantages to be drawn from our financial intervention in Brazil and Argentina, we must create rapid means of communication between France and these two great South American republics, up to date in every way and luxurious enough to induce Brazilians and Argentines to come to Europe and return to their own country in French vessels rather than English, German, or Italian ones.

---

4. The Traveling Expert ～ Henry Stephens*

Progress was also the theme of Henry Stephens, a U.S. traveler who journeyed through South America on the eve of World War I. Here, we see how Stephens reacted to what he saw in the Andean highlands of Peru. He describes Henry Meiggs's railway and the Cerro de Pasco Mining Company, two famous examples of neocolonial enterprise. Stephens exemplifies the fascination of many European and U.S. travelers with the minute details of the technological transformations that they observed. In addition, during the century before World War I, travel books were the primary source of information of all kinds about Latin America for readers abroad. Moreover, Stephens and others like him clearly enjoyed the role of expert-on-virtually-everything.

The famous railway ascending the Andes to Oroya was built in 1870 by the remarkable engineer and fortune hunter, Henry Meiggs, an American. It is one hundred and thirty-eight miles long, and is the best-

---

*From Henry Stephens, *South American Travels* (New York: The Knickerbocker Press, 1915), 58–60, 66–68.

constructed mountain railroad in the world. Its gauge is standard, and the rolling stock is American, although it belongs to the Peruvian government. Meiggs conceived the original idea of ascending the mountains by means of switchbacks, where the train actually reverses direction, instead of by the ordinary method of broad curves and curved tunnels, as in the St. Gotthard [in Switzerland], or of rack-and-pinion, as on the Brazilian coast railways. The ascent begins in earnest forty-five miles from Lima, at the village of San Bartolomé. From this point to the next station, which is Verrugas, where the Rimac River is crossed on an iron bridge, the distance is only five miles, but in these five miles the tracks climb a thousand feet.

This is the district of verrugas fever, which was thought to be indigenous only to this locality, but which more recent observations have shown to exist at this height along the whole chain of the western Andes. The Peruvian city of Arequipa marks the southern limit of the fever zone, and it doubtless extends as far north as Ecuador. This verrugas fever is a peculiar, but by no means fatal, disease. It begins with a high fever, and later, warts, sometimes nearly an inch long, tapering and bloody, grow all over one's anatomy. I saw several cases of this. The natives tie black silk threads around the bases of these warts, which then, in time, fall off. [Daniel A.] Carrion and [A. L.] Barton proved the inoculability of this disease, the former by experiment upon himself, and the latter upon dogs.

The Verrugas bridge, the longest and highest on the Oroya Railroad, is 575 feet long and 225 feet high, and from its top the river in the canyon below looks like a silver snake. A tunnel named the Cuesta Blanca is entered, and from its eastern entrance begins panorama after panorama of great and rugged mountains. The slopes of these are covered with stunted bushes, and, in more favorable places, heliotrope abounds, as well as other plants whose roots do not need excessive moisture. A few miles farther on, Surco is reached, altitude 6600 feet, and then, at about eleven o'clock, Matucana, where everybody alights to eat breakfast. The train stops here for half an hour in the ascent, and a whole hour in the descent. I did not feel hungry, and, having been advised that overeating was the main cause of altitude sickness, I strolled around the little town, instead of going into the dining hall. There is little to see in the place, which is a health resort with a sanitarium. It lies in a canyon hemmed in by high mountains, and has groves of eucalyptus and a few pines. A battle was once fought here against the Spaniards in the War of Liberation, and a conquered flag is on exhibition in the little church of the village. Foolishly, I had forgotten to bring with me heavy underclothing and I now began to feel the effects of the chill of the atmosphere. I had on only the lightest kind of knee underdrawers and armless undershirt worn by the inhabitants of the tropics.

The next leg of the journey, from Cerro de Pasco from Oroya, ascends over two thousand feet, but it is gradual and presents little of interest. It was dark before we reached the great smelter of the Cerro de Pasco Mining Company, which is at La Fundición. Cerro de Pasco is a "bum" town, although by a supreme decree of 1840 it was entitled to the euphonious name of the "Opulent City of Cerro de Pasco." It was founded in 1771 and belonged to the Department of Tarma from which it became separated to be the capital of the Department of Junín. Its name means "Hill of Peace," but there is no peace there, either for its inhabitants or strangers. The inhabitants have to work too hard to enjoy themselves, and the strangers are kept awake all night by the barking of dogs and the ribald voices of drunken natives. There are over 15,000 people in the place, and all make a living by following the mining trade, as here are the great copper and silver mines with their innumerable chimneys, furnaces, and smelters. The altitude is 14,295 feet, and the air is chill and raw, while a strong wind is generally blowing. The natives call the reddish silver ore *cascajo*, meaning pebbles. There is scarcely any ore, whether it is silver or copper, that lacks some gold as well. The mining company is owned largely by [Henry Clay] Frick, [James] Haggin, and the successors of J. P. Morgan and so far has been unprofitable, largely on account of the costly operations and the cost of transportation.

At Cerro de Pasco, there is a German named Herold, who a few years ago managed to borrow enough money to start a small brewery. In a short time he paid back his debt and is now on the way towards "easy street." His brewery, the Cervecería Herold, is the highest brewery in the world. Although there is a lively and sociable bunch of Americans at La Fundición, one hour's time is enough for any tourist to devote to the Cerro de Pasco Mining Company unless he has business there, such a desolate place it is. I spent most of my time at the Smelter Hotel, opposite to the railroad station, waiting for the next train to pull out.

---

5. Amazonian Exotica ∼ H. M. Tomlinson*

Some travelers visited Latin America in search of a world where progress had not yet arrived. They wished to see untamed nature and viewed native people almost as a variety of wildlife. When the Englishman H. M. Tomlinson voyaged through Amazonian Brazil in 1909, he knew that he was retracing the steps of the distinguished English naturalist Henry Bates, who had visited and written about the Amazon in the 1850s. In the following excerpt, Tomlinson relates his disappointment at finding postcard vendors and electric streetcars in the capital

---

*From H. M. Tomlinson, *The Sea and the Jungle* (New York: E. P. Dutton & Co., 1913), 120–27.

of the Brazilian province of Pará, where, years earlier, Bates had described "an
isolated community of strange but kindly folk" lost in the jungle.

Occasionally the river narrowed, or we passed close to one wall, and
then we could see the texture of the forest surface, the microstructure
of the cliff, though we could never look into it for more than a few yards,
except where, in some places, habitations were thrust into the base of the
woods, as in lower caverns. An exuberant wealth of forms built up that
forest which was so featureless from a little distance. The numerous palms
gave grace and life to the façade, for their plumes flung in noble arcs from
tall and slender columns, or sprayed directly from the ground in emerald
fountains. The rest was inextricable confusion. Vines looped across the
front of green, binding the forest with cordage, and the roots of epiphytes
dropped from upper boughs, like hanks of twine.

In some places the river widened into lagoons, and we seemed to be
in a maze of islands. Canoes shot across the waterways, and river schooners, shaped very like junks, with high poops [decks] and blue and red
sails, were diminished beneath the verdure, betraying the great height of
the woods. Because of its longitudinal extension, diminishing visually to
a point in the distance, the elevation of the forest, when uncontrasted,
looked much less than it really was. The scene was so luminous, still, and
voiceless, it was so like a radiant mirage, or a vivid remembrance of an
emotional dream got from books read and read again, that only the unques-
tionable verity of our iron steamer, present with her smoke and prosaic
gear, convinced me of the scene's reality. Across a hatch a large butterfly
hovered and flickered like a flame. Dragonflies were suspended invisibly
over our awning, jewels in shimmering enamels.

We anchored just before breakfast, and a small launch flying a large
Brazilian flag was soon fussing at our gangway. The Brazilian customs
men boarded us, and the official who was left in charge to overlook the
vessel was a tall and majestic Latin with dark eyes of such nobility and
brooding melancholy that it never occurred to me that our doctor, who has
traveled much, was other than a fellow with a dull Anglo-Saxon mind
when he removed some loose property to his cabin and locked his door,
before he went ashore. So I left my field glasses on the ice-chest; and that
was the last I saw of them. Yet that fellow had such lovely hair, as the
ladies would say, and his smile and his courtesy were fit for kings. He
carried a scented pink handkerchief and wore patent-leather boots. Our
surgeon had but a faint laugh when these explanations were made to him,
taking my hand fondly, and saying he loved little children.

Pará, a flat congestion of white buildings and red roofs in the sun, was
about a mile beyond our anchorage, over the port bow; its name to me had
the appeal of the world not ours, like Tripoli of Barbary, Macassar, the

Marquesas, and the Rio Madre de Dios. The ride in the agent's launch, as it took us towards the small craft lying immediately before the front of that spread of houses between the river and the forest, was so momentous an occasion that I scarcely heard the small talk of the dainty Englishmen in linen suits, a gossiping group around the agent and the skipper. The launch rudely hustled through a cluster of gaily painted native boats, the dingiest of them bearing some sonorous name, and I landed in Brazil. There was an esplanade, shadowed by an avenue of mangoes. We crossed that, and went along hot narrow streets, by blotched and shabby walls, to the office to which our ship was consigned. We met a fisherman carrying a large turtle by a flipper. We came to a dim cool warehouse. There, some Negroes and half-breeds were lazily hauling packages in the shadows. It had an office railed off where a few English clerks, in immaculate white, overlooked a staff of natives. The warehouse had a strange and memorable odor—evasive, sweet, and pungent, as barbaric a note as I found in Pará, and I understood at once I had come to a place where there were things I did not know. I felt almost timorous and yet compelled when I sniffed at those shadows; though what the eye saw in the squalid streets of the riverside, where brown folk stood regarding us carelessly from openings in the walls, I had thought no more than a little interesting.

The people of Pará, passing by at a lazy gait—which I was soon compelled to imitate—in the heat, were puzzling folk to one used to the features of a race of pure blood, like ourselves. Portuguese, Negro, and Indian were there, but rarely a true type of one. Except where the black was the predominant factor the men were impoverished bodies, sallow, meagre, and listless, though there were some brown and brawny ruffians by the shore. But the women often were very showy creatures, certainly indolent in movement, but not listless, and built in notable curves. They were usually of a richer color than their mates, and moved as though their blood were of a quicker temper. They had slow and insolent eyes. The Indian has given them the black hair and brown skin, the Negro the figure, and Portugal their features and eyes. Of course, the fashionable ladies of Pará society, boasting their straight Portuguese descent, are not included in this insulting description. And I do not think I saw them—unless, indeed, they were the ladies who boldly eyed us in the fashionable Pará hotel, where we lunched, at a great price, off imported potatoes, tinned peas, and beef which in England would be sold to a glue factory.

After lunch some disappointment and irresolution crept into our holiday. There had been a time—but that was when Pará was only in a book; that was when its mere printed name was to me a token of the tropics. You know the place I mean. You can picture it. Paths that go but a little way into the jungle which overshadows an isolated community of strange but kindly folk, paths that end in a twilight stillness; ardent hues, flowers of vanilla, warm rain, a luscious and generative earth, fireflies in the scented dusk of gardens, and mystery—every outlook disappearing in the dark of the unknown.

Well, here I was, placed by the ordinary moves of circumstance in the very place the name of which once had been to me like a chord of that music none hears but oneself. I stood in Pará, outside a picture postcard shop. Electric cars were bumping down a narrow street. The glitter of a cheap jewelry store was next to the stationer's shop, and on the other side was a vendor of American and Parisian boots. There have been changes in Pará since Bates wrote his idylls of the forest. We two travelers went to the Nazareth that Bates had described. In 1850 it was a mile from the town. It is part of the town now, and an electric tram took us there, a tram which drove vultures off the line as it bumped along. The heat was a serious burden. The many dogs, which found energy enough to limp out of the way of the tram only when at the point of death, were thin and diseased, and most unfortunate to our nice eyes. The Brazilian men of better quality we passed were dressed in black cloth suits, and one mocked the equator with a silk hat and yellow boots. I set down these things as the tram showed them. The evident pride and hauteur, too, of these Latins, was a surprise to one of a stronger race. We stopped at a street corner, and this was Nazareth. Bates's pleasant hamlet is now the place of Pará's fashionable homes—pleasant still, despite the overhead tram cables and the electric light poles which interrupt the avenues of trees.

We passed through by-ways, where naked brown babies played before the doors. We happened upon the cathedral, and went on to the little dock where native vessels rested on garbage, the tide being out. Vultures pulled at stuff beneath the bilges. The crews, more Indian than anything, and men of better body than the sallow fellows in the town, sprawled on the hot stones of the quays and about the decks. There was a huge black woman, arms akimbo, a shapeless monument in black India rubber draped in cotton print, who talked loudly with a red boneless mouth to two disregarding Indians sitting with their backs to a wall. She had a rabbit's foot, mounted in silver, hanging around her neck. The schooners, ranged in an arcade, were rigged for lateen sails, very like Mediterranean craft. The forest was a narrow neutral tinted ribbon far beyond. The sky was blue, the texture of porcelain. The river was yellow. And I was grievously disappointed; yet if you put it to me, I cannot say why. There was something missing, and I don't know what. There was something I could not find; but as it is too intangible a matter for me to describe even now, you may say, if you like, that the fault was with me and not with Pará. We stood in a shady place, and the doctor, looking down at his hand, suddenly struck it. "Let's go," he said. He showed me the corpse of a mosquito. "Have you ever seen the yellow fever chap?" the doctor asked. "That is he." We left.

6. The Athens of South America ⁓ H. J. Mozans*

A fourth traveler of the early twentieth century, H. J. Mozans, aimed to plug a gap in readers' knowledge of Latin America. Explaining that "meritorious books" had already provided satisfactory coverage of the Caribbean, he lamented that parts of Venezuela and Colombia remained as unknown as "the least explored portions of darkest Africa." Unlike many travelers, Mozans had read considerably in Spanish, especially the chronicles of the Conquest—hence his title Following the Conquistadors Up the Orinoco and Down the Magdalena, *the chief rivers of Venezuela and Colombia, respectively. Mozans glowingly describes the Colombian capital, Bogotá, as "the Athens of South America." What impressed him so much about the city?*

Great as has been the change that it has undergone during the last few decades, Bogotá preserves much of the quaintness of colonial times. Indeed, it is not difficult, in certain parts of the city, to fancy one's self carried back to a typical Spanish town of the time of Charles V or Philip II. The city is adorned by a number of broad and beautiful streets and several plazas and parks. Aside from a few government buildings, the edifices that attract the most attention are the monasteries and churches. The cathedral is a noble building that compares favorably with any similar structure in South America. An object of interest to the traveler, within these sacred precincts, is the tomb of the illustrious conquistador, Gonzalo Jiménez de Quesada.

The residences of the people are usually two stories high with a balcony on the second story facing the street. All of the older houses, as well as many of the modern ones, are of the well-known Moorish style of architecture, with a single large entrance, the *portón*, and a courtyard or two onto which the rooms open. This style of building is well adapted to tropical climates. We were surprised to see the number of foreign flowers grown in these patios. One would naturally expect to find representatives of the rich and beautiful Colombian flora, but the ladies of Bogotá seem to prefer the flowers of Europe and the United States. We found roses, camelias, pinks, and geraniums in abundance. Our hotel, however, was an exception to this rule. Here we delighted with a veritable exhibition of orchids of many species and of the most wonderful forms and colors.

Some of the streets and houses have recently been lighted by electricity, but horses or mules are still used to move the few streetcars that traverse the principal thoroughfares. As nearly all the streets are paved with

---

*Adapted from H. J. Mozans, *Following the Conquistadors Up the Orinoco and Down the Magdalena* (New York and London: D. Appleton and Co., 1910), 287–303.

cobblestones, driving is anything but a pleasure. As a matter of fact, the only passable drive in the city is the one that leads to the charming little suburb of Chapinero. The is one of the showpieces of Bogotá, and its houses are in marked contrast with those found in the older parts of the city. Most of them are entirely different in style from the enclosed Moorish-style structures of which mention has been made. Here one is introduced to cozy Swiss chalets in the midst of delightful flower gardens and picturesque French chateaux that carry one back to the Seine and the Loire.

Aside from the churches and monasteries, many of which have been converted into government offices, there were two buildings that possessed a special interest for us. One of these was the old Colegio del Rosario— now known as the School of Philosophy and Letters—founded in 1553, nearly a hundred years before the University of Harvard. This institution has long been fondly spoken of by the people of Bogotá as the country's special glory, *la gloria de la patria*. The other building was the astronomical observatory, the first structure of its kind in the tropics, erected in 1803. After the observatory of Quito, it is said to be the highest in the world. Colombia counts many sons who have contributed greatly to our knowledge of nature.

The names of the poets and prose writers of Colombia that have achieved distinction make a long list. Many of them enjoy an international reputation, and their productions compare favorably with the best efforts of the writers of the mother country, Spain. The number of public and private libraries now existing in the city of Bogotá justifies its claim to be a chief center of South American culture. Another evidence of the intellectual atmosphere that reigns there is the number of second-hand book stores. In browsing among these storehouses of old and precious tomes. I quite forgot, for the time being, that I was so far from the busy world of action, and I could easily fancy myself among the bookshops of Florence, Leipzig, or Paris. Indeed, some of the most prized volumes of my Latin American collection I picked up in the book stalls of Bogotá.

Mr. W. L. Scruggs, a former diplomat in Bogotá, writes: "Most of the educated classes have, or think they have, a literary ability. They are particularly fond of writing (what they call) poetry and of making after-dinner speeches. An average high school student there writes poetry by the yard and can speak impromptu for an hour. He never shows the least embarrassment before an audience. His adjectives and adverbs flow in sluices of unbroken rhythm, and the supply of sweet-sounding words and hyperbolic phrases seems inexhaustible."

In Colombia there seem to be as many "doctors," that is, men who have the degree of Doctor of Laws, as there are generals in Venezuela. Most of them are politicians or contributors to the various newspapers of the country, or they are professors in the numerous educational institutions of the Colombian Republic. The number of newspapers published in Bogotá is also surprising, more than there are in Boston or Philadelphia. Of course, their circulation is extremely limited. Most are party newspapers or literary journals remarkable, the majority of them, for long poems, verbose editorials, and translations of the latest French novels.

Any city in the United States or Europe, having in its immediate vicinity such attractions as Bogotá has, would immediately put them within easy reach of the public. An electric railway would be constructed to the great waterfall of the Tequendama, the largest in Colombia and among the most celebrated in South America. Incredible as it may seem, few Colombians have ever seen the falls. Although the people of Bogotá love to talk about them, as among the greatest wonders of their country, one rarely encounters a person who has actually visited them. And yet they are not more than twelve miles from the capital. How different this would all be if the place were of easy access and if the visitor, on arriving there, could find the comforts to be obtained in similar places in the United States and Europe.

---

7. Our Ugly Little Backyard ~ Fredrick Palmer*

Our last travel writer, U.S. journalist Fredrick Palmer, made his trip to Central America for the Chicago Tribune, *which published his reports serially in 1908. Palmer viewed Central America as a festering sore, a land of not only potential trouble but also opportunity for the United States. He asserted that the countries he visited "may be called, for want of a better word, Indo-American," which he thought very unfortunate. Palmer declared that "rich territories, capable of vast development," merely "a day's sail from the United States," awaited the attentions of an energetic, Protestant race that needed to seize the initiative from other energetic races, such as the Japanese and the Germans, who were advancing imperial projects of their own in these years. Here, Palmer makes his way from Mexico to Guatemala.*

Tourist bureaus seem to draw a dead line at the Guatemalan boundary. In Mexico City, accurate information about travel in Russia was more accessible than details of how to reach the capital of Guatemala. The shipping agents mentioned two lines on the west coast, with sailings once in ten days, but advised me to disregard published time tables, which were more or less a formality. Passengers are a consideration largely subsidiary

*From Fredrick Palmer, *Central America and Its Problems* (New York: Moffat, Yard, and Co., 1910), 44–56.

to that of freight. If the slackness of cargo at one port makes a steamer ahead of time, a large consignment or bad surf at the next may make it behind time. The captain's policy is to get ahead as fast as he can, with the chances that, averaging the whole trip, he will reach his terminus approximately when the agents expect him. On my ship all the regular crew were German, the cargo handlers Chilean.

My only fellow traveler in first class was a Japanese major whom I met before, by chance, in Manchuria. He was busy with his notebook, studying Spanish-seeking knowledge with racial greediness. Later we met yet again in Guatemala City, and the astute dictator [Manuel Estrada] Cabrera, in one of my talks with him, ventured, with true Spanish politeness, a sympathetic remark on the misfortune of an American finding himself associated with a Japanese in his travels. It showed how well informed Central American politicians are of the international differences of the United States, and how quick they are to scent politics and intrigue where nothing of the kind occurs to us. As a matter of fact, the Japanese major became rather bored of his trip, and after witnessing one or two reviews of the Central American soldiers, hastened on to Panama and the canal, where he expected to see something worthwhile. On one occasion when we were riding on the train, as he looked out of the window at the rich, sparsely populated valleys, he exclaimed half to himself: "Much better climate than Kiushu" (the great southern island of the Japanese group). "So much room here. No room in Japan. If the Japanese were here they would cultivate right up to the mountain tops. Beautiful, beautiful country. Too bad!" It was the aching of a highly organized race to develop resources going to waste.

To return to the narrative of my voyage from Mexico to Guatemala, we finally dropped anchor opposite two big buoys, a mile or so out from a billowy white ribbon in front of unpainted buildings, grey against the deep green of the foliage. We were in San Benito, on the Mexican border. After whistling a while to announce our arrival—evidently a lone steamer against the horizon was invisible to official eyes—there was a puff of white ashore. This proved to be the steam from an engine which drew a boat through the surf by a rope run over pulleys on the buoys. Aboard were the doctor, the captain of the port, and the agent of the company—a German who wore leather gaiters, riding breeches, and a Tyrolese cap in the blazing sun, despite which he seemed perfectly cool. Time had seasoned him to the land's delays, though his national characteristic of efficiency was probably little impaired, as I found to be the case with most Germans in Central America, whether afloat or ashore. The inspection of the ship's papers and of the health of passengers was conducted in the cabin over iced Pilsener, which I imagine has saved the steamship company from many officially imposed delays in their affairs.

Another vista of breaking surf, and another group of unpainted buildings, the next afternoon, signified Champerico, the first port of Guatemala. Leaving my heavy baggage to continue on the steamer, I climbed into the big, boxlike chair which lowered me into the boat like so much cargo. After weeks on the Pacific coast of Central America, one becomes as used to this procedure as jumping on a streetcar at home. It is the only way in lands where there are no harbors, and Guatemala has not a single one on the Pacific side. A second pulley lift and I was on a long, spider-like pier—the surf tearing through the meshes of the steel legs—with a government official asking for the traveler's name, occupation, and object of coming to Champerico, and a representative of the company that had the pier concession asking for landing dues.

A dozen soldiers in soiled blue jeans, some with caps but mostly without, saluted as the captain of the port escorted me to the office, where I gave my name, occupation, and object of travel again. Next we sought out the American vice consul, a Jamaican by birth, who lived up a long stretch of steps in a single room, office and cottage combined—built out of the debris after the storms. The last train of the day on the coffee line connecting with the Guatemalan Central Railroad at Mazatenango had gone, and another would not start until day after tomorrow. There was no hotel, though I was offered the vice consul's single bed.

So I inquired about a locomotive to make the journey to Mazatenango that night. The sleepy station agent, after he had been found, sent off a wire to see what could be done, and while we waited for an answer, Mr. Kaufman, business arbiter of the community and agent for the coffee planters up country, himself the owner of a coffee plantation, offered his assistance. Word came that I could have the locomotive. Mr. Kaufman warned the station agent as to what was a reasonable price and saw that I was not cheated in the exchange of my gold for quantities of Guatemalan paper currency of continually fluctuating value. The manager of the railroad was quick with his promises but slow in their fulfillment. Word kept arriving that the locomotive was on its way.

"It's raining. There might be a washout," said the consul, "and maybe they've overlooked telegraphing the fact." This was hardly encouraging news at midnight. But directly we heard the scream of a whistle back in the jungle, and eventually I was put in the hands of an Italian conductor in charge of a venerable railroad car behind a venerable, wood-burning locomotive with an American engineer at the throttle. For two hours, with rain beating against the windows, we hurtled through the darkness, the gleam of the headlight making the wet leaves of the forest glisten, and the swing of an occasional lantern at a station signaling as we passed. Shortly after three o'clock the conductor said "Mazatenango!" and his lone passenger stepped out into the darkness, onto a boardwalk with nothing else in sight. A lantern indicated the approach of two figures.

"Welcome to Mazatenango, señor!" called a voice, and though I could not see his face, I caught the shadow pantomime of a hat being lifted from the head of the speaker with a grand sweep. It was the *jefe político* [the appointed head of the local government] come to meet me. The other man was a friend who had volunteered as an interpreter in the event I did not know Spanish. A carriage was waiting behind some scrawny horses, and, the driver lashing them, we plunged through mud holes until we struck a cobblestone pavement just as uneven and treacherous. With all three of us fairly gasping, we halted before a door that opened into a hotel court, where Señor and Señora were waiting before a table spread for supper. Señora hastened to bring out a tureen of soup. Señor opened beer. The *jefe* and I drank to Guatemala, the United States, and each other's good health. Something of the importance of a Pan American commissioner seemed to attach to my humble self. Later I learned that the name, occupation, destination, and object of travel, whenever slightly unusual, are taken directly to the *jefe*. It is his business to keep a sharp watch on all travelers, in view of possible revolutionary plots. In vain, I begged that polite *jefe* to retire. He insisted on keeping me company while I ate, and finally, with a grand sweep of his hat at the door of my bedchamber, he bade me goodnight a few minutes before dawn broke.

READING IMAGES
U.S.–Latin American Relations

Like other forms of humor, newspaper cartoons offer insight into widely shared attitudes. The four images in this section, published in U.S. newspapers between 1886 and 1962, have been selected from a book-length study, Latin America in Caricature, *which establishes several standard themes in journalistic portrayals of the region. Students should consider the implications of the U.S. attitudes that can be "read" in these portrayals. Such attitudes would have inevitably influenced U.S. policy in Latin America, not only as a dimension of public opinion but also because Washington's policymakers, from the president down, often were bigoted and paternalistic.*

"Uncle Sam and Mexico, 1886." In 1886 a minor diplomatic tiff with Mexico led the famous cartoonist Thomas Nast to contrast an upright, imperious Uncle Sam with a "Mexico" figure whose demeanor was, to put it mildly, not nearly so flattering. What exactly does this negative portrayal tell us? *Source:* Thomas Nast, *Harper's Weekly*, copied from John J. Johnson, *Latin American Caricature* (Austin: University of Texas Press, 1980), 213.

"Uncle Sam and Central America, 1906." In 1906, when the United States mediated a minor conflict between El Salvador, Guatemala, and Honduras, a Seattle newspaper presented a peacemaking Uncle Sam watching benevolently over those nations. Particularly interesting is the racial depiction of those three countries, none of which has a large population of African descent. What overall picture of inter-American relations does this cartoon present? How would you relate this image to the reality of frequent U.S. military interventions in the Caribbean basin during the first quarter of the twentieth century? *Source: Seattle Post-Intelligencer*, copied from Johnson, *Latin American Caricature*, 199.

"Uncle Sam and Latin America, 1923." By 1923 frequent U.S. military interventions had so soured relations with Latin America that hemispheric diplomacy had become strained. Then, too, in the wake of World War I, the United States had taken over from Great Britain as Latin America's dominant foreign trading partner. So, on the occasion of that year's Fifth Conference of American States, Uncle Sam appears as a suitor to an alluring and charming Latin America. If this cartoon is typical, how does the imagery differ when Latin America is portrayed favorably in the U.S. press? *Source: Philadelphia Evening Public Ledger*, copied from Johnson, *Latin American Caricature*, 103.

"Kennedy and Latin America, 1962." The Cold War tensions of 1962 prompted a small-city North Carolina newspaper to depict the Organization of American States (or OAS, a diplomatic body representing the countries of the hemisphere) as the usual Latin American stereotype. In the cartoon, when President John F. Kennedy calls the attention of the OAS to the actions of Cuba's president Fidel Castro, the OAS replies, "Why Theese Excitement? Eet's just a Wooden Horse!" *Source: Greensboro Daily News*, copied from Johnson, *Latin American Caricature*, 243.

VII

Nationalism

Around 1930, neocolonialism gave way to nationalism in Latin America. Twentieth-century nationalism in the region had a double emphasis. Nationalists took a skeptical view of foreign investment and enterprise. For the most part, they believed, such investment and enterprise in their countries amounted to "economic imperialism," which exploited rather than developed the region's potential. Nationalists also officially repudiated scientific racism and, in so doing, overcame Latin America's chronic inferiority complex, the nation-builders' old dilemma.

Problems caused by the neocolonial concentration on exporting raw materials and agricultural commodities became clear in the 1930s. During the Great Depression, people in Latin America lacked the cash to import manufactured products. Meanwhile, raw materials, without buyers, piled up on docks. This disruption of the existing world economy, with its industrialized center and raw materials–producing periphery, was prolonged until 1945 by World War II. Industrialists in Latin America had a fifteen-year-long opportunity to step in and make substitutions for goods that were formerly imported, without competition from other already industrialized countries. The result was import-substitution industrialization, or ISI, which occurred to some degree in most of the region. Oil refineries and steelworks were the pride of Latin American nationalists in the mid-twentieth century.

Once World War II was over, however, U.S. companies were eager to take up where they had left off before the period of economic depression and war. But they found a radically changed political scene in Latin America. In a nutshell, the landowning class, preeminent throughout the region while agricultural exports defined economic prosperity, had lost power after 1929 to an urban coalition of the middle and working classes. Political power had followed economic power from the hands of coffee growers and cattle barons to the hands of industrialists, middle-class voters, and labor unions. The new nationalist consensus was that ISI should be continued, that Latin America must industrialize at all cost. Believing the absence of outside competition essential to the growth of their own manufacturing capacity, Latin American nationalists put up protective tariffs to protect fledgling industries. (For more on these developments, see chapter X.)

Ideologically, the neocolonial fixation on European models had evaporated in favor of a nationalist preference for new expressions of distinctive Latin American identities. The folkways of the poor brown and black people who had always been the majority now became models of national cultures embodied in art, music, and literature. The neocolonial vision of "whitening" was scrapped for a nationalist vision of race mixture emphasizing social and cultural amalgamation over lighter skin color. Latin American nationalists had thus consigned scientific racism and white supremacy to the trash heap of history even before the defeat of Nazism discredited scientific racism throughout the world—at least in theory. White supremacy, in fact, has never disappeared totally from Latin American life. Still, the new nationalist celebration of indigenous American and African roots marked a giant step forward.

At the same time, admiring images of Europe and the United States gave way to angry denunciations of economic imperialism. The period of depression and war had coincided with the Good Neighbor Policy, a major effort by the U.S. government to cultivate friendly relations that had resulted in military alliances throughout Latin America. But after World War II, U.S. foreign policymakers directed their concern, along with considerable resources in aid, to rebuilding Europe and Japan. Indeed, the "Good Neighbor" seemed to forget about its Latin American friends and allies altogether except when defending the profits of a U.S. multinational corporation. In the Cold War climate, the prestige of Marxist ideology, in combination with intensified nationalist sentiment, rose rapidly as a response.

The following texts will exemplify the imagery and spirit of Latin American nationalism during its mid-twentieth-century high tide. If you had been there, would you have been a nationalist?

QUESTIONS FOR ANALYSIS

1. How did the nationalist visions of Gilberto Freyre or Ciro Alegría resolve the old dilemma faced by Latin America's would-be nation-builders?

2. How does the Mexican oil expropriation of 1938 contrast with the behavior of neocolonial governments in Latin America?

3. How does the anti-imperialist view of Washington's activities in Latin America contrast with the view commonly held in the United States?

1. Mestizo Pride ～ Gilberto Freyre*

Brazilian anthropologist Gilberto Freyre was one of the leading spokesmen for the new nationalist vision of racial amalgamation. His 1933 book, Big House and Slave Quarters, *interpreted colonial Brazil as the hemisphere's greatest racial and cultural melting pot. Freyre believed that the overall historical experience of the Portuguese had predisposed them to mix easily with darker people. He concentrated particularly on "The Black Slave in Brazilian Sexual and Family Life," the topic of more than one-third of the book. The importance of race mixture in Latin American history was, of course, not news to anyone in 1933. The difference was that Freyre presented it not as a drawback and not as a hope of "whitening," but rather as a favorable biological and cultural adaptation, the key to positive Latin American identities. Subsequent studies have shown that the Portuguese were far from having few race prejudices, as Freyre asserts. Furthermore, in his nationalist pride, Freyre went so far as to proclaim his country a "racial democracy" (in clear contrast to the United States), as if racism did not exist in Brazil. This wishful denial of the obvious clouded his reputation later in life.*

W hen Brazilian society was first organized socially and economically in 1532, the Portuguese colonizers had already had an entire century of contact with the tropics. Their aptitude for tropical life had already been demonstrated in Africa and India. The colonization of Brazil would put that aptitude to the test by shifting from the easier path of trade, characteristic of Portuguese activities in Africa and India, to the more substantial and arduous practice of tropical agriculture. Cultivation of the land required stable, patriarchal families and a system of slavery to regulate agricultural labor. The sexual union of Portuguese males with indigenous women incorporated local populations into the culture, economy, and society of the invaders.

Portuguese colonies in tropical America became, in their demographic composition, hybrids of European, Indian, and later, African [*sic*]. The societies that developed there were carved out not so much by state action as by the swords of private individuals. They were societies regulated not so much by racial consciousness (of which the flexible, cosmopolitan Portuguese had little) as by religious exclusivity, all subordinated to economic imperatives. . . . Those in charge in Brazil were always the great landowners with their sugar mills, their private chapels and chaplains, their Indian

---

*From Gilberto Freyre, *Casa grande e senzala: Formação da família brasileira sob o regime da economia patriarcal*, 28th ed. (Rio de Janeiro: Editora Record, 1992), 4–10, 283–84. Translated by John Charles Chasteen.

followers armed with bow and arrow or their slaves armed with blunder-busses. These lords of land and labor always spoke with a loud voice when addressing the king's representatives in Brazil or protesting the actions of mother country or mother church.

The singular Portuguese predisposition for this sort of slave-based, demographically hybrid colonization of the tropics can be explained by the historical experience of Portugal—the experience of a people culturally intermediate between Africa and Europe. African influence bubbled beneath the European, giving a special pungency to Portuguese diet, religion, and sexual life. The blood of Moors or black Africans was widespread in the light-skinned Portuguese population when not the dominant strain, as it is to this day in certain regions of Portugal. African winds mitigated the Germanic harshness of the country's law and institutions, the doctrinal and moral rigidity of the medieval church, softening the Portuguese versions of feudalism, Gothic architecture, even its Latin tongue. European culture reigned, but African culture governed.

The tense and often conflictive human relations between Europe and Africa somewhat offset the softening effect of climate. Constant war stiffened the Portuguese character and victory provided labor for agriculture and industry in the form of enslaved war captives. But these conflictive relations did not exclude the possibility of miscegenation and cultural intercourse between Portuguese and Africans. . . . "One looks in vain for a unified physical type," Count Hermann Keyserling recently observed in speaking of Portugal. Instead, he noted diverse and even opposing elements, people with a Scandinavian air and blacks living together in what seemed to him "a state of profound unity." An earlier history of Portugal described "an indeterminate population in the midst of two contending groups, half-Christian, half-Muslim, with relatives and friends in both groups. . . ."

Within this bi-continentalism or dualism of culture and race, there are other, subordinate factors that call for attention. One is the presence of individuals of Semitic origin or stock, people of a mobility and adaptability that one easily detects in the Portuguese navigators and cosmopolitans of the fifteenth century. Hereditarily predisposed to life in the tropics by long experience there, the Semitic element conferred upon the Portuguese colonizers of Brazil some of the principal physical and psychological attributes required for endurance and success. Among these was the economic realism that tended from an early date to correct the excesses of military and religious zeal in the formation of Brazilian society.

Mobility and a disposition to mix with other peoples were the particular secrets of Portuguese success in the colonization of Brazil. Otherwise, how could an under-populated country like Portugal have managed to spread its blood and culture through areas of the world so diverse and so distant from each other—in Asia, Africa, America, and numerous archipelagos? Wherever they settled, the Portuguese took wives and engendered offspring with a fervor due as much to the instincts of individuals as to policies adopted by the state for obvious economic and political reasons.

No other colonizing people in modern times has equaled the Portuguese in their readiness to mix with others. "Mixibility," in a word, was the quality that allowed the Portuguese to compensate for their small population. From their first contact with women of color, the Portuguese mingled with them and procreated children of mixed race. The result was that a few thousand daring males took firm control of vast territories, vying successfully with much more numerous peoples in the extension of their colonial domain and the efficiency of their colonizing activity. Their history of living intimately with darker races in and near their peninsular homeland had prepared the Portuguese for this colonial undertaking.

Significantly, one of these darker races, the Moors of Islamic faith, was more highly skilled technically and possessed an intellectual and artistic culture superior to that of the Christians. Long contact with the Moors had led the Portuguese to idealize the figure of the Moorish enchantress—brown-skinned and black-eyed, enveloped in a sexual mystique, always dressed in red, always combing her tresses or bathing in the river or in the water of an enchanted spring—that the colonizers found almost perfectly reproduced in the indigenous women of Brazil. The indigenous women had dark, flowing hair they were fond of combing, and they adored bathing their ardent, red-painted bodies in the river. The indigenous women were heavy-set like the Moorish women, too. But they were much less aloof and freely gave themselves to the woman-starved colonizers in return for trinkets like small pieces of mirror.

Today, all Brazilians (even the light-skinned, blond ones) carry in their souls (when not in both soul and body) the mark of Africa or indigenous America. Up and down the coast of Brazil, from Maranhão in the far north to Rio Grande do Sul in the far south, as well as inland in Minas Gerais, the predominant of these influences, whether direct or remote, is that of Africa. We reveal it in our tenderness, in the way we illustrate our words with abundant gestures, in our form of Catholic worship that delights the senses, also in our music, our speech, our gait, and our way of singing lullabies. The mark of Africa is on our sincerest forms of self-expression. It is the influence of the slave "mammy" who rocked us to sleep, who breast-fed and then spoon-fed us, after mashing the food to a pulp in her hand. It is the influence of the old woman who told us ghost stories, of the young boy who was our first playmate, of the mulata who groomed us and, in the creaking cot where we felt for the first time the sensation of complete manhood, initiated us in the ways of physical love.

Some have suggested that the inclination of white males toward black women in slave-holding societies resulted from the intimate relations between white children and their enslaved wet-nurses. Scholars may be correct on this point, given that psychologists now emphasize the enormous impact of breast feeding on children. But the truth is that the social conditions surrounding the development of all children on the sugar plantations of Brazil (as on the antebellum plantations of Virginia and the Carolinas) are sufficient explanation of this predilection.

---

2. The Power of Indigenous Community ~ Ciro Alegría*

In countries with large indigenous populations, twentieth-century nationalism brought a reassessment of what it meant to be "Indian." Assimilation into the larger society remained the overall goal, but indigenous culture took on a new meaning. Neocolonial ideologies had cast Indians as brutish and culturally debased beings who had lost all trace of past Inca or Aztec glory. Nationalists, on the other hand, identified distinctive virtues in indigenous villages. Where neocolonial ideology had dictated the dissolution of Indian communities to promote individual ownership of property, nationalist ideology revered the powerful community ethos of indigenous people. Latin American novelists such as Peru's Ciro Alegría made the point in fiction. The following passage from his 1941 novel Wide and Alien Is the World *gives a lyrical picture of indigenous villagers harvesting their crops but then depicts the exploitation of Indian labor outside their communities. Where neocolonial authors had portrayed the Indians as beaten and fatalistic, Alegría paints them as future revolutionaries.* Wide and Alien Is the World *was the most influential in a long line of Latin American* indigenista *novels.*

The villagers of Rumi began the harvest. Men and women, old and young, even children, went out into the cornfield. Their dark faces and brightly colored clothing leapt to the eye amid the pale gold of the ripening crop. The morning was soft, warm, and luminous, and the land itself seemed to glow with satisfaction at having made the grain swell so fat.

The harvesters broke through the heavy leaves encasing each ear of corn with a fingernail or with a wooden point that they carried, attached to their wrists with a string. Then they pulled the leafy casing apart to reveal the dry, shiny grains, yellow and white, but also red and purple, finally pulling the ear free and letting it tumble into the cloth bags that they carried over their shoulders. Other harvesters gathered the bean pods

---

*From Ciro Alegría, *El mundo es ancho y ajeno* (Caracas: Biblioteca Ayacucho, 1978), 108–9, 130–32. Translated by John Charles Chasteen.

that hung from vines that climbed the stalks of corn. Still others gathered the large white melons that grew there, too. The ears of corn were carried to a structure where they were stacked on end and exposed to the sun to dry. The name of the structure (*cauro*) and the name of the operation (*mucura*) were words from Quechua, the language of the Incas. The Spanish spoken by whites and mestizos had tended to displace Quechua in northern Peruvian villages like Rumi, but the agricultural vocabulary had remained Quechua, rooted in people's hearts the way their plants were rooted in the ground. The cauro full of stacked corn stood in front of the mayor's house on Rumi's modest plaza. Other fruits of the harvest were heaped beside the cauro. The harvesters who watched the heaps rise as they returned repeatedly to empty their sacks praised the bounty of the earth.

Everyone harvested, from the very young to the very old. Old Rosendo, the mayor of Rumi, moved more slowly than most, but worked right alongside them. He did not seem like the mayor at all, only a happy, hard-working grandfather. Anselmo, the harp player, seated on a stool to one side of the cauro, his large instrument reclining on his shoulder, played for the harvesters. The notes of the harp, the sounds of laughing voices, the rustling of dry corn shucks, the crack of ears coming loose from the stalk—all mingled to form the happy sound of the harvest. Girls carrying gourds went back and forth between the harvesters in the field and the large earthenware jugs of chicha corn beer, distributing the red, celebratory brew. The chicha sang in the harvesters' veins of its fermented-corn origins. And the cornfield, shorn of its pregnant fruits, was gradually transformed into a patch of forlorn stalks robbed of their former plumes.

And whom did we see chatting over there but Juan Medrano, son of a village official, and Simona, one of the young women we saw helping with the cows on a certain morning. The two were beginning to feel close in the last couple of days. And the afternoon, shimmering with heat, had just begun. A penetrating fragrance was rising from the earth to mingle with the smell of overall ripeness. Juan was strong as a tree limb, Simona, succulent as a fruit, and neither was over twenty years old. They began to tussle, slowly separating from the other harvesters. Simona ran away laughing and Juan pretended he couldn't catch her. Finally, he did catch her, and they looked deeply into each other's eyes.

"Bet I can trip YOU."

"Bet you can't."

They struggled playfully for a moment—Simona was strong, too—finally rolling amid the stalks of corn. The corn patch covered the joyous alliance of their brown bodies with its interminable rustle, its obedient ears, its yellow beard. Above arched the deep blue heavens, bending harmoniously over the earth. Simona discovered the joy of her own body and of a man's, and Juan, who had tripped up many young women in his travels, discovered that powerful call that eventually leads men to settle on just one woman.

The setting sun struck the corn flowers and the brown faces now in profile. The long shadow of the neighboring Andean peak grew longer, creeping over the ground to cover the corn field. The day's work was finished, and the harvesters returned to the village. In the plaza stood the cauro, brim full, and the towering heaps of beans and melons.

The harp is still playing. Someone sings. All the villagers of Rumi feel happy and, without stopping to think about it, they are fulfilled at having used their days for peace, cultivating the earth for the common good.

Meanwhile, far away, Rumi's native son Benito Castro suffered greatly as a salaried hacienda laborer. Benito remembered Rumi and his heart ached. He remembered his horse, Luccro, and his heart ached even more. The agricultural labors of the hacienda were *so* different from those of the indigenous community. In Rumi, people worked quickly, laughing and singing, and their daily labors were a pleasure to them. On the haciendas, they moved slowly and sadly, like stepchildren of the land. They might have a little strength left, but they had no spirit left at all.

Time passed and, not suspecting what grave events were occurring in Rumi, Benito labored with a hundred other indigenous workers in the mud under heavy rains, cultivating the crops of the *patrón* who owned the hacienda. The hacienda was enormous, and the huts provided for the workers were so far away from the field that Benito and the others had to sleep together in a large shed while they worked there. In these quarters, he came to know Indians from all over, people who spoke Quechua (when they spoke, which was not often), and had mostly melancholy things to say. Benito had not been raised speaking Quechua, which sounds sometimes like a raging wind and sometimes like water seeping through the earth, but now he began to learn.

Their stories were rarely the old folktales, but rather, lamentations of their labors and sufferings. In low voices, a tight circle of listeners gathered around them, and the oldest of the group told of the great rebellion led by Atusparia more than a generation earlier.

Here is the story: The year was 1885. The Indians were groaning under the weight of the oppression they suffered. Each of them had to pay a personal tax of two *soles* twice a year. They had to contribute their labor without pay to build roads, barracks, cemeteries, churches, and public buildings in the name of the Republic. The overseers devastated the indigenous communities to force them to work. The Indians had to work for nothing just to escape persecution. They had to endure in silence.

But one time they protested, presenting a petition in Huaraz [Huarás].

No one paid any attention. Instead, Pedro Pablo Atusparia, an indigenous mayor who led the petitioners, was insulted, jailed, and whipped. Fourteen mayors of indigenous communities went to protest this abuse. They, too, were insulted, jailed, and whipped.

They pretended to give in. And then on March first the Indians came down from the mountains toward Huaraz carrying bundles of straw to roof a building—public work for the Republic. But at a signal they pulled clubs and machetes from the bundles of straw, and the fight began. They told this story in the present tense.

The first wave of Indians is thrown back. A squadron of cavalry charges, scattering their forces. Encouraged by this success, the squadron attacks Pumacayán, a steep-walled Inca fortress where the Indians have taken shelter. Pumacayán has beautiful stone carvings of mating pumas on walls that the government prefect of Huaraz intended to dismantle, planning to use the materials for the city cemetery and several private mansions. Pumacayán is defended by Pedro Granados and a handful of brave men. Granados wields a huge leather sling with which he hurls rocks the size of a person's head with deadly accuracy. Alone he topples seventy of the attacking cavalry. The squadron falls back, and the Indians besiege Huaraz. It falls the next day. The Indians drink the blood of the most valiant of their enemies to feed their own valor. They want to destroy the families of the rich who cower in their houses. But Atusparia, the leader of the rebellion, is against that. "I do not want crimes," he says. "I want justice."

The revolution begins to spread. The Indians cover themselves with sheep fleece and crawl on all fours to take the city of Yungay by surprise. The countryside of Huaylas, too, rises up, and assaults all the towns there. In some of them, the rich form "urban guards" and fight bravely. Other indigenous leaders emerge.

Emissaries are sent to other parts of the highlands asking for help, asking for revolution. But the battalions of the government arrive with good rifles, with artillery. They massacre the Indians like so many ants. To save ammunition, the army stands indigenous prisoners in rows to execute six at a time with one bullet. The leaders of the rebellion are captured and executed, too. As the blows and bullets rip the body of José Orobio, the White Condor, he sneers at his executioners: "A little more. Give me a little more." Uchcu Pedro, who brought dynamite from the mines to arm the revolution, turns his bare buttocks to the firing squad and bends over. Atusparia falls wounded, and his bodyguards fall dead on top of him, defending him even in death.

These are the things that were whispered among the workers, exhausted by their days of ceaseless toil, in the nights when they gathered together. They remembered the victories more than the defeats. And the night was filled with hope and tragedy, with images of legendary heroes, with the memory of those who struggled shrewdly and powerfully against their tormenters. They were not yet beaten. Any day now, the revolution would begin again.

3. The Poetry of Anti-Imperialism ∼ Pablo Neruda*

Artists of all kinds gave expression to nationalist sentiments in the middle years of the twentieth century. One of Latin America's most celebrated poets, Chile's Pablo Neruda, voiced the anti-imperialism of the period in a number of his poems. The two featured here are taken from his book-length Canto General *(1950). Neruda depicts U.S. multinational corporations such as Standard Oil operating in Latin America as powerful economic predators, buying governments, stealing national wealth, and using violence to repress any protests against them. The mention of Paraguayans and Bolivians in "Standard Oil Co." refers to the Chaco War, 1932–1935, in which Paraguay and Bolivia disputed a desolate territory where oil had been discovered. In "United Fruit Co.," Neruda refers to the U.S. giant that controlled banana plantations in many countries of the Caribbean basin but particularly on the isthmus of Central America, where it maintained proverbially warm relations with petty dictators whom he scorns as "flies" and "small-time Caesars." In weighing the significance of Neruda's anger, consider that he was probably the most popular Latin American poet of the twentieth century. Also note that, as is often the case in anti-imperialist writings, Neruda's nationalist sentiments do not focus on his own country of Chile alone but extend to Latin America as a whole.*

Standard Oil Co.

> When the drill bored down
> toward the stony fissures
> and plunged its implacable intestine
> into the subterranean estates,
> and dead years, eyes
> of the ages, imprisoned
> plants' roots
> and scaly systems
> became strata of water,
> fire shot up through the tubes

---

*From Pablo Neruda, *Canto General, Fiftieth Anniversary Edition*, ed. and trans. Jack Schmitt (Berkeley: University of California Press, 1991), 176–77, 179. © 1991 by the Fundación Pablo Neruda and The Regents of the University of California. Reprinted by permission of The Regents of the University of California and the University of California Press.

transformed into cold liquid,
in the customs house of the heights,
issuing from its world
of sinister depth,
it encountered a pale engineer
and a title deed.

However entangled the petroleum's
arteries may be, however the layers
may change their silent site
and move their sovereignty
amid the earth's bowels,
whenever the fountain gushes
its paraffin foliage,
Standard Oil has arrived beforehand
with its lawyers and its boots,
with its checks and its guns,
with its governments and its prisoners.

Its obese emperors
from New York are suave,
smiling assassins
who buy silk, nylon, cigars,
petty tyrants, and dictators.

They buy countries, people, seas,
police, legislators,
distant regions where
the poor hoard their corn
like misers their gold:
Standard Oil awakens them,
clothes them in uniforms, designates
which brother is the enemy,
and Paraguayans fight its war,
and Bolivians are undone
in the jungle with its machine guns.

A President assassinated
for a drop of petroleum,
a million-acre
mortgage, a swift
execution on a morning
mortal with light, petrified,
a new prison camp for
subversives, in Patagonia,
a betrayal, scattered shots
beneath a petroliferous moon,

a subtle change of ministers
in the capital, a whisper
like an oil tide,
and zap, you'll see
how Standard Oil's letters
shine above the clouds,
above the seas, in your home,
illuminating their domains.

United Fruit Co.

When the trumpet blared, everything
on Earth was prepared
and Jehovah distributed the world
to Coca-Cola Inc., Anaconda,
Ford Motors, and other entities.
United Fruit Inc.
reserved for itself a juicy part,
the central isthmus of my land,
America's sweet waist.
It rebaptized its lands "Banana Republics,"
and upon the slumbering corpses,
upon the restless heroes
who conquered renown,
freedom, and flags,
it established a comic opera.
It alienated self-destiny,
gave crowns to small-time Caesars,
unsheathed envy, and drew
the dictatorship of flies:
Trujillo flies, Somoza flies,
Carías flies, Martínez flies,
Ubico flies, flies soaked
in humble blood and jam,
drunk flies that drone
over common graves,
circus flies, clever flies
versed in tyranny.

Among the bloodthirsty flies
the Fruit Co. disembarks,
ravaging coffee and fruits
for its ships that spirit away
like serving trays
our submerged lands' treasures.

Meanwhile, in the seaports'
sugary abysses,
Indians collapse, buried
in the morning mist.
A body rolls down, a nameless
thing, a fallen number,
a bunch of lifeless fruit
dumped in the rubbish heap.

4. Economic Nationalism in Action ∼ Lesley Byrd Simpson*

Mass meetings and charismatic leaders were typical of the nationalist style. Like Lázaro Cárdenas of Mexico, whose presidency (1934–1940) is described here, nationalist leaders often put major emphasis on the idea of economic self-determination. Cárdenas boldly put that idea into action when he expropriated the Mexican holdings of foreign oil companies in 1938. He exemplified the nationalist respect for communal values by distributing land in collectively owned ejidos rather than to individual peasant families. Moreover Cárdenas insisted on a foreign policy that did not toe any U.S.-drawn lines. Historian Lesley Byrd Simpson's narrative of the Cárdenas years, first published in 1941, conveys a feeling of their excitement. Would the age-old injustices of Latin America now finally be undone?

During the four effective years of his term, Cárdenas distributed more land to the peasants than had been distributed in all the years since the beginning of the Revolution. In the Laguna district of Durango, a cotton strike gave Cárdenas the opportunity to take 600,000 acres of rich land and begin upon it the famous Laguna cooperative project. He settled 30,000 families in the Laguna and organized them into a multitude of interlocking units, to form the first great state-operated farm. The project required large-scale financing, and a new bank was created for the purpose, the National Bank for Ejido Credit, with a capital of 30,000,000 pesos. This was benevolent despotism with imagination. By the end of 1936 the new bank reported: "In the Laguna region credits were granted to 29,690 family heads organized in ejidos, for the cultivation of 247,000 acres. The total of these loans was 8,124,692 pesos, guaranteed by crops of an estimated value of more than 50,000,000 pesos. During the last week of January 1937, the bank's investment in the region reached a new weekly high of more than a million pesos."

*From Lesley Byrd Simpson, *Many Mexicos*, 4th ed., revised (Berkeley: University of California Press, 1966), 288, 290–91. © 1966 by Lesley Byrd Simpson. Reprinted by permission of the University of California Press.

The most powerful support for the Cárdenas regime came from the new and militant Mexican Workers' Confederation organized in 1936 by Vicente Lombardo Toledano. It became, as it was intended to become, a working-class militia, and, with the backing of Cárdenas, it reached into every field of activity, from federal white-collar workers and schoolteachers to the porters who snatched one's luggage, willy-nilly, at the railroad stations.

The civil war in Spain found Cárdenas and the vigorous Mexican Workers' Confederation firmly supporting the Spanish Republican government, while the rest of the democratic world seemed to be doing its best to insure the victory of General Francisco Franco. President Cárdenas had a clearer vision of the essentials of the conflict than our own government. The arrival of five hundred refugee Spanish children at Veracruz in 1937 was one of the most moving spectacles in the history of the generous Mexican people. Cárdenas was also the first to seize the opportunity of inviting an unlimited number of Spanish Republicans to Mexico after the war and giving them Mexican citizenship, for he recognized the great value to the Mexican economy of those hardy peasants and mechanics. He did the same thing for the exiled intellectuals of Spain, and Mexico was enriched by the cream of Spanish scholars, scientists, writers, and artists. Cárdenas was, of course, condemned as a Red: he was polluting the holy soil of Mexico with the atheistic scum who had been run out of Spain by that paladin of the Faith, Francisco Franco. Fascist organizations joined the traditional conservative elements of Mexico in fighting the whole Cárdenas program. They were soon reinforced by the most formidable enemy that Cárdenas had challenged, the foreign oil companies.

A strike of refinery and field workers had dragged on for two years, with each side making charges and claims so essentially opposed that compromise was out of the question. A Supreme Court decision favored the workers. The companies refused to obey it and were declared to be in a "state of rebellion." On March 18, 1938, President Cárdenas signed his famous order expropriating the oil properties.

In the ensuing dispute an immense amount of literature was circulated by both sides, and epithets such as "Communist" and "imperialist" were freely exchanged. To the oil workers, who were saturated with the xenophobia of the Revolution, the expropriation meant the emancipation of Mexico from the foreign yoke. A monster mass meeting [in Mexico City] was organized by Lombardo Toledano on March 23, 1938, to celebrate Mexico's new "Independence Day." The *Mexican Labor News* became lyrical: "At nine o'clock in the morning the demonstrators began their march toward the central Zócalo, and the last contingents had not passed by the main balcony of the Palace, where President Cárdenas, together with several members of his administration, reviewed the parade, until four in the afternoon. At the height of the demonstration the tremendous square was solidly packed with a mass of wildly cheering humanity celebrating the dawn of what thousands of placards and standards hailed as the economic independence of Mexico."

March 18 was made a national holiday. Two years later I watched the slightly stereotyped celebration of the expropriation. Mexico had been through a lot of trouble with her new baby, but I could not help admiring the spirit, somewhat forced at times by cheerleaders, of the crowd. The faithful *Mexican Labor News* repeated its somewhat shopworn tribute: "All over the country, in cities and towns and villages, workers, peasants, soldiers, and all of the people paraded through the streets with cheers and music and banners that proclaimed: 'The Wealth of Mexico Must Be Possessed by Mexico!' In Mexico City more than a hundred thousand men, women, and children crowded into the great Plaza of the Constitution. Flags were hung from the Palace windows, and flags and enormous pictures of Cárdenas were hung from the cathedral towers. Bells rang; the uniformed drum and bugle corps of the Mexican Workers' Confederation played the marches of the Mexican Revolution; and when the plaza was full to overflowing, the thousands there began to sing the National Anthem with all the strength of their voices. This was Mexico's reiteration of her declaration of independence from foreign imperialism."

---

5. The Shark and the Sardines ～ Juan José Arévalo*

Juan José Arévalo, a former president of Guatemala, spent much of his life in exile from governments supported by the United States. His fable of The Shark and the Sardines *was published in Spanish in 1956 on the heels of a CIA-engineered military overthrow of Guatemala's constitutionally elected nationalist regime. This U.S. intervention was strongly encouraged by the United Fruit Company, whose interests had been injured by the Guatemalan government's nationalist policies. Arévalo's denunciation resonated strongly with Latin American public opinion, but in the United States "the American reader," whom Arévalo addressed in this introduction to the English translation, paid little attention.*

In your hands you hold a controversial book—a book that speaks out against your State Department's dealings with the peoples of Latin America during the twentieth century. It intends neither insult nor offense to the United States as a nation. The future of your country is identified

---

*From Juan José Arévalo, *The Shark and the Sardines*, trans. June Cobb and Raul Osegueda (New York: Lyle Stuart, 1961), 9–13.

with the future of contemporary democracy. Neither does this book seek to cast blame on the North American people—who, like us, are victims of an imperialist policy of promoting business, multiplying markets, and hoarding money.

Very different was the ideology of the men who first governed your country. It was as thirteen widely varying former colonies inspired by ideals of individual freedom, collective well-being, and national sovereignty that the United States came into existence in the world. Protestants, Catholics, and Masons alike, those men of the eighteenth century were moved by an ardent sense of dignity that won for them and for their cause the sympathy and the admiration of the entire world. They recognized worth in all kinds of work, they welcomed to their shores foreigners of every origin, and when their crops and their homes were threatened, they defended their crops and their homes just as they defended the privacy of the individual conscience. They went to church with their heads held high and they founded colleges so that their children might advance along the road to self-improvement.

Moral values served as a motivating force in the days of your independence. Those same values, confirmed by the civilian populace of the young republic, figured among the norms of government. The nation was characterized by its grandeur of spirit and indeed great were the military accomplishments and the thesis of the new law. Amazed, the world applauded.

But as the twentieth century was dawning, the White House adopted a different policy. To North America as a nation were transferred the know-how, sentiments, and appetites of a financial genius named [John D.] Rockefeller. Grandeur of spirit was replaced by greed. The government descended to become a simple entrepreneur for business and protector of illicit commercial profits. From then on, accounting was the science of sciences. The new instrument of persuasion was the gunboat. Now the United States had become different. It was neither a religious state nor a juridical state but, rather, a mercantile state—a gigantic mercantile society with all the apparatus of a great world power. The European juridical tradition was abandoned and North American morality was forgotten. The United States thenceforth was to be a Phoenician enterprise, a Carthaginian republic. Washington and Lincoln must have wept in shame in their graves.

The immediate victim was Latin America. To the North American millionaires converted into government, Latin America appeared an easy prey, a "big moneymaker." The inhabitants of this part of the world came to be looked upon as international *braceros*.* This multiple-faceted

---

*Mexican agricultural workers allowed to enter the United States as part of a U.S.-sponsored program during World War II.

exploitation was carried out with intelligence, with shrewdness, with the precision of clockwork, with "scientific" coldness, with harshness, and with great arrogance. From our southern lands, the river of millions began to flow northward, and every year it increased. The United States became great while progress in Latin America was brought to a halt. And when anything or anyone tried to interfere with the bankers or the companies, use was made of the Marines. Panama, 1903. Nicaragua, 1909. Mexico and Haiti, 1914. Santo Domingo, 1916. Along with the military apparatus, a new system of local "revolutions" was manipulated—financed by the White House or by Wall Street, which were now the same. This procedure continued right up to the international scandal of the assault on Guatemala in 1954, an assault directed by Mr. [Secretary of State John] Foster Dulles, with the okay of Mr. Eisenhower, who was your President at that time. North American friends, this is history, true history, sketched here as briefly as possible.

We Latin Americans, who, more than anybody else, suffered from this change in political philosophy and its consequences, could no longer be friends of the government of the United States. The friendship certainly could be reestablished. But to do so, it would be necessary for the White House to alter its opinion of us, and it would be necessary for its conduct to change. We expect a new political treatment. We do not want to continue down this slope that takes us straight to colonial status, however it may be disguised. Neither do we want to be republics of merchants like the African trading stations of old.

We Latin Americans are struggling to prevent the business mentality from being confused with, or merged into, statesmanship. The North American example has been disastrous to us and has horrified us. We know that a government intimately linked to business and receiving favors from business loses its capacity to strive for the greatest possible happiness for the greatest number of its people. When businessmen become rulers, it is no longer possible to speak of social justice; and even the minimum and superficial "justice" of the common courts is corrupted.

In our resistance to the business mentality, we are still Spanish, stubbornly Spanish. Also, we have not stopped being Catholic, nor have we stopped being romantic, and we cannot conceive of private life without love, nor of public life without chivalry, nor of our children's education without ideals.

If you want to be our friends, you will have to accept us as we are. Do not attempt to remodel us after your image. Mechanical civilization, material progress, industrial techniques, wealth, comfort, hobbies—all these figure in our programs of work and enjoyment of life. But, for us, the essence of human life does not lie in such things.

These lines, my North American friends, are meant to explain why I wrote the fable of *The Shark and the Sardines*. This book was written with indignation—indignation wrapped from time to time in the silk of irony. It declares that international treaties are a farce when they are pacted between a "shark" and a "sardine." It denounces the Pan-American system of diplomacy as an instrument at the service of the shark. It denounces the Pan-American idea of "allegiance to the hemisphere"—a juridical device that will inevitably lead to the establishing of an empire from pole to pole. It denounces the relentless and immense siphoning-off of wealth from south to north. It denounces the existence of the terrible syndicate of millionaires, whose interests lie even outside the United States.

It denounces the subordination of the White House to this syndicate. It denounces the conversion of your military into vulgar policemen for the big syndicates. And for the purpose of analysis, it takes up the case of Nicaragua, compelled by the United States to sign (in 1914–1916) a treaty that goes against all written and all moral laws.

This book, friends of the North, has been read all over Latin America. Read it now, yourselves, and accept it as a voice of alarm addressed to the great North American people who are still unaware of how many crimes have been committed in their name.

---

6. In the Eye of the Hurricane Are
120 Million Children ~ Eduardo Galeano*

The original Spanish version of The Open Veins of Latin America *was one of the most influential books on the region in the 1970s and 1980s. It went through many dozens of editions in Spanish and was widely translated. The title exemplifies the author's vivid metaphors as well as his angry criticism of the way more powerful countries bled Latin America economically during much of its history. After finishing the book in late 1970, Galeano was forced to spend many years in exile following a military takeover in his native Uruguay. He was finally able to return home to Uruguay after the restoration of democratic rule in Uruguay in the mid-1980s.*

The division of labor among nations is that some specialize in winning and others specialize in losing. Our part of the world, known today as Latin America, was precocious: It has specialized in losing ever since those remote times when Renaissance Europeans ventured across the ocean and buried their teeth in the throats of the Indian civilizations. Cen-

---

*From Eduardo Galeano, *The Open Veins of Latin America: Five Centuries of the Pillage of a Continent,* trans. Cedric Belfrage (New York: Monthly Review Press, 1973), 11–17. Reprinted by permission of Monthly Review Press.

turies passed, and Latin America perfected its role. We are no longer in the era of marvels, when fact surpassed fable and imagination was shamed by the trophies of conquest—the lodes of gold, the mountains of silver. But our region still works as a menial laborer. It continues to exist at the service of others' needs, as a source and reserve of oil and iron, of copper and meat, of fruit and coffee, the raw materials and foods destined for rich countries which profit more from consuming them than Latin America does from producing them. The taxes collected by the buyers are much higher than the prices received by the sellers; and after all, as Alliance for Progress coordinator Covey T. Oliver said in July 1968, to speak of fair prices is a "medieval" concept, for we are in the era of free trade.

Latin America is the region of open veins. Everything from the discovery until our times has always been transmuted into European—or later United States—capital, and as such has accumulated in distant centers of power. Everything: the soil, its fruits and its mineral-rich depths, the people and their capacity to work and to consume, natural resources and human resources.

The more freedom is extended to business, the more prisons have to be built for those who suffer from that business. Our inquisitor-hangman systems function not only for the dominant external markets. They also provide gushers of profit from foreign loans and investments in the dominated internal markets. Back in 1913, President Woodrow Wilson observed: "You hear of 'concessions' to foreign capitalists in Latin America. You do not hear of concessions to foreign capitalists in the United States. They are not granted concessions." He was confident: "states that are obliged . . . to grant concessions are in this condition, that foreign interests are apt to dominate their domestic affairs, . . ." he said, and he was right. Along the way we have even lost the right to call ourselves Americans, although the Haitians and the Cubans appear in history as new people a century before the *Mayflower* pilgrims settled on the Plymouth coast. For the world today, America is just the United States. The region we inhabit is a sub-America, a second-class America of nebulous identity.

At the beginning of November 1968, Richard Nixon loudly confirmed that the Alliance for Progress was seven years old and that malnutrition and food shortages had nevertheless intensified in Latin America. A few months later, in April, George W. Ball wrote in *Life*: "But at least for the next several decades, the discontent of the poorer nations does not threaten world destruction. Shameful as it undoubtedly may be, the world has lived at least two-thirds poor and one-third rich for generations. Unjust as it may be, the power of poor countries is limited." Ball had headed the U.S. delegation to the First Conference on Trade and Development in Geneva and had voted against nine of the twelve general principles approved by the conference for removing some of the handicaps of the underdeveloped countries in international trade.

Murder by poverty in Latin America is a secret affair. Every day, without making a sound, three Hiroshima bombs explode over communities that have become accustomed to suffering with clenched teeth. This systematic violence is not apparent but it is real and constantly increasing. Its holocausts are not made known in the sensational press but in Food and Agricultural Organization statistics. Ball says that it is still impossible to act with impunity because the poor cannot set off a world war, but the Imperium is worried. Unable to multiply the dinner, it does what it can to suppress the diners. "Fight poverty, kill a beggar!" some genius of black humor scrawled on a wall in La Paz.

In the eye of this hurricane 120 million children are stirring. Latin America's population grows as does no other. It has more than tripled in half a century. One child dies of disease or hunger every minute, but in the year 2000 there will be 650 million Latin Americans, half of whom will be under fifteen: a time bomb. Among the 280 million Latin Americans of today, 50 million are unemployed or underemployed and about 100 million are illiterate. Half of them live in crowded, unhealthy slums. New factories are being built in the privileged poles of development—São Paulo, Buenos Aires, Mexico City—but less and less labor is needed. The system did not foresee this small headache, this surplus of people. And people keep reproducing. They make love with enthusiasm and without precaution. Ever more people are left beside the road, without work in the countryside, where great estates reign with their vast extensions of land, without work in the city where the machine is king. The system vomits people. United States' missionaries sow pills, diaphrams, intrauterine devices, condoms, and marked calendars, but reap children. Latin American children obstinately continue getting born, claiming their natural right to a place in the sun in these magnificent lands which could give to all what is now denied to almost all.

The United States is more concerned than any other country with spreading and imposing family planning in the farthest outposts. Not only the government, but the Rockefeller and Ford Foundations as well, have nightmares about millions of children advancing like locusts over the horizon from the Third World. While intrauterine devices compete with bombs and machine guns to arrest the growth of the Vietnamese population, in Latin America it is more hygienic and effective to kill future guerrillas in the womb than in the mountains or the streets. Various U.S. missions have sterilized thousands of women in Amazonia, although this is the least populated habitable zone on our planet. Most Latin American countries have no real surplus of people. On the contrary, they have too few. Brazil has thirty-eight times fewer inhabitants per square mile than Belgium. Paraguay has forty-nine times fewer than England, Peru has thirty-two times fewer than Japan. Haiti and El Salvador, the human anthills of Latin America, have lower population densities than Italy. No less than half the territory of Bolivia, Brazil, Chile, Ecuador, Paraguay, and Venezuela has no inhabitants at all. No Latin American population grows less than Uruguay's—a country of old folk—yet no nation has taken such a beating in recent years, with a crisis that would seem to drag it into the last circle of Hell. Uruguay is empty, and its fertile lands could provide food for infinitely more people than those who now suffer in such penury. Thus, the pretexts invoked to limit population in Latin America are an insult to the intelligence. The real intentions anger us.

VIII

Women and Social Change

Social change for Latin American women has been a controversial issue during the last century. Women in the region initiated a campaign for equal rights in the late 1800s, but progress has been slow. The early generation of women's rights activists (mostly white, middle-class, educated, and urban) began a new political dialogue that included women and their concerns for the first time. These pioneers considered themselves to be part of a movement that transcended national boundaries. In their program, education in matters of marriage, finances, and family law was an especially important goal. Women's rights activists and their supporters in contemporary Latin America recognize the need to continue this struggle.

Recall for a moment that colonial Latin America was based on patriarchal foundations. Colonial women, except for widows and nuns, faced legal subordination to their fathers or their husbands. Moreover, they had limited options in life. The dictates of "honor" meant that "decent" women were always chaperoned when away from home. Yet poor women often had to work outside the house, sacrificing their honor to help feed their families. Middle- and upper-class women stayed home, made the parish church the center of their public lives, and protected their honor (which, by extension, was also the family's honor). Furthermore, despite its lofty promises about freedom and equality, Independence did little to transform the conditions of women's lives. Some historians have even argued that the creation of the independent Latin American republics did more harm than good to the cause of women's rights. These authors point to the reactionary gender content of Europe's Enlightenment (which gave birth to republican ideology), particularly its emphasis on the "domesticity" of women.

The early movements for women's rights thus challenged four centuries of patriarchy. To build movements on this issue in various nations, Latin American women, like their North American and European counterparts, raised fundamental questions about their roles in society and their relationships with men. In a word, the women's movement gave us a more complicated understanding of *gender*, meaning the extensive set of qualities associated with being male or female. Gender should always be seen in the proper historical context. Masculinity and femininity, the qualities of maleness and femaleness, are constantly shifting in our world. They change over time (consider the gender expectations placed on your grandparents' generation versus your own) and they change from one society to another (consider the recent debate about women and education in some Islamic countries). In other words, gender roles are socially constructed, which is to say that they are created by human history, not generated by the biology of our sexual differences. Today's turn toward gender studies adds depth to the goal of earlier historians, who wished to "restore women to history" by filling in an essentially blank space in the historical record.

To explore the problem of women and social change in modern Latin America, this chapter is organized chronologically, beginning with the origins of the women's movement across the region in the 1870s and concluding with a spokeswoman of 1990s Brazil. Along the way, perceptive students will note both continuities and changes in the movement as well as the remarkable ability of women to manipulate the traditional language, symbols, and images of Latin America's Roman Catholic heritage. Readers will also be introduced to the fascinating Evita Perón, who will reappear in chapter X as part of the problem of populism. Here, as a woman of tremendous power as well as contradictions, she serves as a guide to some of the extremes of gender identity in modern Latin America.

QUESTIONS FOR ANALYSIS

1. How far have Latin American women advanced—socially, economically, and politically—during the last century?
2. How have these advances been achieved? What sorts of strategies have women social reformers devised in Latin America?
3. What remains to be done if women are to become fully equal partners in society?

1. Women and Education in Latin America ～ Francesca Miller*

When Latin American women began to organize the campaign for women's rights in the nineteenth century, they started with female education. In this selec-

*From Francesca Miller, "Women and Education in Latin America," in *Latin American Women and the Search for Social Justice* (Hanover, NH: University Press of New

tion, historian Francesca Miller explains the early history and character of the Latin American women's movement. Since the colonial era, Miller argues, women's education had been controlled by the Church, but Independence (especially classical liberalism) introduced some changes to the status quo. Gradually, upper-class women and an increasing number of urban, middle-class women developed a reform agenda that put female education high on the list of priorities. Liberal governments across the region, Miller argues, had their own reasons to support some of these demands, which coincided with their own reform agendas. Note also the influence of the North American educational model.

The examination of the education of women in a given time and place provides a vivid indicator of what women's proper roles in the larger society are perceived to be and of how those roles—economic, intellectual, cultural, social, political—differ from or coincide with those of the women's male peers. First, to properly measure who in a society was educated and who was not, we must understand what was meant by education in a particular time and place. Then we may ask how access to special kinds of education differed for socioeconomic groups and for women and men.

Female teachers, who are overwhelmingly the teachers of young women in Latin America, come from two distinct traditions: that of the *normalista* (the women trained in normal, or teaching, schools) and nuns and lay members of Catholic female teaching orders. In each country the history of public female education is intimately linked with attempts to secularize, or modernize, the state. Thus, in mid-nineteenth-century Mexico, Benito Juárez's government, which sought to weaken the church, passed legislation providing for public secondary schools for girls; in Argentina, Domingo Sarmiento and the Liberals placed the training of female teachers near the top of their national agenda—a move that incited furious opposition from Catholic female teaching and nursing orders, who regarded education and health care as their domain.

In addition, there is a strong correlation between the advent of public female education, the appearance of *normalistas*, and the rise of feminism in certain Latin American nations. At the end of the nineteenth century in Argentina, Uruguay, Chile, Brazil, Mexico, and Cuba,

> it was the female schoolteachers who formed the nucleus of the first women's groups to articulate what may be defined as a feminist critique of society. Two factors are of great importance: First, the teachers represented a new group in Latin American society, the educated middle sector, which included skilled workers, clerks, and government employees,

England, 1992), 35–51. © 1991 by University Press of New England. Reprinted by permission of University Press of New England.

as well as educators, and they were well aware of their precarious social, economic, and legal status; second, these women were in touch with one another through their training institutions and through a number of *congresos femininos* which took place in this era from Mérida in the Yucatán to Buenos Aires, Argentina.

The story of the education of women in Latin America consists of three interwoven strands: first, the history of the idea of educating females; second, the debate over what the content of that education should be; and third, the establishment of educational institutions that admitted females.

The patterns for female education established in the colonial period, that of the private, usually Catholic, education of the daughters of the privileged classes and the moral and vocational instruction of the daughters of the poor, usually provided by Catholic charitable societies, persisted in nearly all areas of Latin America throughout the nineteenth century. The private education of the elite woman continues today in many countries; the vocational instruction of the lower-class woman is more apt to be under the auspices of the state.

The intellectual ferment that marked the period of the wars of independence included the discussion of the "rights of man," and Latin American women intellectuals joined their North American, British, and French sisters in expanding the debate to the rights of women. The passion for republican ideals and the increased secularization of the institutions of society, including schools and universities, raised the level of debate on the merits of female education to the national level in Argentina, Chile, Brazil, Uruguay, and Mexico. However, little was done to implement reform in the first half of the nineteenth century.

The wars of independence had a significant intellectual dimension, fostered in the secret meetings of the Freemasons and in the discussions of newly founded scientific societies. Although women were generally barred from these masculine enclaves, they did participate in the discussion of ideas and current politics in the salons of Mexico City, Lima, Caracas, and Rio de Janeiro. In the aftermath of the independence movements some changes occurred in formal education. The first was the decline in clerical control of education, a trend begun with the expulsion of the Jesuit teaching order in the 1760s and intensified in the secular climate of the wars of independence, a struggle in which the hierarchy of the colonial church sided with the mother country. Female teaching orders were not expelled from the colonies, but their political sympathies in general had also allied them with the Spanish and Portuguese loyalists; at the dawn of the national period, patriots looked to private finishing schools rather than convents for the instruction of their daughters.

A second trend was the establishment of national universities, a move in keeping with the ideals set forth in the constitutions of the new Spanish American republics. The universities at Buenos Aires (1821), Montevideo (1833), Santiago de Chile (1842), and those of El Salvador, Costa Rica, and Honduras date from this postrevolutionary period, as do the faculties of medicine and law in Brazil. In Mexico, which already possessed a central university, a number of state institutions, most of which offered a bachelor of law degree, were inaugurated. Women were excluded from these formal institutions of learning, which were intended as training grounds for the American-born male elite; however, the result of the broadening of the educated public, even though relatively slight, created a climate in which the subject of educating women could be broached.

Many of the constitutions of the newly independent countries contained articles that proclaimed the state's responsibility to create and support public education at all levels, as did Chile's (1833), which provided that "education is one of the subjects of primary importance of the states." The Brazilian constitution, drafted in 1822, declared the commitment of the nation to the education of children of both sexes, although this clause was deleted from the constitution imposed by the Emperor Dom Pedro in 1823. In Mexico the constitution of 1822 declared elementary education free, and a nascent public education system for the children of the poor was instituted, employing the "Lancastrian" method, where more advanced pupils taught younger students.

However, as has often been noted, these constitutions were more statements of the aspirations of the national leadership than programs that could be immediately put into practice. Even the long-established educational institutions struggled to survive in the political turmoil and economic disruption of the postwar period, which absorbed the attention of the leaders and the scarce resources of the societies.

At mid-century several patterns are visible in female education in the larger Latin American states. First, as had been true during the colonial era, most formal education had a significant religious content. Young women of the upper classes might be tutored at home or might attend a convent school, where the course of instruction was likely to stress accomplishment in the *belles artes*, such as an acquaintance with French, a little musical training in voice or piano, sketching, fine needlework, and religious instruction.

In addition, female charitable societies sponsored schools for female orphans and children of the poor. In Argentina all public education for girls was under the auspices of the Society of Beneficence. In Brazil in 1870, the Society for the Propagation of Instruction of the Working Classes celebrated the opening of a new school in Rio de Janeiro with premises spacious enough to allow separate classrooms for boys and for "the other sex" as girls are consistently referred to in the records. The school was free, and another charitable organization, Protectoresses of the Children of the Poor, provided uniforms and school materials. Similar societies, many with church affiliations, carried on comparable activities in Mexico, Colombia, Venezuela, and Peru. As was true in the colonial period, the charitable schools for girls emphasized training in household skills that would prepare them for domestic service.

The impetus for dramatic reform in the content, availability, and quality of female education—an impetus that in the twentieth century became the drive for universal education—came not from the socially elite women nor from the charitable schools they established but from the women of the emergent middle sectors. These reform-minded women were urban and tended to be the wives and daughters of professional men: lawyers, doctors, magistrates, professors. Their appearance in Buenos Aires, Santiago, Rio de Janeiro, and Mexico City in the 1860s and 1870s is directly proportionate to the degree of political stability and economic expansion attained by these societies by the late nineteenth century. Conversely, in the societies in which small oligarchies continued to exercise exclusive economic and political power and in areas where political instability was the norm, such as Bolivia, Ecuador, and the Central American states, there was little interest in educational reform.

The medium of expression for social criticism was the periodical. In Brazil, for example, as abolitionist and republican sentiments reached a crescendo in the 1870s, there were some 250 papers and journals in print, and though most of them issued from the major urban centers, no region was without its own. The numerous articles written by women represented the whole spectrum of Brazilian political thought, from monarchist to republican, and ranged in subject matter from romantic poetry to advice on childbirth; however, one theme was common to the women's articles: the commitment to education for women. Education is presented as the sine qua non, the road to greater control over their lives, in both the domestic and political spheres.

An excellent example of the spirit of the women's writings is evident in the following passage from *0 Sexo Feminino*, which was published intermittently in Rio de Janeiro between 1873 and 1889. It was dedicated to the principles of education for women and to the elimination of all forms of slavery in Brazil: "It is to you, *Os Senhores* [meaning men in general], that is owed our inadequacy; we have intelligence equal to yours, and if your pride has triumphed it is because our intelligence has been left unused. From this day we wish to improve our minds; and for better or worse we will transmit our ideas in the press, and to this end we have *O Sexo Feminino*, a journal absolutely dedicated to our sex and written only by us. *Avante, minhas patricias!* [Forward, my countrywomen!] The pen will be our weapon."

A brief profile of the editor of *O Sexo Feminino*, Dona Francisca Senhorinha da Motta Diniz, gives an idea of the social and economic background of these literate women. She was married to a lawyer and widowed at a young age; in 1873 she became the directress of a school for girls in the province of Minas Gerais, where she inaugurated her journal. In 1874 she moved to Rio de Janeiro, continued publishing *O Sexo Feminino*, and became headmistress of a secondary school for young women. Motta Diniz had numerous counterparts in Cuba, Mexico, Argentina, Chile, and Uruguay.

The efforts of these early reformers resulted in the establishment of a number of primary schools and a few secondary schools for young women, but the effect for most women in most places of Latin America was negligible. By and large, education remained within the domain of the church and was restricted to a small sector of the population, the majority of whom were male. The more important contribution of these early reformers was in creating a more receptive atmosphere toward the idea of educating women.

It was the introduction of the government-supported normal school that broadened and strengthened the move to educate a larger sector of the population, male and female. From their inception normal schools were overwhelmingly female institutions, although a few should be noted as being among the first coeducational institutions in Latin America. Many were reserved solely for women students (who were identified from the first as "natural teachers") so that girls from good families would be attracted to them. Normal school students were drawn from the newly emergent middle classes; in the societies of the Southern Cone many of them were the children of European immigrants. Teacher-training schools were also open to men, but young men of this emergent middle class had job opportunities in industry, commerce, banking, government, the military, higher education—realms from which young women were excluded. The normal schools offered girls a chance to acquire an education for themselves and a respectable, if poorly remunerated, profession teaching primary school children. In nations where this emergent class did not exist, such as Peru, normal school programs had few advocates and no constituency. The presence or absence of educational opportunities for women in a society provides a valid litmus test of the extent of social change that the society has experienced.

Several factors combined to favor these new secular institutions in societies where education had traditionally been under the auspices of the Catholic church. One was the exemplary pace of economic growth and industrialization being enjoyed by the United States, where public education was widespread. A second factor was the gradual change in public opinion about the value of an educated society, male and female. Less tangible but significant was the belief that the New World experiments in political democracy, whatever their present imperfections, offered the opportunity to build better societies than had previously existed and that an educated citizenry was essential to the realization of this ideal. Although there were parallel movements in Chile, Uruguay, Brazil, and Mexico, the most famous normal school program was carried out in Argentina. In 1870, President Domingo Sarmiento founded Argentina's first public, coeducational normal school at Paraná. Sarmiento's enthusiasm for educational reform influenced the development of public education, not only in Argentina but throughout Spanish America. His program was modeled on what he had observed in the United States. The school system was to encompass kindergarten through secondary school, and the curriculum, which was entirely secular, would emphasize physical fitness, responsible citizenship, vocational instruction, and skills in reading, writing, and arithmetic. The teaching staff would be drawn from the newly established normal schools, which he envisioned as the keystone of the projected public system. In a singular effort to assure a strong beginning for the system, Sarmiento recruited young women schoolteachers from the Midwestern United States, and between 1869 and 1886 some sixty-five graduates of normal schools in Minnesota and upstate New York went to teach in Argentina. Their dedication to and influence on the fledgling system was considerable; through their efforts and the efforts of those they trained, Argentina's literacy rate rose from less than one-third of the population in 1869 to more than two-thirds in 1914.

---

2. Women's Reform Issues in Late Nineteenth-Century Peru and Mexico ～ Carolina Freyre de Jaimes and *Violetas del Anáhuac**

The women's rights activists of late nineteenth-century Latin America advanced a broad agenda of reforms. The following selections provide three examples of this agenda. The first two, published in the Lima newspaper El Correo del Perú, *were written by the reformer Carolina Freyre de Jaimes, whose articles appeared in newspapers in several other Latin American countries. The third comes from an elite Mexican women's magazine,* Violetas del Anáhuac. *In all three cases, female authors pointed to the need for specific social changes. Note that the model for these changes, particularly in Freyre's articles, is either North American or northern European. Apart from the specific demands they expressed, what*

---

*From *El Correo del Perú* (Lima, 1871 and 1872), trans. Gertrude Yeager, and *Violetas del Anáhuac* (Mexico City, 1889), trans. Daniel Castro. Special thanks to Gertrude Yeager for bringing this material to the previous edition.

makes these selections significant is the way their authors used elements of liber-
alism—such as anticlericalism and state activism—to challenge Latin American
social traditions. Finally, students should be aware of the limited nature of the
demands in this early stage of the women's movement. While Freyre wants to
change the way Peruvian marriages are conducted, she still sees marriage as the
cornerstone of society and women as the "messengers of civilization."

Education and Women (1872)

Women have been admitted to the University of Vermont, all of its classes, and others in Zurich have become doctors. What do you think, ladies? Woman is weak by nature and soft by character? A woman doctor an absurdity? Education and women have never been incompatible ideas to me. Some believe that to change the poetic mission of women for the prosaic occupation of men may be ridiculous.

But there are places where women exercise influence. In the United States they are teachers, journalists, and are demanding the vote. They say in Chile that women administer the post office and telegraph. We need to raise woman's intelligence to the level of men through education or she will continue to be housebound.

Women are those who are called on to regenerate society; they are messengers of civilization. Lima, a great South American city, presents a very sad contrast from the moral perspective because its women lack education. It is available to those with money while ignorance reigns among the masses. The schools offer a rich and varied curriculum for the elites and intellectual misery for the more numerous poor. To form a free society we must elevate women, amplify their educational opportunities, give them professions if they need employment, and inculcate habits of work, sobriety, and good customs.

The Problem with Marriage (1871)

Marriage suffers because the Roman Catholic Church has the poor and incorrect view of women (who were associated with evil). God also created a need for the family. To quote Saint Paul, he who does not give his daughter in marriage is he who would not improve himself. Marriage is necessary according to positivism and progress because it represents the basis of social order. Marriage is not only enjoyment and pleasure, although without sexual attraction it could not continue to function. It is the fulfillment of God's will that marriage is vital to social organization, to educate, to form an honorable society. Marriage is based on intimacy and identification, confidence, and reciprocal caring.

A man who does not have a legal capacity to marry will look for other forms of diversion. He may become a seducer. He would not love truly because he who dishonors does not love truly.

Marriage is a refuge for children and a relief from obligatory celibacy. It is the behavior of married couples which discredits marriage. The failure to complete vows tends to pervert the institution; lack of love is nothing more than mere selfishness. Adultery breaks vows and divides one flesh, but its greatest offense is that it kills love.

People who do not marry are egoists, mere passengers through life, incapable of understanding love and commitment.

Against Drunkenness (1889)

One of the initiatives that should be adopted in Mexico is the creation, at least in the main urban centers, of workshops where journeymen who are prevented from entering their regular place of employment because of tardiness or any other reason can go and spend the day productively. In Mexico it is well known that the workers whose workday is reduced for any reason spend the time going to different *pulquerías* [bars where *pulque* alcohol was served]. We believe that the rules and regulations about to be adopted in some European countries could not be more appropriate, and the following ones could be easily adopted in Mexico:

1. The authorization to open a place to sell alcoholic beverages can only be given to people of proven morality, and the locale must meet certain conditions of hygiene, as well as good light and ventilation;
2. The drinking and consumption of spirits by children and young people under sixteen years of age shall be forbidden in these establishments;
3. There should be official vigilance of these establishments and the drinks being sold therein;
4. [There should be] active vigilance to avoid clandestine sales, particularly in second-class establishments; and
5. Drunkenness must be considered a crime and should not be invoked as an extenuating circumstance, under any circumstances, in the commission of a crime.

Do not label us as pretentious, if we add our weak voices to the universal uproar being raised against such a degrading vice. We are only guided by the desire to see women suffer less, because they are the targets of the excesses of their husbands or their children. Let us take the case of the worker's wife who anxiously awaits her spouse to come to the house with a week's worth of wages. In the course of the day, she will build innumerable castles in the air. She will envision thousands of projects which she will rework constantly to make the money go further. She will buy shoes for the oldest child, who is barefoot and is already going to school, and the littlest one needs a coat, because he is cold crawling on the floor (the mother cannot pick him up because of her household chores). The husband desperately needs another shirt, and whatever is left over will be used for the limited weekly budget of the home. For herself? . . . Oh, well! Next time. The hour when the husband normally comes home rolls around. He does not come . . . at half past . . . six o'clock; she feeds the children and puts them to bed, more than anything to avoid the spectacle that the father will provide soon, because undoubtedly he will be drunk, scandalously drunk. It was payday, after all!

Finally the hour arrives, no longer anxiously awaited but feared, when the head of the household appears, but in such a condition. My God! The wife does not dare say a word for fear of unleashing a storm. If she asks for the money, aside from justifying the use he found for it, he will argue that "this is why I work," and it is very much *his* to spend with his friends or in whatever way he wants.

The hapless woman can hardly find a voice to ask him if he wants to eat. He does not even answer. He throws himself on the bed and begins to shake the whole house with his loud snoring. The next day, he gives his wife what remains of his salary and leaves as if nothing had happened, as if he had fulfilled his duty as a husband and as a father.

The next Saturday, there will be a repeat performance until the wife is driven to the limit of her patience, and she will demand with harsh words. Then he will abuse her, because he has spent the week working like a dog, and he is not allowed even a single moment of leisure, and they want him to be there under all circumstances. . . . Come on!

There is a different kind of drunk. These are the middle-class ones in frock coats and top hats. Pity the clothes, as the poor would say. These gentlemen do not give a plugged nickel about the death of their ascendants and descendants when they have a bottle and a glass in front of them. These are the ones who drink everything from maguey juice to hard liquor.

---

3. The Lady of Hope and the Woman of the Black Myth ~ Julie M. Taylor*

María Eva Duarte de Perón ("Evita" to those who adored her) is one of the most controversial women in modern Latin American history. Fifty years after her

*From Julie M. Taylor, *Eva Perón: The Myths of a Woman* (Chicago: University of Chicago Press, 1979), 75–81. Reprinted by permission of the University of Chicago Press.

death from cancer, she is still the object of both praise and scorn in her native Argentina. Born into a poor, provincial family, Eva Duarte became a successful radio actress as a teenager. She then began a romantic liaison with politically ambitious Colonel Juan D. Perón. Eventually they married and Juan was elected president of Argentina. As First Lady, Eva was extremely active. She helped women secure the right to vote, organized the Peronist Feminist Party (to make sure that they voted for Juan Perón), created and administered the charitable Eva Perón Foundation, and made countless speeches on behalf of her husband's government. These activities resulted in the controversy surrounding her. In the following selection, anthropologist Julie M. Taylor presents two competing versions of Eva Perón's life and character. On one hand is the "Lady of Hope," the positive version promoted by her admirers and supporters. On the other hand is the "Woman of the Black Myth," the negative version put forth by her critics and detractors. Students should pay particular attention to the values used to judge Evita—either positive or negative—and recall that the anthropologist is expressing the judgment of people on the street rather than her own.

The Lady of Hope

Claiming that she knew nothing about politics, Eva found in social work a sphere for which her womanly intuition and emotional life qualified her perfectly. She dedicated much of this work to children, as would be expected from such an ideally feminine, thus deeply maternal, woman. A woman may involve herself in any area of activity to which her man directs her, but her place and the function for which she was born are in the home. Neither Eva's childlessness nor her death affects this theme in any way. Eva Perón had no sons and daughters of her own; she was mother to the children of Argentina. More than that, she was mother of the nation as a whole, particularly to the common people and the poor and needy of Argentina. It was maternal devotion that motivated her attendance on the poor, her work to raise money for her cause, her conferences with governors of the provinces, and her meetings with labor delegations. In grateful response, popular Peronism dubbed her its Lady of Hope and Good Fairy.

Not even the invitation of the Spanish government to visit her nation's Motherland could make Eva forget the workers and their cause. She continued to stress her interest in social work and to distribute alms throughout her journey. But the deeds of the Good Fairy of the poor now had to share the spotlight with the successful social contacts of the traveling First Lady. The Spaniards welcomed her with protocol usually reserved for royalty. Soon she had become as much a favourite with the Spanish aristocrats as with the hundreds of thousands of anonymous Spaniards who lined the streets to catch sight of her. In Italy, too, she fascinated both the crowds and high society. Only her decision to change her itinerary prevented her arrival in London from being, as sumptuous preparations for it promised, one of the most important events of high society's year. The innumerable rooms of a mansion in the heart of the London frequented by English aristocracy awaited her in vain.

Europe, even France, the supreme authority on matters of feminine taste, marveled at the beauty of Argentina's emissary of good will. She encountered admiration everywhere, confirming her position as a paragon of elegance. Her followers memorized the details of her every change of dress—the fittings, the designers, the gold lamé, the hats, mantillas, even a tiara—and never tired of the rainbow of images that spread over the media of the time and continued glowing in the huge full-coloured photographs of magazines still dedicated, twenty-five years later, exclusively to her.

But Eva did not spend all her time dispensing charity, making calls, and planning her wardrobe. She made a point of visiting museums and attending cultural events, appreciating deeply these works and performances, which she went out of her way to see. As always properly hesitant to express inexpert opinions on politics, Eva Perón expatiated on her preferences in music and literature.

From her triumphal tour of Europe, the First Lady returned to throw herself immediately into her campaign for women's suffrage in Argentina. A week after her arrival in Buenos Aires, she directed an open letter to Argentinian women from the front pages of the newspapers, announcing her plans and the needs for their fulfillment. Eva explicitly differentiated her movement from feminist movements in other, especially Anglo-Saxon, countries, where the Peronists felt that feminism had become a form of competition with men. Eva and Peronism rejected earlier Argentinian campaigns on behalf of women's civil rights as copies of foreign ideas, considering them not only mistaken in content, but the result of ingrained social snobbery and cultural imperialism.

The virtue of the Peronist woman lay in never aspiring to supplant the opposite sex. Rather, Peronist feminism represented an effort to take advantage of women's own special identity and talents in order better to fill their particular place in the world. Peronist women carefully emphasized the point that they had no intention of denying their domestic nature now that they had obtained full citizenship.

Eva Perón's position in the nation exemplified the position of the ideal woman in the home. She, on her level, like the housewife on hers, assumed a role as the chief agent responsible for the transmission of the values which uphold society as a whole. Both carried out functions broader than spiritually and physically nutritive ones. The watchfulness of the Peronist woman over domestic economy and morality extended beyond the home to become one of her special political functions: it was she who, qualified by her feminine nature, could best take up a unique watch against treach-ery within the Peronist movement and threats arising from without. Evita, chief protector of the movement, kept watch as well over its leader and her husband, Juan Perón himself. He, realizing her importance as his shield against betrayal and evil, acknowledged that "Eva . . . with her marvelous judgment has been the guardian of my life, confided to her intelligence and loyalty."

With her successes in Europe and in the campaign for women's rights behind her, Eva's activities grew in importance and number. Her influence depended on her all-enveloping aura more than on specific actions affect-ing particular political situations, despite the fact that the Peronist press of the time offered reports on her activities or particulars of personages, organizations, schedules, gifts, and honours. Eva defined the tone of Peronism as a movement even more than as a party.

As she wore herself out in her office day by day, the symptoms of her final disease began to appear, bearing witness to the gruelling sacrifice that Eva insisted on offering up for her people. "Poor thing," stated a Peronist, referring to the widely known fact that sexual relations were impossible for Eva for two years before her death; "she gave up even her happiness as a woman for us." In her attempts to continue working through her long illness, the Lady of Hope was making her conscious and voluntary sacrifice.

Her renunciation of the vice-presidency formed part of this process. In the mass demonstration of the Cabildo Abierto, the Open Town Hall, Eva's people and her party offered her the highest honour which they could bestow. When she refused this honour, her disappointed followers dedicated the nearby anniversary of October 17 to her in recognition of her selfless renunciation. The words "*Santa Evita*" appeared for the first time in the press in connection with this celebration.

Her death, which loomed before her immediately after the Renuncia-tion, made her martyrdom incontrovertible. Her brokenhearted followers responded to the dead Eva in the only way appropriate to her saintly act: they worshipped her as a saint. They erected altars to her; offered her prayers; called her their Spiritual Chief, Saint Eva, and Spiritual Protector of the Argentine University; believed in her miraculous powers; and waited for her return.

The Woman of the Black Myth

"That woman," "*esa mujer*," was born in the ill-disguised brothel of her mother. During a childhood and adolescence spent helping to run and maintain her family's "boarding house" or "*pensión*," Eva early began to attract the attention of passing clients as well as the townspeople in general. Already aggressive and ambitious at fifteen, she linked herself to the troupe of a tango singer whom she had probably seduced, and travelled to Buenos Aires to establish herself as a prostitute. Her professed occupation on the stage was no more than a disguise of her real activities. The capital offered Eva a whirlwind of affairs with actors, producers, industrialists, and political figures. She possessed a coarse, dark attraction, a typically provincial prettiness. But beyond this, she demonstrated sexual appetites and habits that contributed spectacularly to her notoriety. Exploiting both her liaisons and the special talents that attracted them, Eva was frantically scrambling up the social ladder when she met Juan Domingo Perón and immediately moved in with him. Recognizing his rising star, she held on to this catch—with success which amazed even her: anti-Peronists say that when Perón proposed marriage, Evita Duarte was so astounded that she nearly fell out of bed.

Sometimes the account differs. Eva could magnetize Perón because she, like him, lacked sexuality. Either she was frigid and he, impotent, or both valued power over all. Even sexual attraction became unimportant beside this all-consuming passion. Their distorted values led them to center their lives entirely around the interests of their regime, to the extent that they did not sleep together—Perón, the military man, rising early, and Eva, the bohemian, retiring as he rose.

However she attracted him, Eva Duarte married Juan Perón and immediately began to wear the pants in their relationship. Unlike women such as Eleanor Roosevelt of the United States or Madame [Vincent] Auriol of France who knew how to play "the role of second violin which every woman of real tact assumes," Eva took up the first violin or even the baton of the orchestra. She contrasted dramatically with the ideal wife who "has neither youth, nor fur coats, nor [knows] how to harangue over the radio, but knows how to knit, cooks well, darns the socks and bakes pastries which make you lick your fingers." This perfect wife satisfies any man simply by being "a woman who is quiet, intuitive, and who does not make speeches."

The dominance of this upstart soon extended beyond her marriage. She involved herself in all aspects of government. Perón meekly endorsed her growing interference by asserting that wherever Eva appeared, she represented his own presence and carried his authority. The sun of a radiant Eva began to eclipse Juan's fading moon. Eva was converting the nation into a matriarchy.

Inexorably, she stretched her web of control over the other men in her husband's regime. Some she dominated through the fascination of her own eroticism or through secret sexual practices. Others, Eva Perón castrated— sometimes figuratively and sometimes literally: she dealt with her own underlings by rendering them political eunuchs, and she tortured her opponents with electric shocks that left them impotent. Eva took direct responsibility for the castration of rebel leaders and others, making flamboyant displays of her satisfaction with her deed. She kept a glass receptacle preserving the testicles of her victims in the office where she leaned, young and exquisitely clad in her Parisian suits, over a desk to attend the needs recited by ministers, union delegations, and the poor alike.

Meanwhile, the new First Lady attempted in vain to shoulder her way into social circles closed to her. When her efforts failed, she determined to outdo the aristocratic women who would not accept her. Her envy of these inaccessible social circles had decided her marriage to Perón, a rising young military figure. Now that she was First Lady, her bitter resentfulness intensified. It sent her to Europe; drove her to establish the vast Eva Perón Foundation; goaded her into the acquisition of houses, jewels, and clothes; and, finally, kindled her frustrated appeal to the masses for the recognition denied her by high society.

Early in her husband's regime, she had attended an exclusive fashion show in Harrod's department store, only to be ignored or, according to some accounts, to be left alone with her small party of friends as the distinguished ladies swept out. The same women refused her the traditional honor bestowed upon Presidents' wives, the office of president of their charity organization, the Society of Beneficence. Their acts only exacerbated Eva's long-standing resentment towards those whose social position she could never attain. This rancor became unbearable and prodded her into expressing it in every aspect of her life, accounting for most of her projects; she knit even the beneficial works of her charity into her elaborate plots of retaliation.

Her petty desire for vengeance far outweighed any political convictions or motivations Eva might have claimed. An anti-Peronist with a nondescript surname would run no risk from the same activities for which Eva would jail anyone with one of the aristocratic surnames of Buenos Aires. It was Eva Perón who imprisoned upper-class women and adolescents accused of demonstrating against the government. Knowing that this would inflict greater cruelty on the sheltered members of the upper classes than on middle-class anti-Peronists, Eva jailed the women with prostitutes and drug addicts. In some cases, the First Lady threatened to interfere with the funerals of older women of the aristocracy, preventing their relatives from burying them with their illustrious forebears. However, if the ladies in question invited her to tea in their homes, she promised that the funeral plans would go through.

Eva's drive to obtain the marks of her enemies' social status found its most complete and extravagant expression in her tour of Europe. However, as would have been expected, the lamentable cultural deprivation inherent in her disreputable origins foiled her prodigious efforts.

On her wardrobe alone, in her attempts to surpass her enemies, she lavished millions of dollars. Before Eva's trip to Europe, an anti-Peronist took the trouble to count her different outfits and reported to the press that during the 270 days between June 4, 1946, and April 30, 1947, the First Lady had donned 306 dresses.

Original models began to arrive by official airplane from Paris. Some of these bouffant, gala gowns occupied an entire plane, which the Argentinian government sent to France and brought back at public expense, containing the dress arranged on a solitary standing mannequin.

All of this could not change the Eva who had peered out of one of her first publicity posters, smiling under "a funny little hat from the movies." This Evita, shamelessly and gaudily voluptuous, lurked forever behind the later, more streamlined image that diet and expensive clothes created. At the time of her European trip she still revealed her own true penchant for a wardrobe that was distinctly Hollywood-esque, her taste expressing itself in elaborate falls and rolls of blonde hair and in an addiction to fur wraps even in the hottest Spanish and Italian weather. Even when her clothes lost the stamp of her early career, she could not hide the tell-tale signs of her vulgar origins: her wide hips and thick ankles.

---

4. Peronist Feminism in Argentina ～ Eva Perón*

Eva Perón's political activities, as we saw in document 3, inspired powerful feelings among Argentines. She never flinched when it came to putting herself on public view. During her years as First Lady, she not only gave numerous speeches on behalf of her husband's government but also had her views on Peronism and Argentine society published for all to read. The following selection is taken from My Mission in Life, *a collection of short essays covering various aspects of Peronism, particularly with regard to the role of women in the movement. Two passages have been chosen to indicate the complicated, seemingly contradictory nature of Peronist feminism (at least as it was articulated by the self-proclaimed leader of the Peronist feminist movement). While Argentine women are being called to action, their efforts are still firmly grounded in the traditional feminine ideal of self-sacrifice.*

Women and My Mission

My work in the woman's movement began and grew, just like my work of social service and my trade-union activities, little by little, and more by force of circumstances than through any decision of mine.

*From Eva Perón, *My Mission in Life*, trans. Ethel Cherry (New York: Vantage Press, 1953), 181–83, 205-6.

This may not be what many imagine to be the case, but it is the truth. It would be more romantic or more poetic or more literary, and more like fiction, if I said, for example, that all I do now I had felt intuitively . . . as a vocation or a special decree of fate.

But such is not the case.

All I brought by way of preparation to the scene of these struggles were those same feelings which had made me think of the problems of the rich and the poor.

But nothing more.

I never imagined it would fall to my lot someday to lead a woman's movement in my country, and still less a political movement.

Circumstances showed the way.

Ah! But I did not remain in my comfortable position of Eva Perón. The path which opened up before my eyes was the path I took if by it I could help [Juan] Perón's cause a little—the cause of the people.

I imagine many other women have seen the paths I pursue long before I did.

The only difference between them and me is that they stayed behind and I started. Actually, I should confess that if I girded myself for a struggle it was not for myself but for him . . . for Perón!

He encouraged me to rise.

He took me out of "the flock of sparrows."

He taught me my first steps in all my undertakings.

Afterward I never lacked the powerful and extraordinary stimulus of his love.

I realize, above all, that I began my work in a woman's movement because Perón's cause demanded it.

It all began little by little.

Before I realized it I was already heading a woman's political movement . . . and, with it, had to accept the spiritual leadership of the women of my country.

This caused me to meditate on woman's problems. And, more than that, to feel them, and to feel them in the light of the doctrine with which Perón was beginning to build a New Argentina.

I remember with what extraordinary fondness, as friend and master, General Perón explained to me innumerable women's problems in my country and in the world.

In these conversations I again became aware of the kindliness of his nature.

Millions of men have faced, as he has faced, the ever more acute problem of woman's role in humanity in this afflicted century; but I think very few of them have stopped, like Perón, to penetrate it to its depths.

In this, as in everything, he showed me the way.

The world's feminists will say that to start a woman's movement in this way is hardly feministic . . . to start by recognizing to a certain extent the superiority of a man!

However, I am not interested in criticisms.

Also, recognizing Perón's superiority is a different matter. Besides . . . it is my intention to write the truth.

Women and Action

I firmly believe that woman—contrary to the common opinion held by men—lives better in action than in inactivity.

I see this every day in my work of political service and social welfare.

The reason is very simple. Man can live exclusively for himself. Woman cannot.

If a woman lives for herself, I think she is not a woman, or else she cannot be said to live. That is why I am afraid of the "masculinization" of women.

When that occurs, women become even more egoistic than men, because we women carry things to greater extremes than men.

A man of action is one who triumphs over all the rest. A woman of action is one who triumphs for the rest. Isn't this a great difference?

Woman's happiness is not her own happiness, but that of others.

That is why, when I thought of my feminist movement, I did not want to take woman out of what is so much her own sphere. In politics men seek their own triumph.

Women, if they did that, would cease to be women.

I have not wanted women to look to themselves in the woman's party . . . but rather that right there they should serve others in some fraternal and generous form.

Woman's problem everywhere is always the deep and fundamental problem of the home.

It is her great destiny—her irremediable destiny.

She needs to have a home; when she cannot make one with her own flesh, she does so with her soul, or she is not a woman!

Well, for this very reason I have wanted my party to be a home that each basic unit should be something like a family . . . with its great loves and its small disagreements, with its sublime fruitfulness and its interminable laboriousness.

I know that in many places I have already attained this. Above all, where the women I have appointed are most womanly!

More than political action, the feminist movement has to develop social service. Precisely because social service is something that we women have in the blood!

Our destiny and our vocation is to serve others, and that is social service.
Not that other "social life" . . . which is contrary to all service!

---

5. Women's Reform Issues in Late Twentieth-Century Brazil ∼ Benedita da Silva*

The right to education, to work, to vote: according to Benedita da Silva, these have been the achievements of the Latin American women's movements. But, Da Silva adds, there is still a long way to go before the rights of women can be said to be truly equal to those of men. Da Silva should know. As a black woman in a country where blackness is still a disadvantage, she once worked as a domestic servant. However, as the first Afro-Brazilian woman to serve in her country's Senate, Da Silva has seen the full range of late-twentieth-century Brazilian social life. Her experiences have led her to continue the struggle begun more than a century earlier by women such as Carolina Freyre de Jaimes. Specifically, as she explains in the following selection, Da Silva has promoted legislation to elimi-nate the most abusive aspects of sexism in Brazil. Her words remind us that double standards, sexual and otherwise, remain a troubling aspect of contempo-rary life in Latin America.

Back in sixteenth-century Brazil, the Jesuit priest Antonio Vieira preached that a woman should only leave her home three times in her life—when she was baptized, married, and buried.

Since then, Brazilian women have certainly gotten out of the house. We've struggled for the right to education, and today 60 percent of university graduates are women. We've struggled for the right to work, and today almost half of the workforce are women. We've struggled for the right to vote, and today we are even running for office and winning elections.

Women in Brazil have come a long way, but not far enough. We're still relegated to less prestigious professions—teachers, secretaries, cleri-cal and domestic workers—and we earn half the pay that men do. We may be winning elections, but only 6 percent of the congressional representa-tives are women.

While few men today dare to openly defend the idea that women are inferior, sexism still permeates our society. In the media, women are por-trayed as sexual objects and their bodies are used to sell all kinds of prod-

*From Benedita da Silva, *Benedita da Silva: An Afro-Brazilian Woman's Story of Politics and Love*, as told to Medea Benjamin and Maisa Mendonça (Oakland, CA: Institute for Food and Development Policy, 1997), 103–9. Reprinted by permission of Food First Books.

ucts. Sometimes sexist attitudes appear in more subtle ways—disguised in our schoolbooks or in the words of popular songs. The message is that girls should be well behaved, cute, and sweet, and boys should be smart, sharp, and competitive.

Gender roles are not natural or determined by biological differences. They're socially constructed roles, and vary according to the culture and the time period. Intuitively, I have always questioned these stereotypes since the time I was a child. I liked to build my own toys and do the same things boys did. I played marbles. I climbed trees to pick fruit. I was one of the few girls who worked in the market.

But many women are influenced by the stereotypes promoted by the media. They obsess about their weight—going on crash diets, then gaining the weight back and dieting again. I don't worry about my weight. I'm not going to kill myself because someone thinks I should be skinny. Plus, who says that fat people are ugly? I also don't kill myself doing exercises that are too hard on my body. For me, taking care of my body means taking a shower. I love taking hot showers; that's my kind of exercise.

I'm not interested in looking like everyone else. I refuse to buy certain clothes just because they're in style. I'm also not the type of woman who worries about wrinkles and is afraid of getting old. I'm proud of being a grandmother. I enjoy my age, I don't try to hide anything.

Many times women in positions of power feel they have to act like men to gain respect. We have an expression to describe someone who is assertive. We say they *"põe a pau na mesa,"* which literally means they "put their pecker on the table." I consider myself a feminist, but I don't want to have to act like a man to gain respect. I believe I can be assertive and a true feminist without losing my femininity.

I also don't think that feminist women have to be stiff and hide their emotions. Strong women are women who know how to laugh and cry, women who love with passion, women who nurture. I'm an extremely warm and caring lover. I have a very strong personality but in the privacy of my own home, I express all my feelings, including those considered by some to be a sign of weakness.

I know how to flirt and use my charm. I like to dress well and I know that men admire well-dressed women. I admire men who look sharp, too. Sometimes when I see an attractive man, I think of the romantic song "Girl from Ipanema" that goes, *Olha que coisa mais linda, mais cheia de graça*—Look at that beautiful thing, how full of charm. . . . I certainly appreciate a handsome man, a muscular body. But that doesn't mean that I would ever use a man as a sexual object, like men do to women. The most important thing in a relationship is to feel an intellectual affinity. When that happens, that first impression based solely on physical attraction becomes secondary.

And just because I look at other men doesn't mean I'm unfaithful to Pitanga. I'm faithful to him because I respect and trust him. For me, fidelity has to be a mutual agreement. I can't stand this double standard where people think it's acceptable for men to cheat on their partners, but if women do, it's a big scandal. If it's adultery when a woman sleeps with another man, then it's adultery when a man sleeps with another woman.

In Brazil, the concept of "conjugal fidelity" is actually written into the Civil Code. It's supposed to work both ways, but in reality it only applies to women and so it becomes an instrument to preserve male domination. That's why I'm trying to change the wording of the Civil Code, eliminating any reference to "conjugal fidelity" and replacing it with "mutual respect and consideration." The latter is a more advanced concept and reflects women's struggle for juridical equality. It also reflects my own feelings that the most important element for a good partnership is not fidelity but mutual respect.

You wouldn't believe the controversy that my suggested revision provoked. Some men in Congress were scandalized and said, "If you're going to get rid of fidelity, you might just as well get rid of marriage." They accused me of advocating free love and attacking marriage as an institution. But I really believe that fidelity in marriage should come from reciprocal love, not from the imposition of punitive laws or obsolete rules that are only applied to women.

I have a very liberated attitude when it comes to sex. I always talked to my children about everything. When they wanted to know how babies were born, my husband didn't know what to tell them, so I explained everything. I gave them all kinds of information about sex. One time my son came home with gonorrhea and my husband was horrified. I was the one who had to take care of him, and I had no problem with that. I also don't have a hang-up about my body or nudity. Even today, I take off my clothes in front of my children.

I never put pressure on my daughter to be a virgin when she married, even though that kind of pressure was very common when I was growing up. Most parents were really uptight. They were constantly fretting over whether their daughters "*pularam a cerca*"—jumped the fence. If the girls got caught with their boyfriends, the parents would create a big scandal and sometimes even throw their daughters out of the house. My parents had this type of mentality and my sisters suffered because of it. One of my sisters became a prostitute and had to leave the house. I felt sorry for her, and we continued to have a good relationship.

Although I've always tried to pass these liberal values on to my children, my daughter Nilcea is more conservative than I am. My granddaughter Ana Benedita, however, takes after me. Nilcea says, "This child is going to give us a headache." And I say, "Of course she is, *ela vai botar pra quebrar*—she's going to drive us crazy." She's already very assertive, and I'm sure she's going to be a very independent woman. But I want her to go out in the world with her eyes open to the difficulties that women face.

One of the real difficulties that many women confront is sexual harassment. Sure, it's nice to feel desired by a man. A sexual advance, if it's done respectfully, makes you feel good and is simply part of the game between the sexes. I'm not offended if a man admires me sexually, but I won't accept an aggressive come-on. I know how to throw a bucket of cold water on a guy's advances when I have to, but not all women are able to protect themselves. Many times women have to perform sexual favors in order to get a job. And to get ahead professionally, they have to put up with come-ons and lewd behavior from their bosses.

Sexual harassment not only exists in the workplace, but any place where men and women get together. When men first look at women, they're usually undressing them with their eyes. Men feel powerful through sex, especially if they have sex with a lot of different women.

Many men want to have their *"mulher de casa"*—woman at home—and *"mulher da rua"*—woman on the street. The prostitute is seen as someone with whom they can be more sexually intimate and get greater sexual pleasure. Their wives are expected to be more modest. Taboos and dogmas don't allow the wives to fully explore their sexuality. This pushes the men to play out their sexual fantasies with prostitutes, whom they feel they can exploit in whatever ways they please.

Black women bear the brunt of this exploitation, particularly when it comes to white men. There is this impression that black women are *"mais quentes"*—hotter, so men feel free to exploit them more. Black women are considered more pleasing sexually, but these men usually don't want to make a commitment to them. Black women are considered good enough for screwing, but not good enough to marry.

These sexist attitudes lead to one of the most serious problems in Brazil today, which is violence against women. When I was a federal deputy, I helped organize a special Congressional commission to investigate this issue, and we were shocked by our findings. We discovered that over 300 cases of violence against women were reported every day. In fact, we discovered that Brazil was the world champion in terms of violence against women!

IX

Populism and the Working Class

The twentieth century was a period of great challenges to the traditional societies of Latin America. In its opening decades, profound changes occurred throughout the region as middle-class women and people of color pressed their claims for full and equal citizenship. As the century progressed, yet another new social group emerged to challenge the guardians of social order: the industrial working class.

Workers had always been the majority in Latin American societies. They toiled on the haciendas and plantations, labored in the mines and on the docks, sweated in the workshops, and moved merchandise in the streets and markets. But beginning in the twentieth century, a new type of worker was being created by the industrialization of the region's economies. This new, industrial working class was different. For one thing, these men and women were found primarily in large factories that required expensive machinery and produced vast quantities of manufactured goods. For another, such factories tended to be located in or near large cities, leading to an increased concentration of workers in those areas. Given the urban organization of Latin American industrial development, it is no wonder that the new labor force possessed greater class consciousness than any previous one in Latin American history.

This chapter, in examining the political and social consequences that accompanied Latin America's industrial growth, focuses primarily on a political phenomenon known as populism. In the 1930s and 1940s varieties of populism also appeared in Europe and the United States. At the core of twentieth-century populism was a relationship between a charismatic leader and the industrial working class. Benito Mussolini's Fascist movement in Italy and Franklin Roosevelt's New Deal in the United States both had populist aspects. What linked these movements together was the worldwide crisis of capitalism that began with the Great Depression of 1929.

The Great Depression devastated national economies that depended on international trade. Nowhere was this shock worse than in Latin America, whose countries were completely dependent on the exportation of basic raw materials. As markets for exports shriveled, Latin American economies were thrown into free fall. One example of this trend occurred in the port of São Paulo, where tons of handpicked coffee beans had to be burned for lack of buyers. To deal with the impact of the depression, Latin America needed to transform its entire approach to economic development, but such a transformation also required a radical change in political leadership.

Beginning in the 1930s (and carrying through until the 1950s), effective assaults on the political power of the oligarchs were carried out by populist leaders such as Juan Perón of Argentina and Lázaro Cárdenas of Mexico (both already mentioned) as well as Getúlio Vargas of Brazil and Jorge Eliécer Gaitán of Colombia. Populist leaders often came from relatively humble origins, had a background in the military, and knew how to stir a crowd of workers with rhetoric based on nationalism, class struggle, and traditional gender relationships. In their speeches, the populists created opportunities for workers to identify with the nation in ways that would have been unimaginable only decades earlier. Populists blasted the corruption and privilege of traditional oligarchies closely linked to the shattered import-export system. By equating the oligarchs with the economic devastation brought about by the Great Depression, populists rode to electoral victory.

Once in office, the populists attempted to implement a set of core policies aimed at the further industrial and social development of their countries. On the economic front, they pursued import-substitution industrialization (ISI), a key element of twentieth-century Latin American nationalism. Aggressively protecting fledgling national industries, populists ignored the tenets of laissez-faire liberalism. They also promoted state control of vital sectors of the economy. Many foreign investors lost capital in the "nationalization" of these industries, which generated powerful enemies abroad for the populists. On the social front, their program favored the interests of the urban middle class and the industrial working class. Trade unionism flourished, and though most populist leaders manipulated the unions, Latin American workers generally felt more equitably treated in their relations with management than ever before. The first social security systems were established along with such important benefits as modern labor codes and welfare programs.

QUESTIONS FOR ANALYSIS

1. How did populist leaders such as Perón, Vargas, and Gaitán attempt to achieve their goals? What strategies did they employ?

2. What were the limits on the goals and strategies of the populists? What, if anything, were they unwilling to do?
3. Decide for yourself. Were populist leaders legitimate heroes for the working class or authoritarian demagogues whose main goal was keeping themselves in power?

1. The Peronist Political Vision ～ Daniel James*

The career of Juan Perón of Argentina presents a fascinating case study of the problem of populism. Like the other populists, Perón was a powerful orator and manipulator of imagery. In this selection, historian Daniel James writes about Perón's successful linking, in his political rhetoric and symbolism, of Argentine nationalism with the "concrete, material aspects" of working-class life. Such aspects of workers' daily lives constituted the field in which Peronist language grew and included specific words (such as "los descamisados," *the "shirtless" and thus penniless) and cultural references (such as lyrics from tangos). To begin, James grounds his interpretation of Peronism in the basic schools of thought regarding workers' motivations for participating in the Peronist movement.*

The relationship between workers and their organizations and the Peronist movement and state is clearly vital for understanding the 1943–55 period. Indeed, the intimacy of the relationship has generally been taken as defining the uniqueness of Peronism within the spectrum of Latin American populist experiences. How are we to interpret the basis of this relationship, and beyond that, the significance of the Peronist experience for Peronist workers? Answers to this question have increasingly rejected earlier explanations which saw working-class support for Peronism in terms of a division between an old and new working class. Sociologists like Gino Germani, leftist competitors for working-class allegiance, and indeed Peronists themselves explained worker involvement in Peronism in terms of inexperienced migrant workers who, unable to assert an independent social and political identity in their new urban environment and untouched by the institutions and ideology of the traditional working class, were *disponible* (available) to be used by dissident elite sectors. It was these immature proletarians who flocked to Perón's banner in the 1943–46 period.

In the revisionist studies working-class support for Perón has been

---

*From Daniel James, *Resistance and Integration: Peronism and the Argentine Working Class, 1946–1976* (New York: Cambridge University Press, 1988), 12–14, 21–24.

regarded as representing a logical involvement of labor in a state-directed reformist project which promised labor concrete material gains. With this more recent scholarship the image of the working-class relationship to Peronism has shifted from that of a passive manipulated mass to that of class-conscious actors seeking a realistic path for the satisfaction of their material needs. Political allegiance has, thus, been regarded, implicitly at least, within this approach as reducible to a basic social and economic rationalism. This instrumentalism would seem to be borne out by common sense. Almost anyone inquiring of a Peronist worker why he supported Perón has been met by the significant gesture of tapping the back pocket where the money is kept, symbolizing a basic class pragmatism of monetary needs and their satisfaction. Clearly, Peronism from the workers' point of view was in a fundamental sense a response to economic grievances and class exploitation.

Yet, it was also something more. It was also a political movement which represented a crucial shift in working-class political allegiance and behavior, and which presented its adherents with a distinct political vision. In order to understand the significance of this new allegiance we need to examine carefully the specific features of this political vision and the discourse in which it was expressed, rather than simply regard Peronism as an inevitable manifestation of social and economic dissatisfaction. Gareth Stedman Jones, commenting on the reluctance of social historians to take sufficient account of the political, has recently observed that "a political movement is not simply a manifestation of distress and pain; its existence is distinguished by a shared conviction articulating a political solution to distress and a political diagnosis of its causes." Thus if Peronism did represent a concrete solution to felt material needs, we still need to understand why the solution took the specific political form of Peronism and not another. Other political movements did speak to the same needs and offer solutions to them. Even programmatically there were many formal similarities between Peronism and other political forces. What we need to understand is Peronism's success, its distinctiveness, why its political appeal was more credible for workers—which areas it touched that others did not. To do this we need to take Perón's political and ideological appeal seriously and examine the nature of Peronism's rhetoric and compare it with that of its rivals for working-class allegiance.

The issue of credibility is crucial for understanding both Perón's successful identification of himself with certain important symbols such as industrialism and, more generally, the political impact of his discourse on workers. Gareth Stedman Jones, in the essay to which we have already referred, notes that to be successful "a particular political vocabulary must convey a practicable hope of a general alternative and a believable means of realizing it, so that potential recruits can think in its terms." The vocabulary of Peronism was both visionary and believable. The credibility was in part rooted in the immediate, concrete nature of its rhetoric. This involved a tying down of abstract political slogans to their most concrete material aspects. . . . In the crucial years 1945 and 1946 this was clearly contrasted with a language of great abstraction used by Perón's political opponents. While Perón's rhetoric was capable of lofty sermonizing, particularly once he had attained the presidency, and depending on the audience he was addressing, his speeches to working-class audiences in this formative period have, for their time, a unique tone.

They are, for example, framed in a language clearly distinct from that of classic radicalism, with its woolly generalities concerning national renovation and civic virtue. The language of "the oligarchy" and "the people" was still present but now usually more precisely defined. Their utilization as general categories to denote good and evil, those who were with Perón from those against, was still there, but now there was also a frequent concretizing, sometimes as rich and poor, often as capitalist and worker. While there was a rhetoric of an indivisible community—symbolized in "the people" and "the nation"—the working class was given an implicitly superior role within this whole, often as the repository of national values. "The people" frequently were transformed into "the working people" (*el pueblo trabajador*): the people, the nation, and the workers became interchangeable.

A similar denial of the abstract can be found in Peronism's appeal to economic and political nationalism. In terms of the formal construction from the state of Peronist ideology, categories such as "the nation" and "Argentina" were accorded an abstract, mystical significance. When, however, Perón specifically addressed the working class, particularly in the formative period, but also after, one finds little appeal to the irrational, mystical elements of nationalist ideology. There was little concern with the intrinsic virtues of *argentinidad* nor with the historical precedents of *criollo* culture as expressed in a historical nostalgia for some long-departed national essence. Such concerns were mainly the province of middle-class intellectuals in the various nationalist groups which attempted, with little success, to use Peronism as a vehicle for their aspirations. Working-class nationalism was addressed primarily in terms of concrete economic issues.

Moreover, Peronism's political credibility for workers was due not only to the concreteness of its rhetoric, but also to its immediacy. Perón's political vision of a society based on social justice and on the social and political integration of workers into that society was not premised, as it was, for example, in leftist political discourse, on the prior achievement of long-term, abstract structural transformations, nor on the gradual acquisition at some future date of an adequate consciousness on the part of the working class. It took working-class consciousness, habits, life styles, and values as it found them and affirmed their sufficiency and value. It glorified the everyday and the ordinary as a sufficient basis for the rapid attainment of a juster society, provided that certain easily achievable and self-evident goals were met. Primarily this meant support for Perón as head of state and the maintenance of a strong union movement. In this sense Peronism's political appeal was radically plebeian; it eschewed the need for a peculiarly enlightened political elite and reflected and inculcated a profound anti-intellectualism.

The glorification of popular life styles and habits implied a political style and idiom well in tune with popular sensibilities. Whether it was in symbolically striking the pose of the *descamisado* (shirtless one) in a political rally, or in the nature of the imagery used in his speeches, Perón had an ability to communicate to working-class audiences which his rivals lacked. The poet Luis Franco commented cryptically on Perón's "spiritual affinity with tango lyrics." His ability to use this affinity to establish a bond with his audience was clearly shown in his speech to those assembled in the Plaza de Mayo [in Buenos Aires] on 17 October 1945 at a mass demonstration that marks the rise of the Peronist movement. Towards the end of that speech Perón evoked the image of his mother, *"mi vieja"*: "I said to you a little while ago that I would embrace you as I would my mother because you have had the same griefs and the same thoughts that my poor old lady must have felt in these days." The reference is apparently gratuitous, the empty phraseology of someone who could think of nothing better to say until we recognize that the sentiments echo exactly a dominant refrain of tango—the poor grief-laden mother whose pain symbolizes the pain of her children, of all the poor. Perón's identification of his own mother with the poor establishes a sentimental identity between himself and his audience; with this tone of nostalgia he was touching an important sensibility in Argentine popular culture of the period. Significantly, too, the speech ended on another "tangoesque" note. Perón reminded his audience as they were about to leave the Plaza, "remember that among you there are many women workers who have to be protected here and in life by you same workers." The theme of the threat to the women of the working class, and the need to protect their women, was also a constant theme of both tango and other forms of popular culture.

Perón's use of such an idiom within which to frame his political appeal often seems to us now, and indeed it seemed to many of his critics at the time, to reek of the paternalistic condescension of the traditional *caudillo* figure. His constant use of couplets from "Martin Fierro,"* or his conscious use of terms taken from *lunfardo* slang can grate on modern

---

*The Argentine national epic poem.

sensibilities. However, we should be careful to appreciate the impact of his ability to speak in an idiom which reflected popular sensibilities of the time. In accounts by observers and journalists of the crucial formative years of Peronism we frequently find the adjectives *chabacano* and *burdo* used to describe both Perón himself and his supporters. Both words have the sense of crude, cheap, coarse and they also implied a lack of sophistication, an awkwardness, almost a country bumpkin quality. While they were generally meant as epithets they were not descriptions Peronists would necessarily have denied.

Indeed, this capacity to recognize, reflect, and foster a popular political style and idiom based on plebeian realism contrasted strongly with the political appeal of traditional working-class political parties. The tone adopted by the latter when confronted by the working-class effervescence of the mid-1940s was didactic, moralizing, and apparently addressed to a morally and intellectually inferior audience. This was particularly the case of the Socialist Party. Its analysis of the events of 17 October is illustrative of its attitude and tone:

> The part of the people which lives for its resentment, and perhaps only for its resentment, spilled over into the streets, threatened, yelled, and, in its demon-like fury, trampled upon and assaulted newspapers and persons, those very persons who were the champions of its elevation and dignification.

Behind this tone of fear, frustration, and moralizing lay a discourse which addressed an abstract, almost mythical working class. Peronism on the other hand was prepared, particularly in its formative period, to recognize, and even glorify, workers who did "threaten, yell, and trample with a demon-like fury" Comparing Perón's political approach to that of his rivals one is reminded of Ernst Bloch's comment concerning Nazism's preemption of socialist and communist appeal among German workers that "the Nazis speak falsely, but to people, the communists truthfully, but of things."

Perón's ability to appreciate the tone of working-class sensibilities and assumptions was reflected in other areas. There was in Peronist rhetoric, for example, a tacit recognition of the immutability of social inequality, a commonsense shrug-of-the-shoulders acceptance of the reality of social and economic inequities, a recognition of what Pierre Bourdieu has called "a sense of limits." The remedies proposed to mitigate these inequities were plausible and immediate. Perón, in a speech in Rosario in August 1944, had emphasized the apparently self-evident reasonableness of his appeal, the mundaneness behind the abstract rhetoric of social equality: "We want exploitation of man by man to cease in our country, and when this problem disappears we will equalize a little the social classes so that there will not be in this country men who are too poor nor those who are too rich."

This realism implied a political vision of a limited nature but it did not eliminate utopian resonances; it simply made such resonances—a yearning for social equality, for an end to exploitation—more credible for a working class imbued by its experience with a certain cynicism regarding political promises and abstract slogans. Indeed, the credibility of Perón's political vision, the practicability of the hope it offered, was affirmed on a daily basis by its actions from the state. The solutions it offered the working class did not depend on some future apocalypse for confirmation but were rather directly verifiable in terms of everyday political activity and experience. Already by 1945 the slogan had appeared among workers which was to symbolize this credibility: *"Perón cumple!"* (Perón delivers).

2. Declaration of Workers' Rights ~ Juan Perón*

Populist leaders such as Perón did more than just talk about the working class and its needs. They also created a vast array of new programs and policies aimed at improving the lives of workers. In this primary source selection, many aspects of the Peronist agenda come together as an official "Declaration of Workers' Rights" ("solemnly proclaimed in public on the 24th of February, 1947, by His Excellency, General Juan Perón, President of the Republic"). Note the particular rights granted in the document. What exactly is being promised—and what is not? As with all such declarations and manifestos, students must distinguish between the ideological principles espoused and the practical application of those principles. The document does, nevertheless, reveal a key component of Peronist populism.

I. The Right to Work

Work is the indispensable means of satisfying the spiritual and material necessities of the individual and the community. It is the cause of all the conquests of civilization and the basis of general prosperity. Therefore the right to work should be protected by society, by giving it the dignity it deserves and by providing occupation to all.

*Adapted from Juan Domingo Perón, *Perón Expounds His Doctrine* (Buenos Aires, 1948; reprint ed., New York: AMS Press, 1973), 201–5.

II. The Right to a Fair Wage

As wealth, rent, and the interest on capital are the exclusive results of human labor, the community should organize the sources of production and guarantee the worker a moral and material reward to satisfy his vital needs and to compensate him for his efforts.

III. The Right to Training

The improvement of the condition of mankind and the preeminence of spiritual values make it imperative to raise the standard of culture and professional ability, so that all intellects should be led towards every branch of knowledge; and it is the concern of society to stimulate individual effort by supplying the means which will enable every individual to have an equal chance to exercise the right to learn and perfect his knowledge.

IV. The Right to Proper Working Conditions

The consideration which is due to any human being, the importance of work as a social function, and the reciprocal respect inherent in the productive relationships confer the right of individuals to demand fair and proper working conditions and oblige society to see that these conditions are strictly regulated.

V. The Right to the Preservation of Health

The physical and moral health of the individual should be a constant concern of society. Society is responsible for the hygiene and security of the workplace. Working conditions should not exact excessively heavy effort and should enable the individual to recover his energy through rest.

VI. The Right to Well-Being

Workers have the right to well-being. The minimum expression of this right is an adequate dwelling place and adequate clothing and food. A worker should be able to satisfy his and his family's necessities, work with satisfaction without too heavy toil, rest free of worry, and enjoy spiritual and material freedom. The right of well-being imposes the social necessity of raising the standard of living as far as our level of economic development allows.

VII. The Right to Social Security

The right of the individual to be protected in cases of disability or unemployment requires society to take unilaterally into its charge matters such as social security and workman's compensation insurance.

VIII. The Right to the Protection of the Family

The protection of the family is a part of the natural destiny of the individual, since it is here that his most elevated affections have their origin. The worker's well-being must be stimulated and favored by the community to encourage the improvement of humanity and the consolidation of our spiritual and material principles.

IX. The Right to a Better Economic Situation

Productive capacity and the zeal to excel find their natural initiative in the possibility for economic improvement. Therefore society must support economic initiatives and stimulate the formation and utilization of capital insofar as it constitutes an active element for production and contributes to general prosperity.

X. The Right to the Defense of Professional Interests

The right to group together freely and to participate in other legal activities which promote the defense of their professional interests constitutes an essential right of the workers.

---

3. Many Getúlios ～ Robert M. Levine*

Like Juan Perón of Argentina, Getúlio Vargas of Brazil employed a radically new vocabulary of class-conscious rhetoric and imagery in his long and influential political career. In this selection, historian Robert Levine begins by posing a puzzling contradiction: the Vargas years are remembered by most poor Brazilians as a time of great progress, yet the standard measures of most workers' material lives showed little sign of improvement. The author looks for explanations in two related areas of Brazilian culture. According to Levine, Vargas's political connection to the daily lives of the workers in his country was similar

---

*From Robert M. Levine, *Father of the Poor? Vargas and His Era* (New York: Cambridge University Press, 1998), 100–106. Reprinted by permission of Cambridge University Press.

to the traditional Brazilian kinship role known as padrinho, *or godfather, of an extended family that often might include slaves and other dependents. Levine also examines the Catholicism of the urban poor as a dimension of Vargas's relationship with the workers.*

Throughout the Vargas years, the unmistakable division separating the social classes remained essentially untouched by government reforms. Brazil's "haves," in fact, employed more maids and domestic servants than any country in the Western world, because labor was so cheap. Whether remaining in the rural interior or as migrants to urban areas, these men and women were barely above subsistence level, hidden, in that sense, from the everyday world of the affluent. That the "have-nots" on the whole tended to accept their lot caused them to be treated as if they were children, a by-product of the paternalistic legacy of Brazilian society. They used good-naturedness and resignation as coping mechanisms, although when they snapped, mobs smashed and burned streetcars (*quebra quebra*) or looted storehouses for food. The lower classes, Spanish journalist Ricardo Baeza pontificated, are a "garrulous and laughing people, who do not yet know the poison of thought or the curse of work."

Vargas maintained a sharp distance in his mind between himself and the people he called *populares* in his diary. They loved him nonetheless. During the 1930 election campaign pro–Liberal Alliance crowds overturned streetcars in Salvador. After the Liberal Alliance triumph, thousands lined the tracks to watch Vargas's train proceed from the South to Rio de Janeiro, where he would take office. Street poets called Getúlio the *defensor dos marmiteiros,* the protector of the workers who carried their tin lunchboxes of rice and beans with them to their jobs. At the same time, the growing migration of rural families to the cities of the coast in a desperate search for jobs spawned ever larger slums: foul *mocambos* on the river banks of Recife, shanties in Salvador and Pôrto Alegre, *favelas* (shantytowns) sprouting in São Paulo for the first time, between 1942 and 1945, and a proliferation of new and larger favelas on the hillsides of Rio de Janeiro.

Carolina Maria de Jesus, an indigent black girl in rural Minas Gerais living at the lowest rung of poverty, scorned by the "good families" in her small city and condemned to deprivation, describes in her autobiographical memoirs what the 1930 Revolution meant to her:

> One day I awoke confused to see the streets filled with soldiers. It was a revolution. I knew only revolutions of ants when they moved about. Revolutions by men are tragic. Some killing others. And the people only talked about Getúlio Vargas and João Pessoa. It was the union of the State of Paraíba with the State of Rio Grande do Sul. And the military rebels asked people to arm themselves, that men shouldn't be absent in the hour

of their country's litigation. These seditions occur because of the arrogance of those who want to govern the nation. With Getúlio Vargas we
will have more work.

The soldiers spread through the streets with green, yellow, and white
banners with Getúlio's face in the center. Those who saw the portrait
liked him and said: "Now, Brazil will be watched over by a man!" This
will move the country forward. We are a country without a leader. We
have to wake up. Countries cannot lie down eternally in a splendid cradle.
Our country is very backward. The girls who were domestic servants
didn't leave their employers' houses. I was working in Dona Mimi's
house, the wife of the *gaúcho*.* He was happy it was his state that would
bring order to Brazil.

> I walked the streets. I heard the soldiers sing:
> Long live our Revolution
> Brazil will ascend like a balloon
> With Getúlio, Brazil moves ahead
> With Getúlio, Brazil won't fall
> Let's have more bread on the table
> Getúlio is a friend of the poor.

When she was eighteen or nineteen, in the early 1930s, Carolina went to a
charity hospital. She wrote:

> In the ward the women only spoke about the [1930] Revolution, that it
> was beneficial for the people. That it had changed the rules of the game
> for workers. Salaries were better; they now were able to have bank
> accounts and other benefits from the working-class legislation. A worker
> is able to retire when he is old and be paid for full-time work. Workers
> were content with the laws. And Getúlio was becoming known as the
> "father of the poor." The people were disciplined.

Carolina, who wrote her memoirs during the last years of her life in
the mid-1970s, did not remember that Vargas's social legislation came into
effect only over decades. Unskilled workers were initially excluded from
benefits. Still, Carolina remembered that Getúlio gave young men the
opportunity to join the army and therefore leave the hardscrabble interior.
Many of them got jobs in São Paulo, she said; in their letters home to their
relatives they convinced them to come to São Paulo also. They came to
believe that São Paulo was the paradise for poor people. This was the
moment in which she decided that when she could, she would go to São
Paulo herself, a place that for her, in her words, was "Heaven's waiting
room."

Men in rural Minas Gerais, Carolina said, when they got together,
started to speak about Getúlio being the great protector of the poor. She

---

*A nickname for people from Vargas's home state of Rio Grande do Sul.

later wrote that she thought, "Will this be the politician who is going to improve Brazil for the Brazilians? . . . He had reanimated the people, that people who were lukewarm, apathetic, leave-it-for-tomorrow idealistic dreamers, now moving into action because they believed that this government would not deceive them." Planners, she claimed, said that they were going to Sao Paulo to get a loan from Getúlio and open a plant with fifty workers because Getúlio said that if workers have jobs they won't have time to go astray. "Not only does he give us loans," she wrote, "but his goal is to make workers the beneficiaries. Industry in São Paulo brings immediate profits."

Almost from the outset of his arrival in the public eye, millions of these men and women revered Vargas as a father figure. One reason for this was the importance of fictive kinship in Brazilian society. The descendants of slaves became kin of African tribal ancestors through initiation into spiritist cults. Landless peasants traditionally took powerful figures as godparents [*padrinhos* or *madrinhas*] for their newborn children. In the northeastern backlands in the late nineteenth century, for example, parish birth records list the Virgin Maria as madrinha for thousands of baby girls and the northeastern charismatics Antonio Conselheiro or Father Cícero as padrinhos. Many more families elicited permission of the local landlord to godfather (and therefore protect) their offspring. In the same way, Getúilio Vargas, the first national politician to reach out to all Brazilians, became the nation's padrinho. For ordinary people, Getúlio was accessible, all-powerful, demanding of their loyalty, and willing to intervene on their behalf if they proved him worthy.

Many lower-class Brazilians, including Carolina de Jesus, mixed spiritism with the penitential Roman Catholicism prevalent in the hinterlands. For people with such beliefs, Getúlio was a miracle-working saint, with whom one could commune spiritually. They decorated personal shrines with his photograph, and asked him for personal intervention, as they did to clay statues for Father Cícero, the miracle-working defrocked priest whose backlands Ceará religious community in Joaseiro coexisted with Vargas's government during the 1930s and who exerted considerable influence in state politics.

The life histories of ordinary Brazilians who reached adulthood during the 1930s and 1940s demonstrate incontestably that the Vargas era was pivotal in changing their lives, even if the new opportunities for mobility were more incremental than dramatic. Consider the case of Maurílio Tomás Ferreira, bom in 1915 in rural Espírito Santo:

> I had six brothers, most of them older. I even have a photograph of them. Three were drafted into the Guard, all at once, and they had to go even though they were married and had small children. . . . Before the Vargas government things were out of hand. . . . We lived on my father's land he

had bought, everyone in the family had a little house and a small plot. . . .
He distilled *cachaça* [rum] from sugar cane. . . . I had four sisters also.
My father was angry because he now had to take care of his three daugh-
ters-in-law and their kids. My father had to pay for their uniforms,
shoes—in the countryside you had to provide everything yourself.

I went to a rural school, very rudimentary. After primary school I
studied with a teacher my father hired for all of us. Getúlio regulated lots
of things. Before that, things were disorganized. I was now the oldest boy
living at home. My father decided to send me to the army too, to get it
over with, so I lied about my age. . . . I served in the army in 1930 when
I was fifteen. . . . I was sent first to Vitória and then to Rio, to the Praia
Vermelha barracks. I got out in December. I returned to work with my
father and when I was twenty-two I married, in 1937. I grew corn and
potatoes and coffee beans and raised pigs. There was no place to sell
things, so I had to transport my produce, and this was expensive. We
made very little money. Things grew well; my father sometimes harvested ten thousand sacks of coffee. But we had too little land for all of
my brothers and their families. All of my family were *crentes* [evangeli-
cal Protestants]. There was a church in Córrego Rico. We went. I directed
a choir. We were baptized. I met my wife there when she was twelve
years old.

[In 1942] I decided, overnight, to leave. We had two children already.
We went to [the town of] Muniz Freire and bought a house with my
savings. I had no job, nothing. I worked as a barber but didn't make very
much; the town was too small. I worked for the mayor's office. I got one
job through one of my brothers-in-law who was a driver for an Arab. I
became foreman on his farm but he didn't pay me. I stayed for a year and
then left for another foreman's job. Then I got a job with the railroad. I
got it [in 1945] when I went to Cachoeiro to sell chickens. A fellow I
sold them to told me to try and get a railroad job, that they were hiring
many people. He introduced me to some officials of the Leopoldina Railroad. They hired me. I liked the idea of living in Cachoeiro because there
was a school there my kids could attend. My children all studied, one as
far as the fifth grade, the others to high school. And railroad workers were
eligible for pensions; [we were] one of the first. . . . When I started
working they registered me in the railroad pension institute. There was an
enormous union building in Cachoeiro. The union sold provisions and
merchandise to us at cheaper prices. Later on the union gave a scholarship
for my youngest son to study at high school.

Starting in 1945 my wife and I always voted in elections, every year.
I joined the PTB [Workers' Party] . . . and became active in the union.
. . . I admired Getúlio Vargas, always voted for him. . . . He named the
state interventors. He was leading Brazil forward. . . . When he killed
himself it was an enormous shock. . . . I kept his photograph [the union
had given to us] and a copy of his suicide letter, to remind me of what he
did for poor Brazilians. . . . He was the chief organizer of this country.

Looking back on his life nearly a half century later, Maurílio recognized that this was the turning point in his life. Employment by a state agency meant school for his children, a future. To have a government job meant security and a pension. Perhaps because he understood that so few other workers received these benefits, Maurílio idolized Vargas, considering him his personal benefactor. He would have scoffed at social scientists writing that Vargas's labor measures were enacted to control the labor force, because he knew that he and his family benefited. As long as he belonged to the union, his wife would receive food at reduced prices at the union-run store. He would receive a pension, and his children would be eligible for scholarships available to families of union members. He considered voting for Vargas a natural obligation and something that gave him satisfaction. The union allowed him to advance: when Maurílio started, he was an apprentice brakeman. When he retired in 1970, he held the position of "chief of the train." Such upward mobility would have been impossible before 1930.

---

4. A Consummate Speechwriter ~ Getúlio Vargas*

Lourival Fontes, Getúlio Vargas's press secretary in the 1940s and 1950s, compiled a book based upon the Brazilian president's notes and instructions for speechwriting. He asserted that Vargas, always in control, provided the ideas, editing, rephrasing, polishing, and pacing. The speeches were simple and straightforward, always beginning with "Brasileiros!" Vargas avoided slang and stilted wording and always kept his sentences and paragraphs short. Below are a few comments and criticisms that Vargas sent to Fontes.

There are no superior or inferior races, nor races of masters and slaves.

I am imprisoned by a wall that separates me from the suffering and humble people, who elected me in the hope of a better life. I must fulfill that promise!

I need the support and confidence of the workers, and they in turn will find in me a true friend, ready to help them in their just aspirations. They

*From Lourival Fontes and Glauco Carneiro, *A face final de Vargas (os bilhetes de Getúlio)* (Rio de Janeiro: Edicões O Cruzeiro, 1966), chap. 15. Translated by Michael Conniff. Special thanks to Michael Conniff for bringing this material to the previous edition.

should avoid being misled by agitators and rabble-rousers. They may come to me without fear, and I will lead them to just and equitable solutions, using the official agencies created to accomplish this.

~~~

This is too highfalutin. I don't see here the reference I made to the working classes, as the dynamic element in the social equilibrium and force that is organizing to influence the future, not in a purely political democracy, such as we have, but instead in an economic and social democracy. "Workers in the cities and the countryside: those who drive the factories and till the fields. You are the people who follow me and on whom I depend to frighten the hornets waiting to sting me." I wrote that during the scary plane flight. After we arrived, I reread it more calmly. Reduce it to a concept or phrase and send it back for me to look at.

~~~

This is all right, but only speak of the cultural part and drop the reference to the worker, the laborer, in the most industrialized city in Brazil. We should say something like, "In this city of São Paulo there are as many thousands of organized and enlightened workers as our dreams of greater economic development, a higher standard of living, and social harmony."

~~~

I should appear a victim of persecution. In the Senate I made a number of speeches showing that the government is following an erroneous financial path and creating a nonexistent crisis. . . . Afterward I suffered all manner of pressures from the government. . . . I came here [to Itu, his ranch in Rio Grande] in silence; I isolated myself, and I waited for time and events to show I was right.

~~~

And where's the petroleum? It seems to me that this is a fundamental issue to bring up in Bahia. Did you show João Neves my suggestions? Some of my speeches are incomplete and others are missing.

~~~

I am not very impressed with the tenor of some of these draft speeches that arrived. They are very academic, very correct, but they won't make an impression on the masses [*povo*]. It seems that they are not addressed to the masses. They are more for highbrows. They don't deal with the heart of the social and economic crisis that we are undergoing. The one for São Paulo is good. . . . São Paulo is the largest industrial center and has the largest concentration of workers in the country, yet the speech doesn't deal with the social question: the misery, the high cost of living, the declining wages, the industrial crisis, the lack of bank credit, commodity hoarding, etc. You may say that I can add all that later. But it isn't easy, because I don't have the material. I don't have the data to illustrate or even refer to these statements, and it would mean totally rewriting these speeches. And time is short. They are pressuring me to go on the campaign trail and I don't have speeches, I don't have a travel itinerary, and the committee doesn't have money to pay for its activities. PS: Don't work on the São Paulo speech, I already rewrote it.

---

5. Populism and National Development ~
Fernando Henrique Cardoso and Enzo Faletto*

In their highly influential interpretation of Latin America's position in the modern world economy, sociologists Fernando Henrique Cardoso and Enzo Faletto helped to define what became known as the "dependency" school of Latin American Studies. Dependency theorists, critics, and historians dominated the field in the 1970s–1980s and still carry a great deal of weight today. Such scholars regard Latin America's economic problems as a result of the region's structural dependency on the central economies of the world capitalist system. Dependency theorists favored the nationalist policies of the Latin American populists.† In this passage from their classic study, Cardoso and Faletto assess Brazilian populists' attempt to industrialize their country by leading a "developmentalist alliance" within the country. Note that they indicate the losers as well as the winners in the populist transformation of Brazil.

Populism appeared in Brazil as the link between the new scheme of power and the urban masses, who were either mobilized by industry or driven to the city by the decline of the agrarian sector. It was to change into a policy by which the masses participated politically in a relatively limited way, owing to their weak union structure. This policy affected neither the rural masses nor the whole of the urban popular sector.

In Brazil, unlike in other countries that followed a liberal pattern of industrialization, the state emerged as an instrument not only to regulate the industrial system but also to directly participate in it through the cre-

---

*From Fernando Henrique Cardoso and Enzo Faletto, *Dependency and Development in Latin America*, ed. and trans. Marjory Mattingly Urquidi (Berkeley: University of California Press, 1979), 138–42. © 1979 by The Regents of the University of California Press. Reprinted by permission of the University of California Press.

†In the mid-1990s, when Cardoso became president of Brazil, he abandoned dependency theory and became a neoliberal.

ation of public enterprises, both independent and state-controlled. In Brazil, unlike Argentina, a large sector of nonworker urban masses was added to the lesser weight of the worker sector. This difference became even more marked in the presence of a broad sector of rural masses living in a situation totally removed from that of the urban masses.

Government participation in the emergence of an industry can be explained politically by the existence of masses that were mobilized without effective employment having been created to absorb them. This caused a dangerous situation for those who held power. In an urbanizing country with an agrarian economy in decline and a capitalist sector unable to respond rapidly to massive employment requirements, it was imperative that development be made a national undertaking—that is, one in the interests of all the people—and that the state be charged with leading the nation to prosperity.

The alliance that was to carry out the new policy incorporated at the outset the most backward groups of landholders, the farmers who produced for the domestic market, the urban middle class, the already existing industrial sectors, and the urban masses. Not included were the agro-exporting groups (coffee growers) that had controlled the system before the 1930 revolution, or the rural masses. Although the former were to join this "developmentalist alliance" later, the peasants were to be permanently excluded.

Domestic development in Brazil was supported politically by groups with conflicting interests. To create modern economic sectors capable of employing the masses, it was necessary to make a political alliance with the most backward sectors of the Brazilian production structure, the non-exporting landowners. On the other hand, the viability of such a policy of domestic development came to depend precisely on a division between the urban workers that benefited from development and the rural workers that were marginal to it. The system of accumulation and economic expansion—given their limited rate of growth—could not withstand the wage pressures that would result from incorporating broad rural sectors into the labor market. Moreover, the political strength of the landholding sectors depended on preventing rural workers from receiving the benefits of economic, political, and social participation. Since the "developmentalist alliance" encompassed the hacienda owners, the alliance would be shattered by incorporating the peasants.

It was the excluded sectors that would pay the costs of industrialization. In the early stages, industrialization depended on the power of the state to tax the exporting sector and to exclude the rural and urban masses. Eventually, the export sector became diversified, and certain groups within it began to participate in development by reorienting their capital toward production for the domestic market. Nonetheless, because the rural work-

ers continued to be isolated from the benefits of development, they constituted one of the structural limits to the political possibilities of
development. Attempts to expand the "developmentalist alliance" with
such groups were counterproductive, and populism could not be used as a
base for legitimizing power.

The populism of Vargas was a rather vague movement of people's
incorporation into the nation, but without entailing, as in the case of Perón,
stronger trade unions and increased pressure for higher wages. It was less
an economic definition of workers' rights, which would imply political
participation, than a political movement in favor of the "humble." Since
the emerging worker class was diluted in the urban masses, the need to
accumulate capital did not seem to be much opposed to the pressures for
redistribution during the phase of import-substitution industrialization.
Populist leadership could also be entrepreneurial; hence the state appeared
not only as employer but also, from the viewpoint of the masses, even as
a good employer. At the economic level, popular protest could be taken
care of because it was relatively weak; at the political level, it coincided
with the interests of groups that, having reached power without a solid
economic base of their own, were in favor of development under state
direction.

---

6. Words as Weapons ⁓ Herbert Braun*

*Colombia was another country where populism flourished in the 1940s. There,
the new breed of politician was named Jorge Eliécer Gaitán, a lawyer who carried forward the populist challenge to the traditional oligarchy in Bogotá. Due
to a unique power-sharing arrangement between the Liberals and the Conservatives, the country maintained a fragile stability from the early twentieth century
until the late 1930s, when Gaitán burst onto the scene. He served as mayor of
Bogotá, minister of labor and education, and almost won the presidency in 1946.
His assassination in Bogotá two years later brought about the riot known as the*
Bogotazo *and initiated the long period of violent confrontation,* la Violencia,
*between armed Colombian factions. In this selection, historian Herbert Braun
examines Gaitán's unsurpassed ability to connect with the working people of his
city during his 1946 run for the presidency.*

J orge Eliécer Gaitán became an orator who never doubted his rhetorical
abilities and knew that his power resided in his words. Gaitán was not

*From Herbert Braun, *The Assassination of Gaitán: Public Life and Urban Violence in
Colombia* (Madison: University of Wisconsin Press, 1985), 99–103. © 1985 by the University of Wisconsin Press. Reprinted by permission of the University of Wisconsin Press.

responsible for the prominent place of oratory in Colombian politics. He adopted a traditional practice to create a symbiotic relationship between himself and the crowd.

Gaitán understood that linguistic shock had a subversive quality in Colombia's highly verbal and formalistic culture. He was aware that the baroque and aristocratic texture of the *convivialistas'* orations intimidated barely literate audiences,* and he could sense the liberating effect of direct and popular forms of expression on those audiences. Yet his vulgarity was carefully measured. Gaitán was known as the "orator of the *mamola.*" The term, a rather mild expletive with a meaning similar to the verb "to chuck" in English, was personally insulting and physically aggressive. It was also a play on words and conjured up images of human and animal sucking. Gaitán used it, to the obvious delight of the crowd, every time the convivialistas intimated that he ought to lay his presidential aspirations to rest. The convivialistas were outraged and claimed that they would not permit their children to listen to him.

Tonality and intonation were important ingredients of Gaitán's oratory. Prolonging the vowels and crisply sounding the consonants of key expressions, he made the words fly out of the side of his mouth. "*Pueeeblooo,*" he intoned at the end of his speeches, "*aaa laa caargaa!*" ("Common people, charge!"). Gaitán's heavy and growling delivery was in a marked contrast to the melodic, calm, and lyrical rhetoric of the convivialistas. He appealed to the emotional, subjective sensibilities of his audience. Although he was capable of delivering reasoned and logical arguments on technical subjects before select groups, more often he spoke to fantasies that sparked the imagination of the crowd. To search for a clear line of argumentation in Gaitán's more political speeches is to misunderstand them. The orations were designed for dramatic effect, not intellectual consistency. He often returned to the same point, taking his listeners back and forth from one theme to another, reaching rapid conclusions, and supporting them much later or not at all.

Gaitán's speeches were filled with social and political content. His emotionalism and spontaneity and the simplicity of his words did not mean that he had thrust aside his ideology in order to transfix the crowd. Quite the contrary. His easily understandable phrases were a remarkably complete expression of his world view and a condensation of the ideas he had consistently held since writing *Las ideas socialistas* twenty years earlier. They also tellingly reflected his middle place in society. Few of Gaitán's slogans were his own, as his opponents quickly pointed out, but when they came from his mouth they held new meanings.

---

*The *convivialistas* were the leaders of the rival Liberal and Conservative parties who sought to reduce potential conflict.

Gaitán's words require close attention. He played astutely on the contrasting worlds of the convivialistas and the pueblo. He was best known for popularizing the distinction between the *país político* and the *país nacional** and using it to demonstrate the distance that separated leaders from followers: the convivialistas inhabited the former, the pueblo the latter. But Gaitán reversed the places these two "countries" had for the convivialistas. Gaitán's populist ideology pitted a small, unproductive, and meritless elite against a large majority defined by its need and ability to work. Gaitán returned to his favorite organic image. He likened the país politico to a putrefied organism whose head, voice, and tentacles were strangling the productive impulses of the pueblo. Politics, Gaitán said, was simply "mechanics, a game, a winning of elections, knowing who will be the minister, and not what the minister is going to do. It is plutocracy, contracts, bureaucracy, paperwork, the slow, tranquil usufruct of public office, while the public pueblo is conceived of as grazing land and not a place of work that contributes to the grandeur of the nation."

Gaitán referred to the leaders of the país politico as oligarchs, a term they used to accuse one another of the use of public office for private gain. Gaitán thereby added an economic dimension to his political critique of the convivialistas. As a result of the public corruption and nepotism that characterized the current López regime, the term gained a particular bite during the war years. Coming from Gaitán, the accusation had an added sting. For Gaitán was an outsider, and he was using public office, if not for financial gain, for something much worse: to move from the bottom to the top of society. The crowds understood, on the other hand, that the leader used the term to refer to the system of decision making represented by the closed conversations of the convivialistas as well as the boardroom meetings of corporations, or, as Gaitán referred to them, "monopolies."

Gaitán's slogan *"El pueblo es superior a sus dirigentes"* ("The pueblo is superior to its leaders") took the reversal to its logical conclusions. It was the most far-reaching of all his slogans, for it pointed to an overturning of the social order. The slogan is consistent with Gaitán's habit of speaking highly of the pueblo. In an impromptu speech in Caracas, he went so far as to say that "we have learned to laugh at those decadent generations that see the multitudes of our tropics as beings of an inferior race." He also claimed that Gaitanismo was a "great movement of the Colombian race," and that the crowds on the streets "were exactly the opposite of anarchy," a "normal part of a true democracy." In his oratory the feared *chusma* (mob) became the *"chusma heroica,"* and the despised *gleba* (tillers of the soil) became the *"gleba gloriosa."* But Gaitán was not a demagogue who promised his followers the impossible. He

---

*Roughly, the politicians' country versus the real country.

was harsh and demanding of them, urging them to be honest, moral, and hardworking. He never promised them a reversal of the social order that would place them suddenly at the top, living a life of luxury at the expense of toiling politicians. He was too committed to social order, and too conscious of the dangers of such promises.

Gaitán did not believe, moreover, that followers were naturally superior or equal to their leaders. In a speech to medical doctors, he explained what he meant by the superiority of the pueblo. He admitted that some individuals were able to excel on their own. But "with the multitude the phenomenon is different. . . . Separate, they are insignificant; together, they are the strong basis without which the apex does not exist. . . . If collective processes mediocratize the mind and reduce it, those same processes raise the minimal men and place them at the level of mindfulness." Thus, Gaitán believed that participation in a cohesive and purposeful crowd could make individuals more social. The crowd could civilize the pueblo. He shared the convivialistas' hierarchical vision of society, but his vision of the social pyramid was broader.

Yet another masterfully crafted slogan—"*Yo no soy un hombre, soy un pueblo*" ("I am not a man, I am an entire people")—reunited the two worlds that Gaitán had separated and reversed. He represented a new order with himself as head of the *país nacional*. The slogan contradicted the traditional distinction between private and public life. Gaitán was claiming to be an entirely public figure for reasons that were precisely the opposite of those of the convivialistas: they separated themselves from the pueblo; he was giving himself over to it. For his followers the slogan meant that their leader, a distinguished man with the character to challenge the convivialistas, was returning to the pueblo from which he had come.

Gaitán's other major slogan, "*Por la restauración moral y democrática de la república*" ("Toward the moral and democratic restoration of the nation"), succinctly captured the elusive ideal of a return to a social order that the convivialistas had betrayed. It must have produced an intense feeling of racial isolation in the white elite, which saw any restoration, any return to the past that was not led by them, as a return to the indigenous, pre-Hispanic origins of the nation.

Even Gaitán's simple call to arms—"*A la carga*"—contained a meaning that is not readily apparent. The word *carga* also signifies a physical burden, a heavy weight to be carried. Every time Gaitán called the pueblo to action at the end of his orations, he was eliciting images of the daily world of labor. Gaitán ended most of his speeches by repeating these slogans. As the crowds grew accustomed to the ritual, he would call out, "*Pueblo*," and the crowds responded: "*A la carga!*" "*Pueblo!*" "*Por la restauración moral y democrática de la república!*" "*Pueblo!*" "*A la Victoria!*" "*Pueblo!*" "*Contra la oligarquía!*"

The power of Gaitán's oratory was not lost on the convivialistas. Azula Barrera wrote that he "was the first to speak to the national proletariat in direct language, creating an aggressive class consciousness without the obscure Marxist phraseology, and a more elevated concept of its own worth." Through Gaitán's oratory, the Conservative historian concluded, the poor realized "that behind politics there existed the zone of their rights, the real range of their economic aspirations, the concrete world of misery, and of their collective victory." The Liberal politician Abelardo Forero Benavides could only agree. "He spoke [to the multitude] in a language that could be its own. . . . The boundary of the theater was transposed through the microphones into all the homes, shops, and attics." According to the Conservative Mario Fernández de Soto, Gaitán's oratory did not win him a place in the Academy or the Atheneum. But his "power resided primarily in his extraordinary ability to create between himself and the masses who followed him a community of spirit and emotions and aspirations so intimate that [the crowd] delivered itself completely to him." After the May 5, 1946, election, *Calibán* wrote that Gaitán was a "born caudillo of the multitudes."

Gaitán's oratory was a complete representation of the man. He stood above the crowd, demonstrating his prowess. He forged a unity with the pueblo to lead the nation to a new compromise, a balance between leaders and followers. He spoke proudly and passionately, for he believed that the warmth of emotion was as much the basis of society as was the cold reason of the convivialistas. And he revealed both his public and private selves, for he had nothing to hide. The new order would be built around individuals who stood up openly for their beliefs. Gaitán was like the corner grocer who stood proudly in front of his windows displaying the staples of daily life.

X

Social Revolution

Latin America saw many "revolutions" before 1950, but none was a social one. Before 1950, the word "revolution" in Latin America usually referred to any forceful regime change. Social revolutions, by contrast, bring more fundamental changes to the way countries operate. If a society is like a house in need of repair, then fixing rusted pipes, frayed electrical wiring, or a leaky roof is *reform*. Tearing the house down to redesign and rebuild it is *revolution*. In twentieth-century Latin America, the inspiration for this kind of revolution came overwhelmingly from Marxism-Leninism.

For many decades, Latin Americans have confronted the challenge of social revolution, whether as proponents or opponents. While the region experienced numerous episodes of crisis and reform in its first century of independence, the revolutionary challenges that began in the 1950s were more profound, larger in scale and ambition, more organized, and more ideologically driven. But if social revolutionary movements were widespread in Latin America from the 1960s through the 1980s, successful social revolutions were few. Only in Cuba did a lasting revolution occur, although several other movements achieved real power in their countries for months or even years at a time.

Factions of traditional Latin American elites came together with international allies, primarily the U.S. government and the military, to combat revolutionary outbreaks. The connection between U.S. and Latin American armed forces figures prominently in the next chapter in this book. For now, let us focus on another critical aspect of the problem: how and why Latin Americans themselves participated in the social revolutionary movements of the twentieth century.

While Latin American revolutionaries drew deeply from the well of European social thought, they also revised existing theories to match the unique social conditions and histories of their own national societies. Classical Marxist doctrine suggested that social revolutions would begin in the industrial working class, whose experience and working conditions would be particularly conducive to revolutionary mobilization. As we have seen, industrial workers did play an important political role in the mid-1900s, but more a populist than a revolutionary one. Seeking an alternative strategy, Latin American revolutionaries turned to the countryside. Cuba's Fidel Castro and Argentina's Ernesto "Che" Guevara, for example, started the hemisphere's most successful social revolution in Cuba, an island with one main city and hundreds of villages. The revolutionary model that seemed more relevant in most parts of Latin America was Chinese, not Russian. As Chinese Communist Party chairman Mao Zedong said, revolutionary guerrillas could become like fish swimming in the water of the rural peasantry.

After revolutionaries marched into Havana in 1959, the Cuban example created great excitement in Latin America. Cuban revolutionaries were bolstered by their alliance with the Soviet Union and by the overall strength of the global Communist bloc (including Communist Eastern Europe, the People's Republic of China, North Korea, and North Vietnam as well as some African and Middle Eastern states) during the 1960s. Indeed, the Cubans even went so far as to develop an informal Ministry of Exporting Revolution headed by Guevara, who traveled from the Congo to Bolivia to assist fellow insurgents. Revolutions broke out in the Dominican Republic, Guatemala, Colombia, and Nicaragua, to name only a few of the major cases. Che announced the famous goal of creating "one hundred Vietnams" to challenge the U.S. armed forces. The 1960s were, without doubt, a decade of revolutionary advance in Latin America.

The 1980s, as we will see in the next chapter, were a decade of revolutionary reversals. Between local defeats at the hands of Latin American military governments and the collapse of the international Communist bloc, social revolution in Latin America suffered a punishing blow. After years, sometimes decades, of guerrilla warfare, revolutionary movements throughout the region sought peace (or a cease-fire, at the minimum) and reconciliation in the 1990s. In a few places in Latin America, however, social revolutionary movements are still at war with national armies, paramilitary units, and special forces. As long as social problems continue to fester in the region, we would be foolish to think that social revolutions will never regain momentum.

QUESTIONS FOR ANALYSIS

1. Historians often discuss the implications of revolution "from above" versus revolution "from below." What do the terms mean, and how does leadership "from above" or "from below" affect a revolutionary movement?

2. What leads people to join a revolutionary movement? How much weight should historians give to the testimony of participants in forming their interpretations of the recent past?
3. What kind of oppression, if any, justifies the use of violence to end it? Can oppression that is institutionalized (that is, legal), such as slavery once was, be a kind of violence?

1. Essence of Guerrilla Warfare ∼ Che Guevara*

Ernesto "Che" Guevara, born in Argentina in 1928 and killed by government troops in 1967 while trying to organize a guerrilla movement in Bolivia, was one of the most influential and inspiring revolutionary figures in Latin America in the 1960s. His ideas and personal example had a powerful impact in Cuba, where he served as a medical doctor and military commander in the peasant-based rural insurgency against the dictatorship of Fulgencio Batista. Guerrilla Warfare, published in the year after the Cuban Revolution of 1959, condenses Che's experiences in Cuba and offers practical advice to would-be revolutionaries from across the region. Of particular importance was Guevara's message about how revolutionaries should build relationships with the rural peasant communities and bypass the urban, industrial working class.

The armed victory of the Cuban people over the Batista dictatorship was not only the triumph of heroism as reported by the newspapers of the world; it also forced a change in the old dogmas concerning the conduct of the popular masses of Latin America. It showed plainly the capacity of the people to free themselves by means of guerrilla warfare from a government that oppresses them.

We consider that the Cuban Revolution contributed three fundamental lessons to the conduct of revolutionary movements in [Latin] America. They are:

1. Popular forces can win a war against the army.
2. It is not necessary to wait until all conditions for making revolution exist; the insurrection can create them.
3. In underdeveloped [Latin] America the countryside is the basic area for armed fighting.

*From Ernesto Guevara, *Guerrilla Warfare*, with an introduction by Major Harries-Clichy Peterson, USMCR (New York: Praeger, 1961), 3–10.

Of these three propositions the first two contradict the defeatist attitude of revolutionaries or pseudo-revolutionaries who remain inactive and take refuge in the pretext that against a professional army nothing can be done, who sit down to wait until in some mechanical way all necessary objective and subjective conditions are given without working to accelerate them. As these problems were formerly a subject of discussion in Cuba, until facts settled the question, they are probably still much discussed in [Latin] America.

Naturally, it is not to be thought that all conditions for revolution are going to be created through the impulse given to them by guerrilla activity. It must always be kept in mind that there is a necessary minimum without which the establishment and consolidation of the first center is not practicable. People must see clearly the futility of maintaining the fight for social goals within the framework of civil debate. When the forces of oppression come to maintain themselves in power against established law, peace is considered already broken.

In these conditions popular discontent expresses itself in more active forms. An attitude of resistance finally crystallizes in an outbreak of fighting, provoked initially by the conduct of the authorities.

Where a government has come into power through some form of popular vote, fraudulent or not, and maintains at least an appearance of constitutional legality, the guerrilla outbreak cannot be promoted, since the possibilities of peaceful struggle have not yet been exhausted.

The third proposition is a fundamental of strategy. It ought to be noted by those who maintain dogmatically that the struggle of the masses is centered in city movements, entirely forgetting the immense participation of the country people in the life of all the underdeveloped parts of [Latin] America. Of course, the struggles of the city masses of organized workers should not be underrated; but their real possibilities of engaging in armed struggle must be carefully analyzed where the guarantees which customarily adorn our constitutions are suspended or ignored. In these conditions the illegal workers' movements face enormous dangers. They must function secretly without arms. The situation in the open country is not so difficult. There, in places beyond the reach of the repressive forces, the inhabitants can be supported by the armed guerrillas.

We will later make a careful analysis of these three conclusions that stand out in the Cuban revolutionary experience. We emphasize them now at the beginning of this work as our fundamental contribution.

Guerrilla warfare, the basis of the struggle of a people to redeem itself, has diverse characteristics, different facets, even though the essential will for liberation remains the same. It is obvious—and writers on the theme have said it many times—that war responds to a certain series of scientific laws; whoever ignores them will go down to defeat. Guerrilla warfare as a phase of war must be ruled by all of these; but besides, because of its special aspects, a series of corollary laws must also be recognized in order to carry it forward. Though geographical and social conditions in each country determine the mode and particular forms that guerrilla warfare will take, there are general laws that hold for all fighting of this type.

Our task at the moment is to find the basic principles of this kind of *fighting* and the rules to be followed by peoples seeking liberation; to develop theory from facts; to generalize and give structure to our experience for the profit of others.

Let us first consider the question: Who are the combatants in guerrilla warfare? On one side we have a group composed of the oppressor and his agents, the professional army, well armed and disciplined, in many cases receiving foreign help as well as the help of the bureaucracy in the employ of the oppressor. On the other side are the people of the nation or region involved. It is important to emphasize that guerrilla warfare is a war of the masses, a war of the people. The guerrilla band is an armed nucleus, the fighting vanguard of the people. It draws its great force from the mass of the people themselves. The guerrilla band is not to be considered inferior to the army against which it fights simply because it is inferior in firepower. Guerrilla warfare is used by the side which is supported by a majority but which possesses a much smaller number of arms for use in defense against oppression.

The guerrilla fighter needs full help from the people of the area. This is an indispensable condition. This is clearly seen by considering the case of bandit gangs that operate in a region. They have all the characteristics of a guerrilla army: homogeneity, respect for the leader, valor, knowledge of the ground, and, often, even good understanding of the tactics to be employed. The only thing missing is support of the people; and, inevitably, these gangs are captured and exterminated by the public force.

Analyzing the mode of operation of the guerrilla band, seeing its form of struggle, and understanding its base in the masses, we can answer the question: Why does the guerrilla fighter fight? We must come to the inevitable conclusion that the guerrilla fighter is a social [revolutionary], that he takes up arms responding to the angry protest of the people against their oppressors, and that he fights in order to change the social system that keeps all his unarmed brothers in ignominy and misery. He launches himself against the conditions of the reigning institutions at a particular moment and dedicates himself with all the vigor that circumstances permit to breaking the mold of these institutions.

When we analyze more fully the tactic of guerrilla warfare, we will see that the guerrilla fighter needs to have a good knowledge of the surrounding countryside, the paths of entry and escape, the possibilities of speedy maneuver, good hiding places; naturally, also, he must count on the support of the people. All this indicates that the guerrilla fighter will carry out his action in wild places of small population. Since in these places the struggle of the people is aimed primarily and almost exclusively at changing the social form of land ownership, the guerrilla fighter is above all an agrarian revolutionary. He interprets the desires of the great peasant mass to be owners of land, owners of their means of production, of their animals, of all that which they have long yearned to call their own, of that which constitutes their life and will also serve as their cemetery.

It should be noted that in current interpretations there are two different types of guerrilla warfare, one of which—a struggle complementing great regular armies such as was the case of the Ukrainian fighters in the Soviet Union—does not enter into this analysis. We are interested in the other type, the case of an armed group engaged in a struggle against the constituted power, whether colonial or not, which establishes itself as the only base and which builds itself up in rural areas. In all such cases, whatever the ideological aims that may inspire the fight, the economic aim is determined by the aspiration toward ownership of land.

The China of Mao begins as an outbreak of worker groups in the South, which is defeated and almost annihilated. It succeeds in establishing itself and begins its advance only when, after the long march from Yenan, it takes up its base in rural territories and makes agrarian change its fundamental goal. The struggle of Ho Chi Minh [in Vietnam] is based in the rice-growing peasants, who are oppressed by the French colonial yoke; with this force it is going forward to the defeat of the colonialists. In both cases there is a framework of patriotic war against the Japanese invader, but the economic basis of a fight for the land has not disappeared. In the case of Algeria, the grand idea of Arab nationalism has its economic counterpart in the fact that nearly all of the arable land of Algeria is utilized by a million French settlers. In some countries, such as Puerto Rico, where the special conditions of the island have not permitted a guerrilla outbreak, the nationalist spirit, deeply wounded by the discrimination that is daily practiced, has as its basis the aspirations of the peasants (even though many of them are already a proletariat) to recover the land that the Yankee invader seized from them. This same central idea though in different forms, inspired the small farmers, peasants, and slaves of the eastern estates of Cuba to close ranks and defend together the right to possess land during the thirty-year war of liberation, 1868–1898.

Taking account of the possibilities of development of guerrilla warfare, which is transformed with the increase in the operating potential of the guerrilla band into a war of positions, this type of warfare, despite its special character, is to be considered as an embryo, a prelude, of the other. The possibilities of growth of the guerrilla band and of changes in the mode of fight, until conventional warfare is reached, are as great as the possibilities of defeating the enemy in each of the different battles, combats, or skirmishes that take place. Therefore, the fundamental principle is that no battle, combat, or skirmish is to be fought unless it will be won. War is always a struggle in which each contender tries to annihilate the other. Besides using force, he will have recourse to all possible tricks and stratagems in order to achieve the goal. Military strategy and tactics are a representation by analysis of the objectives of the groups and of the means of achieving these objectives. These means contemplate taking advantage of all the weak points of the enemy. The fighting action of each individual platoon in a large army in a war of positions will present the same characteristics as those of the guerrilla band. It uses secretiveness, treachery, and surprise; and when these are not present, it is because vigilance on the other side prevents surprise. But since the guerrilla band is a division unto itself, and since there are large zones of territory not controlled by the enemy, it is always possible to carry out guerrilla attacks in such a way as to assure surprise; and it is the duty of the guerrilla fighter to do so.

"Hit and run," some call this scornfully, and this is accurate. Hit and run, wait, lie in ambush, again hit and run, and thus repeatedly, without giving any rest to the enemy. There is in all this, it would appear, a negative quality, an attitude of retreat, of avoiding frontal fights. However, this is consequent upon the general strategy of guerrilla warfare, which is the same in its ultimate end as is any warfare: to win, to annihilate the enemy.

Thus, it is clear that guerrilla warfare is a phase that does not afford in itself opportunities to arrive at complete victory. It is one of the initial phases of warfare and will develop continuously until the guerrilla army in its steady growth acquires the characteristics of a regular army. At that moment it will be ready to deal final blows to the enemy and to achieve victory. Triumph will always be the product of a regular army, even though its origins are in a guerrilla army.

Just as the general of a division in a modern war does not have to die in front of his soldiers, the guerrilla fighter, who is general of himself, need not die in every battle. He is ready to give his life, but the positive quality of this guerrilla warfare is precisely that each one of the guerrilla fighters is ready to die, not to defend an ideal, but rather to convert it into reality. This is the basis, the essence of guerrilla fighting. Miraculously, a small band of men, the armed vanguard of the great popular force that supports them, goes beyond the immediate tactical objective, goes on decisively to achieve an ideal, to establish a new society, to break the old molds of the outdated, and to achieve, finally, the social justice for which they fight.

Considered thus, all these disparaged qualities acquire a true nobility, the nobility of the end at which they aim; and it becomes clear that we are not speaking of distorted means of reaching an end. This fighting attitude, this attitude of not being dismayed at any time, this inflexibility when confronting the great problems in the final objective is also the nobility of the guerrilla fighter.

2. Testimony of a Guatemalan Revolutionary ～ María Lupe*

The collection and analysis of oral histories and testimonies have become an important part of the Latin American Studies methodology. As a form of evidence, oral testimonies offer unique, individualized insights into broad historical forces, though they are not without their own interpretative pitfalls. In this selection (an oral testimony taken from a peasant woman in the northern Guatemalan province of El Quiché), María Lupe recounts her experiences as a rural worker, activist, and combatant in the Guatemalan Army of the Poor, which was founded in 1972. She joined the revolutionary movement early in its history, having been recruited in one of the many communities of landless peasants and squatters who occupy the area.

B efore, my husband and I were very poor. We worked for the rich on a plantation. I took care of the young people; I cooked and cleaned from one in the morning until ten o'clock at night. Since there was no electricity everything was done manually. My husband earned $0.50 per day, and I was paid in meals only. Later, we bought a house and a little bit of land, but things became very bad for us and we were always in debt.

About twelve years ago we decided to go and see what we could find in the north, in Ixcan, but there it was even harder for us. There was nothing there, the store was four days from the road. We spent four months eating only *atol* [a drink made from corn] and tortillas. One of the local children died of malnutrition. I was pregnant with my third daughter, and I was very pale and undernourished. She was born in the seventh month, very thin, and I almost lost her. Later the engineers came and they gave us a little plot of land. During that time many people arrived and things improved a little. The people that came were from all over the country, from the coast, from the mountains, from all over.

After two years the first members of the Guerrilla Army of the Poor arrived. I remember just when it was because there wasn't even any corn at that time. I was scared, because I didn't know any better, and because all I had been told by the government was that the guerrillas only came to

*From María Lupe, "María Lupe's Testimony," *Latin American Perspectives* 36, no. 10 (Winter 1983): 105–8. Reprinted by permission of Sage Publications.

rob and to rape our daughters. Even one of my kids was scared, one who is now a guerrilla himself, and he ran and hid the radio.

The compañeros helped everyone to build a house, and it was the first time that we had worked collectively. Later, they explained to us that they were poor too and that they were fighting so that the poor could live a better life and that we were going to win. How are they going to win, I thought, when the towns are all so far apart? But now I see how the struggle has developed all over the country.

We were one of the first families that began to collaborate. I liked to raise chickens and pigs and I sold them at a good price to the compañeros and also gave some to them. Later, we gave them information and bought things for them that they needed. Others took advantage of them; they sold them things at very high prices, but when they realized what the compañeros were doing, that their purpose for being there was to help us and themselves, then these people stopped taking advantage and began to collaborate also.

All the families collaborated although there were times when we could only speak to the woman or only to the man in a family, and then later the one would try to convince the other; but sometimes they could not agree. Many times the men who were participating did not want their women working with the other men in the group, because of jealousy. So we arranged it so that other women worked with them instead. The women organized the preparation and serving of [food]; they brought it to my house, and then we would take it to the mountains where the compañeros were training.

After a year spies began to appear, and later the army placed a military commissioner there. There was a lack of secrecy, so everyone knew about those of us who were collaborating, especially those first families. My husband and oldest daughter, twelve years old, went to train in the mountains, and there my daughter learned to read and write. They stayed there three months and then they returned. But after a month they had to return to the mountains for good because the army was pursuing them. At the time Luis Arenas was executed, a very repressive landowner who was called the "Tiger of Ixcan." This was made public by the organization and then the repression really began.

I continued alone with my six children. I said that I could not work on the plantation, but later they had me doing everything. Since I was now politically aware, I continued collaborating. Information and food were collected from people in the entire area. It was a rare individual who did not know of the compañeros. Since people live far from one another, we began to support one another, working collectively among twenty families or so, forming a network.

Those of us who were organized were given classes, the women and the men separately. A compañera spoke to us about the discrimination against women, about why we had not been able to mix and work with the men, about the lack of trust they had in us. We knew about discrimination within a marriage, apart from the exploitation by the rich; husbands who say we can only be in the home, that we can't do certain things, and generally women, not being conscious of anything else or of any other way of life, believed this to be natural.

The first element we dealt with in our meetings was the problem of women being hit by their husbands. It was very hard to change this custom. At the same time as we were discussing it, the compañeros were explaining to the men how a woman is not a slave and that she should not be beaten. But to stop this practice is very difficult and in some cases impossible. It was also necessary to fight for a woman's right to participate in political work. There were times when she would have to go out at night, for example, and her husband would not want her to leave. Later, they understood that it was because of lack of trust in the relationship that he would not allow her to go out. My husband and I never had problems like this.

Other customs were even harder to change. For example, among small landowners like ourselves, we marry at fifteen years of age and older, but we marry freely. But amongst the Indian population it is different. Some Indian people who lived close by came and offered to buy my twelve-year-old daughter. It was their custom that if this is what our daughter wanted, then it was okay, but if not, then no. They accused us of discriminating against them because they were Indians. We spoke about this with the compañeros of the organization, and they spoke with the Indians later, but one cannot simply change the customs of a people so easily. Finally, the Indian man bought another young woman, an Indian woman. They remained hostile towards us. Later, the young man became a guerrilla, and our two families worked together, but it is very hard to change these customs. It is even harder for the Indian woman than it is for the Indian, because of the hard life she leads. Sometimes when the compañeros of the organization come to their homes, the women hide. They are very timid and since the compañeros do not speak their dialect, they cannot communicate with them.

I was the first compañera to arm herself, because I was pursued by the army; they came to take me away. I left the children with another woman, but she really couldn't care for them well. I had to come down from the mountains into the town (where the army knew me and was looking for me) to take my children away with me. We did this like a military operation, and we went back to the mountains with the children. We lived several months like that, in the encampment, and sometimes I was there alone with the children.

Later, because of security precautions, I left the encampment and went to live in another town. Then I lost contact with the organization. I had very little money and no one from the organization made contact with me. So, with the children, I worked washing other people's clothes and selling tortillas. My oldest daughter worked as a babysitter to make some money. How we survived I don't know. We lived that way for five months, with me telling everyone that my husband had left us, that he was a wretched man, and they believed me.

Already in the encampment they were doing everything: training, studying, going out to the towns and speaking with the people, making necessary purchases, etc. If the men went into the towns alone, the people did not trust them, but if the women also went they saw that there were women participating, women carrying arms, women equal to the men.

We gave talks to the people in the towns about simple things, comparing the growth of the organization to the growth of the corn. The women in the organization gave talks to the women, and the men to the men.

---

3. Christianity and Revolution ~ Margaret Randall*

In the 1970s the small island of Solentiname in Lake Nicaragua became the home of an experimental community inspired by "liberation theology," which had as its goal the liberation of Christian communities from all forms of oppression (both spiritual and material, the linkage between the two being crucial to their theological perspective). Liberation theology arose in Latin America in the wake of the Bishops' Conference at Medellín, Colombia, in 1968, which issued a call for the Catholic Church to take a more active role in demanding respect for human rights and social justice, even when such demands led to direct confrontations with state authorities. At that time, numerous revolutionary movements had produced high levels of government repression, especially among the peasantry. In this selection, several members of the Christian base community at Solentiname talk to researcher Margaret Randall about the way it took shape. A key figure mentioned by the participants is Ernesto Cardenal, a controversial Nicaraguan priest and revolutionary who helped create Solentiname. Note the obstacles that he and the other liberationists had to overcome.

M ANUEL: Ernesto would celebrate the Mass and afterwards he would read the Gospel. Each person would get a book called *God Comes to Man*, which is a very clear translation of the Gospel. We would read it

*From Margaret Randall, *Christians in the Nicaraguan Revolution*, trans. Mariana Valverde (Vancouver: New Star Books, 1983), 68–73. © 1983 by Margaret Randall. Reprinted by permission of Margaret Randall.

and then comment on it verse by verse. Each person would give their opinion. And we arrived at the conclusion that the system we were living under was bad and had to be changed.

NATALIA: Ernesto would ask, "What do you think of what it says here in the Gospel?" And he would listen to everyone's opinion. Some people said what they thought; others didn't say anything. Some didn't agree with Ernesto and would have died before saying anything. One time, someone mentioned Che Guevara. And I said: "Che died, but he didn't die. He remains alive because there are others who followed him."

OSCAR: When I began to participate in the dialogues I felt relief, I felt satisfied. Many people only preached the Gospel in Latin, and of course we didn't understand it. We were so happy to have the opportunity to hear Ernesto talk clearly and to participate ourselves.

I was brought up in a sect called the Seventh-Day Adventists. My family and my grandmother were of that religion. I would hear the Gospel and would pick up a few things about Christianity and the Word of God. But we never had the opportunity of discussing them with the priest or the pastor. They just preached. But Ernesto wanted everyone to discuss the Gospel. He didn't like just speaking or reading. When we participated, each person communicated their ideas, and the Holy Spirit was there in what was being said.

Ernesto tried to get to know the people better. Then he formed a group called "God's family" with the older people. From then on we had more confidence, as though we belonged to the same house. The group was both women and men. We lived as though in a seminary. Ernesto spoke about our vices; that was the kind of thing that he was concerned about. The group had discussions with comrades from Managua and from outside the country.

That experience was very beautiful. The Gospel was spoken there as Jesus Christ had wanted. Christ was a guerrilla fighter, not the sort of person to be kicked around, with the imperialist boot always on top of him. The Gospel was quite clear. It told of the suffering that Christ underwent for a group that was in a similar situation to ours in Nicaragua under [Anastasio] Somoza. Earlier we had thought we could always live like that, with the Book in our hands, without any change. Because many people, even the oldest men, believe that you can be saved by the Bible alone. After hearing the Gospel we saw more clearly what Jesus Christ wanted, what kind of love he had for his people. We saw that you had to overthrow imperialism to live a little better.

I used to think that Somoza had given us something. I didn't feel the need for change, the need to struggle to overthrow the dictatorship. I was quite mistaken. With time, I came to feel hatred against Somoza's rule here. I remember that we were very afraid of the National Guard. Through the Gospel, through dialogue, this fear went away. I also felt a different change. I began to see the possibility of a change for my people, for the human race, a future for Nicaragua and for all the peoples that have suffered.

TERESITA: Everything changed when we began to understand what it really meant to be a Christian. It wasn't so much the prayers and Masses and Communions, but something else. Love, really. Love for others. At the beginning we had daily Masses in Solentiname but afterwards Ernesto said that if we didn't want Mass, we shouldn't have it. He said we could ask him whenever we wanted. From then we didn't have Masses every day but only one or two a week, apart from Sunday Mass. And we never said the Rosary. We would recite the Psalms in the morning, and then read some other book. Prayer was still very important to me.

ALEJANDRO: Father de la Jara, who was active in the Christian base communities in Managua, gave us the idea of taping the commentaries and told us how to do it. Afterwards, Fernando, Ernesto's brother, came and wanted to tape us and make a book with the tapes. Because our commentaries concerned theological questions it was important to write them down. After we did the taping, we saw how we were developing politically. Within the context of the Gospel, we were overcoming theoretical problems. The tapes helped us improve our discussions and made us realize how important they were.

Other influences helped. We had a large library, and lots of visitors, although we were more and more selective. And that helped a lot. University students came with their Christian faith and their Marxism, and all their skills. We soon changed from receiving only Christians to receiving others, too. We discussed all that, and became more politically aware. In this way we kept growing.

OLIVIA: You see, before that I would read the Bible with my daughter and would try to be resigned in my misery, waiting for death in order to enjoy happiness. Now I see that is absurd.

MANUEL: Those who taught us the old religion, and said that we shouldn't hate anybody, had us supporting Somoza's government. In that sense we supported Somoza. Religion taught us that we had to have a dictator there, for God had put him there, that we had to spend our time praying for this man to be healthy. That's what religion taught us, to accept the conditions of life that we had.

OLIVIA: I believe that still happens, even in Nicaragua, in any place where some people still live in conformity, in their misery, expecting to go to their reward. What will they enjoy then? What we have to enjoy is this life here and now, which God made for all of us. I got to the point where I could not live resigned to eating next-to-nothing, bringing up my children in such poverty, with all my childbirths, everything.

MANUEL: They would say: God wants it that way, we have to be on His side. This is a commandment of God. For instance, the evangelists read the verses from the Bible to teach you that each country has to have a government, and that we must help it, protect it, and pray for it. They said that it is a sin to kill a National Guardsman or to join the guerrillas, and if we agreed with the guerrillas or supported "assassins" who went around in the mountains killing, we would burn in Hell.

At that point, for me, Che Guevara was just a creep. But when Ernesto put some politics in the Gospel, we began to realize much of what we had learned was not true, that Che Guevara was better than a priest, better than a bishop, better than the Pope. That this man went around changing the system so we could live better.

Now, there were some people who accepted what Ernesto told them, but some people did not. They did not believe in Ernesto. For example, some didn't believe in the baptisms that he celebrated. When Ernesto was going to baptize a child he said: "Bring some water from the beach to baptize the child." People said that was not right, because the water had not been blessed. It wasn't holy water. And that would not do. But of course what really works are the words, the commitment that you make at a wedding or a baptism. In Christianity, that's what counts; not the rites, which are meaningless.

ERNESTO: Some people complained because we took the statues of saints away. We only left two of them, beautiful antique sculptures. But we burned the others. They were ugly, painted with lead.

NATALIA: Some people said they wouldn't go to Mass because Ernesto was a communist. They would say, "Everybody who goes there is a communist." Ernesto told the people in Mancarroncito that we would all go there in a boat and he would say Mass. They had said they could not come here, and when Ernesto went, there wasn't a soul to be seen. And when we saw that, we said, "Ernesto, let's go, what's the point?" We knew they were afraid to come because people said Ernesto was a communist. The rumor was that anybody coming to see Ernesto was going to end up in jail. Even some of the people here believed it, too.

And then I would ask them: Do you know what a communist is? If Ernesto asks you what it means to be a communist, you won't be able to answer. There are different kinds of communists. To be a communist is to be in a community together. But they would say, what does Natalia know anyway? Ernesto is brainwashing all the old women, after they've already sold their sons to him. They thought he was paying us and that he was turning our sons into communists. That's how they talked.

4. Chile's Revolution from Below ~ Peter Winn*

Chile, unlike Cuba, Guatemala, and Nicaragua, had a proud tradition of electoral democracy and civilian rule going back to the nineteenth century. The views of its most important revolutionary leader, Salvador Allende, differed greatly from those of Che Guevara on how to achieve socialism. Allende believed in the ballot box. He founded a revolutionary electoral coalition, the Unidad Popular or Popular Unity, and called his strategic vision la vía chilena, the Chilean Road. In this selection, historian Peter Winn discusses the way in which Allende's victory in the 1970 presidential election produced a radicalization among workers at the Yarur cotton mill outside Santiago, a bastion of Allende's support. Ultimately, Winn suggests that President Allende's controlled revolution from above was not possible once the uncontrollable revolution from below gained momentum at places such as Yarur.

On the twenty-fifth of April 1971, the workers at the Yarur cotton mill in Santiago seized control of their factory and demanded "socialism." There had been strikes before at the Yarur mill—for better wages, for an independent union, against the Taylor System†—but this was different: This was a strike to rule. Three days later, President Allende reluctantly bowed to their demands and Yarur, Inc., became the first Chilean industry to be requisitioned by the Popular Unity government "for the simple fact of being a monopoly."

It was a historical role that took the workers themselves by surprise. All they had hoped to do was "liberate" themselves from "the yoke of the Yarurs." All they thought they were doing was fulfilling the Popular Unity program and redeeming Allende's campaign pledge. But what they did was enact their own understanding of the Chilean revolution—a model other workers then followed.

In only five months of Popular Unity government, the workers' movement at the Yarur mill had fulfilled its historic agenda and gone beyond it to pose questions of worker power that challenged Amador Yarur's control over his own factory. The Yarur workers may have been bywords for political backwardness in the past, but during the five months of Allende's presidency they had leaped into the vanguard of an accelerating and deepening revolution from below, one significantly different from Salvador Allende's revolution from above.

---

*From Peter Winn, *Weavers of Revolution: The Yarur Workers and Chile's Road to Socialism* (New York: Oxford University Press, 1986), 139–43. © 1986 by Oxford University Press. Reprinted by permission of Oxford University Press.

†Philadelphia engineer and efficiency expert Frederick Winslow Taylor's theory of a scientific approach to factory operations.

The Popular Unity program and the authors of its economic strategy envisioned a carefully controlled revolution from above. The structural changes that would pave the way for socialism were to be carried out legally, using the instruments created by the bourgeoisie and the powers granted the state. At the same time, mandated price controls and wage increases would redistribute income "from the infinitesimal minorities to the overwhelming majority" of Chileans. Together with the Popular Unity government's vastly expanded social programs, the resultant raised real incomes would "solve the basic needs of the people" and make possible Allende's promised "revolution with meat pies and red wine."

These measures—and successes—were also central to the Popular Unity's political strategy, which was to produce an electoral majority for socialism by the end of Allende's six-year presidential term. It was a strategy that counted on the growing support of Chile's workers, peasants, and *pobladores* [urban underclass], who would be won over by the material benefits that they would receive and persuaded by their experience that socialism was a superior system that was in their own self-interest. But in order to succeed, *la vía chilena* also required the support of a sizable sector of the middle classes, who wanted the benefits of *los cambios* ("the changes") that both Allende and [Radomiro] Tomic had proposed but feared the personal and societal costs of a Marxist-led revolution. Most of them had voted for Tomic and change in 1970, rather than for [Jorge] Alessandri and the status quo, and their support could give the Popular Unity the majority that it sought. The solution was to produce the promised revolution without sacrifice while allaying their fears of a violent or authoritarian revolution in which they might become victims.

This required a carefully controlled and phased revolutionary process, which was also necessary for the successful implementation of the Popular Unity's program of structural change. Here the strategy called for dividing the Chilean bourgeoisie, confronting one sector at a time, and enlisting the cooperation or neutrality of the smaller and medium-sized enterprises by confining leftist attacks to the "monopolies." In this delicately balanced strategy of economic and political change, the role of the "masses"— workers, peasants, and pobladores—was to provide political and social support when called on, but otherwise to await patiently the advances and benefits of the revolution from above.

Allende's "popular triumph," however, had a different meaning to his mass base than it had to the politicians and planners of the Popular Unity. To Chile's workers, peasants, and pobladores, the election of a "Popular Government" was a signal for them to take the revolution into their own hands and fulfill their historic aspirations through direct action from below. Allende's promise that he would never use the security apparatus of the state against "the people" freed them from fear of governmental repression, and the Popular Unity's commitment to structural change, redistribution of wealth, and meeting the basic needs of Chile's poor persuaded many that, in acting for themselves, they were fulfilling the Popular Unity program and advancing the revolutionary process. For them, the underlying meaning of Allende's election was that they were now free to pursue their long postponed dreams.

The result was the unleashing of a revolution from below, which sometimes coincided with or complemented, but increasingly diverged from, the legalistic and modulated revolution from above. More spontaneous, it emerged from the workers, peasants, and pobladores themselves, although through a complex process in which certain political groups played an important role. Workers, peasants, and pobladores, however, were the protagonists of this other revolutionary process, and they infused it with their own concerns, style, and worldview. Their aims tended to be concrete—objectives that responded to problems in their daily lives but that they equated with advancing "the revolution." It was an uneven process, with varying dynamics, but it was sufficiently powerful to call into question the speed, priorities, and character of the overall revolutionary process. It was never completely autonomous nor totally spontaneous, but from a passive political base the Chilean masses began to transform themselves into active agents of change, the protagonists of their own destiny.

The hallmark of this revolution from below was the *toma*—the seizure of the sites where people lived or worked—or hoped to live or work. Allende's election was followed by a wave of suburban land seizures by homeless urban workers and recent rural migrants desperate for the housing that successive governments had promised to provide but failed to deliver. Led by leftist activists, squatters seized vacant lots on the edge of Chile's cities, raising the national flag and building cardboard shacks as symbols of legitimacy and signs of possession.

Equally dramatic and even less compatible with Allende's phased revolution from above was the wave of farm seizures that began in the Mapuche Indian areas of the Alpine south and spread rapidly to the rural laborers and poor peasants of the fertile Central Valley, Chile's breadbasket and the economic and political base of Chile's traditional elite. Whether it was "the running of the fences" by Indians to reclaim the lands that European settlers had taken from them during the preceding century or the toma of large estates by peasants who had been disappointed by the speed and scope of [1960s president Eduardo] Frei's agrarian reform, the message was the same. The deprived of Chile had taken Allende's victory as their own and were acting out its meaning in their own direct action. It was at once a sign of faith in the Popular Unity and suspicion of all governmental bureaucracy.

For Chile's industrial workers, Allende's election and inauguration were also a signal: a time to organize, to press for big wage increases, to prepare for the socialization of one's workplace. For the most part, the industrial workers were better organized and better paid, more disciplined and more committed to the Popular Unity than the peasants and pobladores. They interpreted the advent of a Popular Unity government as an opportunity to press for their historic aspirations—higher real wages, an economist orientation ingrained by years of struggle within the legalistic Chilean Labor Code and a politicized labor movement. The workers took the Allende government's wage guidelines—a 36 percent raise, equal to the previous year's inflation—as a starting point for contract negotiations. Taking advantage of their new bargaining leverage—management awareness that government representatives on the tripartite mediation boards would now side with the workers and fear that a labor conflict might lead to a strike that would provoke a factory seizure or government takeover—industrial workers won the largest real wage raises in Chilean history, leading the way to the 30 percent average increase in real incomes that Chilean workers secured for 1971.

For such workers, peasants, and pobladores, the meaning of Allende's presidency was the license to fulfill their aspirations and pursue their dreams. Some were conscious of the broader implications of their actions; others, conscious only of the opportunity to realize the goals of a lifetime. Together, their individual actions transformed Allende's narrow electoral victory into a profound revolution from below. It was a social revolution that confirmed the fears of the elite and awoke the anxieties of the middle classes even as it raised the hopes of the most "revolutionary" factions within the Popular Unity and factions to its left.

The Popular Unity leaders had banked on the increasing radicalization and support of Chile's workers, peasants, and pobladores on their democratic road to socialism, but they had not bargained for a revolution from below. The problem for the Allende government was how to reward the expectations of its mass base while keeping wage increases within noninflationary bounds and land seizures from threatening its political strategy of class coalition.

Although the large raises for 1971 might cause economic problems later on, it was the tomas that most worried the Popular Unity leadership. There had been land seizures before the election of Allende, but never on such a scale. The rural revolution from below, in particular, was playing havoc with the Popular Unity's timetable and image of legality and was threatening the governing coalition's political strategy of class coalition by raising the anxieties of small landowners, a central social base of the Radical party.

Still more worrying to many Popular Unity leaders was the prospect of a deepening revolution from below among the industrial working class.

Except for those few industries whose owners had abandoned the country, failed to meet payrolls, or shut down plants, factory seizures had been conspicuous by their absence before 1971. By March of that year, however, government officials were becoming aware that pressure from below for the socialization of industry was growing. If these pressures could not be contained, the Popular Unity might be forced to choose between its strategy for socialism and its central mass base.

By April 1971, it was becoming clear that Allende's election had set off processes that were calling into question his initial timetable and strategy. A surging revolution from below was threatening to leave the national leaders of the Left behind and to disrupt the Popular Unity's economic and political strategies in the process. Together with the unexpectedly rapid progress of the revolution from above, this unanticipated emergence of a revolution from below was forcing the Popular Unity leaders to reassess the scope, speed, direction, methods, and character of their road to socialism, posing with new urgency the old question: reform or revolution?

---

5. The Chilean Road to Socialism ~ Salvador Allende*

Salvador Allende's democratic road to socialism differed greatly from the road of guerrilla warfare proposed by Che Guevara. In the following selection, Allende explains what he calls the "five essential points" about the Chilean Road. The overall impression given is of a gradual transformation rather than immediate change. Having the electoral majority on his side was obviously crucial to his strategy. Allende believed that majority support allowed him to reorganize institutions such as the judicial system through the democratic legislative process. And on the question of revolutionary violence, Allende clearly differentiated between the conditions his movement faced in Chile versus those found in military dictatorships such as (prerevolutionary) Cuba, Guatemala, and Nicaragua. One of Allende's most popular measures was the government takeover of foreign-owned copper companies, mentioned as his fifth point, despite furious U.S. opposition. Sadly, the Chilean military did not remain neutral in the political struggles of the early 1970s as it had in the past. A coup d'état led by General Augusto Pinochet ended Allende's life and the Popular Unity government in September 1973.

In the revolutionary process in which we are involved, there are five essential points upon which our political and social struggle turns—

---

*From Joan E. Garces, ed., *Salvador Allende on Chile's Road to Socialism*, trans. J. Darling, with an introduction by Richard Gott (Hammondsworth, UK: Penguin Books, 1973), 147–55.

legality, institutionality, political freedom, violence, and the nationalization of the means of production. These are questions which affect the
present and future of each citizen.

The Principle of Legality

The principle of legality now reigns in Chile. It was imposed after the
struggle of many generations against absolutism and the arbitrary use of
the power of the state. It is an irreversible triumph as long as no distinction
remains between the governing and the governed. It is not the principle of
legality which is denounced by popular movements. Our protest is against
a legal order whose principles reflect an oppressive social system. Our
juridical norms, the techniques which regulate social relations between
Chileans, correspond today to the requirements of a capitalist system. In
the transition to a socialist regime, the juridical norms will correspond to
the necessities of a people struggling to build a new society. But legality
there will be.

Our legal system must be modified. This is the main responsibility of
the courts at the present time to see that nothing impedes the transformation of our juridical system.

It depends to a great extent on the realistic attitude of Congress
whether or not the legal system of capitalism can be succeeded by a socialist legal system, conforming to the socioeconomic changes which we are
planning, without there being a violent rupture in the juridical system,
which could give rise to those arbitrary acts and excesses that we wish to
avoid.

Institutional Development

The regard for law and order which marks the constitutional state extends
through all our institutions. The struggle of the popular movements which
now are represented in the government has contributed substantially to
one of the most heartening facts on which the country can rely: we possess
an open institutional system which has withstood attempts to violate the
will of the people.

The flexibility of our institutional system allows us to hope that it will
not present rigid opposition to our proposals, and that it will adapt itself,
as will our legal system, to the new requirements in order to create the
new concept of institutionality needed for the overthrow of capitalism in
a constitutional manner.

The new institutional order will serve the principle which legitimizes
and directs our action: that is, to transfer political and economic power to

the workers. To make this possible, it is essential first of all for society to own the basic means of production.

At the same time it is necessary to accommodate the political institutions to the new reality. For that reason, at the proper time, we shall submit to the sovereign will of the people the question of the need to replace the present Constitution, which has a liberal framework, with a socialist-orientated Constitution, and to replace the two-Chamber system by a single Chamber.

We have promised that our governmental program will put its revolutionary aims into practice with full respect for the rule of law. This is not merely a formal assurance, but the explicit recognition that the principles of legality and institutional order are compatible with a socialist regime, in spite of the difficulties inherent in a period of transition.

To maintain these principles while transforming their class bias during this difficult period is an ambitious task, and of decisive importance for the new social order. Nonetheless, its fulfillment depends solely on our strength of will; it will depend fundamentally on the relationships in our social and economic structure, on their evolution in the short term, and on realistic political behaviour on the part of the people. At the present time, we believe that it is possible, and we are acting accordingly.

Political Freedoms

It is also important for us, as the representatives of popular forces, to remember that political freedom has been won by the people along their arduous road towards emancipation. It is part of what was positive in the historical period which we leave behind us, and it must remain, as our respect also remains for freedom of conscience and of all beliefs. For this reason we are pleased to note the words of the Cardinal Archbishop of Santiago, Raúl Silva Henriques, in his speech to the workers: "The Church I represent is the Church of Christ, son of a carpenter. Thus the Church was born and thus we want her to remain. Our greatest sorrow is when men forget her birthplace, which was and is among the humble."

But we would not be revolutionaries if we were to limit ourselves to maintaining political freedom. The government of Unidad Popular will extend political freedom. It is not enough to proclaim it by word alone, for that leads to frustration and mockery. We shall make it real, tangible, and concrete, and exercise it in the measure that we master economic freedom.

The policies of the Unidad Popular government are inspired by a paradoxical situation. Classes and sectors exist in our society with hostile and exclusive interests, and disparate political levels exist within one and the same class or sector.

In the face of this diversity the government will attend primarily to the interests of all those who earn their living by their own work: labourers and professionals, technicians and artists, intellectuals and clerical workers. These people represent a group which is growing day by day as the result of capitalist development. They are becoming more and more united by their common situation as wage-earners. The government will also support small- and medium-scale businesses. Indeed we shall support all those sectors of society which, with varying degrees of severity, have been exploited by the minorities who own the means of production.

The multi-party coalition of the Unidad Popular government is very conscious of the problems in this situation. In the daily confrontation of its interests with those of the ruling class the government will make use of all the decision-making processes available within the institutional juridical system. We recognize the political freedom of the Opposition and we will conduct all our activities within the terms of the Constitution. Political freedom is the prized possession of all Chilean people.

It is fundamental to our policy to develop the political potential of our country to the maximum, so that in the stage of transition towards socialism we shall be able to dismantle the present system systematically. We shall abolish or reject its negative aspects and strengthen and reinforce its positive factors.

Violence

The people of Chile are acquiring political power without finding themselves forced to use arms. They are advancing on the road of its social liberation without having had to fight a despotic or dictatorial regime. They have had to resist only the limitations of a liberal democracy. Our people hope with deep sincerity to spend the period of transition to socialism without having to fall back on authoritarian forms of government.

Our attitude on this point is very clear. But the responsibility of guaranteeing political evolution towards socialism does not rest solely with the government and the movements and parties that compose it. Our people have risen against the institutionalized violence which the present capitalist system imposed upon them; that is why we are transforming this system at the base.

My government owes its existence to the freely expressed will of the people. It answers only to them. The movements and parties which compose it are the guides of the revolutionary consciousness of the masses and the expression of their hopes and interests. They are also directly responsible to the people.

Nonetheless I must warn you that there are dangers which could obscure the clear path of our emancipation and radically alter for the worse the way which a realistic assessment of our circumstances would recommend. Such a danger would consist of violence done to the decisions of the people.

If violence, internal or external, violence in any of its forms, whether physical, economic, social, or political, were to succeed in threatening our natural development and the achievements of the workers, then the continuity of our institutions, our constitutional state, political liberties, and the chance for pluralism would be in acute danger. The battle for social emancipation, for the free determination of our people, would be forced to take on very different features from those which, we can proudly and truthfully say now, constitute the Chilean road to socialism. The resolute attitude of the government, the revolutionary energy of the people, the democratic strength of the armed forces and police will be our defense in ensuring that Chile advances safely along the highway to socialism.

The unity of the popular forces and the good will of the middle classes represent that infinitely superior strength which ensures that the privileged minority will not easily take to violence. As long as violence is not used against the people, we shall be able to transform the basic structures where capitalism is entrenched in a democratic, pluralistic, and free manner. The transformation will come about without the use of unnecessary physical coercion, without institutional disorder, and without disorganizing production, at a pace set by the government in accordance with the needs of the people and the development of our resources.

Nationalization of the Means of Production

Citizens, during our six months of office, we have taken decisive action on all fronts. Our economic activities aim to remove the barriers which hinder the complete development of our human and material potential. In our six months of office, we have made vigorous advances along a path of irrevocable change. The report which we have just published contains details of our activities.

Chile has begun the definitive recovery of its basic wealth: copper. The nationalization of our copper is not an act of vengeance or of hate towards any group, government, or particular nation. On the contrary, we have taken the positive step of exercising the inalienable right of a sovereign people: the full use of our resources exploited by national labour and effort.

The recovery of our copper is Chile's decision and we have a right to the respect of all countries and governments for the unanimous decision of a free people. We shall pay for the copper if it is fair to pay, or we shall not pay if it is not fair to do so. We shall protect our interests. We shall be totally intransigent if we find that negligence or malevolent acts are being perpetrated by persons, or companies in order to damage the interests of the country.

READING IMAGES
Religion and Politics

Despite the old saying, religion and politics often do mix. In Latin America, Catholic theology provided much of the official ideology of Spanish and Portuguese colonial rule from the sixteenth through the eighteenth centuries. After 1825 liberal doctrines of popular sovereignty, exercised through written constitutions and elected representatives, replaced the divine right of kings as official ruling ideology throughout newly independent Latin America. Yet, for decades, the Catholic Church remained at the center of political conflict in many countries—most notably, in Mexico. Even when the Church was not a political issue, people's habits of thought continued to structure political concepts along religious lines. What can the following images tell us about Latin American political culture in the nineteenth and twentieth centuries?

The Martyr Olaya. The banner at the top reads: "The Patriot Don José Olaya served his country gloriously and honored his birthplace." The inscription at the lower left explains that Olaya was caught carrying letters to patriots inside Spanish-controlled Lima during the Wars of Independence. He died rather than reveal any names. José Gil de Castro, a mulatto painter of society portraits, joined the patriot army as its official artist and painted many of the heroes of Independence. This 1823 rendering of a political martyr does not look like a society portrait. Why is Olaya dressed in immaculate white, displaying the letters that led to his execution and gazing directly into the viewer's eyes? Does the handkerchief tucked into his breast pocket resemble other images that you may have seen? (Hint: the handkerchief is reddish in color.) *Source: The Martyr Olaya,* by José Gil de Castro, 1823, oil on canvas, Museo Nacional de Historia, Lima, Peru. Reprinted by permission of the Museo Nacional de Historia.

"Guatemalan Church." At a church in Guatemala's heavily Mayan Quiché Province in 1983, during the darkest years of military repression in the country, photographer Jean-Marie Simon captured this image of a Roman centurion standing guard beside the crucified Christ—a figure here wearing the uniform of the government's elite counterinsurgency troops. Recalls Simon: "I heard competing stories about the figure. One was that the army dressed it as a soldier in order to intimidate the population. The second was that the villagers did so to protect themselves from the army. I am inclined to believe the latter, not because the army was incapable of such an act, but because it had recently killed a lot of people in the town and did not need religious images to quash any real or imagined dissidence. But I could be wrong." *Source:* photograph by Jean-Marie Simon, 1983.

XI

Latin America, the United States, and the Cold War

In order to combat the rising threat of social revolution in Latin America, the Cold War–era governments of the United States went to extraordinary lengths. Alliances between the U.S. and Latin American governments became increasingly important in the context of the postwar, global struggle between the Communist East and the Capitalist West, between Moscow and Washington. In the previous chapter we explored the problem of Latin American social revolution from the point of view of its participants. In this chapter we will shift perspectives and consider the role of the U.S. government in preventing social revolutionary change in Latin America, which it considered its primary mission in the region.

Since the end of the nineteenth century, U.S. governments had often acted aggressively toward the neighboring republics to the south. The Mexican-American War over Texas and the Spanish-American War over Cuba, Puerto Rico, and the Philippines are two classic examples of this violent early history. Intervention by U.S. forces (usually the Marines) was not unusual in the first half of the twentieth century, although Franklin Roosevelt began to change the pattern of intervention prior to World War II with his Good Neighbor Policy. The term "our backyard" became a fitting description of Latin America's standing relative to the United States.

The outcome of World War II presented a new set of global dynamics for U.S.–Latin American relations. By the late 1940s, old European empires were collapsing around the globe. The United States and the Soviet Union then became the world's two military superpowers, each with nuclear arsenals and extensive military alliances. U.S. policymakers were thrust into a position of responsibility for the preservation of what they saw as "the Free World," that is to say, the non-Communist world. So began the Cold War, so-called because the two sides, though apparently locked in a life-and-death confrontation, never struck at each other directly. Although they came close to armed conflict, the war stayed cold—except in some areas of the Third World, where it got very hot indeed.

In their dealings with Latin Americans, U.S. policymakers looked at the region's upsurge in social revolutionary movements and saw, or thought they saw, the hand of the Soviet Union at work. Their approach to the region was therefore founded on fundamental tenets of Cold War thinking. First was the conviction that the Soviet Union was bent upon the destruction of the Free World and the imposition of a global Communist system. Second was a commitment to "containment," which dedicated U.S. resources to stopping the spread of communism in Europe, East Asia, and the developing world. In Latin America, these tenets translated into staunch support for anti-Communist forces. And who better to combat Communist insurgency than the Latin American armed forces?

Washington's relations with the Latin American armed forces underwent a dramatic intensification during the Cold War decades. The United States provided money, weapons, special agents, advisers, and, occasionally, troops in the antirevolutionary effort. Thousands of Latin American military officers underwent specialized "counterinsurgency" training at the U.S. School of the Americas in the Panama Canal Zone (later moved to Fort Benning in Georgia). Support for the region's military leaders grew especially fast after the Cuban Revolution of 1959. Another wave of intensified funding and assistance came after Nicaragua's Sandinista Revolution of 1979.

In this context of extreme political and ideological polarization, U.S. policymakers sometimes encouraged the Latin American military to seize the reins of civil authority before it was too late. Beginning in Brazil in 1964 and continuing through the 1980s, the U.S. government declared its support for the temporary suspension of civilian democratic regimes in the region's hot spots of guerrilla conflict. Washington's National Security Doctrine justified anti-Communist dictatorships across the region. Chile, for example, which had a nearly unblemished record of democratic succession since the nineteenth century, was taken over by General Augusto Pinochet in 1973, with U.S. support. Not until 1990 would Chile have another elected president.

The United States "won" the Cold War and, in Latin America, achieved its goal of stopping social revolutions (with the nagging exception of Cuba). For most foreign policy decision makers in Washington, victory was what mattered, at any cost to Latin America. The following selections will force you to confront the costs and consequences of that victory and form your own assessment of the history of U.S.–Latin American relations.

QUESTIONS FOR ANALYSIS

1. What was the Cold War strategy of the U.S. government in regard to Latin America? How did the region fit into the bigger, geopolitical picture?

2. How does the Cold War period fit into broader patterns of the historical relationship between the United States and Latin America?

3. In the context of the Cold War, were the means used to combat social revolution in Latin America justified?

---

1. The Lesser of Two Evils ~ David F. Schmitz*

With the coming of the Chinese Communist revolution in 1949 and the Korean War of the early 1950s, U.S. policymakers faced an uncertain era of global commitments. It did not take long for the Cold War to spread from East Asia to Latin America. In the following selection, historian David Schmitz offers a perspective on one of the major challenges facing the Eisenhower administration in this new age of American superpower—how to eliminate the root causes of Communist insurgency in the Third World. Schmitz argues that President Dwight D. Eisenhower and his cabinet (in particular, Secretary of State John Foster Dulles) decided that measures to reform decolonizing societies had to be sacrificed to preserve the more fundamental objective of anti-Communist stability. For this difficult task, military dictatorships seemed the only possible solution. The author also emphasizes the decision to develop the capability for covert (secretive and often illegal) action in pursuit of the anti-Communist victory.

As had all administrations since [Woodrow] Wilson's, Eisenhower's agreed that U.S. interests were best served by the existence of other stable democratic and capitalist nations and spoke publicly about promoting democracy and freedom abroad. The problem, as Eisenhower and Dulles understood it, was in areas lacking a history of free government. New democratic governments tended to be weak and faced a myriad of challenges in their efforts to establish order and create prosperity. It was, therefore, considered a gamble to support such governments when the Soviet Union appeared to be active in all areas and communists were apparently poised to take advantage of instability or nationalist reform movements.

*From David F. Schmitz, *Thank God They're on Our Side: The United States and Right-Wing Dictatorships, 1921–1965* (Chapel Hill: University of North Carolina Press, 1999), 181–87. © 1999 by the University of North Carolina Press. Reprinted by permission of the University of North Carolina Press.

Dictators who protected Western interests, provided stability, and suppressed communism were a much better bet in such a context and had to be supported until their nations matured politically or, given the logic of the domino theory, whole areas would fall to communist forces. With their Manichean view of the Cold War, neither Eisenhower nor Dulles could tolerate revolutionary nationalism and other challenges to the status quo in the Third World.

The fundamental premise for this policy remained the idea that too many of the world's people were not yet trained or were unable to govern themselves democratically. With enough time and tutelage they could possibly develop democratic systems, but communist forces were waiting to take advantage of any signs of instability and the weaknesses of new democratic governments. The time necessary for the transition from colonial status or authoritarian government to democracy was a luxury the United States did not appear to have. In addition, an agent theory of communist activity and revolution saw all disturbances and radical movements as emanating from the Kremlin. Communist forces were seen as having a discipline and zealousness that democratic groups had difficulty matching.

The president mused in June 1953 that the "tricky problem that is posed these days is this: if firm opposition to the spread of Communism requires fighting, as in Korea and Indo-China [now Vietnam], how can the free world turn its attention to the solution of these great humanitarian problems which must be tackled in order to eliminate the conditions that promote Communism?" As Eisenhower's comments indicate, the administration understood the need for social change in the world and recognized that the United States had to adjust its approach to relations within the hemisphere and elsewhere in the Third World. Dulles told the Senate Foreign Relations Committee in April 1953 that he realized social problems and instability would be present in the world without the Soviet Union, "but what makes it a very dangerous problem for us is the fact that wherever those things exist, whether it is in Indo-China or Siam or Morocco or Egypt or Arabia or Iran . . . even in South America, the forces of unrest are captured by the Soviet Communists." In a peaceful world without the threat of the Soviet Union, the United States "could do very much more in the way of promoting . . . reforms and advancing self-government than we can do under present conditions." The secretary of state believed that it was necessary "to take a realistic view of the situation and recognize that at this time, to support a somewhat backward situation, it is the lesser of two evils, because the possibility of a peaceful change is very much diminished by the fact that you have constantly with you, for instance, the tactics of the Soviet Communist forces which take advantage of every opportunity to capture and lead the so-called reform and revolutionary movement." The United States was forced to back dictators. "Syngman

Rhee [of South Korea], Chiang Kai-shek [of Nationalist China], and so forth . . . are not the people, under normal circumstances, that we would want to support." Others would be preferable, "but in times like these, in the unrest of the world today, and the divided spirit, we know we cannot make a transition without losing control of the whole situation."

The solution to the dilemma of how to bring about social change and an evolution toward democracy without setting off revolutions and aiding the spread of communism was to be found in supporting strong leaders who would heed American advice. The rule of various dictators, therefore, was viewed positively by the new administration. For example, Vice President [Richard] Nixon, discussing South Korea, exclaimed in 1953 that "they are hard to work with, but thank God they're on our side. With all the things that are wrong with Rhee, the Communists are a lot worse." Eisenhower commented in June that, given the recurring crises in Paris, "he himself was beginning to feel that only a strongman could save France." Favors and honors were extended to shore up the rule of certain dictators, such as Marcos Pérez Jiménez of Venezuela. The State Department found Venezuela to be an "outstanding example to the rest of the world of cooperation between foreign investors and the government" for the benefit of both sides. For his efforts, Jiménez was invited by Eisenhower for a state visit in Washington in 1956 where he was presented the Legion of Merit medal, the highest award the nation can bestow on a noncitizen. Advocates of greater military aid for [Anastasio] Somoza argued that Latin American military leaders, such as that Nicaraguan dictator, worked more closely with the United States than any other groups, and those who "come to this country and see what we have and what we can do are frequently our most useful friends in those countries."

To enhance this relationship, National Security Council (NSC) resolution 5432/1, adopted in September 1954, called for closer relations with military officers, recognizing that they "play an influential role in government." A National Intelligence Estimate noted that the United States faced a dilemma in the "conflict between 'democracy' and 'dictatorship' in the Caribbean." The dictators "present themselves as guarantors of stability and order and of cooperation with the United States. The reformists, by definition, are an unsettling influence, but they contend that the United States, as a progressive democracy dominant in the area, has a moral obligation to foster social and political development." Conversely, the region's dictators "resent any indication of U.S. support for reformist regimes as a betrayal of the 'true friends' of the United States." Early the next year, Secretary of State Dulles made it clear where the administration stood on this question when he instructed State Department officials to "do nothing to offend the dictators; they are the only people we can depend on."

In a February 1955 discussion on the progress of the implementation of NSC 5432/1, the National Security Council considered the question of communism and dictatorships in Latin America. Secretary of the Treasury George Humphrey told the council that it must realize "that a strong base for Communism exists in Latin America." Moreover, "wherever a dictator was replaced, Communists gained." The United States had to "back strong men in Latin American governments." Nelson Rockefeller responded that the "dictators in these countries are a mixed blessing. It is true, in the short run, that dictators handle Communists effectively. But in the long run, the U.S. must encourage the growth of democracy in Latin America" if it wished to defeat communism in the region. The discussion of relations with dictators reminded the president of a comment made by Portugal's Antonio Salazar, which he did not dispute: "Free government cannot work among Latins." Eisenhower noted his general agreement with Rockefeller "that in the long run the United States must back democracies" without providing any indication of when and how that would come about. It was, however, the short-run challenge of communism that had to be attended to.

In both the crises in Iran and Guatemala, Eisenhower and Dulles believed that the situation had moved from a theoretical problem to an actual danger of communist rule. Both governments exhibited all of the problems policymakers associated with weak and ineffective democratic governments. They were creating a climate of confusion that would either pave the way for a communist takeover or had already permitted communists to penetrate their governments. The evidence for this view was found in Iran's efforts to nationalize the oil industry and Guatemala's pursuit of land reform. These policies, the administration noted, were exactly the same ones that communist nations adopted. Even if the people in power were not communists, they were doing the work of the Kremlin. In these cases, the administration found it necessary to help remove the dangerous government and support leaders who would maintain order, suppress communism, and align the countries with American foreign policy. The Truman administration had allowed the situation in these nations to reach the crisis stage. Establishing and supporting right-wing dictators, covertly and through announced policy, appeared to be the only option outside of direct military intervention to prevent the creation of full-blown communist states.

The administration formally set out its policy on covert action in March 1954 when it adopted NSC 5412. Greater suspicion of nationalist movements required new measures to combat these forces and shore up traditional forms of authority. Based clearly on the bipolar worldview and concern that the Soviet Union had redirected its efforts from Europe to the Third World, the National Security Council believed that "in the interest of world peace and U.S. national security, the overt foreign activities of the U.S. Government should be supplemented by covert operations." The CIA's activities could expand beyond espionage and counterespionage actions to include discrediting and reducing the strength of international communism and its parties; countering "any threat of a party or individuals directly or indirectly responsive to Communist control to achieve dominant power in a free world country"; orienting peoples and nations toward the free world and the United States by increasing the "capacity and will of such peoples and nations to resist International Communism"; and developing resistance movements and covert operations in areas "dominated or threatened by International Communism." These actions were to be coordinated with the State and Defense Departments to ensure that "covert operations are planned and conducted in a manner consistent with United States foreign and military policies" and carried out in such a manner that "any U.S. Government responsibility for them is not evident . . . and that if uncovered the U.S. Government can plausibly disclaim any responsibility for them." The operations would include "propaganda; political action; economic warfare; preventive direct action, including sabotage, anti-sabotage, demolition; . . . subversion against hostile states or groups including assistance to underground resistance groups, guerrillas and refugee liberation groups; [and] support of indigenous and anti-communist elements in threatened countries of the free world."

At the same time, Eisenhower appointed a committee headed by General James Doolittle to conduct a study of the CIA [Central Intelligence Agency] and the need for covert activity. The committee's conclusion, which Eisenhower received in October 1954, set the issues out in stark and dangerous terms:

> It is now clear that we are facing an implacable enemy whose avowed objective is world domination by whatever means and at whatever cost. There are no rules in such a game. Hitherto acceptable norms do not apply. If the United States is to survive, long-standing American concepts of "fair play" must be reconsidered. We must develop effective espionage and counterespionage services and must learn to subvert, sabotage, and destroy our enemies by more clever, more sophisticated, and more effective methods than those used against us. It may become necessary that the American people be made acquainted with, understand, and support this fundamentally repugnant philosophy.

Covert activities were to fill the gap between the need to maintain order and prevent the spread of communism and the desire to avoid direct intervention. The United States was entering a new phase of the Cold War and relations with right-wing dictators.

In a 1956 interview, Secretary of State Dulles captured the intentions and problems confronting the administration. The secretary explained that

American policy was designed to ensure freedom from communism for all the nations of the world. What nations did "with their freedom after they get it is a second problem. We naturally would like them to have the same kind of freedom and exercise it the way we do, with our same democratic processes." This was not, he realized, the case. Nor was it a major concern of the United States. Democracy was the best system, but it "is a system which can only be spread throughout the world gradually, and as I say, today there are not many parts of the world where that particular system prevails." To insist on it, then, would damage American interests and create openings for the Soviet Union to exploit. Better to stay with loyal friends than experiment with change and new people in a dangerous world.

---

2. Statements of U.S. Foreign Policy Doctrine ~ Presidents James Monroe, Theodore Roosevelt, and Harry Truman*

At various critical junctures in U.S. history, American presidents have articulated fundamental statements about the goals and methods of their foreign policy. Historians often refer to such statements as doctrines (or corollaries, when addenda to doctrines are made after the fact). The earliest and most deeply rooted of these doctrines was announced before Congress in 1823 by President James Monroe at the time of the Spanish American Wars of Independence. Monroe called for a policy of noncolonization in the Americas, aiming his message at any European power that might be eyeing the territories soon to be liberated from Spanish control. The next major statement to impact on Latin America came from President Theodore Roosevelt in the early twentieth century. Known as the Roosevelt Corollary (to the Monroe Doctrine), TR's announcement made in Congress in 1904 embraced the idea that the U.S. government would act as the "hemispheric policeman" of the Americas, settling any and all disputes among parties. Four decades later, the most important statement of U.S. policy during the Cold War was announced to Congress by President Harry Truman in 1946. At the time, U.S. ally Greece was being menaced by an internal Communist insurgency, which was seen as part of a Soviet assault on the eastern Mediterranean. The Truman Doctrine pledged U.S. support and protection to Greece and any other government facing a Communist threat. In a word, Truman's doctrine of worldwide "containment" was the foundation of U.S. policy throughout the Cold War.

---

*From James D. Richardson, comp., *Messages and Papers of the Presidents*, 20 vols. (New York: Bureau of National Literature, 1897–1922); and U.S. Congress, Senate Committee on Foreign Relations, *A Decade of American Foreign Policy: Basic Documents*, 1941–1949 (Washington, DC: U.S. Government Printing Office, 1950), 1270–71.

Monroe Doctrine (1823)

In the wars of the European powers in matters relating to themselves we have never taken any part, nor does it comport with our policy so to do. It is only when our rights are invaded or seriously menaced that we resent injuries or make preparation for our defense. With the movements in this hemisphere we are of necessity more immediately connected, and by causes which must be obvious to all enlightened and impartial observers. The political system of the allied powers [Europe's Holy Alliance] is essentially different in this respect from that of America. This difference proceeds from that which exists in their respective Governments; and to the defense of our own, which has been achieved by the loss of so much blood and treasure, and matured by the wisdom of our most enlightened citizens, and under which we have enjoyed unexampled felicity, the whole nation is devoted. We owe it, therefore, to candor and to the amicable relations existing between the United States and those powers to declare that we should consider any attempt on their part to extend their system to any portion of this hemisphere as dangerous to our peace and security. With the existing colonies or dependencies of any European power we have not interfered and shall not interfere. But with the Governments who have declared their independence and maintained it, and whose independence we have, on great consideration and on just principles, acknowledged, we could not view any interposition for the purpose of oppressing them, or controlling in any other manner their destiny, by any European power in any other light than as the manifestation of an unfriendly disposition toward the United States. In the war between those new Governments and Spain we declared our neutrality at the time of their recognition, and to this we have adhered, and shall continue to adhere, provided no change shall occur which, in the judgment of the competent authorities of this Government, shall make a corresponding change on the part of the United States indispensable to their security.

Roosevelt Corollary to the Monroe Doctrine (1904)

Chronic wrongdoing, or an impotence which results in a general loosening of the ties of civilized society, may in America, as elsewhere, ultimately require intervention by some civilized nation, and in the Western Hemisphere the adherence of the United States to the Monroe Doctrine may force the United States, however reluctantly, in flagrant cases of such wrongdoing or impotence, to the exercise of an international police power. If every country washed by the Caribbean Sea would show the progress in stable and just civilization which with the aid of the Platt amendment Cuba has shown since our troops left the island,* and which so many of the republics in both Americas are constantly and brilliantly showing, all question of interference by this Nation with their affairs would be at an end. Our interests and those of our southern neighbors are in reality identical. They have great natural riches, and if within their borders the reign of law and justice obtains, prosperity is sure to come to them. While they thus obey the primary laws of civilized society they may rest assured that they will be treated by us in a spirit of cordial and helpful sympathy. We would interfere with them only in the last resort, and then only if it became evident that their inability or unwillingness to do justice at home and abroad had violated the rights of the United States or had invited foreign aggression to the detriment of the entire body of American nations. It is a mere truism to say that every nation, whether in America or anywhere else, which desires to maintain its freedom, its independence, must ultimately realize that the right of such independence cannot be separated from the responsibility of making good use of it.

Truman Doctrine (1946)

One of the primary objectives of the foreign policy of the United States is the creation of the conditions in which we and other nations will be able to work out a way of life free from coercion. This was a fundamental issue in the war with Germany and Japan. Our victory was won over countries which sought to impose their will, and their way of life, upon other nations. To ensure the peaceful development of nations, free from coercion, the United States has taken a leading part in establishing the United Nations. The United Nations is designed to make possible lasting freedom and independence for all its members. We shall not realize our objectives, however, unless we are willing to help free peoples to maintain their free institutions and their national integrity against aggressive movements that seek to impose upon them totalitarian regimes. This is no more than a frank recognition that totalitarian regimes imposed on free peoples, by direct or indirect aggression, undermine the foundations of international peace and hence the security of the United States.

The peoples of a number of countries of the world have recently had totalitarian regimes forced upon them against their will. The Government of the United States has made frequent protests against coercion and intimidation, in violation of the Yalta Agreement in Poland, Romania, and Bulgaria. I must also state that in a number of other countries there have been similar developments.

---

*An amendment to Cuba's 1901 constitution that gave the United States the right to intervene in Cuban affairs.

At the present moment in world history nearly every nation must choose between alternative ways of life. The choice is too often not a free one.

One way of life is based upon the will of the majority, and is distinguished by free institutions, representative government, free elections, guarantees of individual liberty, freedom of speech and religion, and freedom from political oppression.

The second way of life is based upon the will of a minority forcibly imposed upon the majority. It relies upon terror and oppression, a controlled press and radio, fixed elections, and the suppression of personal freedoms.

I believe that it must be the policy of the United States to support free peoples who are resisting attempted subjugation by armed minorities or by outside pressures.

I believe that we must assist free peoples to work out their own destinies in their own way.

I believe that our help should be primarily through economic and financial aid which is essential to economic stability and orderly political processes.

The world is not static, and the status quo is not sacred. But we cannot allow changes in the status quo in violation of the Charter of the United Nations by such methods as coercion, or by such subterfuges as political infiltration. In helping free and independent nations to maintain their freedom, the United States will be giving effect to the principles of the Charter of the United Nations.

---

3. Alleged Assassination Plots Involving Foreign Leaders ~ Church Committee*

In 1974, Senator Frank Church initiated a series of hearings to look into the covert activities of the U.S. government in regard to the alleged assassinations of five prominent political figures in the Third World. The assassinations (four out of five of which were successful) spanned the years from 1960 to 1970 and took place from the Caribbean to Central Africa to Southeast Asia. What Church found was a shock to some Americans: the Central Intelligence Agency (CIA), set up in the late 1940s to coordinate the large-scale intelligence-gathering and covert operations of the Cold War, was indeed implicated. (See, in particular,

---

*From U.S. Senate, *Alleged Assassination Plots Involving Foreign Leaders: An Interim Report of the Select Committee to Study Governmental Operations with Respect to Intelligence Activities,* with an introduction by Senator Frank Church (New York: W. W. Norton, 1975), 4–7.

the summaries on Cuba's President Fidel Castro and Chile's General Rene Schneider.) Moreover, a footnote to the report stated that the Church Committee had also received some evidence of CIA involvement in plans to assassinate President Sukarno of Indonesia and "Papa Doc" Duvalier of Haiti. The Church Committee demanded and passed legislation curtailing the activities of the "rogue elephant," the senator's term for the out-of-control CIA of the 1950s and 1960s. Nevertheless, the record is clear about the lengths to which the U.S. government would go to stop the spread of communism around the world.

1. The Questions Presented

The Committee sought to answer four broad questions:

ASSASSINATION PLOTS—Did United States officials instigate, attempt, aid and abet, or acquiesce in plots to assassinate foreign leaders?

INVOLVEMENT IN OTHER KILLINGS—Did United States officials assist foreign dissidents in a way which significantly contributed to the killing of foreign leaders?

AUTHORIZATION—Where there was involvement by United States officials in assassination plots or other killings, were such activities authorized, and if so, at what levels of our Government?

COMMUNICATION AND CONTROL—Even if not authorized in fact, were the assassination activities perceived by those involved to be within the scope of their lawful authority? If they were so perceived, was there inadequate control exercised by higher authorities over the agencies to prevent such misinterpretation?

2. Summary of Findings and Conclusions on the Plots

The Committee investigated alleged United States involvement in assassination plots in five foreign countries:

Country	Individual Involved
Cuba	Fidel Castro
Congo (Zaire)	Patrice Lumumba
Dominican Republic	Rafael Trujillo
Chile	General Rene Schneider
South Vietnam	Ngo Dinh Diem

The evidence concerning each alleged assassination can be summarized as follows:

PATRICE LUMUMBA (Congo/Zaire)—In the Fall of 1960, two CIA officials were asked by superiors to assassinate Lumumba. Poisons were sent to the Congo and some exploratory steps were taken toward gaining access to Lumumba. Subsequently, in early 1961, Lumumba was killed by Congolese rivals. It does not appear from the evidence that the United States was in any way involved in the killing.

FIDEL CASTRO (Cuba)—United States Government personnel plotted to kill Castro from 1960 to 1965. American underworld figures and Cubans hostile to Castro were used in these plots and were provided encouragement and material support by the United States.

RAFAEL TRUJILLO (Dominican Republic)—Trujillo was shot by Dominican dissidents on May 31, 1961. From early in 1960 and continuing to the time of the assassination, the United States Government generally supported these dissidents. Some Government personnel were aware that the dissidents intended to kill Trujillo. Three pistols and three carbines were furnished by American officials, although a request for machine guns was later refused. There is conflicting evidence concerning whether the weapons were knowingly supplied for use in the assassination and whether any of them were present at the scene.

NGO DINH DIEM (South Vietnam)—Diem and his brother, Nhu, were killed on November 2, 1963, in the course of a South Vietnamese Generals' coup. Although the United States Government supported the coup, there is no evidence that American officials favored the assassination. Indeed, it appears that the assassination of Diem was not part of the Generals' pre-coup planning but was instead a spontaneous act which occurred during the coup and was carried out without United States involvement or support.

GENERAL RENE SCHNEIDER (Chile)—On October 25, 1970, General Schneider died of gunshot wounds inflicted three days earlier while resisting a kidnap attempt. Schneider, as Commander-in-Chief of the Army and a constitutionalist opposed to military coups, was considered an obstacle in efforts to prevent Salvador Allende from assuming the office of President of Chile. The United States Government supported and sought to instigate a military coup to block Allende. U.S. officials supplied financial aid, machine guns, and other equipment to various military figures who opposed Allende. Although the CIA continued to support coup plotters up to Schneider's shooting, the record indicates that the CIA had withdrawn active support of the group which carried out the actual kidnap attempt on October 22, which resulted in Schneider's death. Further, it does not appear that any of the equipment supplied by the CIA to coup plotters in Chile was used in the kidnapping. There is no evidence of a plan to kill Schneider or that United States officials specifically anticipated that Schneider would be shot during the abduction.

Assassination Capability (Executive action)—In addition to these five cases, the Committee has received evidence that ranking Government officials discussed, and may have authorized, the establishment within the

CIA of a generalized assassination capability. During these discussions, the concept of assassination was not affirmatively disavowed.

Similarities and Differences among the Plots—The assassination plots all involved Third World countries, most of which were relatively small and none of which possessed great political or military strength. Apart from that similarity, there were significant differences among the plots:

1. Whether United States officials initiated the plot, or were responding to requests of local dissidents for aid.
2. Whether the plot was specifically intended to kill a foreign leader, or whether the leader's death was a reasonably foreseeable consequence of an attempt to overthrow the government.

The Castro and Lumumba cases are examples of plots conceived by United States officials to kill foreign leaders.

In the Trujillo case, although the United States Government certainly opposed his regime, it did not initiate the plot. Rather, United States officials responded to requests for aid from local dissidents whose aim clearly was to assassinate Trujillo. By aiding them, this country was implicated in the assassination, regardless of whether the weapons actually supplied were meant to kill Trujillo or were only intended as symbols of support for the dissidents.

The Schneider case differs from the Castro and Trujillo cases. The United States Government, with full knowledge that Chilean dissidents considered General Schneider an obstacle to their plans, sought a coup and provided support to the dissidents. However, even though the support included weapons, it appears that the intention of both the dissidents and the United States officials was to abduct General Schneider, not to kill him. Similarly, in the Diem case, some United States officials wanted Diem removed and supported a coup to accomplish his removal, but there is no evidence that any of those officials sought the death of Diem himself.

3. Summary of Findings and Conclusions on the Issues of Authority and Control

To put the inquiry into assassination allegations in context, two points must be made clear. First, there is no doubt that the United States Government opposed the various leaders in question. Officials at the highest levels objected to the Castro and Trujillo regimes, believed the accession of Allende to power in Chile would be harmful to American interests, and thought of Lumumba as a dangerous force in the heart of Africa. Second, the evidence on assassinations has to be viewed in the context of other, more massive activities against the regimes in question. For example, the plots against Fidel Castro personally cannot be understood without considering the fully authorized, comprehensive assaults upon his regime, such as the Bay of Pigs invasion in 1961 and Operation MONGOOSE in 1962.

Once methods of coercion and violence are chosen, the probability of loss of life is always present. There is, however, a significant difference between a coldblooded, targeted, intentional killing of an individual foreign leader and other forms of intervening in the affairs of foreign nations. Therefore, the Committee has endeavored to explore as fully as possible the questions of how and why the plots happened, whether they were authorized, and if so, at what level.

The picture that emerges from the evidence is not a clear one. This may be due to the system of deniability and the consequent state of the evidence which, even after our long investigation, remains conflicting and inconclusive. Or it may be that there were in fact serious shortcomings in the system of authorization so that an activity such as assassination could have been undertaken by an agency of the United States Government without express authority.

The Committee finds that the system of executive command and control was so ambiguous that it is difficult to be certain at what levels assassination activity was known and authorized. This situation creates the disturbing prospect that Government officials might have undertaken the assassination plots without it having been uncontrovertibly clear that there was explicit authorization from the Presidents. It is also possible that there might have been a successful "plausible denial" in which Presidential authorization was issued but is now obscured. Whether or not the respective Presidents knew of or authorized the plots, as chief executive officer of the United States, each must bear the ultimate responsibility for the activities of his subordinates.

The Committee makes four other major findings. The first relates to the Committee's inability to make a finding that the assassination plots were authorized by the Presidents or other persons above the governmental agency or agencies involved. The second explains why certain officials may have perceived that, according to their judgment and experience, assassination was an acceptable course of action. The third criticizes agency officials for failing on several occasions to disclose their plans and activities to superior authorities, or for failing to do so with sufficient detail and clarity. The fourth criticizes Administration officials for not ruling out assassination, particularly after certain Administration officials had become aware of prior assassination plans and the establishment of a general assassination capability.

There is admittedly a tension among the findings. This tension reflects a basic conflict in the evidence. While there are some conflicts over facts, it may be more important that there appeared to have been two differing perceptions of the same facts. This distinction may be the result of the differing backgrounds of those persons experienced in covert operations as distinguished from those who were not. Words of urgency which may have meant killing to the former, may have meant nothing of the sort to the latter.

While we are critical of certain individual actions, the Committee is also mindful of the inherent problems in a system which relies on secrecy, compartmentation, circumlocution, and the avoidance of clear responsibility. This system creates the risk of confusion and rashness in the very areas where clarity and sober judgment are most necessary.

---

4. Two Centuries Later ～ Lars Schoultz*

Does the historical record show the Cold War to be a unique period in the evolution of U.S.–Latin American relations? Or are there meaningful continuities between it and the century that preceded it? In this selection, political scientist Lars Schoultz argues for a fundamental continuity in the relationship. According to Schoultz, the most important constant since the early national period has been the "mind-set" of U.S. foreign policymakers toward Latin American civilization, which officials such as John Quincy Adams, Theodore Roosevelt, Woodrow Wilson, Jeane Kirkpatrick, and George Kennan viewed as "inferior" to their own. This perception of inferiority was shaped by several factors, including anti-Catholicism, Manifest Destiny, racism, and paternalism. In this unconventional interpretation of U.S.–Latin American relations, Schoultz questions the motivations for what appear to be well-intentioned U.S. policies toward the region.

To obtain a full explanation of United States policy toward Latin America, we have had to add the mind-set that governs the thinking of U.S. officials as they process these concerns. Dominating this mind-set are the underlying beliefs that U.S. officials hold about Latin Americans and, specifically, their belief that Latin Americans are an inferior people.

The origin of this belief is indisputable: the dark shadow of Latin American inferiority crept across our consciousness long before the first U.S. diplomat set foot in Latin America, decades before there was such a thing as United States policy toward Latin America, years before there was an empirical foundation for any belief, one way or the other. John

---

*From Lars Schoultz, *Beneath the United States: A History of U.S. Policy toward Latin America* (Cambridge, MA: Harvard University Press, 1998), 374–80. © 1998 by the President and Fellows of Harvard College. Reprinted by permission of Harvard University Press.

Quincy Adams and his generation were prejudiced in the strict sense of the word: they prejudged Catholics to be inferior to Protestants, Hispanics to Anglos, dark-skinned to light. In adopting this prejudice, early U.S. foreign-policy officials reacted much like any group encountering a different culture; indeed, their reflex prejudice, often called ethnocentrism, is so nearly universal as to be properly considered a part of human nature.

But the belief in Latin American inferiority is no longer a reflex prejudice; it has continued for nearly two centuries, and its sheer persistence has never been explained. The beginning of an explanation almost certainly lies in the initial decades of U.S. relations with independent Latin America, the decades from the early 1820s, when the first U.S. ministers took up their posts, to the late 1850s, when the Civil War interrupted U.S. diplomacy. This was the time when contradictory evidence might have overcome the uninformed prejudice of John Quincy Adams's generation, but the moment was not propitious. As the new U.S. envoys were presenting their credentials in Bogotá and Buenos Aires, the Spanish were just months away from their final defeat at Junín and Ayacucho, preparing to leave the victorious Creoles with devastated economies and a decade-long legacy of militarism, unbalanced by a tradition of self-rule. This was a recipe for instability, and this is what the initial U.S. envoys found. They attributed this instability to the inherent inferior nature of Hispanic culture.

Then in the 1840s the expansionist ideology of Manifest Destiny seized control of United States policy toward Latin America, and a justification was needed for taking land from the Hispanic Europeans who had taken it from the indigenous inhabitants. The rationale that James K. Polk's generation selected was a belief that the Latin Americans who stood in the path of expansion were only a small step above the savages who had blocked the march of civilization across the original thirteen colonies. Now saddled with the instrumental purpose of facilitating growth, Anglo prejudices were confirmed, particularly in Mexico, where the move into Texas began at the very moment of Mexican independence. The Anglos who wanted Mexico's territory took advantage of the fledgling's weakness, cloaking their acquisitive behavior in the mantle of improving upon Hispanic civilization. As Theodore Roosevelt would write years later, "it was inevitable, as well as in the highest degree desirable for the good of humanity at large, that the American people should ultimately crowd out the Mexicans from their sparsely populated Northern provinces."

So it was that the mental mold of U.S. policy toward Latin America was firmly set by the time that the United States descended into its own Civil War. Then late in the nineteenth century, when the United States had recovered and was beginning to renew its interest in Latin America, this mold was once again used to fashion policy by the Young Turks [advocates of change] of Theodore Roosevelt's generation. Identifying Latin America as a convenient site for demonstrating that their adolescent nation had matured into an international power, the United States became involved in disputes in Peru, Chile, Venezuela, Cuba, Colombia, Panama, the Dominican Republic, Haiti, and Nicaragua. In each case, U.S. policy can be explained by a mixture of security concerns, domestic politics, and economic interests, but it was the underlying belief in Latin American inferiority that guided U.S. officials to the specific policies known as the Big Stick and Dollar Diplomacy. In particular, the belief in Latin American inferiority dictated Washington's turn-of-the-century assumption of responsibility for solving Latin Americans' problems, be it their inability to end a war, draw a boundary line, achieve independence, or stabilize their economies.

The decision to help Latin Americans with their foreign debt was especially significant. Shouldering this burden was originally justified by a security argument (the need to keep European creditors out of the Caribbean), but this justification was based on the underlying belief that the region's profligate leaders were unable to manage their own money. Poised at the top of a slippery slope, U.S. officials argued that security required economic control, took one step in that direction, and immediately slid into the conclusion that economic control required political tutelage, a requirement based on the assumption that Latin America's corrupt, chaotic politics were the cause of the region's economic problems. Having learned from Europe how a powerful nation should behave, U.S. leaders seemed almost eager to accept their share of the White Man's Burden,* which in Latin America manifested itself in the appointment of proconsuls, often accompanied by detachments of Marines.

As this proconsular policy gathered momentum, it quickly became the norm. By 1913, when Woodrow Wilson entered office, the new President saw nothing unusual about assuming responsibility for teaching Mexicans not simply how to handle their economy, but how to behave democratically, a task that the preceding generations—Benjamin Harrison or a Grover Cleveland—would never have considered for a moment. Wilson instructed his new secretary of state that "we consider it our duty to insist on constitutional government there and will, if necessary . . . take charge of elections and see that a real government is erected." Secretary of State [Robert] Lansing responded by upping the ante, suggesting that the entire Caribbean region receive U.S. tutelage, again blending a security rationale with an assumption of Latin American inferiority: "Within this area lie the small republics of America which have been and to an extent still are the prey of revolutionists, of corrupt governments, and of predatory foreigners. Because of this state of affairs our national safety, in my opin-

---

*Rudyard Kipling's phrase.

ion, requires that the United States should intervene and aid in the establishment and maintenance of a stable and honest government." In this way, Washington's early-twentieth-century leaders grafted a new belief in the need for hegemony onto the pre–Civil War belief in Latin American inferiority. It was no longer simply that Latin Americans were inferior, but that their inferiority threatened U.S. security—everything from a cutoff of vital supplies and transit routes to the establishment of military bases by powerful European rivals.

After that, the decades passed quickly—the Roaring '20s, the Great Depression, another World War, and then the Cold War, while one significant corner of the minds of U.S. officials remained frozen in time. In 1832 a U.S. envoy had written that Argentines "have all the vices of men and all the follies of children, without the virtues or the sense of either," and so he closed the U.S. legation in Buenos Aires and went home. More than a century later, as the Eisenhower administration was coming to a close, the minutes of a meeting of the National Security Council indicate that "Mr. Allen Dulles pointed out that the new Cuban officials had to be treated more or less like children. They had to be led rather than rebuffed. If they were rebuffed, like children, they were capable of doing almost anything." Soon the U.S. embassy in Havana was also closed.

The generation of officials who padlocked the embassy in Argentina did not share the hegemonic vision of the generation that severed relations with Cuba, and so subsequent policies toward these two governments were quite different. But both generations compared Latin Americans to unruly children—immature, emotional, and needing supervision. To our generation this comparison seems hopelessly quaint, so politically incorrect that readers will not be surprised to discover that in 1832 Minister Francis Baylies knew next to nothing about Argentines, and that in 1959 CIA Director Allen Dulles was uninformed about Cubans. What we have here, we tell ourselves, are two more examples of John Quincy Adams's uninformed prejudice.

But however much we might wish it were otherwise, this prejudice remains today at the core of any explanation of United States policy toward Latin America. It was especially evident during the spasm of U.S. attention to Central America in the 1980s, and can be seen most clearly in the writings of Jeane Kirkpatrick, whose articles in *Commentary* magazine served as the intellectual foundation for the Reagan administration's policy. The first of Ambassador [to the United Nations] Kirkpatrick's two articles developed the distinction between totalitarian and authoritarian regimes, and provided the rationale for continuing U.S. support of Latin America's anticommunist authoritarian governments; the second explained the region's importance to U.S. security, emphasizing the global balance of power. Laced into both articles is the assertion that Latin

Americans are pathologically violent. "Violence or the threat of violence is an integral part of these political systems—a fact which is obscured by our way of describing military 'interventions' in Latin political systems as if the system were normally peaceable. Coups, demonstrations, political strikes, plots, and counterplots are, in fact, the norm." To Kirkpatrick, the particularly vicious Salvadoran civil war reflected the fact that "El Salvador's political culture . . . emphasizes strength and machismo and all that implies about the nature of the world and the human traits necessary for survival and success. Competition, courage, honor, shrewdness, assertiveness, a capacity for risk and recklessness, and a certain 'manly' disregard for safety are valued."

Since Ambassador Kirkpatrick never visited El Salvador before writing about its political culture, her views had to come from some source other than direct observation. Their precise origin is unknown, for she mentioned no sources and provided no citations, but since her ideas obviously flowed from the 1940s tradition of national character analysis, she probably relied heavily upon the work of the leading contemporary exponent of that tradition, Howard Wiarda, who at the time was her colleague at the American Enterprise Institute in Washington. Wiarda's writings contained precisely Kirkpatrick's argument, cloaked in academic regalia, and, like Kirkpatrick, Wiarda used his view of Latin American culture as the foundation for policy advice. "El Salvador has had a long tradition of political violence," he wrote; indeed, "*machetismo*, or the butchering of one's personal and political foes, is a way of life. Such endemic, persistent violence is very difficult for Americans to understand or come to grips with. The entire political culture—governance, challenges to it, the circulation of new and old groups in and out of power—is based on the display and use of violence."

Like Kirkpatrick, Wiarda never conducted research in El Salvador. His ideas are also of second-hand provenance and, although their exact pedigree is uncertain, they are remarkably similar to those of the preceding generation of scholars who pursued Ruth Benedict's national character approach to cultural analysis. They especially resemble the ideas of historian Richard Morse, who contended that "Latin America is subject to special imperatives as an offshoot of postmedieval, Catholic, Iberian Europe which never underwent the Protestant Reformation." Like Kirkpatrick and Wiarda, Morse then jumps ahead several centuries to identify the contemporary product of this background: "human laws are frequently seen as too harsh or impracticable or inequitable or simply as inapplicable to the specific case. Hence the difficulty of collecting income taxes; the prevalent obligation to pay fees or bribes to officials for special or even routine services; the apathy of metropolitan police toward theft and delinquency; the thriving contraband trade at border towns; the leniency toward those who commit crimes of passion—all the way down to the nonobservance of 'no smoking' signs on buses and in theaters."

Morse never tells his readers the origin of these ideas, but every word he wrote could have been written by John Quincy Adams. Viewed in historical perspective, it seems clear that contemporary national character analysts borrow their ideas about Latin America from the early-nineteenth-century Anglo view of Hispanic culture, then adapt that view to the special circumstances of their day. Kirkpatrick's special contribution was to simplify—to discard the academic mumbo jumbo that only confuses fast-reading Washingtonians—and to highlight the cultural commitment to "*machismo* and all that implies." Then, knowing where Washington focuses its attention, she drew out the implications for U.S. policy: we may respect human rights here in the United States, she wrote, but the Carter administration should never have expected Latin Americans, heir to a violent culture, to share the same values: "Hurried efforts to force complex and unfamiliar political practices on societies lacking the requisite political culture, tradition, and social structures not only fail to produce desired outcomes; if they are undertaken at a time when the traditional regime is under attack, they actually facilitate the job of the insurgents."

The history of U.S.–Latin American relations is overflowing with this type of thinking. Perhaps the best example is that of George Kennan, the intellectual father of containment, whose only exposure to Latin America was a hopscotch tour of the region's capitals in 1950. His trip report focused on Latin Americans' "exaggerated self centeredness and egotism" and their "pathetic urge to create the illusion of desperate courage." Written by a lame duck in the Truman-Acheson State Department, Kennan's report received little attention, but one cannot help but wonder how much of early Cold War policy toward Latin America was influenced by these ideas while Kennan was serving as director of State's Policy Planning Staff (1947 to 1949) and as Counselor (1949 to 1950). What we need not wonder is the origin of his beliefs about Latin Americans: just as Kirkpatrick could not possibly have uncovered the secrets of Salvadoran political culture without stepping foot in the country, Kennan could not have learned enough in his whirlwind visit to justify his analysis of Latin American personality. Instead, he modernized the thinking of John Quincy Adams, adding the Freudian argot popular at the time.

The Kennans and the Kirkpatricks are crucial to an understanding of United States policy toward Latin America, simply because every administration seems to have a quota for this type of person—like JFK's Richard Goodwin, who revealed that prior to helping formulate the Alliance for Progress, "I had never set foot south of the border (aside from one orgiastic night just beyond the Texas border during the campaign which had little to do with high policy, but which an exceptionally imaginative psychiatrist might conclude had planted the seed of my love affair with Latin America)." However shallow they and their knowledge of Latin America may be, it is important to know what this type of official believes, because their beliefs often determine policy.

XII

Globalization

This chapter, and the one that follows, offer two perspectives on the complex dynamics that define contemporary Latin America. With the collapse of the Soviet Union in 1991, the period known as the Cold War came to an end. The few Marxist-Leninist-inspired social revolutionary movements that lasted into the 1990s were clearly on the retreat worldwide. New patterns of trade, migration, and communications began to reshape the globe, including the areas of Latin America that had been racked by decades of civil war, military rule, and accelerating national debt. A new period in Latin American history seemed to be taking shape. But would this new period really change the damaging dynamics of the Cold War era and allow the region to overcome its most burdensome legacies?

While historians are naturally cautious about attempts to characterize contemporary trends, they have wholeheartedly embraced the concept of globalization in defining the present moment in world history. Globalization is the name of the process by which relationships of all sorts—social, environmental, cultural, and, above all, economic—are cut loose from their local points of origin to float freely in the emerging "global" space created by new transportation and communications technologies. Because of its decentered, borderless, planetary nature, globalization threatens to undermine the basic concept of national sovereignty that has existed in the world for centuries.

Historians of Latin America have sought new perspectives from which to gauge the complicated process of globalization. The dominant perspectives of the 1960s, 1970s, and 1980s do not seem adequate for the task. For one thing, the prospects of social revolution, a primary concern of Latin American historians during the Cold War, look very different now. Most of the revolutionary insurgents of the 1980s laid down their arms and returned to their fields, factories, churches, and schools in the 1990s. Fidel Castro's brand of social revolution continued in Cuba but grew more and more isolated. The problem of U.S.–Latin American relations also looks different in the post–Cold War era. As the wave of revolutionary energy subsided, U.S. policy shifted away from anticommunism toward regional economic integration. The starkly divided, bipolar world of the Cold War period had become more closely interconnected than ever.

The classical liberal model of economic development, which had been eclipsed in Latin America around the 1930s, returned to its earlier position of dominance in the 1990s. As we will see below, *neoliberalism* (the newly revitalized classical liberalism) was implemented in many countries beginning in the 1980s, often under military rule. Many of the civilian governments that took over in the 1990s were even more fervent neoliberals than their military predecessors. They pressed hard for reforms, in fulfillment of the International Monetary Fund's prescriptions for "structural adjustment" and the demands of the so-called Washington Consensus, which usually included the selling of state-owned enterprises (called *privatization*, undoing the earlier process of *nationalization*), the reduction of state spending in the public sector, the active courting of foreign investment, and the aggressive exploitation of untapped primary resources.

Two other aspects of globalization stand out with respect to the selections that follow. The first is the importance of regional economic integration in the process of globalization. The North American Free Trade Agreement (NAFTA), implemented in 1994 under Bill Clinton, is a major example of this trend. Others include the South American Common Market (MERCOSUR/MERCOSUL) and the Central American Free Trade Agreement (CAFTA). The controversial Free Trade Area of Americas (FTAA), however, faces stiff resistance from several South American governments.

The other aspect of the problem that needs to be considered is the rising importance of China in the global economy. North Americans are well aware of the impact of Chinese production on the U.S. consumer economy, but where does China get the raw materials it needs to be the world's mass manufacturer? The answer, for now, is that they get what they need from every possible source on the planet, including Latin America. This new relationship, something that would have been unthinkable just a few decades ago, is providing Latin American leaders with a whole new set of diplomatic and economic options. As you work through the following documents, think about how Latin America relates to that larger, global arena.

QUESTIONS FOR ANALYSIS

1. What are the dynamics that define globalization? Is it a single process, or is it more accurate to talk about globalizations?
2. How does regional integration contribute to globalization? What is its impact on nation-states?

3. Is globalization really helping to further social and economic development goals in Latin America, or is it a third conquest?

1. Reagan in Cancún, or the Third Conquest of Latin America ~ Greg Grandin*

According to historian Greg Grandin, the neoliberal takeover of Latin American governments opened the door to a "third conquest" of the region by outside forces, comparable to those of the sixteenth and nineteenth centuries. This new conquest was led initially on the U.S. side by President Ronald Reagan (1981– 1989), whose election victory in 1980 signaled a major shift in U.S. government policy with regard to the global economy. Reagan embraced a highly conservative† economic philosophy that made him an orthodox free-trader and deregulator. In 1981, he took that message to an international meeting held in Cancún, México. In the selection Grandin begins by pointing out how Reagan's economic policies went against the "developmentalist" recommendations of the UN Economic Commission on Latin America and its most prominent economist, Raúl Prebisch, whose ideas on the economics of developing nations were extremely influential in the 1960s and 1970s. Reagan set in motion a process that would be carried forward under his Democratic successor, Bill Clinton, in the 1990s.

R eagan unveiled the outline of this new system at the International Meeting on Cooperation and Development, held in Cancún, Mexico, in late 1981. At the time, discussions of the international economy were still permeated with the language of developmentalism. Throughout the preceding decade, third-world leaders had expanded on ideas elaborated by the Argentine economist Raúl Prebisch, who headed the U.N. Economic Commission on Latin America, to propose a radical restructuring of the terms of global trade. Their vision of a New International Economic Order included increasing financial assistance to developing countries, negotiating the transfer of first-world technology and industry to poor nations, lowering tariff barriers to third-world manufacturing, recognizing each state's full sovereignty over its natural resources and economic activities (which would legitimate industrial expropriations and nationaliza-

---

*From Greg Grandin, *Empire's Workshop: Latin America, the United States, and the Rise of the New Imperialism* (New York: Metropolitan Books, 2006), 185–90. Reprinted by permission of Henry Holt and Company, LLC.
†Conventional definitions of "liberal" and "conservative" in the political culture of the United States can be confusing. In terms of economic philosophy Reagan's conservatism was really a return to classical liberal principles.

tions), and setting just prices for ten core commodities—cocoa, coffee, tea, sugar, hard fibers, jute, cotton, rubber, copper, and tin. A majority of third-world countries called for the establishment of new international institutions, such as an affiliate to the World Bank that would help make energy costs more manageable for non-OPEC countries, and began to organize themselves as a single bloc to press their interests on the floor of the U.N. General Assembly.

[. . .] But the economic ground under such proposals had already evaporated. "Trade, not aid," is how Reagan's Treasury secretary Donald Regan said development would take place, backed up by a 15 percent cut in U.S. foreign assistance. In a run-up speech to the Cancún meeting in Philadelphia, Reagan chided those who "mistake compassion for development and claim massive transfers of wealth somehow will produce new well-being." Reagan agreed with his critics that "development is human fulfillment" but lectured that such development would be achieved not through regulation or re-distribution but by "free people" building "free trade." The *Boston Globe* urged the president to avoid repeating in Mexico such "doctrinaire one-liners and homespun homilies about the virtues of free enterprise, the necessity of self-reliance and the need of underdeveloped countries to emulate the methods of American capitalism."

But homespun became the core of America's economic policy in the third world. In Cancún, Reagan rejected outright the call to create new institutions and establish fixed commodity prices, along with other non-market mechanisms to promote third-world industrialization. Development, he said, would come about by "stimulating international trade, . . . opening up markets," and rolling back regulations to "liberate individuals by creating incentives to work, save, invest, and succeed." Without a "sound understanding of our domestic freedom and responsibilities . . . no amount of international good will and action can produce prosperity."

This was a radical break with past U.S. policy, one that had been based on the strategy that the Cold War would be won by providing a more equitable and successful model of development than did the Soviet Union. In contrast, Reagan in Cancún exalted the unrestrained market as both the end and the means of reform, laying out a vision of the world not as a kind of global welfare state but as a competitive arena. Success was the responsibility not of a community of nations but of each nation alone. Rather than encouraging nations to travel together on a "path to equity," as Raúl Prebisch called on the world's leaders to do, the new system would have winners and losers. And since throughout the previous two decades a generation of Latin America's democrats and economic nationalists had been exiled, executed, or tortured into silence by U.S.-backed military regimes, there were few left to argue.

Compelled by the debt crisis, one country after another implemented a program that was the mirror opposite of what was called for in the nonaligned movement's program for a New International Economic Order. They slashed taxes, drastically devalued their currencies, lowered the minimum wage, exempted foreign companies from labor and environmental laws, cut spending on health care, education, and other social services, did away with regulations, smashed unions, passed legislation that allowed up to 100 percent repatriations of profits, cut subsidies designed to protect national manufacturing, freed interest rates, and privatized state industries and public utilities. Rather than fostering unified efforts to set commodity prices and force fairer terms on the industrialized world, as poor countries were just beginning to do, the debt crisis forced a race to the bottom to attract foreign capital. It was every nation for itself.

In Latin America, the sale of state enterprises was one of the largest transfers of wealth in world history. In the second half of the nineteenth century and early part of the twentieth, Latin America experienced what some historians have described as a "second conquest." The first was, of course, the plundering of American gold and silver by the Spanish and Portuguese. The second entailed the initial phase of U.S. corporate expansion, as extractive firms like United Fruit Company, Standard Oil, and Phelps Dodge turned to the region as a source of raw materials and agricultural products, coming to control most of the continent's railroads, electric companies, ports, mines, and oil fields. "When the trumpet blared everything on earth was prepared," wrote the Chilean poet Pablo Neruda, capturing the Job-like scope of this dispossession, "and Jehovah distributed the world to Coca-Cola Inc., Anaconda, Ford Motor and other entities."

The third conquest, beginning full scale in the early 1980s, was no less epic. Railroads, postal service, roads, factories, telephone services, schools, hospitals, prisons, garbage collection services, water, broadcast frequencies, pension systems, electric, television, and telephone companies were sold off—often not to the highest but to the best-connected bidder. In Chile, everything from "kindergartens to cemeteries and community swimming pools were put out for bid." Between 1985 and 1992, over two thousand government industries were sold off throughout Latin America. Much of this property passed into the hands of either multinational corporations or Latin America's "superbillionaires," a new class that had taken advantage of the dismantling of the state to grow spectacularly rich.

In Mexico, even as the average real minimum wage plummeted, the number of billionaires, according to *Forbes*, increased from one in 1987 to thirteen in 1994 and then nearly doubled the next year to twenty-four. Much of this wealth was concentrated during an orgy of "unprecedented corruption," as a PBS documentary described the privatization program of Carlos Salinas, the Mexican president who sold off over a thousand state industries, many of them to his political cronies. Today, the assets of Carlos Slim Helú, whose acquisition of Mexico's national telephone system catapulted him into the rank of Latin America's richest man, equal that of the seventeen million poorest Mexicans.

Free marketeers today single out state industries as hothouses of corruption and waste yet, as historian Mark Alan Healey and sociologist Ernesto Semán observe, a "vast web of bribes, subsidies, deals and swindles" accompanied the selling off of Latin American "state assets, involving many top government officials and major corporations like IBM, Citibank, and Telefónica"—all winked at by Washington and the IMF. In Argentina, the government agreed to absorb much of the debt of the privatized companies, many of which, such as Aerolíneas Argentinas, were disassembled and had their profitable assets resold. Much of the money from these transactions, write Healey and Semán, "vanished into a tangle of private accounts and offshore banks"—a disappearing act, it should be added, made possible through the magic wand of the financial deregulation that went with privatization. Even Pinochet, despite his reputation for severe rectitude, used his close ties with Riggs Bank and other U.S. financial houses to squirrel away millions of illicit dollars in hundreds of accounts and offshore shelters.

In Chile, public enterprises were sold at roughly 30 percent below value on terms, according to one economist, "extremely advantageous to the buyers," many of whom had close connections with the Chicago alums and with military officers. In Bolivia, between 1995 and 1996, the government auctioned off the oil company, the telephone system, the national airline, and the electric company. Much of the national railroad was dismantled and sold for parts. The following year, the World Bank informed Bolivia that future debt relief was dependent on unloading its water company as well, which it duly did to Bechtel. Nearly overnight, families getting by on barely sixty dollars a month were told that their water bill would average fifteen dollars a month, a 200 percent hike. Bolivians were even outlawed from capturing rainwater for their personal use. The whole deal disquietingly echoed the fate of the Caribbean nation in Gabriel García Márquez's *Autumn of the Patriarch*, which suddenly found itself no longer an island, having had its surrounding sea sold off to dark-suited U.S. businessmen.

2. NAFTA and the U.S. Economy ~ Clinton Administration*

After the Cold War ended and most social revolutionary groups put down their guns, U.S. governments changed their approach to Latin America. Whereas Reagan had pushed for the "liberation" of Latin American markets, the Clinton administration (1993–2001) took the idea a step further and moved boldly for regional economic integration in North America. Such a move was designed to strengthen the U.S. economy at a time when a single, unified European Union was already coming into existence. The Clinton administration pushed the North American Free Trade Agreement through Congress in 1993. In this primary source selection, the administration argues its case for NAFTA's passage. The case was largely an attack on Mexico's last remaining tariff barriers on U.S. imports. The government of President Carlos Salinas had already begun dismantling such barriers (a vestige of Mexico's earlier experiment with populist economic nationalism) by the mid-1980s, but that was not good enough. Who, according to this selection, was NAFTA designed to help? In the decade since its implementation, have predictions about NAFTA proven accurate?

Every generation of Americans has embraced the challenge of its times. None has shrunk from the task. Our biggest challenge today is economic—to channel a changing international economy to our benefit.

The Clinton Administration is committed to rebuilding the U.S. economy from the ground up. We must prepare our entire work force to compete in the global economy and make sure that nobody gets left behind in the process. We look at trade—and every other issue—from the viewpoint of what is best for ordinary Americans who work hard, play by the rules, and want a chance to get ahead. The key building blocks are economic growth and jobs.

The North American Free Trade Agreement (NAFTA) is a part of this forward-looking strategy. This Administration supports NAFTA because it will create high-wage U.S. jobs, boost U.S. growth, and expand the base from which U.S. firms and workers can compete in a dynamic global economy.

Creating the Biggest Market in the World

With NAFTA, the United States, Canada, and Mexico will create the biggest market in the world—a combined economy of $6.5 trillion and 370 million people:

*Adapted from *The NAFTA, Expanding U.S. Exports, Jobs, and Growth: Clinton Administration Statement on the North American Free Trade Agreement* (Washington, DC: Executive Office of the President, 1993), 3–5.

- Our competitors are expanding their markets in Europe and Asia. NAFTA is our opportunity to respond and compete.
- By increasing our export opportunities, NAFTA will enable us to take advantage of U.S. economic strengths and remain the world's biggest and best exporter.

Immigration

To the extent that our workers compete with low-paid Mexicans, it is as much through undocumented immigration as trade. This pattern threatens low-paid, low-skilled U.S. workers.

The combination of domestic reforms and NAFTA-related growth in Mexico will keep more Mexicans at home.

- It is likely that a reduction in immigration will increase the real wages of low-skilled urban and rural workers in the United States.

Leveling the Playing Field

Mexico's trade barriers are now much higher than ours. NAFTA will level a playing field now tilted heavily in Mexico's favor.

- Mexico's average tariff against U.S. exports is currently 2.5 times higher than the equivalent U.S. tariff against imports from Mexico.
- By contrast, over 50 percent of our imports from Mexico already enter duty-free. Our average tariff on imports from Mexico is only 4 percent.
- Complex Mexican domestic-licensing requirements further impede imports into Mexico from the United States.
- Mexico currently has no obligation to continue recent market-opening moves on which thousands of U.S. jobs already depend. NAFTA will not only lock in current access but expand that access.
- NAFTA will eliminate especially burdensome tariffs and non-tariff barriers in a number of key sectors where the United States is competitive vis-à-vis Mexico—such as autos and agriculture.

NAFTA will require relatively little change on our part—while requiring Mexico to sweep away decades of protectionism and overregulation:

- Half of all U.S. exports to Mexico will be eligible for zero Mexican tariffs when NAFTA takes effect on January 1, 1994.
- U.S. exports eligible for tariff-free entry into Mexico include some of our most competitive products.

- Within the first five years after NAFTA is implemented, two-thirds of U.S. industrial exports will enter Mexico duty-free.
- Under NAFTA, Mexico will open its market significantly to U.S. manufactured exports. For example, for automotive parts, Mexico will eliminate 75 percent of its duties over five years and phase out the rest over ten years.
- NAFTA also will require Mexico to open its market to U.S. service exports (U.S. service exports to Mexico were $8.9 billion in 1992). This will benefit such industries as enhanced telecommunications services, insurance, banking, accounting, and advertising.

Removing Mexican restrictions against U.S. exports means that U.S. companies no longer will have to invest in Mexico or manufacture in Mexico to supply the Mexican market. NAFTA will eliminate Mexican requirements that force our companies in Mexico to:

- Purchase Mexican goods instead of U.S.-made equipment and components;
- Export their production, usually to the United States, instead of selling directly into the Mexican market; and
- Produce in Mexico to sell in Mexico. For example, the current Auto Decree has the effect of barring automotive imports from the United States through a complex series of investment requirements that will be phased out under NAFTA.

---

3. NAFTA Should Have Stopped Illegal Immigration, Right? ∼ Louis Ochitelle*

In early 2007, more than a decade after NAFTA's implementation, New York Times *reporter Louis Ochitelle took a look back at some of its promises. The results of the trade deal, he found, were mixed. There was some good news (wages for U.S. workers were up 14 percent between 1994 and 2004), some bad news (wages for Mexican workers were down 14 percent for the same period), and several faulty assumptions on the part of policymakers were exposed. Among the various assumptions made by NAFTA's creators was that, by creating better jobs in Mexico, NAFTA would stop, or at least slow, illegal immigration across the Mexico–United States border. After all, why were hundreds of thousands, if not millions, of Mexican workers coming north? According to the economists interviewed by Ochitelle, nothing of the sort happened. Why was that? In con-*

From "NAFTA Should Have Stopped Illegal Immigration, Right?" New York Times, Week in Review Section, March 19, 2008, 4. All rights reserved. Used by permission.

cluding the piece, Ochitelle asks us to consider what real regional integration might look like in North America.

The North American Free Trade Agreement, enacted by Congress 14 years ago, held out an alluring promise: the agreement would reduce illegal immigration from Mexico. Mexicans, the argument went, would enjoy the prosperity and employment that the trade agreement would undoubtedly generate—and not feel the need to cross the border into the United States.

But today the number of illegal migrants has only continued to rise. Why didn't NAFTA curb this immigration? The answer is complicated, of course. But a major factor lies in the assumptions made in drafting the trade agreement, assumptions about the way governments would behave (that is, rationally) and the way markets would respond (rationally, as well).

Neither happened, yet NAFTA remains the model for trade agreements with developing Latin countries, including the Central American Free Trade Agreement, passed by Congress in 2005. Three more NAFTA-like agreements are now pending in Congress—with Panama, Columbia and Peru.

When NAFTA finally became a reality, on Jan. 1, 1994, American investment flooded into Mexico, mostly to finance factories that manufacture automobiles, appliances, TV sets, apparel and the like. The expectation was that the Mexican government would do its part by investing billions of dollars in roads, schooling, sanitation, housing and other needs to accommodate the new factories as they spread through the country.

It was more than an expectation. Many Mexican officials in the government of President Carlos Salinas de Gortari assured the Clinton administration that the investment would take place, and believed it themselves, said Gary Hufbauer, a senior fellow at the Peter G. Peterson Institute for International Economics in Washington who campaigned for NAFTA in the early 1990s.

"It just did not happen," he said.

Absent that investment, foreign factories congregated in the north, within 300 miles of the American border, where some infrastructure already existed. "Monterrey is quite good," Mr. Hufbauer said, "but in a lot of other cities the infrastructure is terrible, not even enough running water or electricity in poor neighborhoods. People get temporary jobs, but that is all."

Meanwhile, Mexican manufacturers, once protected by tariffs on a host of products, were driven out of business as less expensive, higher quality merchandise flowed into the country. Later, China, with its even-cheaper labor, added to the pressure, luring away manufacturers and jobs.

Indeed, despite the influx of foreign-owned factories, total manufacturing employment in Mexico declined to 3.5 million by 2004 from a high of 4.1 million in 2000, according to a calculation of Robert A. Blecker, an American University economist.

As relatively well-paying jobs disappeared, Mexico's average wage for production workers, already low, fell further behind the average hourly pay of production workers in the United States, and Mexicans responded by migrating.

"The main thing that would have stemmed the flow of people across the border was a rapid increase in wages in Mexico," said Dani Rodrik, an economist and trade specialist at Harvard's John F. Kennedy School of Government. "And that certainly has not happened."

Something similar occurred in agriculture. The assumption was that tens of thousands of farmers who cultivated corn would act "rationally" and continue farming, even as less expensive corn imported from the United States flooded the market. The farmers, it was assumed, would switch to growing strawberries and vegetables—with some help from foreign investment—and then export these crops to the United States. Instead, the farmers exported themselves, partly because the Mexican government decided to reduce tariffs on corn even faster than NAFTA required, according to Philip Martin, an agricultural economist at the University of California, Davis.

"We understood that the transition from corn to strawberries would not be smooth," Professor Martin said. "But we did not think there would be almost no transition."

A financial crisis also dashed expectations. One expectation was that the Mexican economy, driven by NAFTA, would grow rapidly, generating jobs and keeping Mexicans home. The peso crisis of 1994–95, however, provoked a steep recession, and while there was some big growth later, the average annual growth rate over NAFTA's lifetime has been less than 3 percent.

The financial crisis struck just months after NAFTA came into existence, undermining, early on, the Mexican government's ability to spend money on roads, education and other necessary government functions.

"We underestimated Mexico's deficits in physical and human infrastructure," said J. Bradford DeLong, an economist at the University of California, Berkeley, and a Treasury official in the Clinton administration.

But, he says, without NAFTA the migration would have been even greater. For instance, he says, there would not have been as much investment in the north of the country.

Finally, the steady flow of Mexicans to the United States has produced a momentum of its own—what Jeffrey Passel, a demographer at the Pew Hispanic Institute, calls a "network effect," in which young Mexicans travel to the United States in growing numbers to join the growing number of family members already here.

The upshot is that Mexican migration to the United States has risen to 500,000 a year from less than 400,000 in the early 1990s, before NAFTA, Mr. Passel estimates. Roughly 80 percent to 85 percent of immigrants are here illegally, he says.

The peso crisis, recession, the network effect—their impact may have been beyond anyone's control, but not the assumptions about how the market and the government would act.

"We have indeed had one disappointment after another on this score," Mr. Rodrik said, noting that the same assumption about government spending is part and parcel of the agreements, now before Congress, with Columbia, Peru and Panama.

While there is opposition to these proposals, it is mainly from Democrats who want a better safety net for American workers who might be hurt.

The European Union, in contrast, assumes little about government spending on the part of economically weaker nations joining it. The union itself has hugely subsidized the improved services needed by entering countries like Portugal, Spain, Greece and Poland, rather than leave financing to the relatively meager resources of entering countries.

The money is used not only for public investment, Mr. Rodrik noted, but also to subsidize companies setting up operations in the new countries and to support government budgets.

"I am not saying NAFTA was a bad agreement," Mr. Rodrik said. "But more than a trade agreement is required for countries to converge economically. And NAFTA has been viewed as a shortcut to convergence without having to do all the other stuff."

---

4. China's New Role in Latin America ~ Jorge I. Domínguez*

Beginning in the 1980s, the People's Republic of China under Deng Xiaoping embarked on a radical new path away from Maoist communism toward a form of state-run modernization that accepted the supremacy of the capitalist marketplace. In the new China, the Communist Party maintained political power in a one-party system while the economy was gradually opened to foreign investment and limited competition. China, in short, became more deeply integrated into the global economy, as both a producer and a consumer. In the following selection,

*From Jorge I. Domínguez, "China's Relations with Latin America: Shared Gains, Asymmetric Hopes," *Inter-American Dialogue Working Paper*, June 2006, 1–3, 18–21. Used by permission of Inter-American Dialogue.

Latin American politics and government expert Jorge Domínguez describes the state of the relationship between China and Latin America and examines the economic factors behind "Sino–Latin American" relations at the beginning of the twenty-first century. At the center of the selection is a discussion of the various mineral and agricultural commodities produced by the Latin American nations. It's clear that China's huge demand for things like soy, copper, and oil has driven up prices to unprecedented levels, but how long will that situation last?

The relations between the People's Republic of China (PRC) and nearly all Latin American countries blossomed during the first half of the first decade of the twenty-first century. "China fever" gripped the region. Latin American presidents, ministers, business executives and journalists "discovered" China and its rapidly growing impact on the world's economy and on Latin America itself.

The principal explanation for this boom in "China fever" was China's own economic boom and its widening and deepening worldwide spread. In the current decade, Sino–Latin American trade, and economic relations more generally, have grown at a spectacular pace. Improved political relations were a necessary part of the expansion in economic relations because intergovernmental agreements facilitate economic relations, but the exuberance of the economic boom outpaced the improvement in political relations. Military or militarily sensitive relations changed little, notwithstanding the fears of some in the United States and elsewhere over this question.

The expansion of relations with China has long had substantial cross-ideological and multi-partisan domestic political support in the major Latin American countries. It long precedes the emergence of social-democratic governments in Latin America during the current decade. The political foundations for good Sino–Latin American relations were set under right-wing military dictatorships in Latin America in the 1970s. Thus Latin America had long been ready for a boom in its relations with China, but only in the current decade did China achieve the capacity to capitalize on such opportunities.

There was substantial variation, however, in the cross-country characteristics of Sino–Latin American relations in the early twenty-first century. The domestic economic opportunities in each Latin American country as well as the political strategies of their governments explain this variation. The domestic economic explanation is simple: Sino-Brazilian economic relations are much more important than Sino-Cuban economic relations because Brazil is one of the world's largest economies, while Cuba's economy is in dire straits. China imports mainly non-petroleum commodities from Latin America, and the economic importance of countries varies accordingly.

[. . .] Explaining Variation in Sino–Latin Relations: Economic Factors

Sino–Latin American relations vary for several reasons, among them overall economic importance, the importance of key commodities, and trade regime openness.

One aspect of variation is the relative economic importance of Latin American countries for China. In 2004, Latin America's three principal non-petroleum worldwide exporters were Brazil, Argentina, and Chile, in that order, with Brazil accounting for nearly three times the value of Argentina's worldwide exports. That is a perfect match with the relative ranking of China's imports from Latin America in 2004. Also in 2004, Latin America's three principal worldwide importers were Mexico, Brazil, and Chile. That was a near perfect match with the relative ranking of China's exports to Latin America: Mexico, Brazil, Panama, and Chile (Panama's imports from China were re-channeled to third countries via its free-trade zones, however). Therefore, political explanations are unnecessary to explain the main outlines of variation in the value of trade between China and its principal Latin American partners. The main explanation for variation in the salience of trade relations is the participation of specific Latin American countries in non-petroleum world trade.

Another dimension of variation is specific to key products. China has seemingly limitless demand for energy. Rolling blackouts are a fact of life for many Chinese. China has not turned to Latin America to address its energy needs, however. China imports little petroleum from Mexico. China's largest energy trading partner in Latin America is Venezuela, but Venezuela's share of China's oil imports was only 1.1 percent in 2003. For Venezuela, this makes China a significant trading partner but the comparison underscores the asymmetry in hopes and leverage in Sino-Venezuelan relations. In short, Latin America has a trivial role in addressing China's energy needs.

This could change. SINOPEC, one of China's state-owned oil firms, has signed two deals with Petrobras,* one for $1 billion to build a pipeline linking the north and south of Brazil and another for $7 billion to find, produce, and refine oil. It has signed a contract with Cuba to explore for oil offshore and it has joint ventures to explore for petroleum in Venezuela. These are medium-term prospects at best, however.

Copper is considerably different. Chilean copper accounts for about one-fifth of China's total copper imports while China represents about one-sixth of Chile's copper exports (second only to Japan in its importance for Chile). Copper remains Chile's most important export. This bilateral relationship is balanced.

---

*Petrobras is short for Petróleo Brasileiro, Brazil's national oil company, which was founded by Getúlio Vargas in 1953, then partially privatized in 1997.

China is no longer self-sufficient in food but it so far imports only a small fraction (about 5 percent) of the food that it consumes; this proportion may grow, however. China has turned to Latin America—mainly to Argentina and Brazil—as a major source of its food imports. In 2003, Latin America accounted for about a third of China's agricultural imports; Argentina represented about 15 percent and Brazil about 14 percent of China's total agricultural imports.

Much of this trade has been in soy-based products that, in the form of tofu, are important in the Chinese diet. Soybeans account for about half of Argentina's total exports to China, with other agricultural and livestock products accounting for nearly all of the remainder. In 2004, soybeans constituted about 30 percent and soybean products another 9 percent of Brazil's exports to China; these combined soybean product exports, however, represented only 2.2 percent of Brazil's total worldwide exports but 30 percent of China's total soybean imports. Thus the agricultural trade relationship between China and both Argentina and Brazil seems relatively balanced. China imports a small fraction of its needs but soybeans are a sensitive food product; Argentina and Brazil retain a sufficiently diversified trade export portfolio.

A third major source of economic variation is the relative openness of each country's trade regime. Autarchic economic strategies, which were once employed by China, and to a lesser extent, Latin America, do not foster trade. Chile, however, has an open international trade regime. Mexico and China do, too, with China surpassing Mexico in recent years. In contrast, Argentina and, especially, Brazil lag behind other countries in terms of their openness to trade. This also implies that China would gain much from a successful Doha Round of the World Trade Organization (WTO)* that might open up the Argentine and Brazilian markets. China also has an interest in trade agreements with the southern common market countries (MERCOSUR) led by Brazil and Argentina. Should changes occur in these trade regimes, Sino-MERCOSUR trade could grow further.

In short, Argentina, Brazil, and Chile are Latin America's principal non-petroleum exporters and thus China's key import partners. Along with Mexico (and Panama's free-trade zones), they are also China's most important export markets. Argentina, Brazil, and Chile have also developed reasonably balanced trade relations with China. China matters more to these three countries than they do to China but they export products either in proportions (copper) or sensitivity (soybean) for Chinese imports to accord them some bargaining leverage. China's decision to meet its

---

*The Doha Development Round or Doha Round of the WTO, which refers to the most recent round of negotiations to liberalize the global economy, takes its name from Doha, Qatar, where the talks began in 2001.

energy needs from sources other than Latin America deprives Latin America's petroleum exporters, especially Venezuela, of significant leverage in relations with China. Finally, the relative trade regime openness of Chile, Mexico, and China indicates that governmental barriers are not severe obstacles to trade, but that changes in trade regime openness in Argentina and especially Brazil could foster trans-Pacific trade.

5. The Buenos Aires Consensus ~ Néstor Kirchner and Luiz Inácio Lula da Silva*

In October 2003 in the Argentine capital of Buenos Aires the presidents of South America's two largest economies, Néstor Kirchner of Argentina and Luiz Inácio Lula da Silva of Brazil, signed a document known as the Buenos Aires Consensus. The name of the document was a way of indicating its rejection of the so-called Washington Consensus on neoliberalism, the set of economic policies outlined by Grandin earlier in the chapter. Buenos Aires was also significant because it was the site of intense political protest and popular mobilization in the previous two years during the Argentine economic crisis of 2001–2002. At that time, the government defaulted on its loans and the currency had to be massively devalued, bringing the neoliberal experiment of the 1990s to a painful conclusion. The document included twenty-two points of understanding and agreement between the two neighbors. What is remarkable about the document is the extremely high priority that it put on regional integration in MERCOSUR, the South American Common Market. The two presidents, who were part of what some Latin Americanists have labeled the "new Left turn" in Latin American politics (the subject of the next chapter of this book), also embraced the multilateralism of the United Nations. Does this document suggest to you that Latin American governments are catching on to the new rules of globalization?

1. We, the presidents of Argentina, Néstor Kirchner, and Brasil, Luiz Inácio Lula da Silva, convinced that the well-being of our people constitutes the top priority of both governments, reaffirm our commitment to intensify bilateral and regional cooperation in order to guarantee all citizens the full enjoyment of their fundamental rights and liberties, including the right to development, in a framework of liberty and social justice, and according to the values, purposes, and objectives established by the Millennium Summit.†

*From "Consenso de Buenos Aires," available at http://www.resdal.org/consenso-bsas.html. Accessed on July 30, 2008. Translated by James A. Wood.
†The Millennium Summit, held at the United Nations in New York in September 2000, aimed to stimulate economic growth in poor countries and find ways for them to share in the benefits of twenty first-century globalization.

2. We recognize the transcendent importance of consolidating political democracy in our region, as well as our common purpose to strengthen it, as we assume the historic responsibility of combating poverty, inequality, unemployment, hunger, illiteracy, and illness, [factors] that lead to the loss of autonomy and dignity for those affected, creating serious obstacles for the full exercise of citizenship. [. . .]

4. We express our conviction that—in a global context marked by the acceleration of the process of globalization that has enlarged the field of human possibilities but, at the same time, generated new forms of economic concentration—our nations should define their futures within a framework that responds to the needs, possibilities, and challenges that are unique to each country at the start of the twenty-first century.

5. We commit ourselves to implementing public policies that encourage sustained growth and the equitable distribution of its benefits, favoring fairer tax and fiscal measures.

6. We are certain that the scourge of poverty is not resolved with mere public assistance plans. While such plans constitute an obligatory palliative until an effective solution to the problem is found, they should not be allowed to crystallize into a society divided between those who work and those on public assistance. Therefore, we propose to promote all necessary actions to reduce the high rates of unemployment that are punishing our societies, generating favorable conditions for the development of businesses and productive investments. [. . .]

8. We recognize that our common aspiration for development means putting an absolute priority on education as a tool for social inclusion since its capacity to integrate and equalize is unsurpassed by any other social policy. In that sense, through educational policy our governments will try to guarantee all citizens the acquisition of learning capacities that allow for lifetime personal development in a changing society that demands the constant updating of skills and abilities.

9. We reaffirm our commitment to construct an information society oriented toward the goals of social inclusion, the eradication of hunger and poverty, and the improvement of health and education, with the aim of achieving development that is economically and socially balanced.

10. We know that the information revolution brings new opportunities for participation and access to knowledge, but it also presents new dangers of exclusion, creating a technological gap between our nations and the highly industrialized countries. In this framework, our peoples should be incorporated into the digital world and so we propose to develop the necessary infrastructure in such a way that all citizens and businesses, especially small ones, are in a position to participate in the advantages offered by the information society.

11. We will redouble our efforts to increase the number of and link-

ages between our universities and institutes of science and technology, with the aim of generating a regional scientific-technological pole that deepens basic and applied research, with the criteria of sustainability and social equity.

12. We believe that many of the problems that plague us today are rooted in the strong regional imbalances and inequalities that exist in our societies. Accordingly, we propose to implement regional development policies that recognize and respect the diversity within our territory.

13. We reaffirm our conviction that decent work, as defined by the International Labor Organization, is the most effective instrument for raising the standard of living of our peoples and assuring their participation in the fruits of material and human progress. [. . .]

14. We reiterate our adherence to the principles consecrated in the Rio Declaration on the Environment and Development . . . We express our firm intention to pursue cooperation and coordinated actions with the aim of promoting the objectives outlined in multilateral environmental agreements, such as the UN Convention on Climate Change and its Kyoto Protocol and the Convention on Biological Diversity, among others. We will continue uniting our efforts in search of sustainable solutions for the integrated use of our shared water resources, with the intention of promoting the sustainable development of our population.

15. We ratify our deep conviction that MERCOSUR is not just a commercial bloc, but, rather, that it serves as a catalyzing space for shared values, traditions, and futures. In this way our governments are working to strengthen it by improving both the commercial and political aspects of our institutions and by incorporating new member countries.

16. We understand that regional integration gives us a strategic option for strengthening the position of our countries in the world, increasing their negotiating capacity. Greater autonomy of decision making will permit us to confront more efficiently the destabilizing movements of speculative financial capital and the opposing interests of the bloc of the most advanced countries, making our voice louder in various forums and multilateral institutions. In this sense, we insist that South American integration should be promoted in the interest of everyone, with the objective of forming a development model in which growth, social justice, and the dignity of citizens go hand in hand.

17. We reaffirm our desire to continue with the negotiations of the Doha Round on an equal footing and with a realistic perspective of success, in particular in the field of agriculture . . . We reaffirm our commitment to the objectives of the Doha Round and we urge the developed countries to cooperate effectively in reaching them, so as to consolidate a multilateral system of free trade without distortions and discrimination. Likewise, we declare our intention to generate new alliances and joint

strategies with countries with which we share similar interests and concerns.

18. We reiterate our commitment to the continued tight coordination of our positions in search of balanced agreements to increase MERCO-SUR's relations with other member states, in particular the Andean Community, with the aim of greater prosperity for all. We concur on the need to continue participating through MERCOSUR in the negotiations on the Free Trade Area of the Americas, with the goal of reaching a balanced agreement that respects the dissimilar interests of the participants and endows the process with the flexibility necessary to negotiate an accord that conforms to the situation of each one of the countries and blocs involved. [. . .]

19. We declare that the administration of public debt should have as its goal the creation of wealth and employment, the protection of savings, the reduction of poverty, the promotion of education and health, and the possibility of maintaining policies favoring sustainable economic and social development.

20. We emphasize our historic commitment to strengthening a multilateral order founded on the sovereign equality of all states and we reject any exercise of unilateral power inconsistent with the principles and purposes consecrated in the United Nations Organization.

21. We understand that multilateralism and respect for the norms and principles of international law should be a top priority in all efforts related to international security and, in particular, the objectives of disarmament and non-proliferation. We reaffirm the central role of the United Nations and its Security Council in international relations as the main global instrument for maintaining international peace and security, and the promotion of economic and social development in a sustainable manner. We underscore the need for the strict observance of the UN Charter and the universally recognized norms and principles of international law by all members of the international community. [. . .]

22. We affirm our desire to work jointly towards the realization of this consensus and to extend the invitation to all Latin American countries in order to bring about a more just, equitable, and supportive society that strengthens democracy in the region.

XIII

The New Left Turn

The signing of the Buenos Aires Consensus in October 2003 was a clear indication that the tide was turning in Latin American politics. Indeed, opponents of the neoliberal path of development were taking charge of governments across the continent. Brazilian president "Lula," for example, a former autoworker and union representative from São Paulo, was first elected in 2002 on a Workers' Party platform that had as one of its top priorities "zero hunger" in Brazil. Lula was part of a wave of democratically elected leaders variously labeled by the U.S. news media—because of their roots in the popular social movements and/or their willingness to use government to aggressively regulate capitalist markets—as "leftist," "populist," or "socialist," usually without any clear analysis of what those terms meant in the context of modern Latin American history. This final chapter of the book aims to rectify that problem by providing a set of perspectives that help to clarify the defining characteristics of the new Left turn, especially with regard to its problematic relationship with the region's strong populist tradition.

From the fall of the Berlin Wall in 1989 to the dismantling of the Soviet Union in 1991 the world witnessed a pivotal moment in world history. Communism as it was known in the twentieth century came to a sputtering collapse (with a few notable exceptions). That historic transformation, coupled with developments inside formerly communist China, posed an ontological challenge to the Latin American Left, or, more accurately, to what remained of it. Recall for a moment the dark side of Cold War anti-communism that we explored in a previous chapter. The death squads and dirty wars took a huge toll on the membership of the guerrilla organizations, political parties, labor unions, and civil society groups that had opposed military rule. That grueling experience, for those who survived, led to some serious rethinking about a wide range of issues. They looked more closely, for example, at the nature of Latin American democracy and its lack of racial and ethnic inclusiveness. They looked anew at the question of managing open, globalized markets. As the neoliberal wave of globalization rolled across the region in the 1990s, Latin Americans on the Left began organizing to oppose it.

Leading the way in that fight was the Zapatista Army of National Liberation, the guerrilla army of poor, Mayan peasants in the southern Mexican state of Chiapas who had (symbolically) initiated their armed struggle against the federal government on the day that NAFTA went into effect in 1994. While the Zapatistas, who took their name from the legendary indigenous peasant leader of the Mexican Revolution, Emiliano Zapata, did not win that war, they did contribute to the growing forcefulness of the resistance to neoliberalism. By the late 1990s it was becoming clear to a majority of Latin Americans that IMF-imposed structural adjustment programs were generating lopsided results, favoring the business elite while punishing wage earners and the poor. Income inequality was skyrocketing. Calls for a new economic direction, usually infused with a strong dose of anti-globalization sentiment, grew louder.

The election of Hugo Chávez as president of Venezuela in 1998 marked the next major step in the new Left turn. Chávez, a poor boy who rose through the army to become a national figure, has done more than any other Latin American leftist leader to spread the new approach—what he calls the Bolivarian Revolution—to his Latin American neighbors. He is also the most energetic, as we will see in one of the following documents, in his condemnation of the George W. Bush administration, admiration for Fidel Castro, and his view of U.S. imperialism. During his presidencies (1998–present) Chávez has openly supported his political allies in the region, even to the point of getting dragged into damaging controversies over campaign financing. He has also been connected to the Revolutionary Armed Forces of Colombia (FARC), the last major guerrilla army in South America, in ways that have hurt him politically. Chávez has been able to play such a high-stakes game primarily because of Venezuela's status as one of the world's largest exporters of crude oil. In fact, Chávez, recognizing early on that oil was a "geopolitical weapon," made the fundamental reform of the oil industry his top priority after taking office.

Among the regional leaders Chávez supported was the Bolivian leftist Evo Morales, who was elected to his country's presidency at the end of 2005. Morales, like Lula and Chávez, was not born into the traditional political class of his country. Before his political career he was a coca farmer who became the leader of the *cocaleros*, the association of Bolivian coca farmers who were locked in a bitter dispute with the U.S. Drug Enforcement Agency over the continuation of coca production in Bolivia. Despite active U.S. efforts to prevent it, Morales won the presidency and became the first indigenous head of state (he is Aymara) since the fall of the Inca Empire (in a country where the indigenous population is currently estimated at 55 percent). Morales and his political movement-turned-party, the Movement toward Socialism, have followed Chávez's lead in renegotiating government contracts with all of the multinational corporations that have a stake in Bolivia's natural gas industry. Are Lula, Chávez, and Morales part of the same political phenomenon? What defines this new Latin American Left?

QUESTIONS FOR ANALYSIS

1. How do the first two selections, Castañeda and Roberts, make sense of the new Left turn? How do they subdivide the group?
2. Chávez and Morales were nonprofessional politicians who came from outside their countries' traditional party systems to win power. How does that experience influence their political style and rhetoric?
3. What role does the world's increasing demand for energy play in the success of the new Latin American Left?

1. A Tale of Two Lefts ~ Jorge G. Castañeda*

In the following selection Jorge Castañeda, world-renowned author, political scientist, and former foreign minister of Mexico, lays out his view of the leftist trend in Latin American politics in a leading scholarly journal of international relations. Castañeda argues for splitting the group of recently elected leaders into two categories. What are those categories? In making his case for the two Lefts, Castañeda takes us back to some of the book's other principal problems. He reminds us, for example, that the classic Latin American populists— Cárdenas, Vargas, Gaitán, and, of course, Perón—were successful not just because they did things for the poor but also because they built powerful, personalized patronage networks that could mobilize the urban masses. He also explains the evolution of the formerly Communist and Castroist Lefts in the wake of the Soviet Union's disintegration. Which of these two Lefts does Castañeda prefer, and why?

Just over a decade ago, Latin America seemed poised to begin a virtuous cycle of economic progress and improved democratic governance, overseen by a growing number of centrist technocratic governments. In Mexico, President Carlos Salinas de Gortari, buttressed by the passage of the North American Free Trade Agreement, was ready for his handpicked successor to win the next presidential election. Former Finance Minister Fer-

*From Jorge G. Castañeda, "Latin America's Left Turn," *Foreign Affairs* 85:3 (May/June 2006), 28–43. © 2006 by the Council on Foreign Relations, Inc. Reprinted by permission of *Foreign Affairs*.

nando Henrique Cardoso was about to beat out the radical labor leader
Luiz Inácio Lula da Silva for the presidency of Brazil. Argentine President
Carlos Menem had pegged the peso to the dollar and put his populist
Peronist legacy behind him. And at the invitation of President Bill Clinton,
Latin American leaders were preparing to gather in Miami for the Summit
of the Americas, signaling an almost unprecedented convergence between
the southern and northern halves of the Western Hemisphere.

What a difference ten years can make. Although the region has just
enjoyed its best two years of economic growth in a long time and real
threats to democratic rule are few and far between, the landscape today is
transformed. Latin America is swerving left, and distinct backlashes are
under way against the predominant trends of the last 15 years: free-market
reforms, agreement with the United States on a number of issues, and the
consolidation of representative democracy. This reaction is more politics
than policy, and more nuanced than it may appear. But it is real.

Starting with Hugo Chávez's victory in Venezuela eight years ago
and poised to culminate in the possible election of Andres Manuel López
Obrador in Mexico's July 2 presidential contest, a wave of leaders, parties,
and movements generically labeled "leftist" have swept into power in one
Latin American country after another. After Chávez, it was Lula and the
Workers' Party in Brazil, then Nestor Kirchner in Argentina and Tabaré
Vazquez in Uruguay, and then, earlier this year, Evo Morales in Bolivia.
If the long shot Ollanta Humala wins the April presidential election in
Peru and Lopez Obrador wins in Mexico, it will seem as if a veritable left-
wing tsunami has hit the region. Colombia and Central America are the
only exceptions, but even in Nicaragua, the possibility of a win by Sandin-
ista leader Daniel Ortega cannot be dismissed.*

The rest of the world has begun to take note of this left-wing resurgence, with concern and often more than a little hysteria. But understanding the reasons behind these developments requires recognizing that there
is not one Latin American left today; there are two. One is modern, open-
minded, reformist, and internationalist, and it springs, paradoxically, from
the hard-core left of the past. The other, born of the great tradition of Latin
American populism, is nationalist, strident, and close-minded. The first is
well aware of its past mistakes (as well as those of its erstwhile role models
in Cuba and the Soviet Union) and has changed accordingly. The second,
unfortunately, has not.

Origins of the Species

The left—defined as that current of thought, politics, and policy that
stresses social improvements over macroeconomic orthodoxy, egalitarian

---

*Humala and López Obrador did not win those elections. Ortega, former leader of the
revolutionary Sandinistas, did win in Nicaragua.

distribution of wealth over its creation, sovereignty over international cooperation, democracy (at least when in opposition, if not necessarily once in power) over governmental effectiveness—has followed two different paths in Latin America. One left sprang up out of the Communist International and the Bolshevik Revolution and has followed a path similar to that of the left in the rest of the world. The Chilean, Uruguayan, Brazilian, Salvadoran, and, before Castro's revolution, Cuban Communist Parties, for example, obtained significant shares of the popular vote at one point or another, participated in "popular front" or "national unity" governments in the 1930s and 1940s, established a solid presence in organized labor, and exercised significant influence in academic and intellectual circles.

By the late 1950s and early 1960s, however, these parties had lost most of their prestige and combativeness. Their corruption, submission to Moscow, accommodation with sitting governments, and assimilation by local power elites had largely discredited them in the eyes of the young and the radical. But the Cuban Revolution brought new life to this strain of the left. In time, groups descended from the old communist left fused with Havana-inspired guerrilla bands. There were certainly some tensions. Castro accused the leader of the Bolivian Communist Party of betraying Che Guevara and leading him to his death in Bolivia in 1967; the Uruguayan and Chilean Communist Parties (the region's strongest) never supported the local Castroist armed groups. Yet thanks to the passage of time, to Soviet and Cuban understanding, and to the sheer weight of repression generated by military coups across the hemisphere, the Castroists and Communists all came together—and they remain together today.

The origin of the other Latin American left is peculiarly Latin American. It arose out of the region's strange contribution to political science: good old-fashioned populism. Such populism has almost always been present almost everywhere in Latin America. It is frequently in power, or close to it. It claims as its founders historical icons of great mythical stature, from Peru's Victor Raul Haya de la Torre and Colombia's Jorge Gaitán (neither made it to office) to Mexico's Lazaro Cardenas and Brazil's Getulio Vargas, both foundational figures in their countries' twentieth-century history, and to Argentina's Juan Perón and Ecuador's Jose Velasco Ibarra. The list is not exhaustive, but it is illustrative: many of these nations' founding-father equivalents were seen in their time and are still seen now as noble benefactors of the working class. They made their mark on their nations, and their followers continue to pay tribute to them. Among many of these countries' poor and dispossessed, they inspire respect, even adulation, to this day.

These populists are representative of a very different left—often virulently anticommunist, always authoritarian in one fashion or another, and much more interested in policy as an instrument for attaining and conserving power than in power as a tool for making policy. They did do things for the poor—Perón and Vargas mainly for the urban proletariat, Cárdenas for the Mexican peasantry—but they also created the corporatist structures that have since plagued the political systems, as well as the labor and peasant movements, in their countries. They nationalized large sectors of their countries' economies, extending well beyond the so-called commanding heights, by targeting everything in sight: oil (Cardenas in Mexico), railroads (Perón in Argentina), steel (Vargas in Brazil), tin (Victor Paz Estenssoro in Bolivia), copper (Juan Velasco Alvarado in Peru). They tended to cut sweetheart deals with the budding local business sector, creating the proverbial crony capitalism that was decried much later. Their justifications for such steps were always superficially ideological (nationalism, economic development) but at bottom pragmatic: they needed money to give away but did not like taxes. They squared that circle by capturing natural-resource or monopoly rents, which allowed them to spend money on the *descamisados*, the "shirtless," without raising taxes on the middle class. When everything else fails, the thinking went, spend money.

The ideological corollary to this bizarre blend of inclusion of the excluded, macroeconomic folly, and political staying power (Perón was the dominant figure in Argentine politics from 1943 through his death in 1974, the Cárdenas dynasty is more present than ever in Mexican politics) was virulent, strident nationalism. Perón was elected president in 1946 with the slogan "Braden or Perón" (Spruille Braden was then the U.S. ambassador to Buenos Aires). When Vargas committed suicide in 1954, he darkly insinuated that he was a victim of American imperialism. Such nationalism was more than rhetorical. In regimes whose domestic policy platform was strictly power-driven and pragmatic, it was the agenda.

These two subspecies of the Latin American left have always had an uneasy relationship. On occasion they have worked together, but at other times they have been at war, as when Perón returned from exile in June 1973 and promptly massacred a fair share of the Argentine radical left. In some countries, the populist left simply devoured the other one, although peacefully and rather graciously: in Mexico in the late 1980s, the tiny Communist Party disappeared, and former PRI (Institutional Revolutionary Party) members, such as Cuauhtemoc Cárdenas, Porfirio Muñoz Ledo, and the current presidential front-runner, López Obrador, took over everything from its buildings and finances to its congressional representation and relations with Cuba to form the left-wing PRD (Party of the Democratic Revolution).

More recently, something funny has happened to both kinds of leftist movements on their way back to power. The communist, socialist, and

Castroist left, with a few exceptions, has been able to reconstruct itself, thanks largely to an acknowledgment of its failures and those of its erstwhile models. Meanwhile, the populist left—with an approach to power that depends on giving away money, a deep attachment to the nationalist fervor of another era, and no real domestic agenda—has remained true to itself. The latter perseveres in its cult of the past: it waxes nostalgic about the glory days of Peronism, the Mexican Revolution, and, needless to say, Castro. The former, familiar with its own mistakes, defeats, and tragedy and keenly aware of the failures of the Soviet Union and Cuba, has changed its colors.

---

2. Latin America's Populist Revival ～ Kenneth M. Roberts*

To what extent does the recent political shift to the Left resemble the classic Latin American experience with populism? In this passage from an article published in the journal of the School of Advanced International Studies, political scientist Kenneth Roberts takes on the question directly. Roberts briefly reviews the history of populism in the region and its complicated relationship with both liberal and statist economic programs. What Roberts finds is that populism is definitely on the rise once again. But he also suggests that not all of the recently elected leftist governments were populists. How does he distinguish one group from the other? In addition, Roberts traces the source of the recent leftist wave to what he calls the region's "dual transitions" of the late 1990s and 2000s, the transitions toward greater democracy and, simultaneously, greater market openness. What economic policies, in Roberts' view, were responsible for the populist revival?

Although populism in its myriad forms has appeared in many parts of the world, its most indelible imprint may be on the political landscape in Latin America. Since the onset of mass politics in the early-to-mid-20th century, repeated waves of populist mobilization have convulsed the region. In some countries these waves had an ephemeral existence, but in others they proved to be extraordinarily resilient, producing long-lasting political and institutional legacies. Indeed, the region has provided fertile terrain for some of the world's most quintessentially populist political experiments; leaders like Argentina's Juan Perón and Venezuela's Hugo Chávez are virtually synonymous with populism, endowing the concept with vivid images of charismatic rulers who energize the masses, chal-

*Kenneth M. Roberts, "Latin America's Populist Revival," *SAIS Review* vol. XXVII no. 1 (Winter–Spring 2007), 3–4, 9–12. © The Johns Hopkins University Press. Reprinted with permission of the Johns Hopkins University Press.

lenge traditional elites, and assert national autonomy in the international arena.

Even in Latin America, however, populism has ebbed and flowed in its political prominence, and it is far from homogeneous in its political, economic, and institutional expressions. Historically, Latin American populism was affiliated with the state-led model of capitalist development known as import substitution industrialization (ISI), which allowed interventionist states to extend material benefits to organized working and lower class constituencies. Consequently, many presumed populism had run its course when ISI collapsed in the 1980s, the victim of a region-wide debt crisis and inflationary and balance of payments pressures that bankrupted developmentalist states. The crisis culminated in near universal adoption of austerity programs and free market (or "neoliberal") economic reforms, as states retreated from a broad range of developmental and social welfare roles historically associated with populism. Deeply embedded in the notion of a region-wide "Washington Consensus" for political and economic liberalism was the belief that populism—along with the two "-isms" that followed, statism and nationalism—had been eclipsed in a new era of democracy, fiscal austerity, and market globalization. Conventional wisdom held that henceforth public policies would be determined by responsible technocrats who understood the laws of the marketplace, rather than by social mobilization or the political pressures applied by organized, rent-seeking interest groups.

The demise of populism, however, proved to be short-lived. By the middle of the 1990s, scholars had begun to focus attention on new forms of populist leadership that coexisted with—or even implemented—neoliberal structural adjustment policies, thus challenging the assumption that populism as a political phenomenon was necessarily coupled with a particular model or stage of socioeconomic development. And by the end of the 1990s, the explosive rise of Hugo Chávez in Venezuela demonstrated that even more traditional, statist variants of populism remained potentially potent in Latin America's neoliberal era. Indeed, the early years of the new millennium produced a broader trend of left-leaning parties and populist figures in national office in Chile, Brazil, Argentina, Uruguay, Bolivia, and Peru, reopening historic debates about alternative modes of development that the technocratic Washington Consensus largely had foreclosed during its heyday. Although the populist label is hardly appropriate for some of these new governments, as discussed below, there is little doubt that populism has experienced a revival in post-adjustment Latin America.

[. . .] The dual transitions towards political democracy and market liberalism that swept across Latin America during the waning decades of the 20th century created a series of contradictory effects with profound implications for political representation. On one hand, new democratic regimes extended basic citizenship rights where they had often never reached before—in particular, delivering voting rights and the recognition of cultural autonomy for indigenous peoples. On the other hand, the highly uneven application—both socially and geographically—of the rule of law often impaired broader civil rights. Simply put, large swaths of the population in many countries lived on the margins of legal and administrative structures that could enforce equal rights of citizenship, from access to the courts to protection against police brutality.

Furthermore, rights of social citizenship were often retracted as economic crises and market-based structural adjustment programs forced states to relinquish some of the regulatory, redistributive, and social welfare functions that they had assumed during the ISI era. In particular, economic restructuring and labor market liberalization eroded employment security, caused wages to stagnate or fall in much of the region, and swelled the ranks of informal and temporary contract sectors of the workforce that were excluded from the social safety net. At the same time, antiinflationary austerity programs often forced cuts in public spending, which had long cushioned popular living standards. Sadly, in 2004—more than twenty years after the debt crisis, and following two decades of growth-oriented market reforms—more than 40 percent of Latin Americans continued to live below the poverty line, 46.5 percent of the workforce toiled in the informal sector, and the average Gini index of inequality stood at .542, far above the world average of .381.

[. . .] The election of Chávez in 1998 symbolized the revival of populism's historic nationalist and anti-market thrust, as well as the renewed capacity of popular factions to mobilize politically against market-generated insecurities. In subsequent years, mass protest movements toppled a series of pro-market presidents in Ecuador, Argentina, and Bolivia, and new left-of-center governments were elected into office throughout much of South America. Suddenly, and often unexpectedly, the Washington Consensus was in tatters, and a social backlash had repoliticized development policy, offering group solidarity, collective action, and an interventionist state as alternatives to the material insecurities of market individualism.

Renewed popular mobilization thus brought to the forefront the latent contradictions of Latin America's dual transitions—in particular, the tensions between the extension of democratic political rights and the retraction of social citizenship rights. In countries with relatively strong institutions for mediating conflict, like Chile, Brazil, and Uruguay, "renovated" or post-Marxist social democratic parties articulated and managed these tensions, gradually accumulating electoral support, gaining access to national executive power, and pragmatically seeking to address their "social deficits" within the constraints of globally integrated market economies. Institutionalized channels of political representation thus restrained populist tendencies in these countries and moderated their political expression. In much of the region, however, parties with popular bases were less institutionalized or more easily captured by dominant personalities, and political space existed for new social and political movements to channel popular discontents. These discontents were expressed in strikingly diverse ways, however, and not all of them warrant the appellation of populism.

---

3. Address to the United Nations ~ Hugo Chávez*

In September 2006 Venezuelan president Hugo Chávez, along with many other world leaders, attended the sixty-first session of the United Nations General Assembly in New York to make remarks during the annual general debate period. Speaking the day after President George W. Bush (as well as newly elected Bolivian president Evo Morales), Chávez lit up the hall with bold theatrics. Chávez, typically, framed his remarks in a way that made his voice into the voice of the world's oppressed peoples, the peoples of the global South, and Bush's voice into the voice of the emperor who sought to dominate and control them. In so doing, he dipped into the deep reservoir of nationalist, anti-imperialist sentiment that runs through the Latin American experience, and revealed another connection between the new Left and the classic populists. In making such a speech, who do you think Chávez viewed as his main audience?

The hegemonic pretension of U.S. imperialism puts at risk the very survival of humankind itself. We continue to warn the world about this danger, and call upon the people of the United States and worldwide to halt this danger, which is like the sword of Damocles.

I was thinking of reading a chapter from this book,† but in order to respect the time limit, I will rather leave it merely as a recommendation. This is an easy-to-read book, a good reading, and surely you are familiar with it, Madam President. I am certain it has been published in English, German, Russian, and Arabic [applause]. I believe that the first to read this book should be our brothers and sisters of the United States, because the

---

*From "Statement by H. E. Hugo Chávez Frías, President of the Bolivarian Republic of Venezuela," at the 61st United Nations General Assembly, September 20, 2006, available at http://www.un.org/webcast/ga/61/pdfs/venezuela-e.pdf. Accessed on July 30, 2008.
†Chávez was referring to the book, *Hegemony or Survival: America's Quest for Global Dominance,* by the U.S. linguist and left-wing political activist Noam Chomsky.

main threat is on their homeland. The devil is here. The devil; the devil himself is in their homes.

The devil came here yesterday [laughter and applause]. Yesterday, the devil was here in this very place. The rostrum still smells like sulfur. Yesterday, ladies and gentlemen, from this podium, the President of the United States, whom I refer to as the devil, came here talking as if he owned the world. It would take a psychiatrist to analyze the speech he delivered yesterday.

As the spokesperson for imperialism, he came to give us his recipes for maintaining the current scheme of domination, exploitation and pillage over the peoples of the world. His speech perfectly fit with an Alfred Hitchcock movie, and I could even dare to suggest a title: *The Devil's Recipe.* That is to say, the U.S. imperialism, as stated by Chomsky in a very clear, evident, and profound manner, is making desperate efforts to consolidate its hegemonic system of domination. We cannot allow this to happen. We cannot allow a world dictatorship to be installed or consolidated.

The statement by the tyrannical president of the world was full of cynicism and hypocrisy. Basically, it is with imperial hypocrisy that he attempts to control everything. They want to impose upon us the democratic model they devised, the false democracy of elites. And, moreover, a very original democratic model, imposed by explosions, bombings, invasions, and bullets. What a democracy! In light of this, Aristotle's and those theories made by the first Greek thinkers who spoke about democracy shall be reviewed, so as to analyze what kind of democracy that is, one which imposes itself through marines, invasions, aggressions, and bombs.

Yesterday, the United States' president said in this same hall the following. I quote, "Wherever you look, you hear extremists telling you that violence, terror, and torture can help you escape from misery and recover your dignity." Wherever he looks, he sees extremists. I am sure he sees you, my brother, with your skin color, and he thinks you are an extremist. With his color, the Honorable president of Bolivia, Evo Morales, who came here yesterday, is also an extremist. Imperialists see extremists everywhere. No, we are not extremists. What happens is that the world is waking up, and people are rising up everywhere. I have the feeling, Mister Imperialist Dictator, that you are going to live as if in a nightmare the rest of your days, because no matter where you look at, we will be rising up against the U.S. imperialism. They call us extremists, since we demand total freedom in the world, equality among peoples, and respect for the sovereignty of nations. We are rising up against the Empire, against its model of domination.

4. Chávez's Oil Reforms ~ Dick Parker*

One thing Chávez currently has in his favor is the high price of a barrel of oil. Venezuela, a founding member of the Organization of Petroleum Exporting Countries (OPEC) and huge supplier of oil to the United States, is home to the western hemisphere's largest conventional oil reserves, some of the largest in the world. The Venezuelan state nationalized oil resources in 1976 in the wake of OPEC's 1973 embargo, which drove up the price per barrel worldwide. The new enterprise was called Venezuelan Petroleum, Inc. (often referred to by its Spanish acronym, PDVSA). But then Venezuela, like many export-dependent countries, got caught in a bad cycle of debt and currency devaluation as oil prices plunged downward in the 1980s. By the 1990s Venezuela and PDVSA became one of the showcases of neoliberal reform, as the company was opened to foreign investment. But that was prior to Chávez's coming to power. In the following selection, Dick Parker, a sociologist who teaches at a Venezuelan university, lays out the basics of Chávez's oil reforms. How, according to Parker, has he changed things?

The experience of seven years of the Chávez government in the areas of oil reform, social policy, and development models puts in evidence the broad outlines of an alternative to neoliberalism. From the beginning, the Chávez movement has linked its new development model to oil policy. The Chávez government contributed to a rapid recovery of oil prices by strengthening OPEC. This achievement depended on one of the few aspects of oil policy that still remained firmly in the hands of the national executive, namely, intergovernment agreements. The revitalization of OPEC made possible the search for feasible social and economic alternatives in Venezuela.

Since the government considered a degree of macroeconomic stability a prerequisite for structural changes, it rejected the option of directly confronting the international financial institutions. Nonpayment of the foreign debt was ruled out, currency reserves were maintained high, and macroeconomic policy was designed to bring inflation under control. Indeed, it was precisely these "orthodox" aspects of economic policy that led some analysts to conclude that the balance was neoliberal. Other academics suggested that economic policy, far from responding to Chávez's antineoliberal rhetoric, simply retained the measures previously implemented under the recommendations of the international financial institutions, and

---

*From Dick Parker, "Chávez and the Search for an Alternative to Neoliberalism," in *Venezuela: Hugo Chávez and the Decline of an "Exceptional Democracy,"* edited by Steve Ellner and Miguel Tinker Salas (Lanham, MD: Rowman & Littlefield, 2007), 64–66. Reprinted with permission of Rowman & Littlefield.

on this basis they expressed fears that the regime might be heading in the same direction as Fujimori's and Menem's.* These criticisms, however, failed to consider sufficiently the government's pressing immediate objectives. The fact is that during the first two years, the government's priority had to be increasing oil revenues to previous levels to avoid an economic disaster.

In addition to strengthening links to OPEC, the government immediately attempted to reestablish the role of the Energy and Mines Ministry in the formulation of oil policy. Under Alí Rodriguez Araque† and his successors, the ministry began to prepare legislation designed to promote national interests.

The government was hardly reverting to previous policies. It is true that it honored contracts with foreign investors, despite their unfavorable terms, and continued to accept foreign investments in order to expand productive capacity, but it modified the terms under which foreign capital would be accepted in the future. At the same time, the plans for expanding production were reformulated not as an alternative to OPEC but to strengthen Venezuela's position during the periodical adjustments of the organization's member-nation quotas.

The administration designed a major legislative initiative to undermine PDVSA's capacity to manipulate its records to minimize fiscal contributions. The Organic Law of Hydrocarbons, promulgated as part of a controversial package of forty-nine laws in November 2001, reduced taxes and increased royalties because the latter were easier to calculate than the former. The law also mandated state possession of a majority of stocks in all mixed companies engaged in primary activity in the oil industry.

Initiating reforms within PDVSA proved much more difficult. The company executives inherited from the Giusti era had been invested with a "corporate spirit" and were accustomed to absolute control of the industry. The successive PDVSA presidents appointed by Chávez during the first three years of his administration did little to modify the company's functioning; its third president, General Guaicaipuro Laineda, actually became the spokesman for the executives who criticized the government's new Hydrocarbon Law. Indeed, the executives, organized as *Gente de Petroleo*, played a major role in the opposition's subsequent attempts to overthrow Chávez. They participated discreetly in the one-day strike called by the Venezuelan Federation of Chambers and Associations of Commerce and Production and the Venezuelan Workers' Confederation

---

*Here the author is referring to Alberto Fujimori, president of Peru from 1990–2000, and Carlos Menem, president of Argentina from 1989–1999, both of whom were fervent neoliberals.

†Alí Rodríguez, a former communist guerrilla, was Chávez's controversial pick to head the ministry, replacing the neoliberal privatizer of PDVSA, Luis Giusti.

on December 10, 2001, which set the stage for the work stoppage that preceded the coup in April 2002. They also played a central role in the December 2002 lockout, which resulted in the dismissal of eighteen thousand mainly white-collar employees. The relative ease with which production levels were restored after the two-month lockout suggested that the industry did, in fact, maintain an inflated labor force.

Once the government assumed control of the industry, new changes were introduced. PDVSA went ahead with plans to increase production and facilitate the participation of foreign capital. PDVSA's new president, Alí Rodríguez Araque, announced that the company would spend US$40 billion by 2007 to increase its potential output from three to five million barrels per day and that more than US$18 billion was expected from foreign investors. These plans were more modest than those proposed by Giusti. At the same time, the government stiffened the terms of foreign participation.

The government also revamped PDVSA's organization and introduced measures designed to favor local entrepreneurs, especially small and medium-sized firms. In the aftermath of the two-month lockout, workers' cooperatives and community organizations provided services in areas such as the distribution of gasoline, maintenance, and the supply of food and work clothes in order to generate employment beyond the confines of the oil industry. At the same time, PDVSA extended its social programs, particularly for neighborhood communities, and supported the missions dedicated to education, health, and endogenous development. The change has been dramatic. Between 1999 and 2003, PDVSA's average annual expenditure on social programs was US$48 million. In 2004, it was US$1.7 billion and in 2005, US$ 2.4 billion. Nevertheless, it remains to be seen whether the government will be able to combine its ambitious investment plans with a surplus sufficient to finance its social agenda and whether it will resist the temptation to subject the industry to the clientelistic practices that opposition spokesmen have anticipated.

5. The Chávez-Morales Axis ~ Nikolas Kozloff*

In this selection historian and author Nikolas Kozloff examines the relationship between two of the main members of the new Left turn in Latin American politics, presidents Chávez of Venezuela and Morales of Bolivia. According to Kozloff,

*From Nikolas Kozloff, *Hugo Chávez: Oil, Politics, and the Challenge to the United States* (New York: Palgrave Macmillan, 2006), 164–66, 170–71. Reprinted with permission of Palgrave Macmillan.

*the two men met several years before Morales rose to become president. The
story shows, in fact, how shrewd Chávez has been in gaining allies in his fight
against "the Empire." Kozloff also provides some highlights from Morales's
2005 election campaign, focusing especially on its historic significance for Bolivian race relations. He also makes note of the United States' worried reaction to
his victory. Does the United States have something to fear from governments
such as these?*

Elected as the first wholly indigenous president in Latin America in
December 2005, Morales is the embodiment of a new indigenous
awakening that could inspire social movements across the region. Such a
prospect further emboldens Chávez and concerns the White House.

Events stand to fortify Chávez's hand. The Venezuelan leader has
always had a certain following in Bolivia among indigenous peoples. As
early as 2000, Chávez traveled to Bolivia, whose population is two-thirds
indigenous and is the poorest country in South America. There, he was
greeted by an outpouring of support. During his official state visit, a popular demonstration in favor of the Bolivarian process took place. The *Miami
Herald* published a piece alleging that Chávez had financed a road block-
ade in Bolivia organized by the Aymara Indian leader Felipe Quispe.
Chávez denied the accusations, saying that the reports constituted a "ferocious international campaign" to isolate Venezuela. The U.S. State Department said it was concerned that the Venezuelan leader was supposedly
offering support to violent indigenous movements.

In the presidential elections of 2002, charges of Chávez's supposed
interference in Bolivia's internal affairs resurfaced. This time it was the
turn of *La Prensa*, a Bolivian daily, which claimed that Chávez had
offered $300,000 to Evo Morales to finance the indigenous leader's presi-
dential campaign. Again, Chávez denied the reports. Whether he actively
supported Morales's campaign is unclear, but the Venezuelan leader certainly did not attempt to hide his warming diplomatic ties with the coca
grower. When Sánchez de Lozada won the election, Chávez returned to
Bolivia to attend the inauguration. While staying in his hotel in the capital
of La Paz, Chávez was received by Morales, who had come in second
in the election. Later, both men declared the need for strengthening the
indigenous movement within the *altiplano*, a broad upland plateau located
in southwest Bolivia. In a sign of the friendly ties, Chávez personally
invited members of Morales's party, the Movement Towards Socialism
(known by its Spanish acronym of MAS) to Venezuela to observe the
deepening of the Bolivarian process. Morales returned the favor by helping
to organize a street march in Caracas to support Chávez, then in the midst
of the oil lockout of 2002–2003.

Once Chávez had survived the disruptions caused by the Venezuelan opposition, he met personally with Morales, who was then a Bolivian congressman, in April 2003. According to one journalist who was present, the meeting was jovial and went smoothly. Chávez received Morales at Miraflores at about one in the morning, along with Blanca Chancoso, an indigenous leader from Ecuador, and Rafael Alegria, a peasant farmer activist from Honduras. "From an unlit garden, Chávez emerged from the shadows wearing jeans, a t-shirt and blue sneakers," and the three greeted him excitedly. The activists sat down at a table with Chávez and the Venezuelan president announced, "I don't drink but let me offer you some wine." Someone called, "We know how to drink, and to make a toast. To Bolivarian unity!"

As they sat and talked, Chávez and the activists discussed the issue of security of leaders and activists opposed to U.S. policies. As the time came to say good-bye, the men shook hands, embraced, and took a group photo as a souvenir. "The hurricane of revolution has begun," Chávez remarked, "and it will never again be calmed."

"We'll keep the flame burning, comandante" Alegría added.

"We will return, and there will be millions of us," said Chancoso.

"Thank you, President Chávez," said Morales. "I leave here full of ideas for the struggle ahead."

A scant two and a half years later, Morales's opportunity finally arrived. Wearing a short-sleeved shirt and jeans, he sat down with local inhabitants in the tropical lowland province of Chapare before going to vote in the presidential election. As he enjoyed a breakfast of fish and boiled yucca, a campesino sporting a cowboy hat rode a buffalo through the village, brandishing a checkered, rainbow-colored Aymara flag called a *wiphala*. The Indians say the flag should become the new emblem of a reborn Bolivia. During Morales's campaign for president, the wiphala flew from every one of his campaign vehicles.

Scenes like this one horrify Bolivia's European and mixed-race elites. For centuries, they have ruled over the impoverished Indian majority who have had to endure entrenched racism. A recently released study by the World Bank suggests that not much has changed for the Aymara. According to the study, 74 percent of Bolivia's Indians live in poverty. What is more, Bolivia's indigenous population has 3.7 fewer years of schooling than the non-Indian population. Additionally, the incidence of child labor is four times higher among Indians than nonindigenous children.

Nevertheless, in recent years the Aymara, Bolivia's largest ethnic group, have achieved significant political gains. From 1993 to 1997, an Aymara Indian served as the country's vice president, and indigenous mobilization has only increased under Morales. According to the London *Independent*, Morales cultivates indigenous support and "litters his conversation with Aymara references and reminders that Europeans have been exploiting the indigenous people for 500 years." Indigenous gains have alarmed the non-Indian population. Racism now seems to be moving out into the open, with cases of light-skinned youths harassing indigenous protesters and yelling racial epithets. The protesters in turn pull the neckties from people and call them "white men."

[After Morales's 2005 election victory,] Chávez sent Morales a note of congratulation. The Bolivian election, Chávez declared, had been a "battle for dignity and sovereignty." Chávez was ecstatic that, in his view, the patriotism of Bolívar and Sucre, one of the Liberator's generals sent to rule over Bolivia, had finally triumphed. As he had before with Lula, Chávez offered a replica of Bolívar's sword to the new Bolivian president. For Chávez, Morales's election came as a true geopolitical triumph. In an earlier interview, Morales had declared, "If I was president of Bolivia, I would like to accompany the people of Cuba and Venezuela, and two men, Fidel Castro and Hugo Chávez, who are liberating forces in America." Such declarations alarmed the U.S. State Department, which in June 2005 warned of growing links between Chávez and Morales at the Organization of American States. General James Hill, commander of the U.S. Southern Command in Miami prior to General Craddock's arrival, went even further. He stated that Morales received direct financial support from Chávez. For his part, Morales denies receiving any financial support from Chávez. The coca leader, who identifies himself as a "Bolivarian," said that he had never requested external assistance. "Those accusations always occur," he declared. "Evo Morales is accused of everything, in Bolivia I am responsible for everything, if I am outside of the country I am a problem for the government, if I was in the cemetery surely I would continue to be a problem." Nevertheless, Morales makes no effort to hide his sympathies. He has remarked that he shares Chávez's desire to liberate Latin American countries from the yoke of the United States.

The prospect of a Chávez-Morales axis is cause for worry for the Bush administration. Not only does Morales oppose the drug war, but he has taken a hard line on Bolivia's energy policy. A key plank of the Morales campaign was the nationalization of the hydrocarbon industry. Bolivia contains significant oil reserves and the second largest gas reserves in South America, after Venezuela. Currently six multinational companies control the gas industry in Bolivia, the so-called *transnacionales* (Bolivians, according to one correspondent, practically spit out the word), including Exxon. Many of Morales's supporters speculate that he will expropriate oil and gas facilities within a couple of months after assuming the presidency. Morales himself talks tough, saying "we cannot give away what was given to us by Pachamama."*

---

*Pachamama means "Mother Earth" in the indigenous cultures of the Andes.

6. On Bolivian Sovereignty ~ Evo Morales*

Just days after the UN General Assembly session in which President Chávez called President Bush "the devil," Evo Morales was interviewed in New York by the independent media outlet Democracy Now! *Conducted by hosts Amy Goodman and Juan Gonzalez, the interview covered topics like the failure of the Bolivian political system, U.S. foreign policy toward Bolivia and the Andean region, and the role of Bolivia's indigenous peoples in the new government. In the following selection taken from that (translated) interview, Morales makes sure listeners know that he is not a professional politician. More important, he also lets listeners know where he stands with regard to Bolivia's lucrative natural gas resources. What is that stance, and why did President Lula yell at him? How did he respond to his "elder" ally?*

JUAN GONZALEZ: Mr. President, in the United States voters here are accustomed to leaders promising much, but when they get into office delivering very little. Since you have become president in Bolivia, you have moved rapidly to make changes. You've cut your own salary. You've raised the minimum wage by 50 percent. What is the message you are trying to send to your own people and to Latin American leaders in general?

PRESIDENT EVO MORALES: I never wanted to be a politician. In my country, politicians are seen as liars, thieves, arrogant people. In 1997 they tried to get me to run for president. I rejected that idea, even though that brought me problems with my own grassroots organizations. Then I was later obligated to become a member of the lower house of parliament. I didn't want to do that at the time, either. I preferred to be the head of a rat than the tail of a horse. I preferred to be the head of my own organizations fighting for human rights and fighting for the rights of the members, and not getting involved in electoral political processes and wind up not fulfilling promises.

But what I was learning in that period in '95, '96, '97, is that to get involved in politics means taking on the responsibility, a new way of looking at politics as serving the people, because to get into politics means service. And after hearing the demands, the broad demands of our grassroots organizations, I decided finally to run for president.

And for the last elections, we had a ten-point program. And of those ten, we've fulfilled six already. The austerity measures that you mentioned

*From *Bolivian President Evo Morales on Latin America, U.S. Foreign Policy, and the Role of the Indigenous People of Bolivia*, September 22, 2006, available at http://www.democracynow.org/article.pl?sid=06/09/22/1323211. Accessed on July 30, 2008.

a moment ago, I cut my own salary by more than 50 percent, and the ministers' as well as also the members of congress, and that money has been redirected to health and education, convinced of the idea that to arrive at the presidency means that you're there to serve the people. And we said we were going to do a consultation for a referendum on autonomy, greater autonomy for the regions, and we've done that. 58 percent of the population said no to greater autonomy, although it is important to secure more autonomy for the regions and the indigenous communities.

We said we were going to nationalize the gas and oil sector. We did, without expropriating or kicking out any of the companies. We said it's important to have partners, but not bosses. And we did it. The investor has the right to recuperate their investment and to a reasonable profit, but we can't allow for the sacking of the country and only the companies benefiting, not the people. I just came from a meeting of political analysts, foreign policy analysts here, and they seemed to understand our proposals.

The struggle against corruption, it's a key issue in my country. We're starting that campaign aggressively, starting with members of the executive branch. The judicial branch still is not accompanying this process. And I can talk a lot about the other things that we're doing to meet the demands that were accumulated over time. For example, the centers for eye treatments and surgery, the literacy work that we're doing to meet the demands that were accumulated over time.

JUAN GONZALEZ: I'd like to ask you, in many poor countries around the world, it is said that the most powerful official in the country is the U.S. ambassador, but in your campaign, you actually ran against, not just the other opponents, but against the role of the U.S. embassy and the U.S. ambassador in Bolivia. What is the role that the United States has played historically not only in Bolivia, but in Latin America, as far as you're concerned?

PRESIDENT EVO MORALES: The arrogance of an ambassador or the arrogance of others, including a president, is always an error. This arrogance creates greater rebellion, greater resistance. In 2002, former U.S. ambassador to Bolivia, Manuel Rocha, said, "Don't vote for Evo Morales." And after that, people came out massively to vote for me. I said he was my best campaign chief. And a number of things were said about what would happen if I came to the presidency, that international cooperation would be reduced, we would no longer have access to markets, but in fact I've come to the presidency and we've seen a lot more support from other governments.

The United States embassy tried to effect the changes in the military high command. I said, "That's not going to be changed. That's a sovereign decision that we make." So for that, we have obvious differences, but we want to work out those differences. Even though we're an underdeveloped country, we're a sovereign country, a country with dignity. One of the advantages that we have is that we begin to return dignity to the country. The name Bolivia is now understood. Our peoples need a strong sense of self-esteem. We want relations with all the countries that will be based on mutual respect, relations of complementarity, balance, solidarity, and for now, cooperation so that we can assure the changes that we're trying to achieve.

JUAN GONZALEZ: In your nationalization, one of the groups in the gas companies that you nationalized were also Brazilian companies, as well. How have you been able to negotiate or deal with some of these inter-regional problems of the Brazilian companies also having such a huge say in your gas reserves?

PRESIDENT EVO MORALES: At first, there were protest and resistance, even from compañero Lula—well, perhaps more the company. There was an emergency meeting of the four presidents in Iguassu in Argentina. We had a closed-door meeting between the four presidents. No minister's presence, without any press. This is the first time I've told anybody this. I was attacked. Lula was rough with me. "Where is our partnership? Where is that cordiality? Why didn't you consult me before the nationalization?"

But I defended myself, and I said that on a sovereign basis our country has every right to make decisions about the future of our strategic resources. We are generous. We are compañeros. We are in solidarity. And as my older brother, and as the leader of a more developed country in the region, we recognize that and we respect that. I accept him as an older brother, because he too is a union leader. He's older than me. And he's older than I am, and in the Indian culture we respect our elders very much. But finally, he understood very well, because we were neither expropriating nor kicking out Petrobras.

What I explained is that after the supreme decree that did the nationalization, we were guaranteeing greater security, because the new contracts were going to be transparent and ratified through congress, because previously the contracts were kept under wraps, secret, and never ratified in congress. And we also showed technically, financially, with numbers, that the company was going to be able to recover their investment and would have a reasonable profit. They weren't going to have as much profit as before, because the largest oil fields—excuse me, from the largest gas fields, the companies only gave 18 percent of royalties to the state and took 82 percent in profit. But now, with the new law we've changed that around, now 82 percent for the government, for the state, and 18 percent for the companies. They're staying. There are no problems. And from that large field that Petrobras is managing, we've already seen $150 million coming into government coffers now.

About the Editors

James A. Wood is an associate professor of history at North Carolina A&T State University in Greensboro. His areas of specialization include modern Latin American and world history. He has published several articles on Chile's nineteenth-century history. His first book is *The Society of Equality: Political Citizenship, Popular Republicanism, and the Public Sphere in Santiago de Chile, 1818–1851* (University of New Mexico Press, forthcoming).

John Charles Chasteen has taught Latin American History at the University of North Carolina at Chapel Hill since 1990. He is the author, editor, and translator of numerous books on Latin American history, among them *Heroes on Horseback: A Life and Times of the Last Gaucho Caudillos* (1995); *Born in Blood and Fire: A Concise History of Latin America* (2001, second edition 2005); *National Rhythms, African Roots: The Deep History of Latin American Popular Dance* (2004); and, most recently, *Americanos: Latin America's Struggle for Independence* (2008).